Jim Crow in North Carolina

CAROLINA ACADEMIC PRESS
Legal History Series
H. Jefferson Powell, Series Editor

AMERICAN CONSTITUTIONAL LAW
Selected Essays
Henry Paul Monaghan

THE BIRTH OF AMERICAN LAW
An Italian Philosopher and the American Revolution
John D. Bessler

FEDERAL JUSTICE IN THE MID-ATLANTIC SOUTH
United States Courts from Maryland to the Carolinas 1836–1861
Peter Graham Fish

THE FETHA NAGAST
The Law of the Kings
Abba Paulos Tzadua, translator, and Peter L. Strauss

GENTLEMEN OF THE GRAND JURY
*The Surviving Grand Jury Charges from Colonial, State,
and Lower Federal Courts Before 1801*
Stanton D. Krauss, editor

JIM CROW IN NORTH CAROLINA
The Legislative Program from 1865 to 1920
Richard A. Paschal

LAW IN WAR, WAR AS LAW
*Brigadier General Joseph Holt and the Judge Advocate General's
Department in the Civil War and Early Reconstruction, 1861–1865*
Joshua E. Kastenberg

LOST IN TRANSLATIONS
*Roman Law Scholarship and Translation in
Early Twentieth-Century America*
Timothy G. Kearley

LOUIS D. BRANDEIS'S MIT LECTURES ON LAW
(1892–1894)
Robert F. Cochran, Jr., editor

NEWSPAPER REPORTS OF DECISIONS IN COLONIAL, STATE, AND LOWER FEDERAL COURTS BEFORE 1801
Stanton D. Krauss, editor

OUR CHIEF MAGISTRATE AND HIS POWERS
William Howard Taft
with Foreword, Introduction, and Notes
by H. Jefferson Powell

THE QUOTABLE BRANDEIS
Peter Scott Campbell, editor

THREE NEGLECTED PIECES OF THE DOCUMENTARY HISTORY OF THE CONSTITUTION AND BILL OF RIGHTS
Remarks on the Amendments to the Constitution by a Foreign Spectator, Essays of the Centinel, Revived, and Extracts from the Virginia Senate Journal
Stanton D. Krauss, editor

A VIEW OF THE CONSTITUTION OF THE UNITED STATES OF AMERICA
Second Edition
William Rawle
with Foreword, Introduction, and Notes
by H. Jefferson Powell

Jim Crow in North Carolina

The Legislative Program from 1865 to 1920

RICHARD A. PASCHAL

North Caroliniana Society Imprint, No. 60

CAROLINA ACADEMIC PRESS
Durham, North Carolina

Copyright © 2021
Richard A. Paschal
All Rights Reserved

Library of Congress Cataloging-in-Publication Data

Names: Paschal, Richard A., author.
Title: Jim Crow in North Carolina : the legislative program from 1865 to 1920 / by Richard A. Paschal.
Description: Durham, North Carolina : Carolina Academic Press, LLC, [2020] | Series: Legal History Series.
Identifiers: LCCN 2020031827 (print) | LCCN 2020031828 (ebook) | ISBN 9781531017712 (paperback) | ISBN 9781531017729 (ebook)
Subjects: LCSH: Segregation--Law and legislation—North Carolina—History. | African Americans—Segregation—North Carolina—History. | African American—Legal status, laws, etc.—North Carolina—History. | Legislation—North Carolina--History. | United States—Race relations—History.
Classification: LCC KFN7420 .P37 2020 (print) | LCC KFN7420 (ebook) | DDC 342.75608/73—dc23
LC record available at https://lccn.loc.gov/2020031827
LC ebook record available at https://lccn.loc.gov/2020031828

Carolina Academic Press
700 Kent Street
Durham, North Carolina 27701
Telephone (919) 489-7486
Fax (919) 493-5668
www.cap-press.com

For
Catherine Noelle
and
Richard Allen

Non nobis solum nati sumus

Nations reel and stagger on their way; they make hideous mistakes; they commit frightful wrongs; they do great and beautiful things. And shall we not best guide humanity by telling the truth about all this, so far as the truth is ascertainable?

—W. E. Burghardt Du Bois (1935)

Contents

Acknowledgments xiii

A Word on Terminology xv

Introduction 3

1 | Jim Crow in Books and Jim Crow in Action 31

2 | Woodward's *Strange Career* and Subsequent Scholarship 43

3 | Vile Ambitions and Low Instincts 57

4 | *De Jure* Discrimination in North Carolina 103

5 | State Institutions and Legislative Appropriations 169

6 | Conclusion 189

Table 1: North Carolina Constitutional and Statutory Provisions that Discriminated Based on Race, 1865 to 1920 195

Table 2: North Carolina Constitutional and Statutory Provisions that Affirmed Legal Equality and/or Benefited Racial Minorities, 1865 to 1920 247

About the Author 269

Index 271

Acknowledgments

I want to offer my gratitude for the assistance I received throughout the process of researching and writing this book. First, I want to acknowledge the financial support of the Oliver H. Orr Fund of the North Caroliniana Society and the personal encouragement offered to me by the late Dr. Orr. I want to give a special note of thanks to Willis Whichard and Martin Brinkley, the North Caroliniana Society's president emeritus and its secretary-treasurer, respectively, who first suggested that I undertake this project. They gave careful readings to drafts and offered support throughout. I am also exceedingly grateful to others who read and commented upon various iterations of this study at different points in time: Al Brophy, Jeff Crow, John Orth, and Jeff Powell.

I am indebted to the many librarians who responded to inquiries and helped in innumerable ways over the years. The ones deserving special mention are Robert Anthony, curator of the North Carolina Collection, and Sarah Carrier, research librarian, at the Wilson Library at the University of North Carolina, who both answered numerous questions and shared scans of pages from nineteenth-century newspapers. The images of the Raleigh *News and Observer* reproduced here are courtesy of the North Carolina Collection, Wilson Special Collections Library, University of North Carolina at Chapel Hill. Also, I want to thank Librarian Tom Davis and Assistant Librarian Barrett Fish at the N.C. Supreme Court Library for assistance with the various codifications and city ordinances, to Denise Chachula of the Wake County Public Libraries for help with numerous interlibrary loan requests, and to Fam Brownlee of the North Carolina Collection at the Forsyth County Public Library for sharing his knowledge of the City of Winston's ordinances. In addition, thanks go to Amy Cummings, a paralegal with the Town of Mooresville, who located the Mooresville ordinance discussed in Chapter 4. The book also benefited from the design and production expertise of Jennifer Hill at Carolina Academic Press and from the skillful indexing by Enid Zafran.

Finally, my greatest debt is to my family for enduring this project for so long. Thanks go to my children, to whom this book is dedicated, and unending gratitude to my wife, Jennifer. They brighten my days and with mirth and laughter let my old wrinkles come.

A Word on Terminology

Here, at the outset, a word should be said about what I mean in this book by "Jim Crow." I use the phrase "Jim Crow in North Carolina" to refer to all forms of *de jure* discrimination—that is, discrimination "of right" or by government—and not simply with reference to physical segregation or separation based upon race. This book is about discrimination pursuant to law and the operation of law rather than mere spatial separation or *de facto* discrimination by private entities or individuals.[1] There was certainly segregation by private actors that we associate with Jim Crow—think of a theater owner requiring blacks to sit in the balcony—but the focus of this study is on discrimination by and through government and governmental actors.

The precise origins of the phrase "Jim Crow" are difficult to pinpoint, but it came into widespread use in the 1830s with a song, "Jump Jim Crow," written in its original form and most famously performed by Thomas

---

1. It should be noted that the U.S. Supreme Court has defined *de jure* segregation in the public school context as "a current condition of segregation resulting from intentional state action." *Keyes v. School District No. 1, Denver, Colorado*, 413 U.S. 189, 205 (1973). Relying on this intent standard, the Court has held "that 'the Constitution is not violated by racial imbalance in the schools, without more.'" *Parents Involved in Community Schools v. Seattle School District No. 1*, 551 U.S. 701, 721 (2007) (quoting *Milliken v. Bradley*, 433 U.S. 267, 280 n.14 (1977)). In the present study, however, while virtually all of the laws and their application during the Jim Crow era would qualify as intentional discrimination, the phrase *de jure* discrimination is being used here without regard to intent and, thus, is simply used to distinguish governmental action from nongovernmental action.

Dartmouth "Daddy" Rice.² In performing the song, the white Rice was in blackface and he hopped around on stage with one stiff leg and a "laughable limp" and, in between the song's many verses, he sang the refrain:

> Wheel about, turn about,
> Do jis so,
> An ebery time I wheel about,
> I jump Jim Crow!³

The song and Rice became famous both in the United States and abroad, leading a Boston newspaper to claim in 1838 that the "two most popular characters in the world at the present time are [Queen] Victoria and Jim

---

2. Challenge, *Louisville Daily Journal* (Louisville, Ky.), Jan. 5, 1831, at 3 (letter by "Daddy Rice, Comedian, of the Kentucky Theatres"). See Sol Smith, *Theatrical Management in the West and South for Thirty Years* 65 (1868) (Smith described moving to Louisville for the 1830 fall season at the theater where Rice was a member of the company and who was "busily engaged in composing and arranging his *Jim Crow* songs").

Although other scholarly works have given various dates for the first performances of the song, the newspaper record suggests that the first performance of the "comic Negro Song, of 'Jim Crow'" was on May 21, 1830. Advertisement, *Louisville Public Advertiser* (Louisville, Ky.), May 20, 1830, at 3 (performance scheduled for "Friday Evening, May 21 [1830]").

3. Quoted in An Old Actor's Memories: What Mr. Edmon S. Conner Recalls About His Career, *N.Y. Times*, June 5, 1881, at 10. Rice wrote numerous verses of the song, performed in blackface, and danced in a comedic imitation of an elderly slave with "the left leg stiff and crooked at the knee, giving him a painful, but at the same time, laughable limp." Id. at 10. The accounts of people, such as Edmon Conner, who knew and worked with Rice suggest that there was a slave named or nicknamed Jim Crow who worked in a stable behind the Louisville theater and who sang a similar type of song and danced in an unusual manner and whose song, dance, and name were appropriated by Rice. Id. at 10. See Frederic R. Sanborn, "Jump Jim Crow!"—The Opening of an Era, *N.Y. Times*, November 13, 1932, at 8, 15 (describing Rice as "dancing his peculiar step, and rocking his left heel in the manner which generations of his successors have imitated").

The song had many verses and, eventually, many versions that were not penned by Rice, but the other versions often varied the language and spellings of the refrain in small ways. As for the many different versions of the song, one scholar notes that sheet music to the song published in New York in 1833 had 44 verses; a publication in Boston contained 66 verses; and one published version claimed "50 Verses: The only Correct Copy of the Extravaganza of Jim Crow." Dale Cockrell, *Demons of Disorder: Early Blackface Minstrels and Their World* 71 (1997). An important cultural study of the song reprints many of the different versions of the lyrics. W.T. Lhamon, Jr., *Jump Jim Crow: Lost Plays, Lyrics, and Street Prose of the First Atlantic Popular Culture* 95–145 (2003).

Crow."[4] Despite the popularization of the song, the use of the name "crow" for African Americans antedated Daddy Rice, and earlier references to "Jim Crow" and "John Crow" can be found.[5] "Crow" was and still is an offensive term for African Americans.[6] While the song "Jump Jim Crow" popularized the name and made it synonymous with the stereotyped Negro dancing a jig, the name became a placeholder for both slaves and free blacks and, as such, it quickly came into use to signify the segregated areas of antebellum America, often in the Northern states.[7]

---

4. Cockrell, supra note 3, at 161 (quoting *Boston Post*, July 22, 1838).

5. In 1828, two years *before* Rice wrote and performed the first version of his song, there is criticism of a "Jim Crow poet" who wrote a letter or editorial in a newspaper in support of Andrew Jackson because, in reply, another writer argued that the "Jim Crow poet" intentionally misled people about Andrew Jackson's commitment to the Union—this being the time that John C. Calhoun was arguing in favor of nullification of the Tariff of 1828. *The Torch Light and Public Advertiser* (Hagerstown, Md.), Aug. 14, 1828, at 4 (internal quotation marks omitted).

See also Selections, *Edenton Gazette* (Edenton, N.C.), Sept. 2, 1830, at 1 (story referring to "John Crow the black . . . singing at the top of his pipe") (reprinting Heat and Thirst,—A Scene in Jamaica, 27 *Blackwood's Edinburgh Magazine* (Edinburgh, Scotland), June 1830, at 861 (the spelling used here in original was "Johncrow")).

6. See *Webster's Third New International Dictionary* 544 (2002) (definition 7 for crow is "Negro—usu. taken to be offensive"); 1 *Random House Historical Dictionary of American Slang* 528 (J.E. Lighter ed., 1994) (definition 2 for crow is "a black person.—used contemptuously"). See also Maya Angelou, *I Know Why the Caged Bird Sings* 106 (Random House 2002) (1969) ("It was a dangerous practice to call a Negro anything that could be loosely construed as insulting because of the centuries of their having been called niggers, jigs, dinges, blackbirds, crows, boots and spooks."). In 1823, James Fenimore Cooper in *The Pioneers* had the character Billy Kirby, a white wood cutter, tell the black character Abraham Freeborn, also known as Brom, to "Shut your oven [i.e., mouth], you crow." James Fenimore Cooper, *The Pioneers*, in James Fenimore Cooper, *The Leatherstocking Tales: Volume 1*, at 198 (Library of America ed. 1985).

A broader view of the early nineteenth century suggests that Jim Crow was a phrase in general use in America outside of that one particular song and that it was often a disparaging generic name for African Americans. In addition, the phrase was often invoked in Northern abolitionist newspapers such as William Lloyd Garrison's *The Liberator*, which noted in 1839 that "there is usually attached to rail-road trains what is called a 'Jim Crow' car, in which colored persons . . . are compelled to ride." Mean Conduct, *The Liberator* (Boston, Mass.), Sept. 20, 1839, at 3. There continued to be references to "the Jim Crow car," Communications, *Anti-Slavery Bugle* (Lisbon, Oh.), June 26, 1858, at 2, and "the 'Jim Crow' pew in the churches," Progress of 'Fanaticism' in Rhode Island, *The Liberator* (Boston, Mass.), July 2, 1858, at 4, throughout the decades before the Civil War.

7. A word on the use of racial terminology in this book is in order. While I generally use the modern, preferred terms African American and black and American Indian and

While there was a post-Civil War period when to "jump Jim Crow" meant an inconstancy of beliefs or vacillation as to political policy posi-

Native American in my general analysis sections, I use idiomatic terms such as Negro and colored and Indian in other sections of the book. I do this for several reasons. First, the statutes and census reports from the period covered by this book used these words, often with specific meanings and, for me, the use of the statutory terminology maintains a verbal consistency. For example, when the laws from this period aimed to define who counted as a "Negro" for issues of marriage and admission to schools, it is problematic to transcribe the terms into modern phrasing, as it would be rendered as "the law defined African Americans as anyone of Negro ancestry to the fourth generation inclusive." See 1871–72 N.C. Sess. Laws 328, ch. 193, § 2 ("negro" defined with relation to marriage). Similarly, publications from this period such as the U.S. Census often use "colored" to mean all non-whites and did not always separate out the numbers for different minorities. But, in addition, I use these terms precisely because they are idiomatic and tied to the period under review. These terms anchor the statutes, political campaigns, and culture that are the subject of this book. To mix the statutes and language from 1895 with "African American," in particular, would unduly mix modern and distant sensibilities. To say that "the North Carolina White Supremacy Campaigns of 1898 and 1900 aimed to marginalize African Americans" is more jumble than accurate. Thus, these terms are used with regard to historical context and not as general terms of reference. In his study of this period, historian Leon Litwack set out a similar nomenclature: "For the purposes of this work, the terms 'Negro' and 'black' are both employed, though 'Negro' is generally confined to black people as the objects of white concerns, attitudes, and policies." Leon F. Litwack, *Trouble in Mind: Black Southerners in the Age of Jim Crow* at xvii (1998). See also Randall Kennedy, *Race, Crime, and the Law* xii n.* (1997).

It should also be acknowledged that this book reflects the socially constructed idea of "race" which was especially evident during the period that is the focus of this book and which lingers in America to the present day. The idea and definition of black and white and Indian during the period under review were created by the society and not by nature or biology. See, e.g., 1866 N.C. Sess. Laws 99, ch. 40, § 1 ("That negroes and their issue, even where one ancestor in each succeeding generation to the fourth inclusive, is white, shall be deemed persons of color."); 1871–72 N.C. Sess. Laws 328, ch. 193, § 2 ("All marriages between a white person and a negro or Indian, or between a white person and a person of negro or Indian descent, to the third generation inclusive . . . shall be void."). As Barbara Fields recognized, "To assume, by intention or default, that race is a phenomenon outside history is to take up a position within the terrain of racialist ideology and to become its unknowing—and therefore uncontesting—victim." Barbara J. Fields, Ideology and Race in American History, in *Region, Race, and Reconstruction: Essays in Honor of C. Vann Woodward* 143, 144 (J. Morgan Kousser and James M. McPherson eds., 1982). However, it should be noted that there are scientists who currently maintain that there may be some link between peoples and genetics. With the advent of DNA sequencing technology, geneticist David Reich has stated that "we are learning that while race may be a social construct, differences in genetic ancestry that happen to correlate to many of today's racial constructs are real." David Reich, "Race" in the Age of Modern Genetics, *N.Y. Times*, Mar. 25, 2018, at SR1, SR4.

tions,[8] that particular meaning faded from view in favor of the one referencing racial segregation and discrimination, and yet the phrase "Jim Crow" has never been defined with precision. Connotatively, Jim Crow evokes segregation and separate facilities based on race. However, I use the phrase "Jim Crow" in this book to mean any law or governmental action that discriminated based on race.[9] Jim Crow is often associated with segregation, but there is no way to disentangle any analysis of racial segregation from the larger patterns of discrimination against non-whites. Even in his book *The Strange Career of Jim Crow*, C. Vann Woodward was inexact in how he used the phrase. Woodward wrote that his study was on segregation and the "physical separation of people for reasons of race."[10] Nevertheless, among the subjects of *de jure* discrimination he examined, Woodward devoted the most space to disenfranchisement, which is a subject that is not, strictly speaking, about physical space.[11] There were never white voting booths and colored voting booths. But, it seems perfectly appropriate to refer to disenfranchisement as a part of Jim Crow in North Carolina. In addition, in *Strange Career*, Woodward highlighted "jury service . . . and other matters that go well beyond mere separation."[12] Thus, as Leon Litwack concluded, "What the white South insisted upon was not so much separation of the races as subordination, a system of controls in which whites prescribed the rules of racial conduct and contact and meted out the punishments."[13] Trying to define some distinction between

---

8. See, e.g., Republicans Jumping Jim Crow, *Brooklyn Daily Eagle* (Brooklyn, N.Y.), Sept. 11, 1877, at 1. See also *The Tennessean* (Nashville, Tenn.), Sept. 3, 1875, at 1 ("Senator Oglesby, of Illinois, is to make a speech in Cincinnati to-day [sic]. It is expected he flopped on the currency question at the same time with Senators Morton and Ferry, and will publicly stultify himself accordingly. [Senators] Morton, Oglesby, Brownlow—whew! how they jump Jim Crow.").

9. Cf. *Black's Law Dictionary* 964 (10th ed. 2014) ("Jim Crow law" defined as "[a] law enacted or purposely interpreted to discriminate against blacks, such as a law requiring separate restrooms for blacks and whites").

10. C. Vann Woodward, *The Strange Career of Jim Crow* at xi (3d rev. ed. 1974).

11. Id., at 83–85.

12. Howard N. Rabinowitz, More than the Woodward Thesis: Assessing *The Strange Career of Jim Crow*, 75 Journal of American History 843, 847 (1988).

13. Leon F. Litwack, Jim Crow Blues, *OAH Magazine of History*, Jan. 2004, at 7, 9. The phrase is often used in this broader, more inclusive way today, as with Michelle Alexander's important book on the racially disparate impact of the American criminal justice system. Michelle Alexander, *The New Jim Crow: Mass Incarceration in the Age of Colorblindness* (2010). The value of the Jim Crow analogy to the criminal justice system has

segregation and subordination is not a particularly worthwhile exercise, at least for present purposes. Thus, this book on the Jim Crow laws of North Carolina is concerned with the ways that *de jure* discrimination negatively impacted people of color, *simpliciter*.

---

been questioned in James Forman, Jr., Racial Critiques of Mass Incarceration: Beyond the New Jim Crow, 87 *N.Y.U. Law Review* 21 (2012). The phrase "Jim Crow" continues to be employed in other contexts, as well. For example, it is used to describe how the foster care system and delinquency impact the education of African Americans. Ellen Marrus, Education in Black America: Is It the New Jim Crow?, 68 *Arkansas Law Review* 27 (2015). And, similar to Woodward's emphasis on disenfranchisement, the recent spate of restrictive voter laws have been described as "Jim Crow 2.0." Keith G. Bentele and Erin E. O'Brien, Jim Crow 2.0? Why States Consider and Adopt Restrictive Voter Access Policies, 11 *Perspectives on Politics* 1088 (2013).

Jim Crow in North Carolina

Introduction

In Wilmington, North Carolina, in December 1865, "two negros [sic]" convicted of larceny in the county court were sentenced to be "sold" into "servitude," according to the local newspaper report, for five years.[1] The national press picked up the story and more forthrightly observed that these men were "sentenced to slavery for a term of years."[2] This criminal sentence was handed down over seven months after the end of the Civil War, after the North Carolina state convention of 1865 moved to abolish slavery, and after the state had ratified the Thirteenth Amendment to the U.S. Constitution.[3] Subsequently, in December 1866, crowds of over

---

1. A Conflict of Authorities, *Wilmington Herald*, Dec. 27, 1865, at 1. The sentence was apparently vacated by the Freedmen's Bureau. Id.
2. Our Duty to the Freedmen, *Harper's Weekly*, Jan. 6, 1866, at 2.
3. Hugh Talmage Lefler and Albert Ray Newsome, *North Carolina: The History of a Southern State* 484 (3d ed. 1973); *Cleveland (Oh.) Daily Leader*, Dec. 4, 1865, at 1 (reporting that "[b]oth houses of the North Carolina legislature have passed the Constitutional Amendment").

While the Thirteenth Amendment distinguishes between "slavery" and "involuntary servitude," both are allowed under the amendment "as a punishment for crime." U.S. Const. amend. XIII, sec. 1. As is clear from the Wilmington example, the distinction between slavery and involuntary servitude was nebulous after 1865. One study has observed, "Involuntary servitude . . . was a phrase of broad and indeterminant content—deliberately so." John V. Orth and Paul Martin Newby, *The North Carolina State Constitution* 65 (2d ed. 2013). After the Civil War, there was clearly a drive on the part of many white Southerners to abide by the text of the Thirteenth Amendment but use the criminal law to re-enslave the freedmen. Peter Wallenstein, Slavery Under the Thirteenth Amendment: Race and the Law of Crime and Punishment in the Post-Civil War South, 77 *Louisiana Law Review* 1, 10 (2016) (concluding that "public authorities in southern

400 people in Raleigh "on every day during about a month" witnessed the public whipping "of colored men [brought outside] as fast as they were convicted and sentenced to be whipped" by the state court.[4] The main impetus for the whipping was not as punishment for the crime itself, because many of the convictions were for "paltry offenses,"[5] but were, rather, aimed at a future when the former slaves *might* be extended the right to vote. Why? Because public whipping made their crimes infamous and it thus operated as "as a civil disqualification, so that none of these victims . . . could ever vote, even if the suffrage were extended to colored men."[6]

[sic] states moved quickly to adopt some form of selling or leasing of convicts to private citizens"). However, the Wilmington example here was well before the advent of convict labor in North Carolina and it antedated the statute which permitted counties to hire out convicts "to any company, corporation or individual." 1872–73 N.C. Sess. Laws 290, 292, ch. 174, § 10.

4. Whipping and Selling American Citizens, *Harper's Weekly*, Jan. 12, 1867, at 18 (emphasis omitted).

5. The True Problem, *Atlantic Monthly*, March 1867, at 371, 374. The essay stated:
   Already we learn that the public whipping of negroes for paltry offenses is carried on in North Carolina on a large scale, for the reason that by the laws of that State every man who has been publicly whipped is excluded from the right of voting; so that, if equal suffrage should be imposed upon that State by the [Thirteenth] Constitutional Amendment, or other legislation not sufficiently guarded, a large proportion of the colored population would find itself disfranchised by the mere infliction of a barbarous punishment. How much time it would require thus to disfranchise every negro in the State is a mere arithmetical problem for the consciences of slavery-loving and negro-hating juries . . . .

The True Problem, *Atlantic Monthly*, March 1867, at 371, 374.

6. Whipping and Selling American Citizens, *Harper's Weekly*, Jan. 12, 1867, at 18. What constituted an "infamous" crime under both the common law and statutory law was notoriously imprecise. Rather than "infamous" being tied to the nature of the crime, the North Carolina Supreme Court held that an infamous crime was one which subjected the person "to infamous punishment." *Gudger v. Penland*, 108 N.C. 593, 599 (1891). Conviction of an infamous crime was considered a moral stain on the person and required "his incapacitation as a witness and the suppression of his political rights." Francis Wharton and William Draper Lewis, *A Treatise on Criminal Law* § 22a, at 30 (10th ed. 1896). In North Carolina, an offense punishable by imprisonment did not necessarily constitute infamy and, as long as the offense was not infamous, the person "would retain his *liberam legem* [essentially, one's free law or the ability to take an oath]" and, thus "belong to the *boni et legales homines* of society [good and lawful men]." *Skinner v. White*, 18 N.C. (1 Dev. & Bat.) 471, 474 (1836) (emphasis in original). Thus, conviction of an infamous crime would take away the person's *liberam legem* and generally (although a great deal of discretion was used), remove the person's ability to hold office or sit on juries or vote. See

In a speech in the U.S. House of Representatives the following month, Representative Thaddeus Stevens described a report from officials in the Freedmen's Bureau that "in North Carolina . . . they are now every day whipping negroes for a thousand and one trivial offenses" in order to deprive the freedmen of the vote.[7] Stevens had received word that in one county "they had whipped every adult male negro whom they knew of."[8]

As seen in these two examples, the racial enmity in the application of the criminal law to the freedmen was overt and easily comprehended. The national press and even other governmental officials recognized the reality of what occurred. However, the discriminatory impact of law or the application of law is not always so clear or convincing. On some occasions, the evidence of unequal treatment through law is more diffuse and only achieves clarity with a greater appreciation for how law was administered at the ground level. While the ideal is Lady Justice sitting with a blindfold and balanced scales, the reality is that law is always a reflection of the times and of the people, for better and for worse.

The words of a constitution or a statute only get you so far, and that has been especially true with regard to the field of *de jure* race discrimination. Following the U.S. Supreme Court's decision in 1880 that a statute's explicit exclusion of African Americans from jury service was unconstitutional,[9] white-majority legislatures have often relied on non-explicit language to accomplish the same racially discriminatory ends. Thus, to understand how law has functioned in actuality, it is necessary to look at both the

---

Battle's Revisal of the Public Statutes of North Carolina ch. 59, § 1 (1873) (conviction of infamous crime "whereby the rights of citizenship are forfeited"); Revised Code of North Carolina ch. 58, § 1 (1855) (conviction of infamous crime "whereby the rights of citizenship are forfeited"). The vagueness of the relationship between infamy and citizens' rights was clarified as to voting and officeholding by the 1868 North Carolina Constitution and the 1875 amendments to the Constitution. See Amendment of 1875, ch. 24, to N.C. Const. of 1868, art. VI, sec. 1 ("But no person who, upon conviction or confession in open Court, shall be adjudged guilty of felony, or of any other crime infamous by the laws of this State, and hereafter committed, shall be deemed an elector . . . ."); N.C. Const. of 1868, art. VI, sec. 5 (disqualifying from holding office "[a]ll persons who shall have been convicted of treason, perjury or any other infamous crime").

7. *Congressional Globe*, 39th Congress, 2d Session 324 (Jan. 7, 1867).

8. Id. For an extended discussion of the post-Civil War whipping campaigns across the South, see Pippa Holloway, *Living in Infamy: Felon Disfranchisement and the History of American Citizenship* 33–53 (2014).

9. *Strauder v. West Virginia*, 100 U.S. 303 (1880).

positive law, that is, the text of constitutions and statutes, as well as the operation of the law. Further study and detailed historical research can provide a more comprehensive understanding of the relevant law and how it was put into practice. There is enduring value to legal history which gets down into the proverbial weeds. That is especially true for the subject of racial discrimination, whether by the State of North Carolina or by states and municipalities on both sides of the Mason-Dixon Line.

An example of legal history illuminating the complexity of this process might be instructive, and one such example pertains to the governmental role in exacerbating residential segregation and how the U.S. Supreme Court, in the school desegregation case of *Milliken v. Bradley*, failed to comprehend the ways that law, in various guises, impacted the racial geography of a metropolitan region.[10] *Milliken* involved the segregation of the Detroit, Michigan, school system. Detroit is within Wayne County, Michigan, and the city and county share the same corporate geographical limits to the north. On the other side of that northern boundary line are Macomb and Oakland counties, with communities that are part of "the three-county Detroit metropolitan area"[11] which all share one transit system, one water and sewer system, and park authority.[12] Detroit completely encircles two separate municipalities, with their own school districts.[13] In addition to the Detroit school system, though, there were 85 other school districts in Wayne, Macomb, and Oakland counties at the time that *Milliken* was before the courts.[14]

By the 1970s, when the *Milliken* case was being litigated, the racial geography of the region was of a majority-black central city surrounded by a ring of overwhelmingly white suburbs in Macomb, Oakland, and in the part of Wayne County south of Detroit.[15] Residential segregation based upon race was exceedingly high because, based on the 1970 census figures, Detroit was the sixth most segregated metropolitan area in the nation.[16] This fact meant that the school districts were racially distinct, as

---

10. *Milliken v. Bradley*, 418 U.S. 717 (1974).
11. Id. at 729.
12. Id. at 804 (Marshall, J., dissenting).
13. Id. at 765 (White, J., dissenting).
14. Id. at 729.
15. Id. at 739 (quoting *Bradley v. Milliken*, 484 F.2d 215, 249 (6th Cir. 1973)).
16. Thomas L. Van Valey, Wade Clark Roof, and Jerome E. Wilcox, Trends in Residential Segregation: 1960–1970, 82 *American Journal of Sociology* 826, 836 (1977) (using

well. In 1970, the Detroit school system was 64 percent African American and 35 percent white, while the breakdown for the school-age population in the metropolitan area was 81 percent white and 19 percent African American.[17]

The Supreme Court's holding in *Milliken* was that the remedy for the *de jure* segregation in the Detroit school system—that is, segregation resulting from action by government or law—could not encompass the other school districts and communities without a showing of *de jure* segregation in those districts and communities.[18] Thus, although the Detroit school population was overwhelmingly African American and the suburban school populations were overwhelmingly white, the Court majority reasoned that no remedy involving multiple school districts was permissible when there was no proof that the racial composition of the other 85 school districts in the metropolitan area was the result of discrimination based on race. The Court concluded that the lower federal courts had sanctioned "an interdistrict remedy in the face of a record which shows no constitutional violations . . . except within the city of Detroit."[19]

Without relitigating all of the specifics of *Milliken*, it is reasonably clear that the Court majority's factual premise was mistaken, because *de jure* discrimination existed which impacted the public schools across the Detroit metropolitan area. Richard Rothstein points to *Milliken* in his book, *The Color of Law*, as an example where actions taken by government at all

---

figures for the standard metropolitan statistical area).

17. *Milliken*, 418 U.S. at 765, 765 n.1 (White, J., dissenting).

18. In this book, what I mean by *de jure* discrimination is discrimination rooted in law or actions by any level of government, state or federal. In contrast, what I mean by *de facto* discrimination is discrimination generally originating in actions of private actors such as persons or business entities or other private organizations. It should be noted that, as was the case in *Milliken*, the U.S. Supreme Court has defined *de jure* segregation in the public school context as "a current condition of segregation resulting from intentional state action." *Keyes v. School District No. 1, Denver, Colorado*, 413 U.S. 189, 205 (1973). Relying on this intent standard, the Court has held "that 'the Constitution is not violated by racial imbalance in the schools, without more.'" *Parents Involved in Community Schools v. Seattle School District No. 1*, 551 U.S. 701, 721 (2007) (quoting *Milliken v. Bradley*, 433 U.S. 267, 280 n.14 (1977)). In the present study, however, *de jure* discrimination is used more broadly to separate governmental action from nongovernmental action. The phrase *de jure* is also employed because, for the Jim Crow era, there is little question that discriminatory intent was present in the enactment and implementation of the laws under review here.

19. *Milliken*, 418 U.S. at 752.

levels reinforced and even encouraged the racial segregation that led to a majority-black Detroit surrounded by majority-white communities.[20] It is not that residential segregation based on race did not exist before 1930 but, rather, that federal, state, and local governments created programs and implemented official policies that not only accepted existing segregation, but actually increased its levels in Detroit and throughout America.[21] Starting in 1910, explicit residential restrictions were enacted by cities whereby blocks and neighborhoods were off limits to African American residents, but this approach was struck down by the Supreme Court in 1917.[22] Private individuals subsequently turned to racially restrictive covenants in which contracts or the recorded deeds would prohibit the sale of property to African Americans.[23] And, unquestionably, financial considerations and the actions of private individuals impacted residential housing patterns, but the actions of federal, state, and local governments in the twentieth century worked in tandem to exacerbate the level of residential segregation based upon race.

Many of these governmental policies were not silent about the subject of race and they were applied in ways that caused racially disparate results, and one of the most prominent examples involved the policies of the Federal Housing Administration (FHA). The FHA was established in 1934 as part of the New Deal; it insures mortgages for lenders such as banks, and it has had an indelible impact upon home financing in the United States.[24] As Kenneth Jackson observed in 1985, "No agency of the United States government has had a more pervasive and powerful impact on the American people over the past half-century than the Federal Housing

---

20. Richard Rothstein, *The Color of Law* at xii–xiv (2017).

21. Id. at 23.

22. *Buchanan v. Warley*, 245 U.S. 60, 82 (1917) (invalidating, under Fourteenth Amendment's Due Process Clause, Louisville, Kentucky, ordinance prohibiting the sale of property based on race when majority of residents on block were of another race). See Michael J. Klarman, *From Jim Crow to Civil Rights* 79–83 (2004).

In North Carolina during the years under study, the Town of Mooresville, the City of Winston (prior to its merger with Salem), and the City of Greensboro enacted residential segregation ordinances. See infra Chapter 4.

23. The judicial enforcement of racially restrictive covenants in state courts was held to be state action violative of the Fourteenth Amendment's Equal Protection Clause. *Shelley v. Kraemer*, 334 U.S. 1 (1948). See Clement E. Vose, *Caucasians Only: The Supreme Court, the NAACP, and the Restrictive Covenant Cases* (1959).

24. The FHA was created by Title II of the National Housing Act of 1934, Pub. L. 73-479, 48 Stat. 1246 (1934).

Administration."[25] Mortgage insurance would only be issued if the mortgage and the property itself conformed to guidelines set out by the FHA. With a mortgage guaranteed by the FHA, lenders would be covered by the federal government if the loan went sour. However, for decades, the FHA openly discriminated against minorities—African Americans, in particular—and its policies worked to increase residential segregation.

Prior to providing mortgage insurance on properties, the FHA created standards in the various editions of its *Underwriting Manual* by which to assess the value or creditworthiness of properties and neighborhoods, and the original standards formulated in the 1930s mandated racial discrimination. Indeed, in a section on "Adverse Influences" on properties, the *Underwriting Manual* was explicit that race was one such adverse influence. In advocating for racial covenants in deeds so as to "provid[e] protection from adverse influences," the FHA stated that "[w]here the same deed restrictions apply over a broad area and where these restrictions relate to types of structures, use to which improvements may be put, *and racial occupancy*, a favorable condition is apt to exist."[26] The FHA's April 1936 *Underwriting Manual* stated that high ratings for properties were only warranted where zoning regulations and racially restrictive covenants existed because "these provide the surest protection against undesirable encroachment and inharmonious use."[27] If there was any doubt about what was undesirable and inharmonious, one of the FHA's recommended deed restrictions made it clear: "Prohibition of the occupancy of properties except by the race for which they are intended."[28] Racial homogeneity in neighborhoods was the gold standard to the FHA. But beyond the preference for racially restrictive covenants, the FHA was clear as to its view of mixed-race neighborhoods, generally, and of white neighborhoods bordering African American neighborhoods: "The Valuator should investi-

---

25. Kenneth T. Jackson, *Crabgrass Frontier* 203 (1985).
26. Federal Housing Administration, *Underwriting Manual* ¶ 228 (Apr. 1, 1936) (emphasis added). The section entitled "Protection from Adverse Influences" can be found at id. ¶¶ 226–233.
27. Federal Housing Administration, *Underwriting Manual* ¶ 284(1) (Apr. 1, 1936).
28. Id. ¶ 284(3). To understand how retrograde the FHA was as to fair housing, the federal-government entity continued to advocate for racially restrictive covenants in deeds for two years *after* the U.S. Supreme Court held such restrictions to be unenforceable under the Fourteenth Amendment in *Shelley v. Kraemer*, 334 U.S. 1 (1948). The FHA finally refused to insure properties with restrictive covenants recorded after February 15, 1950. Jack Greenberg, *Race Relations and American Law* 299 (1959).

gate areas surrounding the location [of the highly-rated neighborhood] to determine whether or not *incompatible racial and social groups* are present, to the end that an intelligent prediction may be made regarding the possibility or probability of the location being *invaded* by such groups."[29] Moreover, racial homogeneity was not only desirable, but it was to be permanent in the FHA's eyes: "If a neighborhood is to retain stability it is necessary that properties shall continue to be occupied by the same social and racial classes. A change in social or racial occupancy generally leads to instability and a reduction in values."[30] To the FHA, any neighborhood with black homeowners—even a homogenous one—was not entitled to a high rating for credit worthiness. In practice, there was no allowance for the possibility that middle- or upper-class African Americans could move into a neighborhood without destroying the housing values.[31] A street or

---

29. Id. ¶ 233 (emphasis added). The 1936 language was not an aberration, and it was maintained in later iterations of the Underwriting Manual, as in this case: "Areas surrounding a location are investigated to determine whether incompatible racial and social groups are present, for the purpose of making a prediction regarding the probability of the location being invaded by such groups." Federal Housing Administration, *Underwriting Manual* ¶ 937 (Feb. 1938).

30. Id.

31. 1 Gunnar Myrdal, *An American Dilemma: The Negro Problem and Modern Democracy* 625 (1944) ("The fact is neglected by the whites that there exists a Negro upper and middle class who are searching for decent homes and who, if they were not shunned by the whites, would contribute to property values in a neighborhood rather than cause them to deteriorate."). It was clear to Myrdal, in 1944, what the consequences of the FHA policies were: "The Federal Housing Administration, in effect, extends credit to Negroes only if they build or buy in Negro neighborhoods and to whites only if they build in white areas which are under covenant not to rent or sell to Negroes." Id. That observation, however, was ultimately too rosy, as Thomas Sugrue recognized decades later: "[W]hite owned banks were ... largely unwilling to make safe loans in areas that attracted well-to-do blacks. And they systematically refused to lend to blacks who were among the first to move to all-white neighborhoods or to developers building new homes for blacks.... Because of bankers' racial conservatism, blacks found it almost impossible to get conventional home financing." Thomas J. Sugrue, *The Origins of the Urban Crisis: Race and Inequality in Postwar Detroit* 46–47 (1996).

The standards created by the FHA, at least in the very first editions of the *Underwriting Manual*, were distinct from the residential security maps created by the Home Owners' Loan Corporation (HOLC) of 239 cities between 1935 and 1940. Louis Lee Woods, II, The Federal Home Loan Bank Board, Redlining, and the National Proliferation of Racial Lending Discrimination, 1921–1950, 39 *Journal of Urban History* 1036, 1041 (2012). These HOLC maps are well known today because of the fact that they shaded the lowest-graded urban areas in red, and they are almost certainly the referent for the practice known as

neighborhood occupied by non-whites equaled low valuations, with no exceptions, and a "reject" rating was the result.[32] Even in 1961, the United States Commission on Civil Rights recognized the racial inequity: "Fed-

---

"redlining" whereby mortgage decisions were made based on the neighborhood where the property was located rather than an individualized review of the property. There were four grades for neighborhoods, and the lowest grade of "hazardous" was given to neighborhoods where a mortgage loan was thought to be a dangerous investment. Id. at 1043. The four levels of neighborhood quality were the highest rating A (colored green on the maps), B (blue) was "still desirable," C (yellow) was "definitely declining," and D (red) was where the decline was supposedly complete. Jackson, supra note 25, at 197–198. However, even apart from the consideration of the neighborhoods, there was a clear correlation between the maps' areas of red and the race of the occupants of the neighborhoods: "Areas with African Americans, as well as those with older housing and poorer households, were consistently given a fourth grade, or 'hazardous,' rating and colored red." Amy E. Hillier, Redlining and the Home Owners' Loan Corporation, 29 *Journal of Urban History* 394, 395 (2003). HOLC's residential security maps are now well known and have been frequently reproduced because they provide a clear visual representation of the areas which were cut off from investment and were allowed to decay and because they were, unsurprisingly, areas populated by African Americans. It is unclear as to what degree the HOLC maps themselves were used in subsequent decades. While there has been debate over whether the HOLC maps were shared with other federal agencies and lenders, it seems clear that HOLC's appraisal methods were an outgrowth of a close connection between private lenders and HOLC. There was clearly cross-pollination between HOLC's standardization of appraisals, FHA assessments, and lender decisions because the local agents of these federal agencies who helped make the determinations about the relative "quality" of neighborhoods were often local bankers, realtors, and appraisers. Jackson, supra note 25, at 199. HOLC, as an arm of the Federal Home Loan Bank Board (FHLBB), exerted a powerful influence over standardizing appraisal methods across the country: "FHLBB incorporated the HOLC appraisal standards and insisted that they be used as the national 'professional standard' that would become the 'uniform appraisal policies' that governed the lending activities of all federal banks across the country and their member lending institutions." Woods, *supra*, at 1044. One recent study has demonstrated that the HOLC neighborhoods maps' designation of the two lowest grades—"hazardous" or red and "definitely declining" or yellow—directly led to a drop in private lending in those areas and that it impacted the degree of racial segregation on each side of these boundaries. Daniel Aaronson, Daniel Hartley, and Bhashkar Mazumder, The Effects of the 1930s HOLC "Redlining Maps," Working Papers of the Federal Reserve Bank of Chicago, WP 2017-12, Revised February 2019, available at https://www.chicagofed.org/publications/working-papers/2017/wp2017-12 (last visited July 30, 2019). While the FHA created its own detailed neighborhood maps of at least some metropolitan areas, only a limited number of these maps have been found. Jackson, supra note 25, at 365 n.56.

32. Federal Housing Administration, *Underwriting Manual* ¶ 226 (Apr. 1, 1936) ("Where little or no protection is provided against adverse influences the Valuator must not hesitate to make a reject rating of this feature.").

eral policy in the housing field reflected and even magnified the attitudes of private industry. The FHA indeed encouraged racial discrimination."[33]

On the ground in Detroit, these underwriting standards not only hurt African Americans' ability to obtain conventional mortgages, but they led to visible segregation of black from white. A definite and tangible line of segregation occurred in the Eight Mile-Wyoming neighborhood where a twelve-inch-thick, six-foot-tall concrete wall's erection was necessary before the FHA would insure the loan for a new white development on the west side of the divide.[34] In the 1940s, a small enclave of African Americans lived in this neighborhood on the northern edge of Detroit, but the surrounding areas were majority white.[35] The developer had been unable to secure the loan for the new development because of its proximity to the African American section, but a compromise was reached with the FHA. In exchange for the loan and mortgage guarantees, a six-foot-tall wall extending a half mile was built to separate the races.[36] The irony was that by 1950, the white exodus to the suburbs was so prevalent that "the expanding black population jumped the infamous 'dividing wall' and moved in to the formerly white neighborhood in the west."[37] The wall remains to this day, between Birwood Avenue and Mendota Street, as a reminder of the federal government's policy.

The FHA's esteem for racial homogeneity and its uniformly low valuations of minority neighborhoods did not alone lead to the great metropolitan exodus of whites to the suburbs with African Americans simultaneously tied to an increasingly black central city. There were several governmental policies driving the development of the more-affluent suburbs, not the least important of which was the federal government's com-

---

33. U.S. Commission on Civil Rights, *Housing* at 16 (1961).
34. Sugrue, supra note 31, at 63–72.
35. Id. at 63.
36. Id. at 64. The FHA noted in the *Underwriting Manual* that natural and artificial barriers between areas occupied by "inharmonious" racial groups might weigh in favor of guaranteeing the loan: "Natural or artificial established barriers will prove effective in protecting a neighborhood and the locations within it from adverse influences. Usually the protection against adverse influences afforded by these means include prevention of the infiltration of business and industrial uses, lower-class occupancy, and inharmonious racial groups." Federal Housing Administration, *Underwriting Manual* ¶ 229 (Apr. 1, 1936).
37. Sugrue, supra note 31, at 71.

mitment to allowing the deduction of mortgage interest payments and real estate taxes from the federal income tax of owners of single-family homes.[38] But the increasing residential segregation by race was also being driven by the complementary forces of the FHA's favoritism toward new single-family homes over multifamily apartment buildings and the suburban municipalities' zoning ordinances which mirrored the FHA's preferences. The FHA's relative valuations and localities' zoning rules combined to exclude middle- and low-income African Americans from the suburbs, and many zoning rules were enacted with the goal of excluding African Americans but in the language of single-family homes and setbacks and lot requirements.

The FHA was explicit about its preference toward new suburban developments relative to the underwriting of multifamily structures or existing houses in the city itself. New developments were proclaimed to be "the best mortgage-lending areas"[39] while individuals "of all income levels usually desire to live away from the crowded, older sections of the town."[40] The new single-family houses in the suburbs provided "sufficient light, air, and ground space for play and gardening. For the medium and upper income levels this desire to move to suburban locations is easily possible of fulfillment."[41] At the same time, to the FHA, the desire for houses in these new developing areas meant that the neighborhoods where families were moving *from* could not maintain stable valuations, but were automatically "accompanied by declines in desirability and value."[42] The FHA saw a direct line between a neighborhood's decline in desirability and the genesis of boarding houses and crowded tenements: "In this manner the older districts gradually lose the aspects of owner-occupied communities

---

38. Jackson, supra note 25, at 191.

39. Federal Housing Administration, *Underwriting Manual* ¶ 281 (Apr. 1, 1936). Compare this viewpoint with the following: "Proximity to the center of any major city ... has a tendency to produce rooming houses, boarding houses, or crowded tenements." Id. ¶ 236.

40. Id. ¶ 241.

41. Id.

42. Id. ¶ 305(2). As to the automatic and inescapable nature of this process, the 1936 *Manual* states: "A superficial examination of residential areas in any American city reveals the fact that, with practically no exception, such districts decline in desirability with the passage of substantial periods of time." Id. ¶ 305(1).

and take on the aspects of tenant-occupied districts."[43] It should come as no surprise that the FHA's assumptions became self-fulfilling prophesies, boosting the value of the suburban developments and gutting the value of more densely populated center-city neighborhoods which, in turn, made the latter even less worthy of mortgage guarantees.

The practical effect of the FHA's preferences was to underwrite mortgages in the new (white) metropolitan suburbs for single-family homes while not supplying mortgage guarantees for apartments and more affordable housing in either the suburbs or the urban center. These policies drove the booming new subdivisions and, at the same time, they allowed for the decay and overcrowding of the city and the pathologies that accompanied those. In 1940, the FHA reported that 98 percent of the subdivisions it had underwritten "were restricted to single-family detached homes."[44] The same report noted that from 1934 through 1940, the number of apartment buildings underwritten by the FHA across the country totaled 317, while all other residential mortgage guarantees totaled 634,023.[45] Since the FHA pushed racial homogeneity and wanted to preserve the value of the new suburban developments, apartments were not being built in the suburbs but, at the same time, money was not flowing to the increasingly crowded enclaves of the city cores. As Kenneth Jackson recognized in his pathbreaking book, *Crabgrass Frontier*: "[T]he Federal Housing Administration allowed personal and agency bias in favor of all-white subdivisions in the suburbs to affect the kinds of loans it guaranteed—or, equally important, refused to guarantee."[46]

---

43. Id. ¶ 305(1).

44. Federal Housing Administration, *Seventh Annual Report of the Federal Housing Administration* 23 (1941).

45. Id. at 7. The numbers were for Section 207 mortgage insurance on apartment rental projects and Section 203 mortgage insurance on non-apartment residences, respectively. The trend continued. For the totals for 1934 through 1955, the FHA had underwritten the mortgages on only 765 multifamily apartment projects compared to 3,160,929 homes. Federal Housing Administration, *Twenty-Second Annual Report of the Federal Housing Administration* 19 (1957). Again, these numbers were for Section 207 mortgage insurance on apartment rental projects and Section 203 mortgage insurance on non-apartment residences, respectively.

46. Jackson, supra note 25, at 207. See also id. at 206 ("[The FHA] favored the construction of single-family projects and discouraged construction of multi-family projects through unpopular terms.").

Beyond the mortgage guarantees, though, the FHA's policies drove the suburban townships to adopt zoning rules which ensured, in a comprehensive manner, that their communities would be composed of single-family homes on large lots and with few apartments in order to restrict the number of people who could rent and not buy. The FHA *Underwriting Manual* said that for "a homogenous and harmonious neighborhood,"[47] zoning was the best option: "Carefully complied zoning regulations are the most effective because they not only exercise control over the subject property but also over the surrounding area."[48]

Suburbs took the suggestion and enacted zoning ordinances that worked, in different ways, to ensure homogenous and harmonious townships outside of the urban city core. The suburbs' zoning laws tilted the scales against the less economically well off, which overlapped with the set of "incompatible racial and social groups."[49] Zoning ordinances either banned outright or severely restricted multifamily apartment buildings.[50] Suburbs enacted zoning ordinances for the new subdivisions which often

---

47. Federal Housing Administration, *Underwriting Manual* ¶ 284(2) (Apr. 1, 1936).
48. Id.
49. Id. ¶ 233.
50. The zoning restrictions on apartments avoided the language of race, but multifamily buildings "are often not permitted to have more than one or two bedrooms. A common zoning restriction provides that at least 80 percent of the dwelling units in a multi-family development must have only one bedroom, with up to 20 percent permitted to have two bedrooms." Roger A. Cunningham, The Interrelationship Between Exclusionary Zoning and Exclusionary Subdivision Control—A Second Look, 6 *University of Michigan Journal of Law Reform* 290, 305 (1973). The result was clear: "[E]xclusion of or restrictions on multi-family dwellings tend to perpetuate both economic and racial or ethnic segregation." Id. Suburban bans on apartment buildings through zoning were eventually challenged in the courts. *Park View Heights Corp. v. City of Black Jack*, 467 F.2d 1208 (8th Cir. 1972) (challenge to zoning ordinance which "effectively prohibit[ed]" multifamily dwellings in suburb of St. Louis, Missouri); *Appeal of Girsh*, 437 Pa. 237, 263 A.2d 395 (1970) (challenge to zoning ordinance that did not provide for multifamily apartments in suburb of Philadelphia, Pennsylvania). See also David M. P. Freund, *Colored Property: State Policy and White Racial Politics in Suburban America* 216 (2007) ("[Z]oning itself provided a powerful, court-tested tool for excluding types of residential development—apartments and public housing, especially—that might give racial minorities access to white neighborhoods."). It is worthy of note here that in the U.S. Supreme Court's first major decision on a zoning ordinance, the Court described the apartment building as "a mere parasite" which destroys "the residential character of the neighborhood and its desirability" and that apartments come "very near to being nuisances." *Village of Euclid v. Ambler Realty Co.*, 272 U.S. 365, 394–395 (1926).

mandated detached single-family houses, minimum lot sizes, and setback requirements, all of which worked silently to set the financial bar too high for many African Americans.[51] By zoning the majority of property in the city or township for single-family homes, suburbs thereby constricted all other types of residential development.[52] And, there were zoning regulations that defined what constituted a "family" for the category of single-family residences in order to prevent extended family members or others from living together as a household.[53] While many such zoning laws limited households to those family members related by consanguinity, or

---

51. E.g., *Lionshead Lake, Inc. v. Township of Wayne*, 10 N.J. 165, 89 A.2d 693 (1952), appeal dismissed, 344 U.S. 919 (1953) (upholding minimum-size requirements for houses in Passaic County, N.J.); *Flora Realty & Inv. Co. v. City of Ladue*, 246 S.W.2d 771 (Mo.), appeal dismissed, 344 U.S. 802 (1952) (upholding three-acre lot minimum in St. Louis suburb). See also Freund, supra note 50, at 229 ("[L]arge-lot zoning fast became the trademark suburban land-use strategy. Setting a minimum size for residential plats—generally a quarter acre or more, or twice the size of the typical prewar lot—helped communities maintain low population densities and required the construction of larger, more costly homes."). Although there were (and are) numerous reasons underlying zoning requirements of large lots and setbacks, historically, one of them was race, as noted in 1969:

> Many homeowners also want to exclude families of an economic status lower than their own, perhaps on the assumption that poorer or darker-skinned neighbors will hinder the education of their children, commit more crime, or make living in the suburbs less prestigious. Large lot zoning serves this exclusionary purpose by making residency in the suburb more expensive.

David S. Schoenbrod, Large Lot Zoning, 78 *Yale Law Journal* 1418, 1420–1421 (1969).

52. See Freund, supra note 50, at 230–231 ("The net result was the limitation, strict segregation, and often total exclusion of multiple-family dwellings in the nation's fast-growing suburbs.... By 1970, municipalities in Bergen County, New Jersey, had zoned 27,000 acres of undeveloped land exclusively for single-family homes, compared with 131 acres for apartments."). See also Emily Badger and Quoctrung Bui, Housing Scarce, Cities Erase Single-Family Lots, *N.Y. Times*, June 19, 2019, at A1 (noting that today "[i]t is illegal on 75 percent of the residential land in many American cities to build anything other than a detached single-family home.").

53. National Institute of Municipal Law Officers, *NIMLO Model Zoning Ordinance* 4 (1954) (model zoning ordinance defined "family" as "a single individual, doing his own cooking, and living upon the premises as a separate housekeeping unit, or a collective body of persons doing their own cooking and living together upon the premises as a separate housekeeping unit in a domestic relationship based upon birth, marriage, or other domestic bond").

by blood, some went even further in an attempt to restrict residents who were parts of nontraditional families.[54]

The use of zoning requirements by suburban townships to limit renters and increase the costs of homeownership had the effect of restricting the African American populations of the suburbs, and that result was often intentional. There are certainly good and race-neutral reasons why cities and townships have zoning ordinances, but there was a large degree of overlap between many of the zoning rules adopted in the mid-twentieth century and the desire to keep suburban townships overwhelmingly white. City officials knew that "[i]n effect, economic segregation is not only the easiest but also the most effective form of racial and ethnic segregation."[55] Zoning law was being used to exclude indirectly: "[Z]oning's preference for single-family homes—when seen in the context of a racially segmented mortgage market—meant that most ordinances effectively prescribed racial restriction without ever addressing the issue of race directly."[56]

---

54. It was just that type of zoning law that led to the criminal charge against Mrs. Inez Moore for violating a zoning ordinance because she had two grandsons who were first cousins, rather than brothers, living under her roof. The U.S. Supreme Court invalidated her conviction, holding that the zoning law's cramped notion of "family" violated the Due Process Clause, but the intent behind the ordinance was to prevent extended family members from living together in a rapidly integrating suburb. *Moore v. City of East Cleveland*, 431 U.S. 494 (1977). In his concurrence, Justice Brennan concluded, "The Constitution cannot be interpreted, however, to tolerate the imposition by government upon the rest of us of white suburbia's preference in patterns of family living." Id. at 508 (Brennan, J., concurring).

55. Norman Williams, Jr., Planning Law and Democratic Living, 20 *Law and Contemporary Problems* 317, 330 (1953). Charles Abrams wrote: "Communities no longer resort to the clumsy device of [explicit] racial zoning laws, thereby exposing themselves to judicial attack. The methods are more subtle, motives less discernible, and exclusions more effective. Thus, an ordinance might be written to permit no more than one building to an acre or otherwise make any housing development impractical." Charles Abrams, *Forbidden Neighbors* 210 (1955).

56. Freund, supra note 50, at 227. In 1953, Charles Haar recognized that zoning law was being used to exclude indirectly to "preserve rigidly the character of certain neighborhoods in the interest of preserving property values.... [S]egregation is being increasingly accomplished in terms of levels of prices and rentals, of home ownership versus renting." Charles M. Haar, Zoning for Minimum Standards: The Wayne Township Case, 66 *Harvard Law Review* 1051, 1062–1063 (1953). See also J. Peter Byrne, Are Suburbs Unconstitutional? (Book Review), 85 *Georgetown Law Journal* 2265, 2277 (1997) ("Although it is sometimes asserted that exclusionary practices result merely from the pur-

It should not come as a surprise, then, that the suburbs around Detroit enacted zoning restrictions which worked, under the guise of density, to exclude African Americans and other minorities. In Bloomfield Hills in Oakland County, the attitude was that apartments were "[m]onstrosities" and even if only "scattered" along the major trunk-line road, Woodward Avenue, their presence would "deface Bloomfield."[57] This suburban attitude toward renters and apartments was written into zoning codes. Thus, the City of East Detroit (now Eastpointe), in Macomb County, mandated that apartments were permitted to be built only on stretches of two roads which intersected with one another, in an area that was otherwise zoned for commercial businesses, and the apartments could not be erected "to a height exceeding thirty-five (35) feet."[58] The 1948 zoning map for East Detroit shows that somewhere between 50 and 75 percent of the city was zoned R1 for one-family dwellings.[59] Similarly, in Clinton Township, also in Macomb, multifamily apartments were limited to terrace apartments, "[r]ow houses and multiple dwellings not to exceed eight (8) dwelling units" and multiple family dwellings "in excess of eight units subject to the approval of the Township Planning Commission."[60] Whatever multifamily buildings were constructed could also not "exceed two stories or thirty-five feet in height."[61] With regard to "family," the City of Troy, in Oakland County, defined "family" in its zoning ordinance to be restricted to parents and "direct lineal descendants and adopted children . . . together with not more than two persons not so related."[62] In terms of pushing the

---

suit of economic self-interest by suburban residents, the history of suburban expansion makes the conclusion that it is also driven by a desire for racial isolation inescapable.").

57. Saarinen, Swanson & Saarinen and City Planners of Bloomfield Hills, Michigan, *A General Development Plan for Bloomfield Hills* n.p. (1947).

58. City of East Detroit, *Official Zoning Ordinance* § 10.2, at 13 (1948). The two roads were "Gratiot Avenue only, [and the north side of] Nine Mile Road only." Id. § 10.1(3), at 13.

59. Id. at 18–21.

60. Township of Clinton, *Township of Clinton Official Zoning Ordinance, Number 74*, §§ 4:04-1 and 4:05, at 17 (1958).

61. Id. § 4:04–5, at 17 (referring back to regulation in § 4:01-7, at 16).

62. City of Troy, *City of Troy Zoning Ordinance* § 5.2(30), at 2 (1965). The Troy ordinance went on to state: "Every additional group of two or less persons living on [sic] such housekeeping unit shall be considered a separate family for the purposes of this Chapter." Id. This ordinance would, therefore, work in the following manner: If the renters or owners were to be a husband and wife and, if the wife's divorced sister and her child

size of lots, the City of Warren in Macomb County required one-family residential lots to be between 10,980 square feet and 8,400 square feet in area.[63] The City of Lavonia, in Wayne County, mandated that single-family homes contain a minimum of "one thousand (1000) square feet of usable floor space."[64] But the large lot and house-size minimums were really maximized in other area communities such as Bloomfield Hills, where for single-family dwellings, front-yard setbacks were 40 feet, the minimum dwelling size was 25,000 square feet and the minimum lot size in the five single-family categories varied from three-quarters of an acre to two acres.[65]

Apart from the language of these zoning ordinances, the intent was to make it hard for even middle-class African Americans to move across the city limits from Detroit and into the suburban communities. The attitude was summed up by Dearborn Mayor Orville Hubbard at a December 1944 community meeting: "Housing the Negroes is Detroit's problem."[66] Similarly, a 1954 publication of the Royal Oak Chamber of Commerce, in Oakland County, extolled the zoning work of "professional city planning engineers, architects, and topographers" which had led to a city where "a high

---

intended to live with the couple, along with the wife's mother, that grouping of people would constitute two families under this definition. Thus, apart from the number of bedrooms in the apartment or house, this grouping was technically to be excluded from single-family dwellings.

63. City of Warren, *City of Warren Zoning Ordinance No. 30*, §§ 5.03, 6.03, 7.03, at 10–11 (1960).

64. City of Livonia, *Zoning Ordinance of the City of Livonia* § 4.05, at 8, § 4.32, at 14 (1952). The 7,200 square foot requirement was for 33 of 36 zoned residential sections. Id. § 4.05, at 8.

65. City of Bloomfield Hills, *Zoning Ordinance*, art. XI—Schedule of Regulations at 22 (1964). It should be noted that, from the 1940s through the 1960s, Michigan's Supreme Court stood out nationally as being somewhat hostile to the application of zoning rules to property owners in many situations. Roger A. Cunningham, Zoning Law in Michigan and New Jersey: A Comparative Study, 63 *Michigan Law Review* 1171, 1184–1185 (1965) (noting history of Michigan Supreme Court "giving weight to exactly the same factors local governing bodies should take into account when they enact a zoning ordinance. In short, the court was acting as a 'super zoning commission,' despite the fact that it was normally able to consider only one parcel of land at a time."). The court finally paid heed to a presumption that zoning rules were valid exercises of the police power in *Padover v. Township of Farmington*, 374 Mich. 622, 132 N.W.2d 687 (1965), upholding average minimum lot sizes for single family residential dwellings of 20,000 square feet.

66. Mayor Orville Hubbard, Dec. 18, 1944, quoted in Sugrue, supra note 31, at 76.

percentage of workers residing in this area own their own homes" and, thus, a city that was "nearly 100% white."[67] By 1970, the Detroit suburbs were so racially segregated that the City of Warren, in Macomb County, became the focus of a federal Department of Housing and Urban Development drive "to crack suburban zoning laws and local attitudes that have the effect of keeping blacks out of housing beyond the central cities."[68] At a community meeting with HUD Secretary and former Michigan Governor George Romney, "Warren councilmen ... made it clear they wanted the Federal money but not black residents from the city."[69] These attitudes in the Detroit suburbs were made manifest in the zoning ordinances and, as Thomas Sugrue concluded in his study of post-war Detroit, "It was far more difficult for African Americans to cross suburban lines than it was for them to move into white urban neighborhoods."[70]

The FHA's underwriting policies and these suburban zoning laws worked together to maintain and exacerbate the degree to which the Detroit suburbs were racially monochromatic. But, even so, the numbers are striking. In 1950, East Detroit, in Macomb County—which, along its southern boundary, abutted the City of Detroit—had a total population of 21,461 but only 12 "nonwhite" residents.[71] In 1960, East Detroit's total population had grown to 45,756 but with only 41 nonwhites.[72] Similarly, in 1950, Livonia had a total population of 17,534 but only 21 nonwhites.[73]

---

67. Royal Oak Chamber of Commerce, *Royal Oak: Michigan's Most Promising Community* (1954), quoted in Freund, supra note 50, at 239.

68. Jerry M. Flint, Michiganites Jeer Romney Over Suburbs' Integration, *N.Y. Times*, July 29, 1970, at 27.

69. Id. A group protesting the integration plan formed outside of this meeting and when Romney left the meeting, "hundreds of persons jeered him and some banged against his car as the police cleared a path." Id. See also Jerry M. Flint, Blue Collar Workers of Warren, a Detroit Suburb, Fight to Keep Negroes Out, *N.Y. Times*, Aug. 17, 1970, at 18 ("Most [Warren residents] are factory workers who say they were driven from their old homes [in Detroit] by blacks moving into their neighborhood. They say that now that they have moved to Warren they will not run again.").

70. Sugrue, supra note 31, at 266.

71. U.S. Bureau of the Census, *U.S. Census of Population: 1950, Vol. II, Characteristics of the Population, Part 22, Michigan* at 22–68 (1952) (hereinafter "U.S. Census 1950"). "Nonwhite" was the term used and, in 1950, was not broken down further.

72. U.S. Bureau of the Census, *U.S. Census of Population: 1960, Vol. 1, Characteristics of the Population, Part 24, Michigan* at 24–60 (1963) (hereinafter "U.S. Census 1960"). "Nonwhite" was, again, the general term employed.

73. U.S. Census 1950, supra note 71, at 22–71.

In 1960, those numbers for Livonia were 66,702 total and 140 nonwhites.[74] In Royal Oak, in Oakland County, there was the same imbalance: in 1950, 46,898 total and 69 nonwhites,[75] while in 1960, there were 80,612 residents but only 142 nonwhites.[76] For Macomb and Oakland counties, the overall numbers were lopsided, as well.[77] All the while, Detroit's nonwhite population grew from 303,721 in 1950[78] to 487,174 in 1960.[79]

It is against this history that the factual underpinning for the Supreme Court's decision in *Milliken v. Bradley* was so blinkered and divorced from reality. The Court concluded that for a multi-district remedy, there "must first be shown that there has been a constitutional violation within one district that produces a significant segregative effect in another district."[80] For the Court majority to base its decision on the supposed absence of governmental action affecting the racial imbalances across the dozens of school districts in the Detroit metropolitan area was to ignore the history and expert consensus that existed at that time. Detroit's schools were overwhelmingly black and the suburban schools were overwhelming white and that situation did not exist solely because of individuals' unfettered choices as to where they lived. For the Court to hang its decision on the lack of "an interdistrict violation and interdistrict effect"[81] missed the fact that the various suburban school districts did not have to shift school boundaries in order to keep themselves white because that had already been accomplished through zoning laws and a racially discriminatory mortgage underwriting system.[82] The numerous suburban districts

---

74. U.S. Census 1960, supra note 72, at 24–67.
75. U.S. Census 1950, supra note 71, at 22–74.
76. U.S. Census 1960, supra note 72, at 24–71.
77. In 1950, Macomb County had 184,961 total and 4,429 nonwhites, U.S. Census 1950, supra note 71, at 22–123, and, in 1960, the population was 405,804 with 6,798 nonwhites. U.S. Census 1960, supra note 72, at 24–157. For Oakland County, in 1950, the total population was 396,001 with 18,388 nonwhites, U.S. Census 1950, supra note 71, at 22–125, while in 1960, it had a total population of 690,259 and only 24,078 nonwhites. U.S. Census 1960, supra note 72, at 24–158.
78. U.S. Census 1950, supra note 71, at 22–68.
79. U.S. Census 1960, supra note 72, at 24–60.
80. *Milliken*, 418 U.S. at 744–745.
81. Id. at 745.
82. James E. Ryan, The Supreme Court and Voluntary Integration, 121 *Harvard Law Review* 131, 140 (2007) ("[Proof of school district gerrymandering] was hard to come by, in part because housing discrimination kept most African Americans out of the suburbs,

were not packing whites and blacks into different schools because, given the numbers of African Americans in many of the Detroit suburbs, that was a virtual impossibility. Not only did the Supreme Court majority push aside the specific findings of fact on this issue by the district court,[83] but it ignored a vast literature that already existed about how these laws and governmental policies had impacted where people lived and where their children went to school. Thus, in one of the most consequential school desegregation cases after *Brown v. Board of Education*,[84] the Supreme Court ignored the history of how law and governmental action left their imprint on the world.

As with the ways that FHA policies and local zoning laws affected residential segregation, there is great value in legal history that examines,

---

so there was no need to play around with school district boundaries in order to keep suburban schools mostly white.").

83. On the issue of the governmental responsibility here, the district court found:
   Governmental actions and inaction at all levels, federal, state and local, have combined, with those of private organizations, such as loaning institutions and real estate associations and brokerage firms, to establish and to maintain the pattern of residential segregation throughout the Detroit metropolitan area.... The policies pursued by both government and private persons and agencies have a continuing and present effect upon the complexion of the community as we know, the choice of a residence is a relatively infrequent affair. For many years FHA and VA openly advised and advocated the maintenance of "harmonious" neighborhoods, *i.e.*, racially and economically harmonious. The conditions created continue. While it would be unfair to charge the present defendants with what other governmental officers or agencies have done, it can be said that the actions or the failure to act by the responsible school authorities, both city and state, were linked to that of these other governmental units. When we speak of governmental action we should not view the different agencies as a collection of unrelated units. Perhaps the most that can be said is that all of them, including the school authorities, are, in part, responsible for the segregated condition which exists. And we note that just as there is an interaction between residential patterns and the racial composition of the schools, so there is a corresponding effect on the residential pattern by the racial composition of the schools.
Bradley v. Milliken, 338 F. Supp. 582, 587 (E.D. Mich. 1971). In response, the Supreme Court took refuge in the fact that the Court of Appeals had not relied upon this finding in affirming the district court's decision: "Accordingly, in its present posture, the case does not present any question concerning possible state housing violations." *Milliken*, 418 U.S. at 728 n.7.

84. *Brown v. Board of Education*, 347 U.S. 483 (1954).

with specificity, how law and society interact. Whether in the form of a constitution, a statute, an administrative regulation or the interpretation and application of any one of these, law is the central process for organization and decisionmaking in a democratic state. And it is important to know or uncover or perhaps recover the ways, in granular detail, that the law has both operated on and been impacted by the society in which it operates. Law—in all of its forms—does not come into existence in a vacuum and it is not interpreted and applied in a vacuum. That is to say, law is not autonomous, and external factors like economic and social and political forces will impact what the law is. As Justice Benjamin Cardozo recognized, speaking with regard to judges, "The great tides and currents which engulf the rest of men do not turn aside in their course and pass the judges by."[85] Constitutions and statutes are written within the tides and currents of their times and they are, in turn, interpreted and applied within those same waters. The same can be said for federal mortgage underwriting policies, local zoning ordinances, and every other action of the human institution known as government.

This book is a study of the history of Jim Crow in North Carolina between 1865 and 1920. The primary focus here is on law and on the application of the law in that place and during that period of time. The empirical spadework undertaken here is an attempt to catalog all of the racially discriminatory laws enacted by the State of North Carolina during this time period. But, in addition, I examine how those laws are applied in disparate ways along the racial divide. The Jim Crow laws in North Carolina created a baroque system of *de jure* discrimination, and the ultimate impact in the state and on the state's residents was because of the cumulative effect of those laws, their interpretation, and their operation. The sum was, indeed, greater than the parts. The history of how these laws were implemented is an important gauge for how law works and how, sometimes, what is in the statute books fails to fully capture what is going on in the world.

Since the 1955 publication of C. Vann Woodward's monumental book, *The Strange Career of Jim Crow*, the historical study of racial discrimination has been a growth industry.[86] And, no wonder, both because of how multifaceted race discrimination has been in this country and because

---

85. Benjamin N. Cardozo, *The Nature of the Judicial Process* 168 (1921).
86. C. Vann Woodward, *The Strange Career of Jim Crow* (1955).

of how important this history is to America's present. Woodward argued that the legal, physical separation of the races had not always existed in the South and that there was no system of Jim Crow at the end of the Civil War because it was not needed in a slave society. Woodward went on to argue that there were "forgotten alternatives," paths not taken in the treatment of African Americans by the white South in the decades after 1865, and that the hardened system of *de jure* discrimination that existed in the first half of the twentieth century had not been an inevitability.[87] Law was central to *The Strange Career of Jim Crow* and, even with subsequent scholarship in the field, Woodward observed over thirty years after the book's initial publication that "further research is needed on the Jim Crow statutes themselves."[88]

Some of the most important scholarship following Woodward focused on the origins and geography of racial segregation, both in law and with regard to custom. Assumptions have frequently been turned on their heads. The first uses of what were termed "Jim Crow railroad cars" can be found in the North in the 1840s.[89] In addition, segregation and racial separation have not always been driven by racial hostility. To modern sensibilities, racial segregation is the manifestation of discrimination because segregation is "inherently unequal."[90] But, in the first years after the Civil War and especially with regard to governmental programs, if integration was viewed as an impossibility, segregation was seen as a half-loaf solution to complete exclusion based on race.[91] Some scholars have argued that the

---

87. C. Vann Woodward, *The Strange Career of Jim Crow* 31–65 (3d rev. ed. 1974).

88. C. Vann Woodward, *Strange Career* Critics: Long May They Persevere, 75 *Journal of American History* 857, 862 (1988). See also Woodward, supra note 87, at xiii ("law has a special importance in the history of segregation"). For a more detailed discussion of Woodward, see infra Chapter 2.

89. See, e.g., The Anti-Slavery Convention, *Boston Post*, June 10, 1843, at 1 ("[Mr. Remond] manifested an almost rabid antipathy against the 'Jim Crow car,' designed expressly for the special accommodation of 'the niggers.'"). See also Leon F. Litwack, *North of Slavery: The Negro in the Free States, 1790–1860*, at 97, 106–107 (1961).

90. *Brown v. Board of Education*, 347 U.S. 483, 495 (1954).

91. Howard N. Rabinowitz, *Race Relations in the Urban South, 1865–1890* (1978). See id. at 144 ("The interest in Negro orphanages or cemeteries suggests that blacks were less concerned with encouraging integration than with ending exclusion. . . . This attitude did not indicate passivity, however. Where blacks were barred, they requested the establishment of Negro departments or separate institutions.").

race line was a matter of custom and rooted in slavery.⁹² A recent study has maintained that the antebellum idea of racial separation through resettlement—both through the colonization movement of sending blacks back to Africa and the idea of creating American Indian or black territories in the West—was viewed by many blacks and whites as the only way minorities could achieve true equality.⁹³ While lacking the racial enmity found in America at large, such apartheid was never advocated by many whites, one reason for that being the need for cheap black labor both before and after 1865. Other studies have buttressed Woodward's claim that the Jim Crow of the early twentieth century was not a foregone conclusion and that the years after emancipation saw examples of interracial, cooperative political movements.⁹⁴ Scholarship focused on particular states and locales, such as North Carolina, have shown in detail the breadth and scope of a multifaceted system.⁹⁵

Of course, racial discrimination imposed by law or governmental action was only one part of the complex world of Jim Crow, and social as well as cultural norms both shaped and reshaped this world.⁹⁶ Gender has been a particularly fertile field of research. Glenda Gilmore demonstrated

---

When a majority of African Americans began to see segregation as unalloyed discrimination is difficult to pinpoint. That viewpoint is at least evident in Tennessee in 1881 when the state legislature passed, over black legislators' objections, a law mandating racial segregation on passenger railroads in the state. Edward L. Ayers, *The Promise of the New South: Life After Reconstruction* 143 (1992). The statute is at 1881 Tenn. Pub. Acts, ch. 155, 211.

92. Joel Williamson, *After Slavery: The Negro in South Carolina During Reconstruction, 1861–1877*, at 298 (1965) ("The real separation was not that duo-chromatic order that prevailed on streetcars and trains, or in restaurants, saloons, and cemeteries. The real color line lived in the minds of individuals of each race, and it had achieved full growth even before freedom for the Negro was born.").

93. Nicholas Guyatt, *Bind Us Apart: How Enlightened Americans Invented Racial Segregation* (2016).

94. Jane Dailey, *Before Jim Crow: The Politics of Race in Postemancipation Virginia* (2000).

95. See, e.g., *Democracy Betrayed: The Wilmington Race Riot of 1898 and its Legacy* (David S. Cecelski and Timothy B. Tyson eds., 1998); Thomas W. Hanchett, *Sorting Out the New South City: Race, Class, and Urban Development in Charlotte, 1875–1975* (1998); Malinda Maynor Lowery, *Lumbee Indians in the Jim Crow South: Race, Identity, and the Making of a Nation* (2010).

96. See, e.g., Leon F. Litwack, *Been in the Storm So Long: The Aftermath of Slavery* (1979).

how middle-class black women in North Carolina became racial intermediaries in the years after the White Supremacy Campaigns, advocating for their families at a time when their men were politically powerless.[97] Gender helps explain how the segregation of passenger railroads came about, with black women being the ones excluded from the first-class ladies' cars.[98] Other studies have highlighted how Southern literature around 1900 both reflected the white enmity of the time, as in the popular fiction(s) of Thomas Dixon which glorified the Ku Klux Klan and, from a different vantage point, provided African Americans with a separate world of black culture with its own points of reference.[99] Similarly, in the decades after the Civil War, at the same time that the iconography of white supremacy relied on distorted and hateful images of blacks, there was the New Negro movement put forward as a counternarrative to show "that

---

97. Glenda Elizabeth Gilmore, *Gender and Jim Crow: Women and the Politics of White Supremacy in North Carolina, 1896–1920* (1996). Other studies have broadened the scope, especially with regard to class. See, e.g., Sarah Haley, *No Mercy Here: Gender, Punishment, and the Making of Jim Crow Modernity* (2016).

98. Barbara Y. Welke, When All the Women Were White and All the Blacks Were Men: Gender, Class, Race, and the Road to *Plessy*, 1855–1914, 13 *Law and History Review* 261 (1995).

99. See, e.g., *Thomas Dixon Jr. and the Birth of Modern America* (Michele K. Gillespie and Randal L. Hall eds., 2006); Anders Walker, *The Burning House: Jim Crow and the Making of Modern America* (2018).

Thomas Dixon, a North Carolina native, wrote books about the supposed indignities visited upon the white South during Reconstruction and whites' "necessary" actions to preserve the social order through groups such as the Klan. His two most famous books were *The Leopard's Spots: A Romance of the White Man's Burden—1865–1900* (1902) and *The Clansman: An Historical Romance of the Ku Klux Klan* (1905). In an introductory "To the Reader" section in *The Clansman*, Dixon wrote:

> In the darkest hour of the life of the South, when her wounded people lay helpless amid rags and ashes under the beak and talon of the Vulture, suddenly from the mists of the mountains appeared a white cloud the size of a man's hand. It grew until its mantle of mystery enfolded the stricken earth and sky. An "Invisible Empire" had risen from the field of Death and challenged the Visible to mortal combat.

Thomas Dixon, Jr., *The Clansman: An Historical Romance of the Ku Klux Klan* n.p. (1905). Dixon made *The Clansman* into a play and, subsequently, a movie script which was used by D.W. Griffith as the basis for the 1915 movie, *The Birth of a Nation*. See Joel Williamson, *The Crucible of Race: Black-White Relations in the American South Since Emancipation* 173–176 (1984).

the disparaging claims about the Negro's beastlike 'nature' were horribly mistaken."[100]

This study focuses on law, however, because of its centrality to the system of racial segregation and discrimination that came to be known as Jim Crow. Law does not explain or encompass the entirety of this system. It does not tell us how folkways in the small towns of the South enforced social deference by blacks on sidewalks and in daily interactions.[101] It does not explain the genesis of the 1873 Colfax massacre in Louisiana.[102] It does not show us agency in the ways that the former slaves left the churches of their former masters to form their own churches and congregations soon after emancipation.[103] It does not explain racial steering by real estate agents or the prolonged exclusion of blacks from labor unions in the North, whether in and around Detroit or elsewhere.[104] But law's importance to the system of racial discrimination is of the first order. This history shows how ostensibly democratic, popular *government* fostered racial discrimination and inequity. Compared to social customs, constitutional provisions and statutes and local ordinances at least provide some metric by which to assess the volume and intensity of interest in the subject by the white majority. With the constant scholarly and popular references to the era of Jim Crow statutes, there is value in a detailed study of those laws in order to achieve some understanding of their importance. How comprehensive were those laws? When were those laws enacted? And what weight did those statutes carry, relative to their interpretation and implementation?

---

100. Henry Louis Gates, Jr., *Stony the Road: Reconstruction, White Supremacy, and the Rise of Jim Crow* 4 (2019).

101. In the aftermath of the Civil War, a Northern journalist visiting Wilmington, N.C., observed as to the city's white residents: "They perceive insolence in a tone, a glance, a gesture, or a failure to yield enough by two or three inches in meeting on the sidewalk." North Carolina: Our Southern Tour, *Philadelphia Inquirer*, August 9, 1865, at 4, quoted in W. McKee Evans, *Ballots and Fence Rails: Reconstruction on the Lower Cape Fear* 79 (1967).

102. LeeAnna Keith, *The Colfax Massacre: The Untold Story of Black Power, White Terror, and the Death of Reconstruction* (2008).

103. William E. Montgomery, *Under Their Own Vine and Fig Tree: The African-American Church in the South, 1865–1900*, at 52 (1993).

104. See, e.g., Herbert Hill, The Problem of Race in American Labor History, 24 *Reviews in American History* 189 (1996).

This book sets out in two tables all of the race-conscious laws enacted in North Carolina between 1865 and 1920, but I argue that the application and operation of the laws was much more important on the ground than the statutory text. Moreover, I contend that the racial contagion which swept the state during the elections in 1898 and 1900—the White Supremacy Campaigns—dramatically changed white attitudes in such a way that the operation of the law changed dramatically, as well. While there can be no denying the profound harm caused by the statutory creation of racially segregated schools in North Carolina and the myth of separate but equal, it was the discretion built into the system that allowed for the different levels of financial support as between the white and black schools. Similarly, the 1900 amendment of the North Carolina Constitution requiring that potential voters be able "to read and write any section of the Constitution in the English language"[105] was race neutral on its face, but its application by the registrars was anything but race neutral. Thus, constitutional amendments and legislative statutes which did not openly discriminate on their face—that is, in the actual wording—were applied in a discriminatory fashion to sustain and expand the system of Jim Crow in North Carolina. After chronicling the statutes gathered, I drill several shafts here into particular areas such as schools, suffrage, and jury service to demonstrate the changes on the ground that occurred in these fields after the White Supremacy Campaigns.

A word should be said about why 1920 was chosen as the end point for this study on the Jim Crow statutes. The 1920 date was chosen because the White Supremacy Campaigns of 1898 and 1900 were a turning point for the state and two decades is a sufficient time period by which to assess the impact of those successive political campaigns, both in terms of legislative output and the societal changes in North Carolina. There is perhaps no better barometer of the tenor of the times than the fact that, in the first decade of the twentieth century, one out of every thirteen African Americans in North Carolina left and moved out of this state to other parts of the country.[106] Also, 1920 is a good stopping point because, after the nu-

---

105. Amendment of 1900 to N.C. Const. of 1868, art. VI, sec. 4 ("Every person presenting himself for registration shall be able to read and write any section of the Constitution in the English language....").

106. Glenda Elizabeth Gilmore and Thomas J. Sugrue, *These United States: A Nation in the Making, 1890 to the Present* 97 (2015).

merous race riots during the summer of 1919, the ensuing decade saw yet another rise in racial discrimination and the rebirth of the Ku Klux Klan across the nation.[107]

Over one hundred years ago, the legal scholar Roscoe Pound drew an important distinction between law in books and law in action.[108] This book reveals the distance between the law in books and the law in action with regard to the *de jure* system of Jim Crow in North Carolina.

---

107. John Hope Franklin, *From Slavery to Freedom: A History of Negro Americans* 480 (3d ed. 1967) ("It was the summer of 1919 . . . that ushered in the greatest period of interracial strife the nation had ever witnessed."). Because of the bloodletting during the summer of 1919, it is known as "Red Summer." E.g., Cameron McWhirter, *Red Summer: The Summer of 1919 and the Awakening of Black America* (2011). See also William E. Leuchtenburg, *The Perils of Prosperity, 1914–1932*, at 209 (2d ed. 1993) ("In the early years of the 1920s, the Klan, which had less than 5,000 members as late as 1920, experienced a phenomenal growth, and, with probably a few million adherents at one time or another during this period, made its weight felt in politics."); John Hope Franklin, The Two Worlds of Race: A Historical View, 134 *Daedalus* 118, 128 (2005) ("Racial conflicts swept the country [after World War I], and neither federal nor state governments seemed interested in effective intervention. The worlds of race were growing further apart in the postwar decade.").

108. Roscoe Pound, Law in Books and Law in Action, 44 *American Law Review* 12 (1910).

1
Jim Crow in Books and Jim Crow in Action

It is well known that the United States Supreme Court's 1896 decision in *Plessy v. Ferguson*[1] held that a Louisiana law mandating racially segregated railroad cars did not violate the Equal Protection Clause because the statute directed that the accommodations for each race be the same.[2] With the words reversed, the statute's requirement of "equal but separate" was identified as the constitutional formula for laws touching upon race for many decades.[3] But few people know that almost twenty years earlier, the Supreme Court had reviewed another law—also from Louisiana—which was the mirror opposite of the statute in *Plessy* in that it required common carriers to "make no discrimination on account of race or color" and that the Court struck down that law on the grounds that it imposed an impermissible burden on interstate commerce.[4] Many people do not know that

---

1. 163 U.S. 537 (1896).
2. Id. at 551.
3. Id. at 539 (statute established that "all railway companies carrying passengers in their coaches in this state, shall provide equal but separate accommodations for the white, and colored races") (quoting Act of July 10, 1890, 1890 La. Acts. 152, 153, § 1).
4. *Hall v. DeCuir*, 95 U.S. 485, 486 (1878) (quoting Act of Feb. 23, 1869, 1869 La. Acts. 37, § 1.). *Hall* was effectively overruled by *Louisville, New Orleans and Texas Ry. Co. v. Mississippi*, 133 U.S. 587 (1890), which upheld a Mississippi law that required railroads in the state to "provide equal but separate" accommodations for the races as not being an impermissible burden on interstate commerce. The 1890 Supreme Court claimed

for decades prior to *Plessy*, separate but equal was repeatedly upheld as reasonable by courts under the common law of carriers when railroads and steamboats had existing rules mandating racial separation in order to promote the "comfort" of passengers and to lessen the possibility of social friction.[5] Most individuals are not aware that, prior to *Plessy*, railroad cars were often segregated by both race and gender, with a first-class ladies' car and a second-class smoker, and that black women with first-class tickets were a particular conundrum for both carriers and courts as well as a driving force for a statutory solution.[6] Moreover, few people are aware that *Plessy* itself was a collusive lawsuit between a group of Afro-Creoles and a railway company that wanted to avoid having to haul two first-class railcars on every train just to comply with the law and that Homer Plessy was chosen to participate because he was as white in skin color as the other white passengers in the first-class car.[7] Even fewer people know that the

---

that it was merely distinguishing the cases on the ground that the Mississippi statute applied only to intrastate commerce, id. at 591, but the Louisiana statute in *Hall* was worded in the same fashion—limiting its reach to common carriers operating within the state—and, at the same time, the steamboat trip by Appellant DeCuir in the earlier case was between two points wholly within the state of Louisiana. *Hall*, 95 U.S. at 486. For a thorough study of these cases and the law as to the seating of interstate passengers, see Joseph R. Palmore, The Not-So-Strange Career of Interstate Jim Crow: Race, Transportation, and the Dormant Commerce Clause, 1878–1946, 83 *Virginia Law Review* 1773 (1997).

5. Charles A. Lofgren, *The Plessy Case: A Legal-Historical Interpretation* 116–28 (1987). The key in many of these cases was whether there was an existing rule or regulation of the carrier. See, e.g., *Britton v. Atlanta & Charlotte Air-Line Ry. Co.*, 88 N.C. 536, 543–44 (1883) (holding that because a railway company's policy of providing separate cars for white and colored passengers was not a "fixed or certain rule" enforced with consistency, the railway owed a duty to a colored passenger who was allowed to sit in the smoking car "from the neglect of the company's servants as from the unprovoked assaults of their fellow-passengers").

6. Barbara Y. Welke, When All the Women Were White, and All the Blacks Were Men: Gender, Class, Race, and the Road to *Plessy*, 1855–1914, 13 *Law and History Review* 261 (1995). See id. at 266–267 ("Through the post-emancipation years and into the twentieth century, the ladies' car/ladies' cabin analogy remained fundamental to the legal justification of racial segregation on common carriers.").

7. Williamjames Hull Hoffer, *Plessy v. Ferguson: Race and Inequality in Jim Crow America* 2, 59–66 (2012). Although the 1900 and 1910 federal census forms listed Homer Plessy and his wife as mulattoes, in the last federal census before his death in 1925, Homer Plessy and his wife were recorded as white. Peter Wallenstein, Did Homer Plessy Die a White Man? Race and Southern History—The State of the Field, 94 *Georgia Historical Quarterly* 62, 63 (2010).

1. JIM CROW IN BOOKS AND JIM CROW IN ACTION | 33

Supreme Court Justice who wrote the majority opinion in *Plessy*, Henry Billings Brown, later bluntly recognized that the premise of the Court's decision in *Plessy* was wrong, because the purpose of the Louisiana statute was "not so much to exclude white persons from railroad cars occupied by blacks, as to exclude colored people from coaches occupied or assigned to white persons."[8] In sum, there are many legal and historical facets of *Plessy v. Ferguson* that scholars have brought to light and which supplement and complicate our understanding of the judicial opinion found in Volume 163 of the *United States Reports*.

The common depiction of *Plessy v. Ferguson* as ushering in an era of separate-but-equal state laws is, at the very least, inexact.[9] To even speak of a *Plessy* "period"[10] or "era"[11] seems inapt because, while there was separation by race, there was nothing remotely equal about either the legislative statutes passed in great numbers in the succeeding years, or in the acts of government officials more generally. Indeed, only three years after

---

8. H.B. Brown, The Dissenting Opinions of Mr. Justice Harlan, 46 *American Law Review* 321, 338 (1912), quoted in Mark A. Graber, Judicial Recantation, 45 *Syracuse Law Review* 807, 810 (1994). Brown's opinion for the Court in *Plessy* had asserted that the "underlying fallacy of the plaintiff's [i.e., Plessy's] argument . . . consist[s] in the assumption that the enforced separation of the two races stamps the colored race with a badge of inferiority." *Plessy*, 163 U.S. at 551. In the 1912 law review article, Justice Brown went on to observe about the Court's decision in *Plessy* that "there is still a lingering doubt whether the spirit of the [Reconstruction] amendments was not sacrificed to the letter, and whether the Constitution was not intended to secure the equality of the two races in all places affected with a public interest." Brown, supra, at 336.

9. See, e.g., Richard Cortner, *Plessy* in Perspective: Lofgren's View, 13 *Law & Social Inquiry* 825, 826 (1988) (*Plessy* "is commonly regarded as having placed the imprimatur of constitutional legitimacy upon the rigid system of racial segregation that only began to be dismantled in the 1950s"); Daniel R. Gordon, One Hundred Years After *Plessy*: The Failure of Democracy and the Potentials for Elitist and Neutral Anti-Democracy, 40 *New York Law School Law Review* 641, 641 (1996) ("*Plessy* validated the separate but equal doctrine and provided federal, constitutional and judicial imprimatur to the system of segregation that developed in the late nineteenth century and lasted through the first half of the twentieth century.") (citations omitted); William Bradford Reynolds, Individualism vs. Group Rights: The Legacy of *Brown*, 93 *Yale Law Journal* 995, 997 (1984) ("The separate-but-equal doctrine formulated by the *Plessy* majority held sway in America for over half a century . . . .").

10. John P. Roche, Plessy v. Ferguson: Requiescat in Pace?, 103 *University of Pennsylvania Law Review* 44, 44 (1954).

11. Michael J. Klarman, *From Jim Crow to Civil Rights* 8–9 (2004). It should be noted that for the purposes of his book, Klarman's *Plessy* era runs from 1895 to 1910. Id. at 9.

Plessy, the Supreme Court allowed a Georgia school board's closure of a black high school to stand, even though a high school for whites was kept open.[12] After *Plessy*, statutes that did not speak in overt racial terms were applied in such a way as to exclude African Americans from juries and voting booths and schools. And in the years before *Plessy*, state laws did not often pretend to treat the former freedmen equally or equitably, either. Just as the Court in *Plessy* relied on a reasonableness standard to hold that the legislature "is at liberty to act with reference to the established usages, customs, and traditions of the people,"[13] it was generally thought to be perfectly reasonable for legislative enactments to result in the unequal treatment of African Americans. Statutes that were explicit in excluding African Americans were held to violate the Fourteenth Amendment, but state discrimination in actuality was allowed to stand.[14] *Plessy* was an attempt by the appellant and other Afro-Creoles in New Orleans to bring a halt to state legislation mandating racial segregation and discrimination, but separate-and-unequal legislation was the order of the day both before and after 1896.

The prevalence of state *de jure* discrimination—that is, discrimination "of right" or by government—both before and after *Plessy* has been a focus of ongoing scholarly debate ever since the publication of C. Vann Woodward's groundbreaking book, *The Strange Career of Jim Crow*.[15] Woodward acknowledged that the ambit of racial discrimination and segregation was necessarily greater than what was enacted by the Southern legislatures, but he put law at the center of his study.[16] Yet, as one scholar

---

12. *Cumming v. Richmond County Board of Education*, 175 U.S. 528, 544–45 (1899) (holding that closure of black high school "for economic reasons," while maintaining high school for white children, was not a denial of equal protection of the laws).

13. *Plessy*, 163 U.S. at 550.

14. Compare *Strauder v. West Virginia*, 100 U.S. 303 (1880) (invalidating statute that excluded African Americans from jury service) with *Virginia v. Rives*, 100 U.S. 313 (1880) (holding that the evidence that no African Americans had ever served on jury in county did not prove the existence of racial discrimination).

15. C. Vann Woodward, *The Strange Career of Jim Crow* (3d rev. ed. 1974) (hereinafter *Strange Career*). Woodward's book was first published in 1955. Scholarship on racial discrimination after the Civil War remains a fertile field of inquiry. See, e.g., Davison M. Douglas, *Jim Crow Moves North: The Battle over Northern School Segregation, 1865–1954* (2005); Klarman, supra note 11; Barbara Y. Welke, *Recasting American Liberty: Gender, Race, Law, and the Railroad Revolution* (2001).

16. Woodward, *Strange Career*, supra note 15, at xiii.

has pointed out, even with the studies on the history of *de jure* discrimination, there "has been remarkably little interest in the Jim Crow statutes themselves, and . . . [on] the effects of implementation."[17] To be sure, there have been important studies on discrimination by states after the Civil War.[18] And Pauli Murray performed truly herculean work in the late 1940s by compiling the laws on race then in force that could be found in the state codes of the era.[19] But, when Murray did her work, the quality of the state codifications was especially reliant on the thoroughness of the compilers, and the research itself was dependent upon the quality of the index at the back of the code. Moreover, because compilations are aimed at setting out "current statutes of general and permanent application,"[20] the codes are less concerned with the ebbs and flows of statutes over previous decades and they entirely miss local laws and private laws that are not of sufficient generality to include when systematizing multiple years of session laws. As will be seen in Chapter 4, many discriminatory statutes in North Carolina applied only to one city or county.

The present study began by setting out to catalog and assess, in totality, what North Carolina enacted in every legislative session from the end of the Civil War to 1920 on the subject of race, whether the statute was discriminatory or promoted equality. No other study of which I am aware has taken on the task of examining the session laws from each successive

---

17. Howard N. Rabinowitz, More than the Woodward Thesis: Assessing *The Strange Career of Jim Crow*, 75 Journal of American History 843, 850 (1988).

18. See, e.g., Frenise A. Logan, *The Negro in North Carolina, 1876–1894* (1964); Joel Williamson, *After Slavery: The Negro in South Carolina During Reconstruction, 1861–1877* (1965); Charles E. Wynes, *Race Relations in Virginia, 1870–1902* (1961).

19. *States' Laws on Race and Color* (Pauli Murray ed. 1997) (reprint of 1951 edition). In her autobiography, Murray described going to the New York County Law Library and "laboriously copying" the laws by hand and then typing out what she had copied. Pauli Murray, *Pauli Murray: The Autobiography of a Black Activist, Feminist, Lawyer, Priest, and Poet* 286 (1987). Given that Murray started the project after a November 1948 inquiry from a Methodist church group and that the work was originally published in March 1951, id. at 284–287, Murray primarily used the North Carolina General Statutes compiled by Michie Publishing in 1943, *States' Laws on Race and Color*, supra, at 329, and the cumulative supplements published by Michie in 1947, id., and 1949. Id. at 342. It is also apparent that Murray consulted at least the N.C. session laws from 1949. Id. at 333, 341.

20. Morris L. Cohen and Kent C. Olson, *Legal Research* 161 (9th ed. 2007). The quality of codes varies, especially at the state level, because as Cohen and Olson point out, "[s]ome codes are more thorough and comprehensive than others." Id. at 178.

legislative session of a state on the issue of race over such a long period, but it is only by understanding the scope and chronology of the statutes in their entirety that one can assess both the reach of *de jure* discrimination and the relative importance of the statutes themselves. This inventory of statutes touching upon race is contained in two tables that accompany this book: Table 1 lists all of the session laws of North Carolina from this period that discriminated on account of race, and this collection of statutes forms the primary focus of the present study. Table 2 compiles all of the session laws that advanced the cause of racial equality in North Carolina, in some fashion. Hopefully, both of these tables will be a resource for future scholarship. These lists of individual statutes from North Carolina tell a more complete story of the treatment of minorities over time than the code compilations do. The spadework here provides what can be called "the tyranny of intractable facts"[21] by which we are better able to understand the impact and dynamics of the Jim Crow system in one Southern state.

The North Carolina session laws compiled here are not an end in themselves but, rather, a means by which to assess *de jure* racial discrimination. Specifically, these statutes provide a baseline by which to judge the degree to which discrimination was imposed on minorities—African Americans and Native Americans—and, also, some account of the degree to which these statutes fail to account for the extent of inequality and harm by the state. By *de jure* discrimination, I mean discrimination by the state, whether through the words of a statute or the actions of a governmental official. There has always been more racial discrimination than what is found in the state statute books because of actions by private persons and institutions in the society at large, outside of government. But *de jure* discrimination has always been greater than what appears in the session laws or the state codes, as well. The interpretation and application of the Jim Crow statutes by government officials added another layer of discrimination. Statutory text has to be administered by governmental actors and there is often discretion in how law is put into action. Law is a human institution, and it will inevitably reflect majoritarian priorities and popular biases in interpretation and application. The constitutional provisions and statutes compiled here are a metric by which to assess the interest of the (majority white) North Carolina legislators in drawing ra-

---

21. Oscar Handlin, *Truth in History* 110 (1979).

cially discriminatory lines during the years under study but, as will become evident, there is a disconnect between the chronology, number, and scope of these statutes and the harms visited upon racial minorities in the state. In this book, I argue that the White Supremacy Campaigns waged during the elections of 1898 and 1900 were the real turning point for *de jure* discrimination in North Carolina, not in terms of a flood of new Jim Crow statutes enacted after those elections, because there was not one, but because the application of law turned so dramatically against racial minorities after 1900.[22]

I entered upon this study as someone well versed in constitutional law and constitutional and legal history and, thus, with a good familiarity of the general history of the Jim Crow laws in the Southern states. But I always had a question in the back of my mind about this era: Why did African Americans' access to the voting booth effectively vanish in an instant?

In North Carolina, to say that black voting was eliminated by the 1900 amendment to the state constitution which imposed a literacy test and required the payment of a poll tax is not strictly accurate.[23] The literacy test, ostensibly, should have encompassed what that phrase means. Even as late as 1959, the U.S. Supreme Court concluded that this literacy test in the North Carolina Constitution was valid under federal constitutional standards and the requirement that a voter be able to read and write any section of the Constitution was a "fair way of determining whether a person is literate, not a calculated scheme to lay springes for the citizen."[24] Yet there was no connection between the literacy rates of African Americans between 1900 and 1920 and the virtually complete removal of these citizens from the voting booths of North Carolina. The United States Census for 1900 calculated the illiteracy rate of voting-age colored males in North

---

22. I use the word "Campaign" here and throughout this book because of its martial spirit and because it was used at the time by Josephus Daniels in reference to 1898 and 1900 precisely because of its military overtones. Lee A. Craig, *Josephus Daniels: His Life & Times* 178 (2013).

23. Amendment of 1900 to N.C. Const. of 1868, art. VI, § 4 (final version proposed at 1900 N.C. Sess. Laws 54, ch. 2). Section 4 of the Amendment stated: "Every person presenting himself for registration shall be able to read and write any section of the constitution in the English language, and before he shall be entitled to vote he shall have paid ... his poll tax as prescribed by law for the previous year."

24. *Lassiter v. Northampton County Bd. of Elections*, 360 U.S. 45, 54 (1959). See also id. at 53 ("We do not sit in judgment on the wisdom of that policy. We cannot say, however, that it is not an allowable one measured by constitutional standards.").

Carolina to be 53.1 percent.[25] The United States Census for 1910 calculated the illiteracy rate of voting-age Negro males to be 38.6 percent.[26] Given that the percentage of African Americans voting in North Carolina during those decades came fairly close to zero, this discrepancy was not a rounding error. Large numbers of blacks should have been able to vote under this standard. Even assuming some fuzziness at the margins of the census numbers, it still should have been the case that at least 40 percent of African Americans should have been able to meet the legal standard in the first two decades of the twentieth century. Yes, obviously, this is about the application of the literacy test rather than the text of the amendment and about the intimidation of potential black voters by both white social pressure and even violence. But it is the application that is so confounding: the virtual elimination of blacks was immediate and not gradual (as seen in the figures for the 1902 election), it was uniform from one end of the state to the other, and this posture toward African American voters changed very little over the succeeding five decades.[27] The level of disenfranchisement stunned even Henry G. Connor, the Speaker of the N.C. House when the amendment was drafted, who thought that at least 25,000 blacks would still be able to vote under the literacy test.[28] Furnifold Simmons, the Democratic "political leader perhaps most responsible . . . for the disfranchisement,"[29] believed before its implementation that around

---

25. 1 Bureau of the Census, *Census Reports, Twelfth Census of the United States, Taken in the Year 1900: Population*, Part I, at ccv (1901). "Colored" here included persons "of negro descent, Chinese, Japanese, and Indians." Id. The Report also calculated that the number of voting-age colored males in North Carolina was 128,315, of which 128,315 were "Negro." Id. at cxix.

26. 1 Bureau of the Census, *Thirteenth Census of the United States Taken in the Year 1910: Population* at 1258 (1913). In the 1910 census, "Negro" was separated out from "Indian, Chinese, and Japanese" who, as a combined group, had an illiteracy rate of 51.4 percent. Id. The 1910 Census also calculated that the number of voting-age Negro males in North Carolina was 146,752, while the combined number of voting-age "Indians, Chinese, and Japanese" was 1,771. Id. at 1044.

27. For the full analysis of this history, see Chapter 4.

28. Gregory P. Downs, University Men, Social Science, and White Supremacy in North Carolina, 75 *Journal of Southern History* 267, 294 (2009).

29. Richard L. Watson, Jr., Furnifold M. Simmons and the Politics of White Supremacy, in *Race, Class, and Politics in Southern History* 126, 133 (Jeffrey J. Crow et al. eds., 1989).

30,000 blacks would still be able to vote.³⁰ The fact that the (white) registrars who implemented the literacy test discriminated against African Americans without exception and throughout every corner of the state is extraordinary, given that these officials were to enforce state law. It is not surprising that the elections officials were personally racially prejudiced but, instead, that they were all so willing to completely ignore the legal mandate and discriminate in this fashion. The sociologist Robert Merton recognized the potential gap between opinion and behavior—between prejudice and discrimination—in a typology that demonstrated how behavior can be different from belief because of social pressure and conformity.³¹ Merton's "prejudiced nondiscriminator"³² is someone who possesses racial enmity but would, for example, not discriminate in enforcing a law because of the cultural norm that one should follow the law. That is, a person who was a government official would be more likely to act in a fair manner on the job—because of a belief in the idea of law—than that same person would behave and act as a private citizen. Law, thus, exerts its own social pressure: "Law, as an accomplished fact, is likely to be taken as something already established and it influences even those opposed to it."³³ But the presumption that the law would be followed as written was laid to waste in the aftermath of the White Supremacy Campaigns, where racial animus among whites was so intense and so uniform that it overrode any cultural norm in the sanctity of law among state and county election officials.

As I will show, this disconnect between the text of the law and the magnitude of discrimination for African Americans was not unique to the voting booth. Indeed, it was the discriminatory uses of law after the White

---

30. Id. at 137 (Simmons concluded that 25,000 to 30,000 blacks would be able to vote because literate, and more than 2,000 might vote pursuant to the amendment's grandfather clause because they were lineal descendants of free Negroes who voted in North Carolina or other states prior to 1867). U.S. Senator Marion Butler, a Populist, believed that about 50,000 literate blacks would still be qualified to vote under the amendment. Id. at 138.

31. Robert K. Merton, Discrimination and the American Creed, in *Discrimination and National Welfare* 99 (R.M. MacIver ed., 1949).

32. Id. at 103.

33. Morroe Berger, *Equality by Statute: Legal Controls over Group Discrimination* 187 (1952). For a perspective on the effect of law from the field of psychology, see Tom R. Tyler, *Why People Obey the Law* (rev. ed. 2006).

Supremacy Campaigns of 1898 and 1900 that changed so dramatically because there was no surge of Jim Crow statutes passed by the General Assembly in the succeeding years. After the Democrats regained control of the legislative and executive branches following the White Supremacy Campaigns, no new Jim Crow law of any great import was enacted for seven years, that statute being the one mandating racial segregation in streetcars,[34] and there is not another law of similar significance until 1913, when employers were required to maintain racially separate bathrooms for employees.[35] Yet, during this same time period, *de jure* racial discrimination in North Carolina became worse and more pronounced in ways that are demonstrable and measurable. It is only by compiling the racially discriminatory laws up to 1920 that one can confirm that the shift to a more virulent and boundless system of racial oppression was not a function of the Jim Crow laws alone, but was evidence of a sea change in the cultural attitudes of the white population toward the status and welfare of blacks and other minorities in the state of North Carolina.

Just as many studies have added to our understanding of the well-known case of *Plessy v. Ferguson*, the goal of this book is to add depth and complexity to the history of *de jure* racial discrimination in one Southern state.[36] There are three primary conclusions advanced in this book. First, *de jure* discrimination existed in an unbroken chain in North Carolina from the late 1860s and it did not begin in the 1890s or with the White Supremacy campaigns of 1898 and 1900.[37] Second, contrary to the scholarly literature and to what one might think, there was not a great wave of discriminatory statutes enacted immediately after African Americans effectively lost access to the voting booth and political power following the

---

34. 1907 N.C. Sess. Laws 1238, ch. 850.

35. 1913 N.C. Sess. Laws 127, ch. 83, § 1.

36. I do not address the inequitable application of the criminal statutes, given that criminal prosecutions and trials are so fact specific. It remains a fertile field of scholarship for this era, of course. See, e.g., Richard C. Cortner, *A Mob Intent on Death: The NAACP and the Arkansas Riot Cases* (1988).

37. Cf. Joseph G. de Roulhac Hamilton, *Reconstruction in North Carolina* 309 (1914) ("The laws of the State, after May 10, 1866, made little discrimination between the races ...."); Logan, supra note 18, at 215 ("North Carolina did not enact any Jim Crow laws ... during the period under study [1876–1894]"). With regard to Hamilton, supra, I think that the date used (May 10, 1866) was wrong or a misprint because I suspect that Hamilton was alluding to the state's so-called Black Code, which was passed as one statute on March 10, 1866. See 1866 N.C. Sess. Laws 99, ch. 40.

ratification of the 1900 constitutional amendment and the implementation of the literacy test and poll tax.[38] Third, at least with regard to the time period under consideration and given that there were no consequential Jim Crow laws enacted for several years after 1900, there was still a substantial increase in discrimination through the operation of the laws, not through the statutory language, but because of the (mis)administration of the laws by local white officials. People such as white voting registrars and officials turned against blacks with increased enmity because of the cultural impact of the white supremacy dogma preached in the 1898 and 1900 campaigns. Statutes are not self-enforcing, and the cultural tenor of the times affected how the laws were applied. Ultimately, perhaps the reason that there was no great burst of Jim Crow legislation after 1900 was because it was unnecessary, given the ways that the white officials increasingly imposed discrimination and exclusion under existing statutory frameworks.

---

38. Cf. Jeffrey J. Crow, Paul D. Escott, and Flora J. Hatley, *A History of African Americans in North Carolina* 95 (1992) ("A vicious white-supremacy campaign in 1898 launched this process [of disenfranchisement] in North Carolina, and the adoption of a constitutional amendment in 1900 completed it. Immediately, new 'Jim Crow' laws began to appear on the books . . . ."); Sarah Caroline Thuesen, *Greater Than Equal: African American Struggles for Schools and Citizenship in North Carolina, 1919–1965*, at 7 (2013) ("Voters passed this disfranchisement amendment in 1900 by popular referendum. . . . The General Assembly then enacted a series of segregation statutes that codified racial exclusion and separation in most public places."); David Zucchino, *Wilmington's Lie: The Murderous Coup of 1898 and the Rise of White Supremacy* 311–312 (2020) ("The train car segregation law [of 1899] was just the beginning of a deluge of Jim Crow laws in North Carolina. Over the next few years, new legislation would mandate separate black and white facilities from the cradle to the grave . . . ."); Thomas W. Hanchett, The Rosenwald Schools and Black Education in North Carolina, 65 *North Carolina Historical Review* 387, 391 (1988) ("Disfranchisement was accompanied by a rising tide of Jim Crow laws, which ordained racial segregation in public places."). Speaking of this era throughout the South and after disenfranchisement was achieved, Joel Williamson maintained that "the passage of segregating legislation reached a crescendo between 1897 and 1907." Joel Williamson, *The Crucible of Race: Black-White Relations in the American South Since Emancipation* 256 (1984).

2

Woodward's *Strange Career* and Subsequent Scholarship

To write on the subject of post-Civil War *de jure* discrimination is to enter upon well-trod ground because race is, *pace* Gunnar Myrdal, *the* American dilemma.[1] At the same time, historical scholarship on race and racial discrimination was virtually invisible up until the middle of the twentieth century.[2] To the degree that African Americans were a part of

---

1. Gunnar Myrdal, *An American Dilemma: The Negro Problem and Modern Democracy* (two vols., 1944).

2. The historian John Hope Franklin, who earned his Ph.D. in 1941, wrote in his autobiography that he set out to focus on "new areas of study" which was "how I happened to get into African American history, in which I never had a formal course but that attracted an increasing number of students of my generation and many more in later generations." John Hope Franklin, *Mirror to America: The Autobiography of John Hope Franklin* 7 (2005). Although it received little-to-no attention from (white) scholars, institutions, and historical groups, there was scholarship on African American history prior to the 1930s. See, e.g., H.F. Kletzing and W.H. Crogman, *Progress of a Race or The Remarkable Advancement of the Afro-American* (1903). There was, of course, scholarship by African Americans in other fields. See, e.g., W.E. Burghardt Du Bois, *The Souls of Black Folk* (1903) (sociology).

A white historian who wrote on the African American experience was John Spencer Bassett at Trinity College in Durham (now Duke University). However, Bassett's writings on the subject were relatively short essays in the *South Atlantic Quarterly* and were not scholarly articles or monographs. See John Spencer Bassett, Stirring Up the Fires of Race Antipathy, 2 *South Atlantic Quarterly* 297 (1903); John Spencer Bassett, Two Negro Leaders, 2 *South Atlantic Quarterly* 267 (1903).

the story of America, it was often as adjuncts to the currents of (white) political and social history. The early published histories of Reconstruction, products of what is termed the Dunning School of scholarship, often described the South in the years after the Civil War in terms of the struggles of the downtrodden white majority to regain its economic and political footing in the face of avaricious carpetbaggers and scalawags and the "ignorant negroes" that were propped up and elevated to positions of political power.[3] In 1914, writing about North Carolina after the Civil War, University of North Carolina Professor Joseph G. de Roulhac Hamilton described Reconstruction as a period "when selfish politicians, backed by the federal government, for [Republican] party purposes attempted to Africanize the State and deprive the people through misrule and oppression of most that life held dear."[4] There was an eventual shift by the 1930s and 1940s away from this myopic historical perspective on race and the

---

3. See, e.g., William Archibald Dunning, *Reconstruction, Political and Economic: 1865–1877*, at 212 (1907) (arguing that the power of the federal government in the South was transformed "into the support of a social and political system in which all the forces that made for civilization were dominated by a mass of barbarous freedmen"); James Wilford Garner, *Reconstruction in Mississippi* 295 (1901) (observing, in reference to the leaders of the state House of Representatives, that "[i]t is not to be supposed, however, that all the colored speakers were men of ignorance and incompetency"). Dunning, who taught at Columbia University, guided a generation of historians such as Garner and Joseph Gregoire de Roulhac Hamilton, and they all advanced a particular vision of Reconstruction in the American South. This group is now referred to as the Dunning School. See *The Dunning School: Historians, Race, and the Meaning of Reconstruction* (John David Smith and J. Vincent Lowery eds., 2013). C. Vann Woodward argued that this view of Reconstruction "preceded Dunning and was more the product of a regional white consensus than of a school or of a scholar." C. Vann Woodward, *Thinking Back: The Perils of Writing History* 24 (1986).

4. J.G. de Roulhac Hamilton, *Reconstruction in North Carolina* 667 (1914). Hamilton's view of Reconstruction was typical of the Dunning School and of white historians in this era:

> From the presence of the negro in politics grew one of the greatest evils for which Reconstruction was responsible, namely, the inevitable blunting of the political moral sense of the white people.... But during these two years of Radical misrule, when the ideals of the community were shattered, when an ignorant, inferior, and lately enslaved race, controlled by selfish and corrupt aliens, held the balance of power ... then the practical necessities of the case overcame scrupulous notions of political morality, and a determination to rule by any method possible possessed the mass of the white people....

Id. at 422.

South, as evidenced by scholars such as W.E.B. Du Bois, Howard K. Beale, and John Hope Franklin.[5] But the publication of C. Vann Woodward's *The Strange Career of Jim Crow* in 1955 was a milestone in advancing a new and unjaundiced understanding of racial discrimination since the Civil War.[6] While a complete chronicle of the immense literature that relies upon, responds to, and builds upon Woodward's work is beyond the scope of the present study, it is important to set out Woodward's thesis, in brief, and to highlight some of the most important subsequent work in order to understand the place of the current study in this scholarly field.

The Strange Career of Jim Crow originated as a lecture series at the University of Virginia in the fall of 1954. The date is significant, because those lectures were after the Supreme Court's May 1954 decision in *Brown v. Board of Education*[7] striking down state-mandated segregated schools, but before the implementation decision—how to enforce that ruling—in what is termed *Brown II* in 1955.[8] The lectures were not intended as polemics, but Woodward, at this time already a leading historian of the American South,[9] was preparing these lectures and the resulting book at the time when the white South was reacting to the initial *Brown* decision.[10]

Woodward put forward two primary arguments in *Strange Career*: first, that contrary to widespread belief, Jim Crow discrimination had not always existed in the American South and, second, that there were "forgotten alternatives" and, thus, a fluidity in race relations after 1865 that differed significantly from the rigid system of statutory segregation and

---

5. Howard K. Beale, *The Critical Year: A Study of Andrew Johnson and Reconstruction* (1930); W.E. Burghardt Du Bois, *Black Reconstruction* (1935); John Hope Franklin, *The Free Negro in North Carolina: 1790–1860* (1943).

6. C. Vann Woodward, *The Strange Career of Jim Crow* (1955). Woodward published four editions of the book and two of those editions revised the original text in significant ways to account for subsequent scholarship. All quotations and substantive references herein will be to the 1974 third revised edition.

7. 347 U.S. 483 (1954).

8. *Brown v. Board of Education*, 349 U.S. 294 (1955).

9. E.g., C. Vann Woodward, *Origins of the New South: 1877–1913* (1951).

10. One example is the response of Georgia Governor Herman Talmadge, who declared less than a week after the *Brown* decision was handed down: "We're going to do whatever is necessary in Georgia to keep white children in white schools and colored children in colored schools." Herman Talmadge, quoted in Talmadge Defies High Court Ruling, *N.Y. Times*, May 24, 1954, at 19.

discrimination that began around the turn of the century.[11] Both of these arguments were essentially about chronology, as Woodward recognized, because they were about when state legislation first appeared on the books and about when discriminatory laws were enacted in great bulk against African Americans: "Time and origins thus took precedence over place and circumstances."[12]

Woodward argued that there had not always been state-sanctioned hostility to the former slaves in the form of Jim-Crow-style statutes and, moreover, that there was a long period of racial cross currents which preceded the surge of discriminatory legislation starting in 1890. He pointed out that, contrary to white Southerners' assumptions at the time he was writing, *de jure* segregation—that is, segregation resulting from action by government or law—had not existed in the South since time immemorial.[13] Instead, the Jim Crow system of laws was of a much more recent

---

11. C. Vann Woodward, *The Strange Career of Jim Crow* (3d rev. ed. 1974). See id. at 12–14 (on absence of *de jure* segregation during time of slavery) and at 31–65 (on forgotten alternatives). Woodward also wrote on the reasons why blacks became the political and societal scapegoats of white Southerners toward the turn of the century. He maintained that (1) Northern opinions on race became much more similar to those in the South following the American expansion through Cuba, Puerto Rico, the Philippines, and other places in the Pacific because of the question of what America was to do about the millions of non-Anglo Saxons that came along with those annexations; (2) Southern conservatives, political allies even if not full-fledged boosters of blacks in many majority-black counties following Redemption, turned against blacks to combat the rise of the agrarian Populists with charges of "Negro domination" and the call for white supremacy; and (3) the Populists' eventual repudiation of blacks as the reason for their own political downfall. Id. at 69–82.

12. C. Vann Woodward, *Strange Career* Critics: Long May They Persevere, 75 *Journal of American History* 857, 860 (1988).

13. Again, what I mean by *de jure* discrimination is discrimination rooted in law or actions by any level of government, state or federal. In contrast, what I mean by *de facto* discrimination is discrimination generally originating in actions of private actors such as persons or business entities or other private organizations. It should be noted that the U.S. Supreme Court has defined *de jure* segregation in the public school context as "a current condition of segregation resulting from intentional state action." *Keyes v. School District No. 1, Denver, Colorado*, 413 U.S. 189, 205 (1973). Relying on this intent standard, the Court has held "that 'the Constitution is not violated by racial imbalance in the schools, without more.'" *Parents Involved in Community Schools v. Seattle School District No. 1*, 551 U.S. 701, 721 (2007) (quoting *Milliken v. Bradley*, 433 U.S. 267, 280 n.14 (1977)). In the present study, however, *de jure* discrimination is used more broadly to separate governmental action from nongovernmental action.

vintage. Woodward argued that in the first two decades after 1865, there was great variability in the status of blacks with regard to civil, political, and social rights. Referring to the period after white Conservatives (i.e., soon-to-be Democrats) "redeemed" Southern governments from scalawags, carpetbaggers, and the freedmen, Woodward saw a distinct shift in the 1890s: "Race relations after Redemption were an unstable interlude before the passing of these old and new traditions and the arrival of the Jim Crow code and disfranchisement."[14] Although his claims were qualified and nuanced, especially with regard to public schools, Woodward drew a clear distinction between an era of *de facto* discrimination during Reconstruction and Redemption and, then, a later era of state-sanctioned *de jure* discrimination. He concluded that there "was much segregation and discrimination of an extra-legal sort before the laws were adopted in all the states."[15]

While it is clear from the evidence he presented that there was an era with a lack of uniformity and hardened racial attitudes, and that alternative paths forward were available in the South, Woodward argued that there were few racially discriminatory statutes prior to the 1890s and that what followed was a relatively quick shift to an extensive body of Jim Crow laws. He acknowledged that discriminatory attitudes and folkways "frequently exceeded" the law.[16] But, Woodward wrote of "the relative recency of the Jim Crow laws."[17] He concluded that the "policies of proscription, segregation, and disfranchisement" did not extend back to Reconstruc-

---

14. Woodward, supra note 11, at 32. In North Carolina, the Redeemers—those that redeemed and restored the native whites (i.e., Conservatives) to political power—were in control of the General Assembly after 1870 and, with a brief interlude in 1887 when the legislature was divided between the parties, the Democrats controlled the General Assembly until the fusionists won a majority with the 1894 election. See infra Chapter 3.

15. Woodward, supra note 11, at 34. Woodward did acknowledge that there might be more complexity following Redemption: "Separation of the races continued to be the rule in churches and schools, in military life and public institutions as it had been before. And as the new governments added what few new public services they built—schools, hospitals, asylums, and the like—they applied existing practices of segregation, sometimes by law and sometimes without." Id. at 31.

16. Id. at xiii. See also id. at 41 ("It is clear at least that the newer states were inclined to resort to Jim Crow laws earlier than the older commonwealths of the seaboard, and there is evidence that segregation and discrimination became more generally practiced before they became law.").

17. Id. at xv–xvi.

tion or even Redemption because "they did not originate in those times."[18] Moreover, he emphasized what he called the "bulk and detail" of the later laws.[19] He wrote that the numerous new laws "constituted the most elaborate and formal expression of white sovereign opinion upon the subject."[20] Again, in a study that was about discrimination by law, Woodward emphasized timing and chronology and the multitude of subjects addressed by the new statutes.

Beyond the timing and degree of discrimination and segregation, one important revision to Woodward's original argument was the recognition that segregation was an urban phenomenon or, if not strictly an urban phenomenon, one driven by population concentration. The insight came from Leon Litwack's study of discrimination in the antebellum North and Richard Wade's work on segregation in the cities of the South prior to the Civil War.[21] Litwack documented racial discrimination and segregation in the North, with cities having larger populations of free persons of color than the rural areas. It was in the urban areas where there were streetcars and theaters and restaurants and where free blacks were, naturally, coming into daily contact with whites. Litwack noted *de jure* discrimination at the state level which prohibited free blacks from voting in Pennsylvania, the laws in states prohibiting blacks from testifying in court against whites, and Oregon's laws preventing blacks from owning property or entering into contracts.[22] Even racially progressive Massachusetts outlawed interracial marriage, as did most states.[23] But Litwack also documented the extralegal racial segregation on trains, omnibuses, and steamboats in the form of what were termed Jim Crow sections or separate Jim Crow cars in the cities of the North, often demanded by white riders and acquiesced to by the transportation operators.[24] In his

---

18. Id. at 65.
19. Id. at 7.
20. Id.
21. Leon F. Litwack, *North of Slavery: The Negro in the Free States, 1790–1860* (1961); Richard C. Wade, *Slavery in the Cities: The South 1820–1860* (1967).
22. Litwack, supra note 21, at 84–86 (exclusion from vote in Pennsylvania), at 93 (states prohibiting testimony of blacks and Oregon statutory prohibitions).
23. Id. at 104.
24. Id. at 97, 106–109. See, e.g., The Anti-Slavery Convention, *Boston Post*, June 10, 1843, at 1 ("[Mr. Remond] manifested an almost rabid antipathy against the 'Jim Crow car,' designed expressly for the special accommodation of 'the niggers.'"). It is notewor-

book on the antebellum South, Wade demonstrated that the cities treated slaves and the few free blacks differently, and that segregation by law was in place well before 1865. While not focused upon state statutes, Wade noted the existence of city ordinances which separated the races in many facets of daily life. Even though there were both slaves and free blacks in Southern cities, "race became more important than legal status."[25] A Richmond ordinance banned all blacks from Hackney coaches and carriages unless the black person was a servant.[26] Wade found that ordinances in Savannah, Richmond, and Charleston excluded blacks from certain parks and promenades.[27] He even found a New Orleans ordinance from 1816 that segregated the races at "any public exposition or theatre."[28] Wade concluded, "[I]n the cities a public etiquette was needed to govern the relation of races when the blacks were beyond the supervision of their owners."[29]

In rural areas where population is diffuse, folkways on racial subordination were enforced outside of law because people were more likely to know one another and enforce these rules through social norms, with words and eye contact. In cities, where people are more anonymous, more formal social regulations such as ordinances and the policies of private businesses were used to segregate. Unlike the cities, in rural areas there is less population and naturally less demand for hotels, theaters, restaurants, public parks, and streetcars. The most frequent gathering places in rural nineteenth-century America would have been churches and, in some locales, courthouses. The connection between population centers and *de jure* segregation was succinctly captured by John Cell in his oft-quoted observation that Jim Crow "was not born and bred among 'rednecks' in the country. First and foremost he was a city slicker."[30] While acknowledging the work of Litwack and Wade, Woodward initially re-

---

thy that by the late 1840s, in Massachusetts, "constant abolitionist pressure, the growing impact of public opinion, and the threat of legislative action prompted the railroad companies to abandon segregation." Litwack, supra note 21, at 108.
  25. Wade, supra note 21, at 266.
  26. Id. at 267.
  27. Id.
  28. New Orleans Ordinance, June 8, 1816, quoted in Wade, supra note 21, at 269.
  29. Wade, supra note 21, at 266.
  30. John W. Cell, *The Highest Stage of White Supremacy: The Origins of Segregation in South Africa and the American South* 134 (1982).

mained unconvinced that the urban experience was of great importance to *de jure* discrimination because so few people in the nineteenth-century South lived in the cities.³¹ But Litwack revealed *de facto* physical segregation in the cities of the North, and Wade showed that cities had enacted ordinances enforcing racial segregation prior to the Civil War, and that body of scholarship was a significant amendment to Woodward's initial argument in *Strange Career*.

It is worthy of note for the present study that, prior to the twentieth century, North Carolina was one of the least urban states in the South. In 1890, there were 17 cities in the states of the former Confederacy with populations greater than 25,000, but there was not one city of that size in North Carolina.³² The lack of sizeable cities meant that, in North Carolina, there were not as many streetcars and theatres and the other places that the larger Southern cities would have targeted for segregation. For example, by January 1890, there were at least 154 electric streetcar systems in the United States but only one in North Carolina, in Asheville, with one in Winston beginning operations later that year.³³

In a study on race in post-Civil War South Carolina, Joel Williamson argued that a clear race line was drawn from 1865 onward and that *de*

---

31. Speaking of both the ante- and post-bellum South, Woodward observed that "it would be a mistake to place too much emphasis on the urban experience, either as evidence of segregation or the opposite tendency. For the civilization of the Old South was overwhelmingly rural, and urban life was quite untypical of it." Woodward, supra note 11, at 16.

32. Bureau of the Census, *Report on Population of the United States at the Eleventh Census: 1890*, Part I, at 54-351 (1895). In 1890, Wilmington, N.C., had a population of 20,056. Id. at 259. Five Southern cities (New Orleans, Richmond, Nashville, Atlanta, and Memphis) had populations greater than 60,000. Id. at lxvii. As a point of comparison, in 1890, North Carolina had four cities with populations of at least 10,000 (Wilmington, Raleigh, Charlotte, Asheville) while Texas had ten such cities. Id. at 253–262 (for N.C.), 328–341 (for Tex.). The only Southern states in 1890 without a city of at least 25,000 and with fewer cities than North Carolina of at least 10,000 were Florida and Mississippi. Id. at 253–262 (for N.C.), 83–87 (for Fla.), 206–211 (for Miss.).

33. William D. Middleton, *The Time of the Trolley* 73 (1967). Asheville's electric railway began operations in 1889. A Brilliant Opening: The Asheville Electric Railway, *Asheville Citizen-Times*, Feb. 1, 1889, at 4. Winston's electric railway, which ran from the Winston courthouse to Salem, opened in the summer of 1890. Winston's Electric Railway, *State Chronicle* (Raleigh, N.C.), July 15, 1890, at 1.

facto segregation existed uninterrupted until it was codified in the 1890s.[34] Williamson maintained that by the end of Reconstruction, South Carolina "had become, in reality, two communities—one white and the other black."[35] He wrote: "By 1868, the physical color line had, for the most part, already crystallized. During the Republican regime, it was breached only in minor ways. Once the whites regained political power, there was little need to establish legally a separation which already existed in fact."[36] This thesis was a challenge to Woodward's arguments that the era before Jim Crow lacked definitive color lines and that the Jim Crow statutes were a new and distinct change.

Williamson certainly presented important evidence for his thesis and his book was solely about South Carolina, but I think that his stated conclusions exceeded his empirical evidence to some degree. Williamson was absolutely correct that there were always concerns, even among Radical Republicans, that full integration in certain areas would result in a complete withdrawal of native whites and the possible collapse of public institutions.[37] Public schools were the preeminent concern on that score. And Williamson convincingly demonstrated how, even with a state antidiscrimination law in South Carolina, blacks did not always press the issue of integration because of economic and social realities as well as an apparent desire to avoid private establishments where they were not welcome.[38] However, despite the historical record he marshals, there is evidence in the book of instances where the color line was not drawn. Thus, while an elderly native white is quoted as saying that he will avail himself of a law that exempts people from jury service on the basis of age, the man's reason for avoiding jury service is that the juries were composed of *both* whites and blacks.[39] And a Northern visitor in 1874 groused about how Northerners who had moved to the state would share drinks with blacks

---

34. Joel Williamson, *After Slavery: The Negro in South Carolina During Reconstruction, 1861–1877* (1965).
35. Id. at 299.
36. Id. at 298.
37. Id. at 290–291.
38. Id. at 287–288. See id. at 287 ("Indeed, after 1870, even the Negro leadership hardly seemed inclined to press further their political and legal advantage to end separation.").
39. Id. at 291. Williamson highlights the racial inclusivity of juries on several occasions. Id. at 329–330, 334.

at bars and would host them at their homes.⁴⁰ These instances obviously hint at a more fluid racial world, and Williamson concedes that "complete separation of the races was physically impossible."⁴¹ But, even so, I think it overstates the case to say that that "separation had crystalized into a comprehensive pattern which ... remained unaltered until the middle of the twentieth century."⁴² For his part, Woodward responded to Williamson's argument by saying that while attempts at integration in public and private institutions were not necessarily the norm, the fact "that they could happen at all ... was important."⁴³

Another scholarly amendment to Woodward's *Strange Career* thesis was by Howard Rabinowitz, who contributed the important historical insight—counterintuitive to modern sensibilities—that racial segregation after the Civil War was not viewed as an unmitigated evil by many blacks and was often supported by black leaders because the alternative to segregation was not integration but total exclusion. Rabinowitz fleshed out the history of this viewpoint in his study of five Southern capitals in the decades after the Civil War, one of those cities being Raleigh.⁴⁴ Racial exclusion antedated the war in that there were often no hospitals or hotels or asylums for slaves or free blacks. However, Rabinowitz demonstrated that the Freedmen's Bureau and the U.S. Army, as well as local Republicans, pursued policies in the aftermath of the war that relied on segregation rather than integration or equality because this tactic was the path of least resistance to aid the freedmen and it was far better than exclusion.⁴⁵ While residential segregation was not necessarily a good thing for the black community, segregated schools and welfare services such as hospitals for the blind and insane were actually a step forward.⁴⁶ It meant that

---

40. Id. at 294.
41. Id. at 296.
42. Id. at 275.
43. Woodward, supra note 11, at 27. See also id. at 25 ("[R]ace relations during Reconstruction could not be said to have crystalized or stabilized nor to have become what they later became. There were too many cross currents and contradictions, revolutionary innovations and violent reactions.").
44. Howard N. Rabinowitz, *Race Relations in the Urban South, 1865–1890* (1978).
45. Id. at 127.
46. Id. As Rabinowitz pointed out, residential segregation existed in Southern cities before the war because free Negroes and fugitive slaves often lived in distinct areas on the outskirts of the cities and those communities were eventually annexed by the cities and came in as segregated communities with their own schools and other entities serving

blacks would be entitled to government services such as education and treatment for the handicapped and mentally ill. As Rabinowitz observed, "Negroes themselves favored this policy [i.e., segregation] over exclusion. Along with their white allies, they believed, or at least hoped, that separate treatment would be equal."[47] Segregation was the partial solution that many, but not all, African Americans were willing to accept rather than no public services at all: "The professed policy of separate but equal had the benefit of minimizing white hostility while still presenting the blacks with a significant improvement over their treatment at the hands of earlier administrations."[48] Rabinowitz observed that "[t]he interest in Negro orphanages or cemeteries suggests that blacks were less concerned with encouraging integration than with ending exclusion."[49] One problem became that the separate institutions did not receive the same resources.[50] Thus, over time, the ongoing differential in support meant that segregating schools and other public institutions was a method of discrimination in and of itself. Separate but equal was the promise never delivered.[51]

In addition, Rabinowitz's study set out in unique detail the racial complexity of Southern cities following the Civil War, and he concluded that

---

that community. Id. at 100–101. See id. at 101 ("[T]hese new areas of the city would be brought in essentially as segregated communities. Like giant amoebas the spreading cities absorbed these foreign entities; unlike the amoebas' prey the entities were not broken down and consumed but rather remained as units within the larger body."). One such community was Oberlin (sometimes referred to as Oberlin Village) on the periphery of Raleigh, which was annexed by the city in the late nineteenth century. Id. at 100–101. Rabinowitz recognized the ways that such annexations were attempts to bring black neighborhoods under the control of the larger majority-white cities. Id. at 101.

47. Id. at 127.
48. Id.
49. Id. at 144. It is noteworthy that North Carolina never established a state orphanage of any kind. Arthur E. Fink, Changing Philosophies and Practices in North Carolina Orphanages, 48 *North Carolina Historical Review* 333, 339 (1971). The state did support private orphanages for black and white children, but not equally, as will be seen in Chapter 5.
50. Rabinowitz, supra note 44, at xv ("[A]t no time, even at the height of Radical Reconstruction, were blacks accorded the same rights and privileges as whites.").
51. Because of Rabinowitz's point that separation was initially viewed as a positive first step, I have placed laws which created segregated institutions in Table 2 of this book, where I have listed statutes that advanced racial equality. Thus, for example, I have listed the statute that instituted a separate program for "colored pupils" at the Institution for the Deaf and Dumb and Blind in Table 2. 1872–73 N.C. Sess. Laws 212, ch. 134, § 1. See infra Table 2.

while *de facto* segregation was the norm, there was fluidity prior to the state statutes that were enacted starting in the 1890s. Rabinowitz noted that while there were at least a few city ordinances that furthered segregation, such as ones in Atlanta and Raleigh requiring stricter racial segregation in cemeteries, most of the evidence he put forward demonstrated that it was the private businesses and folkways that drove the segregation after 1865.[52] To some degree, in the privately owned restaurants and hotels, there was a class divide too, whereby the race line was almost never tested in the first-class establishments, but with race mixing in some of the downscale restaurants and bars.[53] Rabinowitz concluded, "When integration did occur, it was only at the initiation of whites and was confined as a rule to the least desirable facilities—cheap, inferior restaurants, second-class and smoking cars on trains."[54] Thus, on this score, Rabinowitz agreed with Woodward that there was at least some racial fluidity, that segregation by custom was the norm in the cities of the South, and that a strict statewide system of *de jure* segregation and discrimination only arrived in the South after 1890.

What has been missing in Woodward and the subsequent scholarship, however, has been a lack of systematic research into the state laws and their implementation.[55] Scholars have undercut Woodward's chronological framework and pushed back the date of the origins of Jim Crow. And research has set out the extent of *de facto* segregation in the Southern cities and some *de jure* segregation in the form of city ordinances on subjects such as cemeteries, parks, and, eventually, streetcars. But those few ordinances do not capture the extent of segregation and discrimination in public accommodations, public services, and public affairs in a state or in the South at large. Moreover, the received wisdom handed down from Woodward to Rabinowitz and others has been that starting in the 1890s,

---

52. Rabinowitz, supra note 44, at 137 (Atlanta and Raleigh cemeteries).

53. Id. at 184 (observing that "[e]xclusion remained the rule in the best restaurants and hotels as well as in many theaters").

54. Id. at 197. See also id. at 188 (noting a report that of Atlanta's 68 saloons, five served blacks but only two served both races).

55. See, e.g., Woodward, supra note 12, at 862 (concluding that "further research is needed on the Jim Crow statutes themselves"); Howard N. Rabinowitz, More than the Woodward Thesis: Assessing *The Strange Career of Jim Crow*, 75 *Journal of American History* 843, 850 (1988) (bemoaning the fact that there "has been remarkably little interest in the Jim Crow statutes themselves, and ... [on] the effects of implementation").

there was a change and that majority whites decided that segregation and discrimination by custom were no longer sufficient and that statutes were needed.[56]

With the compilation of North Carolina's racially discriminatory statutes dating from 1865 in this current study, it will be necessary to reflect upon the foregoing scholarship and to assess how well those arguments hold up for the Tar Heel State. Were there state statutes before the last decade of the nineteenth century? Was there a great wave of new laws after 1890? And do those pages in the statute books tell the whole story? The next chapter provides an introduction to the history of race and politics in North Carolina in the decades after the Civil War.

---

56. Rabinowitz thought that the most important question was why majority whites decided that a system of Jim Crow laws was necessary. He wrote: "Given the extent of *de facto* segregation, however, a better question might be, why after 1890 did Southern whites find it increasingly necessary to substitute a *de jure* system?" Rabinowitz, supra note 44, at 333.

3

Vile Ambitions and Low Instincts

The decades after the Civil War may be the era of this country's history about which the American public knows the least, relative to the era's importance. To the degree that most Americans are even aware of Reconstruction, that period tends to be associated with terms such as carpetbaggers and scalawags and with corruption and misrule. The postbellum decades in the South are misunderstood to this day, at least in part, because of the work of the so-called Dunning School of historians, led by William Archibald Dunning at Columbia University, who interpreted the era through a distorted lens but whose influence lingered in textbooks and popular histories well into the mid-twentieth century. Dunning and his students, such as Joseph Gregoire de Roulhac Hamilton at the University of North Carolina, argued that the former slaves had been put on an equal legal footing as citizens with the end of slavery, but that the freedmen were incapable of intelligently participating in government and that the attempt to allow them to share in governance had led to misrule throughout the South. Dunning wrote that, after the war, "the negroes were in the enjoyment of equal political rights with the whites" but that "the negroes exercised an influence in political affairs out of all relation to their intelligence or property."[1] Yet in North Carolina and throughout the South, the

---

1. William Archibald Dunning, *Essays on the Civil War and Reconstruction and Related Topics* 354 (rev. ed. 1904). See id. at 355 ("[T]he negroes who rose to prominence and leadership were very frequently of a type which acquired and practiced the tricks and

former slaves never truly possessed equal political rights and they were disadvantaged at every turn. Any notion that the former slaves had equal political or legal status once the yoke of slavery was removed is a myth. The white "assumption of black incapacity" is evident at every turn, and it was the justification for the legal and political impediments placed upon the black population from 1865 forward.[2] The post-Civil War history of North Carolina was irretrievably linked to the political power and social standing—or, the lack thereof—of racial minorities. The decades after the war were a time of shifting political fortunes and alliances, both in the state and in the South. It will be helpful, before turning to the statutes, to highlight those changes and the points of political conflict in North Carolina, especially as they touched upon race, as well as to document the racial contagion that swept the state in the White Supremacy Campaigns of 1898 and 1900. This chapter will focus on the shifting legislative power in Raleigh and the racial politics embedded within those tides because, for a study about North Carolina's statutes as they relate to discrimination, it is necessary to have more than a rudimentary understanding of the backdrop to that legislation.

The most distinctive aspects of North Carolina politics during this era are their complexity and heterogeneity. As the historian Richard White has recognized, North Carolina in the second half of the nineteenth century was "a complicated Southern state."[3] The eastern counties with large black populations were very different from the mountain counties with an overwhelmingly white population and both of those were very different from the growing Piedmont cities. What one would assume to be natural political alliances were, instead, difficult to achieve because of divergent interests. While there was a strong base of Unionism and, thus, support for the Republican Party in the majority-white counties of the mountains,

---

knavery rather than the useful arts of politics, and the vicious courses of these negroes strongly confirmed the prejudices of the whites.").

2. Eric Foner, *Black Reconstruction*: An Introduction, 112 *South Atlantic Quarterly* 409, 410 (2013). See also Eric Foner, *The Second Founding: How the Civil War and Reconstruction Remade the Constitution* xxii (2019) ("[The Dunning School's view] was a portrait of Reconstruction meant to justify the times in which it was written. It provided an intellectual foundation for Jim Crow, the racial system of the South and in many ways the United States as a whole, from the 1890s until the civil rights era of the 1960s.").

3. Richard White, *The Republic for Which It Stands: The United States during Reconstruction and the Gilded Age, 1865–1896*, at 739 (2017).

3. VILE AMBITIONS AND LOW INSTINCTS | 59

and while the freedmen were overwhelmingly members of the Republican Party, there were frequently conflicting interests between these groups.[4] Even within geographical sections of the state, generalizations are hard to come by. For example, while the white planters in the eastern part of the state were members of the Conservative Party (what was soon to be the Democratic Party),[5] the blacks in those same counties sometimes crossed the political aisle to support the Democratic candidates—mainly because of the support and political patronage that would redound to the minority community.[6]

In the years immediately after the end of the Civil War, there was immense political instability. On May 29, 1865, a little over a month after taking office, President Andrew Johnson issued two proclamations. One named William W. Holden as the provisional governor of North Carolina and was intended to put the state on a path "to restore said State to its

---

4. See, e.g., Frenise A. Logan, *The Negro in North Carolina, 1876–1894*, at 14 (1964) ("The frequent refusal of white Republicans to support Negro office-seekers, for example, led to acrid and lengthy factional conflict that considerably weakened the party in its battles with a reasonably unified Democratic party."). It is to be remembered that women were not entitled to vote at this time in the United States.

5. The Conservative Party in North Carolina was made up of secessionist Democrats and pre-war Whigs, the latter willing to ally themselves with the white Democrats politically, but not under that name: "The majority of southern Whigs entered the Democratic ranks but did not accept the Democratic label." Thomas B. Alexander, Persistent Whiggery in the Confederate South, 1860–1877, 27 *Journal of Southern History* 305, 318 (1961). See also C. Vann Woodward, *Origins of the New South: 1877–1913*, at 2 (1951) (hereinafter *New South*) ("[S]o repugnant had the marriage with their old enemies been to the Whigs that it was not until eight years after the war that the very name 'Democratic' was avowed by the Conservative party of North Carolina.").

6. See, e.g., James L. Leloudis, *Schooling the New South: Pedagogy, Self, and Society in North Carolina, 1880–1920*, at 7 (1996) ("Under informal agreements with ruling Democrats, black community leaders often claimed at least one, and sometimes all three, of the committee posts attached to their neighborhood schools. White officeholders, mindful of the political clout of black voters, viewed such compromises as the price of power."). A black Baptist minister, Garland H. White, wrote to U.S. Senator Matt Ransom, a Democrat: "The best thing for the colored people to do is to unite with the governing class of white people of this section which are Democrats whom we have to depend upon in every emergency." Garland H. White to Matt Ransom (Apr. 11, 1892), quoted in Logan, supra note 4, at 22. With regard to the benefits to the black community, Logan pointed out that "[d]espite Democratic determination to restrict colored office holding on the county level as exemplified by the system of county government, Negro citizens in a number of eastern counties were given representation by that party in the local government." Logan, supra note 4, at 30.

constitutional relations to the Federal Government."[7] On the same day, Johnson issued another proclamation that granted amnesty and pardon to those who had participated in the rebellion, with specified exceptions, if they were willing to take an oath or affirmation to support the Constitution and the Union.[8] Given that the ability to vote was to be limited to those granted amnesty and pardon, many former Confederates took the oath and they not only voted, but participated as delegates in the October 1865 N.C. convention.[9] This was the period known as Presidential Reconstruction, when Johnson allowed many participants in the rebellion to immediately return to political activity and power while, at the same time, the former slaves were still excluded from the political process and were at the mercy of the white officeholders.[10] Following the October convention, the state elections in November 1865 saw the defeat of Holden by Jonathan Worth, a Unionist and former Whig, as well as the election of a

---

7. Andrew Johnson, Proclamation (May 29, 1865), in 6 *A Compilation of the Messages and Papers of the Presidents: 1789–1897*, at 312, 313 (James D. Richardson ed., 1897).

8. Andrew Johnson, Proclamation (May 29, 1865), in 6 *A Compilation of the Messages and Papers of the Presidents: 1789–1897*, at 310, 310–311 (James D. Richardson ed., 1897). The oath or affirmation was set out:

> I, ——— ———, do solemnly swear (or affirm), in presence of Almighty God, that I will henceforth faithfully support, protect, and defend the Constitution of the United States and the Union of the States thereunder, and that I will in like manner abide by and faithfully support all laws and proclamations which have been made during the existing rebellion with reference to the emancipation of slaves. So help me God.

Id.

9. William A. Link, *North Carolina: Change and Tradition in a Southern State* 218–219 (2009). At the same time, a freedmen's convention took place in Raleigh that sent a document to the all-white convention asking for equal rights, education for their children, and support for families that were broken up under slavery. Jeffrey J. Crow, Paul D. Escott, and Flora J. Hatley, *A History of African Americans in North Carolina* 77–79 (1992). The response of the all-white convention was the endorsement of the creation of a commission to draft new laws with regard to the former slaves, but the result was the discriminatory and oppressive Black Code enacted in early 1866. Link, supra, at 219. On the substance of the state's Black Code, see Chapter 4.

10. Eric Foner observed: "The stark truth was that outside the Unionist mountains, Johnson's policies had failed to create a new political leadership to replace the prewar 'slaveocracy'.... If the architects of secession had been repudiated, the South's affairs would still be directed by men who ... formed part of the antebellum political establishment." Eric Foner, *Reconstruction* 197 (1988).

3. VILE AMBITIONS AND LOW INSTINCTS | 61

legislature that "confirmed the continued dominance of wartime political leadership."[11] This legislature quickly went to work creating the so-called Black Code which, when enacted in the spring of 1866, prohibited the former slaves from offering evidence at trial when the rights of white persons and their property were at issue (unless consented to by the white parties to the case), made contracts by a black person void unless in writing and witnessed by a white person, made the *attempted* rape of a white woman by a black man punishable by death, and created a system of involuntary servitude and, thus, free black labor through laws on apprenticeship and vagrancy.[12] The apprenticeship law gave former slave masters preference over children that the masters previously owned, and it was frequently used without regard to teaching a skilled trade but was "an excuse for providing planters with the unpaid labor of black minors,"[13] while the vagrancy statute allowed adult blacks who were "sauntering about without employment" to be arrested, convicted, and put to work when there was a labor shortage.[14] In a similar vein, Governor Worth and the legislature

---

11. Id.

12. 1866 N.C. Sess. Laws 99, 102, ch. 40, § 9 (persons of color incapable of offering evidence in court); 1866 N.C. Sess. Laws 99, 101, ch. 40, § 7 (contracts involving persons of color void unless in writing and witnessed by a white person); 1866 N.C. Sess. Laws 99, 102, ch. 40, § 11 (attempted rape of white female by person of color punishable by death). The apprenticeship law is found at 1866 N.C. Sess. Laws 99, 100, ch. 40, § 4, and the vagrancy law is at 1866 N.C. Sess. Laws 111, ch. 42. See also the detailed entries in this book's Table A and discussion in Chapter 4, n.64, infra.

13. Foner, supra note 10, at 201. As Foner noted, this so-called apprentice system operated without the consent and, often, knowledge of the black children's parents and, frequently, it did not even involve minors: "[I]n some areas, courts bound out individuals for uncompensated labor who could hardly be considered minors; one tenth of the apprentices in one North Carolina county exceeded the age of sixteen, including an 'orphan' working at a turpentine mill and supporting his wife and child." Foner, supra note 10, at 201. See also Karin L. Zipf, *Labor of Innocents: Forced Apprenticeship in North Carolina, 1715–1919* (2005).

14. 1866 N.C. Sess. Laws 111, ch. 42. See William Cohen, Negro Involuntary Servitude in the South, 1865–1940: A Preliminary Analysis, 42 *Journal of Southern History* 31, 33–34 (1976) ("Broadly drawn vagrancy statutes enabled police to round up idle blacks in times of labor scarcity and also gave employers a coercive tool that might be used to keep workers on the job."). In a jury charge in Wilmington, a Judge Meares was reported to have commented on the "terrible evil [of] vagrancy:"

> Expressing sympathy for those negroes who were industrious and lawabiding in disposition, while desirous of delivering the severest penalties against offenders, he pointed out as a remedy the strict enforcement of

abolished the state school system outright because of a fear that if white children were educated at public expense, as Worth said, "we will be required to educate the negroes in like manner."[15] In light of this approach to the former slaves by North Carolina and the other Southern states, as well as the states' refusal to ratify what was to become the Fourteenth Amendment to the U.S. Constitution, Congress decided to take the reins and ensure that the Civil War had consequences. Thus, Presidential Reconstruction (and Johnson's willingness to keep blacks in their place) was jettisoned by Congress in favor of a much stricter approach to the Southern states, Congressional Reconstruction, which began with the enactment of a federal statute on March 2, 1867.[16]

Congressional Reconstruction brought great changes to North Carolina, the primary one being that the state was "made subject to the military authority of the United States."[17] The state was placed in the Second Military District, along with South Carolina, under the command of Gen. Daniel E. Sickles and, later, Gen. Edward R.S. Canby. The military's duty under the statute was "to protect all persons in their rights of person and property, to suppress insurrection, disorder, and violence."[18] It was during this same time, in March 1867, that the Republican Party was officially formed in North Carolina, composed mainly of native Unionist whites (disparagingly termed "scalawags"), carpetbaggers (non-native whites) and, in the largest number, blacks within the state.[19] Pursuant to Section 5 of the March 1867 act, and excepting those who participated in the rebellion who were disenfranchised under that section, Gen. Canby

---

the vagrancy laws of the State, and believed that this was demanded as much as a matter of justice to the working negroes as to the other classes of our population.

Daily Dispatch (Wilmington, N.C.), Apr. 2, 1867, at 2.

15. Jonathan Worth quoted in Foner, supra note 10, at 208 (internal quotation marks omitted).

16. Act of March 2, 1867, 14 Stat. 428, ch. 153.

17. Id. § 1.

18. Id. § 3.

19. Richard H. Abbott, *The Republican Party and the South, 1855–1877: The First Southern Strategy* 112–113 (1986). As C. Vann Woodward observed, some terms such as scalawags and carpetbaggers, while pejorative and loaded, are "unavoidable": "The historian may deplore the injustice of the term 'carpetbagger' when it falls alike upon the just and the unjust, but [the historian] is no more able to dispense with it than was the carpetbagger himself." Woodward, *New South*, supra note 5, at x.

3. VILE AMBITIONS AND LOW INSTINCTS | 63

ordered that North Carolina hold a constitutional convention with delegates elected "by the male citizens of said State, twenty-one years old and upward, of whatever race, color, or previous condition."[20] This election of delegates resulted in a convention populated with 107 Republicans out of the 120 delegates,[21] and the Constitution of 1868 created the governmental structure that, in the main, exists today in the state. It provided for the direct election of state executive officials such as the secretary of state, treasurer, and attorney general.[22] It enlarged the state supreme court, created superior courts, and provided for the direct election of judges.[23] It created a new entity called the township from which a clerk and two justices of the peace were to be elected.[24] The Constitution of 1868 extended the vote to the freedmen.[25] And, importantly, it directed that the new General Assembly was to provide, through taxation, a "general and uniform system of Public Schools,"[26] but it was silent as to race, neither mandating racial integration of the schools nor requiring racially separate schools. As one black delegate observed, he thought that it was not good for black children "to eat and drink daily the sentiment that they are naturally inferior to whites, which they do in three-fourths of all the schools where they have white teachers."[27]

With the suffrage mandates of Congressional Reconstruction still in force, the state election in April 1868 ratified the new state constitution and swept into office Republicans at every level of government. The inclusion of blacks on the voting rolls instantly created 19 majority-black counties in the eastern part of the state.[28] The election brought back to office William W. Holden, now a Republican, who defeated Worth. The

---

20. Act of March 2, 1867, 14 Stat. 428–430, ch. 153, § 5.
21. Link, supra note 9, at 226. Of the Republican delegates, there were 15 blacks and 77 scalawags. Id. at 228.
22. John V. Orth and Paul Martin Newby, *The North Carolina State Constitution* 20–21 (2d ed. 2013).
23. N.C. Const. of 1868, art. III, § 26.
24. N.C. Const. of 1868, art. VII, § 5. See also Orth and Newby, supra note 22, at 21.
25. N.C. Const. of 1868, art. VI, § 1 ("Every male person born in the United States, and every male person who has been naturalized, twenty one years old or upward . . . shall be deemed an elector.").
26. N.C. Const. of 1868, art IX, § 2.
27. James W. Hood, quoted in Paul D. Escott, *Many Excellent People: Power and Privilege in North Carolina, 1850–1900*, at 144 (1985).
28. Link, supra note 9, at 226.

Republicans won over two-thirds of the seats in the General Assembly, and that delegation included 20 black members.[29] The legislature created a new public school system and quickly ratified the Fourteenth Amendment, which allowed for the readmission of the state to the Union and the effective end of Congressional Reconstruction in North Carolina.[30] Thus, direct military oversight was over. With local offices such as sheriffs and county commissioners and justices of the peace held by large numbers of Republicans (including blacks) who were sympathetic to the large black constituency in their party, the freedmen and women finally achieved some measure of legal protection and fair play from state and local officials.[31] This was a marked change from the injustices that took place from the end of the war until the advent of federal military authority.

Holden and the legislature soon found themselves in political hot water, however. Through a combination of ineptitude and outright corruption, the state debt was increased exponentially by the legislature and bonds were issued and sold at discounts in the North and in Europe, with the desperately poor postbellum state unable to service the debt.[32] This situation led to default and, down the road, a constitutional amendment allowing the state to repudiate the debt.[33] But between the money that had been thrown around in Raleigh to induce the issuance of the bonds and the special taxes levied on the people of the state in order to try to make the interest payments,[34] the Republican incumbents were in political danger with the election of 1870 on the horizon.

---

29. Crow et al., supra note 9, at 85.

30. Link, supra note 9, at 228.

31. Crow et al., supra note 9, at 86. In the 1868 election, Republicans won all five county commissioner seats (including one by a black) in New Hanover County and, in Edgecombe County, two of the five commissioners were black. Escott, supra note 27, at 144.

32. John V. Orth, *The Judicial Power of the United States* 59 (1987). North Carolina was not alone among the Southern states in this regard, as they all issued bonds which could not be serviced. North Carolina, though, not only repudiated the post-war debt but "improved on the occasion by relieving itself of millions more of antebellum debt." Id. at 58.

33. Id. at 60.

34. Id. at 59–60. See also Hugh Talmage Lefler and Albert Ray Newsome, *North Carolina: The History of a Southern State* 493 (3d ed. 1973) ("Later investigations . . . reveal that large commissions had been paid to lawyers and judges by railroad officials or their lobbyists, and that bribery and fraud tainted a few votes for the bond legislation,

3. VILE AMBITIONS AND LOW INSTINCTS | 65

Instead of being focused on corruption and the mismanagement of the state's finances, though, the 1870 election in North Carolina largely took place against a backdrop of brutal racist violence by the Ku Klux Klan and the response of the governor to that violence. The Conservative Party (what would soon become the Democratic Party) and the Klan were not coextensive entities, but many of the Klan's leaders were Conservative Party leaders, and the Klan certainly worked to advance the Conservative Party's fortunes at the ballot box.[35] The Klan had an overt political purpose.[36] In the lead-up to the 1870 election, Klan violence took the form of the assassination of a white Republican, state Senator John W. Stephens, inside the Caswell County Courthouse in May 1870,[37] and the lynching of a prominent black Republican and former town commissioner, Wyatt Outlaw, who was hanged outside the Alamance County Courthouse in February 1870.[38] The Klan focused its violence on the Piedmont counties of the state—like Caswell and Alamance—where the 1868 Republican victories had been narrow and where the black populations in those

---

though a majority of the legislators perhaps knew nothing of the fraud and voted for the bond laws on the basis of merit.").

35. Otto H. Olsen, The Ku Klux Klan: A Study in Reconstruction Politics and Propaganda, 39 *N.C. Historical Review* 340, 352 (1962) (concluding that in both the Piedmont and other parts of state "a veritable galaxy of Conservative luminaries, ranging from State legislators to local policemen, and in some counties half the Conservative voting strength, were Klansmen"). Olsen notes another fact confirming the connection between the Conservative Party leadership and the Klan: "It is also significant that, when they so desired, Conservatives of character and 'responsible position' quickly and easily secured the dissolution of the Klan." Id. at 352–353.

36. Id. at 352 ("The Klan was formed, noted one of its leaders in western North Carolina, not to achieve 'a white man's government only, but—mark the phrase—an intelligent white man's government.'"). See also Escott, supra note 27, at 155. Compare Hamilton's earlier claims: "At any rate, it is clear that the movement [i.e., the Klan] was primarily designed for protection and its influence upon politics was purely incidental. The evidence is overwhelming in support of the theory that the chief purpose of the Ku Klux was to oppose the Union League and check its operations." Joseph G. de Roulhac Hamilton, *Reconstruction in North Carolina* 454 (1914).

37. Olsen, supra note 35, at 358.

38. Carole Watterson Troxler, "To look more closely at the man": Wyatt Outlaw, a Nexus of National, Local, and Personal History, 77 *N.C. Historical Review* 403, 403 (2000). In addition to being a Graham, N.C., town commissioner, Outlaw represented Alamance County at the 1866 Freedmen's Convention, id. at 414, and organized the Loyal Republican League in the county, id. at 416, and was granted a commission to the Union League from Governor Holden. Id.

counties were well shy of being majorities.[39] In Orange County alone, the Klan murdered five people in late 1869 and early 1870.[40] Whipping was also a tool of the Klan, with more than 100 persons whipped in Rutherford County alone and with 21 persons whipped in Caswell County in a little over a month in the spring of 1870.[41] As Klan violence escalated, Governor Holden issued a proclamation after Wyatt Outlaw's murder which declared Alamance County to be in a state of insurrection,[42] called out a militia led by former Union officer George Kirk in late June,[43] and declared Caswell County to be in a state of insurrection on July 8, 1870.[44] The black people in many counties were rightfully scared for their own safety, and many were intimidated from going to the polls during the August 1870 election.[45] In the lead up to the August vote, the Kirk-led troops detained about 100 men, and there was some mistreatment of the detainees by inexperienced officers.[46] Conservatives proclaimed the arrests and detentions of the suspected Klansmen by the militia to be unlawful, and the election "occurred in the midst of the furor over habeas corpus."[47] The Conservative Party and its supporters proclaimed their desire to end

---

39. Link, supra note 9, at 230. See also Paul D. Escott, White Republicanism and Ku Klux Klan Terror: The North Carolina Piedmont During Reconstruction in *Race, Class and Politics in Southern History* 3, 6 (Jeffrey J. Crow et al., eds. 1989) (noting that "most counties in the piedmont had a black population that was less than 40 percent but more than 10 percent of the total population").

40. Olsen, supra note 35, at 353.

41. Proclamation of June 6, 1870, reprinted in *A Report of the Proceedings in the Habeas Corpus Cases* 23, 24 (William H. Battle ed., 1870); Escott, supra note 27, at 154.

42. Proclamation of March 7, 1870, reprinted in *A Report of the Proceedings in the Habeas Corpus Cases* 21 (William H. Battle ed., 1870) (declaring "the civil authorities of the County of Alamance are not able to protect the citizens of said County in the enjoyment of life and property").

43. See, e.g., Holden and Kirk, *The Daily Journal* (Wilmington, N.C.), June 24, 1870, at 2.

44. Proclamation of July 8, 1870, reprinted in *The Daily Standard* (Raleigh, N.C.), July 9, 1870, at 2.

45. Crow et al., supra note 9, at 91.

46. Foner, supra note 10, at 440. See Allen W. Trelease, *White Terror: The Ku Klux Klan Conspiracy and Southern Reconstruction* 219 (1971) (mistreatment of detainees on order of Col. George Bergen at Company Shops, N.C. (modern Burlington), in attempt to extract information about Outlaw's murder).

47. Foner, supra note 10, at 441.

"Negro rule" in the state.[48] Not surprisingly, the black vote from the Piedmont counties was suppressed in the 1870 election, and the Conservative Party took control of the General Assembly.[49] There were fifteen counties that shifted their votes in 1870 to the Conservative Party compared to 1868, and ten of those fifteen counties had experienced significant Klan violence.[50] The victors of the 1870 election were termed the "Redeemers" by many whites, because they "redeemed" white non-Republican rule in the state and, thus, returned political power to those who held it prior to the war. The Conservative members of the legislature almost immediately sought to oust Governor Holden for what they labeled the Kirk-Holden War; he was impeached and, in March 1871, Holden became the first governor in the United States ever removed from office.[51]

While the Conservative Party changed its name to Democratic after 1874 in order to align the state party with the resurgent national party,[52] the party's majority in the legislature after the 1870 election worked to solidify and entrench the Conservative/Democratic Party throughout the state. Although the party had a majority in the General Assembly, it was not overwhelming because of continued Republican strength in both the mountains and the majority-minority counties in the eastern part of the state. The Conservatives/Democrats realized that a small shift in the Piedmont counties could change their electoral fortunes. But the party used

---

48. Escott, supra note 27, at 148 ("[The Conservatives] let no opportunity pass to stress the color line above all other issues."); Lefler and Newsome, supra note 34, at 497 ("All honest, patriotic white men were urged to rally to the Conservative standard and restore 'home rule' and 'white supremacy' in North Carolina.").

49. Escott, supra note 39, at 32 ("In Cleveland County, Republicans lamented the effects of Klan terror, which had reduced black support for their ticket to almost nothing."); Lefler and Newsome, supra note 34, at 498 ("By rallying most of the native whites to its standard and keeping many Negroes from the polls, the Conservative party won an overwhelming victory, electing five of seven representatives to Congress and capturing by large majorities both houses of the state legislature.").

50. Olsen, supra note 35, at 360. Olsen also observed that, in these counties, it was "suggestive of Klan influence that the Conservative victory was due less to an increase in their vote than to a decrease in the Republican vote." Id.

51. Foner, supra note 10, at 441. It is important to note that the Conservative legislature in 1873 passed a law which granted "complete amnesty and pardon" for all crimes committed as a member of the Klan or any similar affiliated organization, the only exceptions being for rape, "deliberate and willful murder," arson, and burglary. 1872–73 N.C. Sess. Laws 298, 299, ch. 181.

52. Lefler and Newsome, supra note 34, at 500.

two tactics that would maximize their power at both the state and local levels: first, by gerrymandering districts along racial lines and, second, by eliminating the local election of township officials.

After the election of 1870 and in succeeding years, the Conservatives/Democrats in the legislature drew legislative district lines in ways to ensure the safe election of members of their party in congressional, state, and local races. They began in 1872 by a reapportionment of the districts of the state senate, with a decided advantage given to Conservatives in the senatorial districts.[53] But the most important reapportionment in this legislative session was the creation of a black congressional district in eastern North Carolina.[54] The second congressional district was a "Republican and black stronghold for the next twenty-eight years."[55] The Conservative legislature packed black Republicans into this one congressional district and, thus, by conceding defeat there, the surrounding counties had reduced numbers of black Republicans and, thus, more white Conservatives/Democrats so those districts were easily won by the Conservative/Democratic candidates. There were ten counties in the second, and all but two had black majorities.[56] This district elected four blacks to the U.S. House of Representatives between 1874 and 1898, and minorities held many other federal and state positions within this district during that same period.[57] Subsequent Democratic legislatures also took aim at New Hanover County and its county seat, Wilmington, to reduce the number of Republican officials elected at the state and local level. First, in 1875, the General Assembly formed a new county, Pender, from the northern and rural two-thirds of New Hanover County, hoping that the Democratic planters in the new county would be able to exert their influence over the

---

53. Hamilton, supra note 36, at 570. The statute is 1871–72 N.C. Sess. Laws 262, ch. 174.

54. 1871–72 N.C. Sess. Laws 259, ch. 171. As originally constituted, the second congressional district was composed of Edgecombe, Wilson, Greene, Wayne, Lenoir, Jones, Craven, Northampton, Warren, and Halifax counties in the eastern part of the state. Id. As Eric Anderson noted, the Black Second changed with this legislation by the removal of three majority white counties (Carteret, Duplin, and Onslow) and the "addition of heavily black Halifax, Northampton, and Warren." Eric Anderson, *Race and Politics in North Carolina, 1872–1901: The Black Second* 35–36 (1981).

55. Anderson, supra note 54, at 5.

56. Id. at 4. Even the two counties that did not have black majorities, Wayne and Wilson, were over 45 percent black. Id.

57. Id. at x.

3. VILE AMBITIONS AND LOW INSTINCTS | 69

still sizable black Republican population.[58] That maneuver left the largest city in North Carolina, Wilmington, "a Republican stronghold,"[59] with an even higher percentage of Republican voters. However, the Democratic-controlled legislature then reduced New Hanover's representation in the state house to two seats (from three) and redrew the city's wards so that 21 percent of Wilmington's population—where the Conservatives and whites overwhelmingly lived—elected 6 city aldermen while the remaining 79 percent of the city population with large Republican and black percentages elected only 3 aldermen.[60] In these ways, Democratic legislatures minimized black and Republican officeholding throughout the state for decades to come.[61]

---

58. W. McKee Evans, *Ballots and Fence Rails: Reconstruction on the Lower Cape Fear* 167 (1966). The statute is 1874–75 N.C. Sess. Laws 96 [sic], ch. 91. While the chapter number of this statute is correct, the page number at the top of the page in the published volume is clearly wrong: the page should actually be 93, as it is between pages 92 and 94 in the published session laws. I have retained the incorrect misprint in the table with "sic" to note the problem. This error is also noted in Table 1, infra.

59. Evans, supra note 58, at 167.

60. Id. at 167–68. The statute that reduced the number of state representatives from New Hanover County is 1874–75 N.C. Sess. Laws 154, ch. 136, § 4. The statute that changed the wards in Wilmington is 1874–75 N.C. Sess. Laws 462, ch. 43, § 4 (Private). However, the Wilmington law was invalidated in *State ex rel. Van Bokkelen v. Canaday*, 73 N.C. 198 (1875) (striking down 1875 statute on grounds that it unconstitutionally changed residency requirements). The legislature responded with another law focused on Wilmington wards and elections. 1876–77 N.C. Sess. Laws 376, ch. 192, § 1 (most black Wilmington residents again packed into two out of the five total wards).

61. Another example of racial districting is the creation of Vance County in 1881, 1881 N.C. Sess. Laws 169, ch. 113, into which black Republican power was packed so that Democratic power would be guaranteed in the counties from which it was created. *News and Observer*, Mar. 6, 1881, at 2 ("[Vance] county will be Republican, but Granville will doubtless be Democratic, inasmuch as the territory taken from Granville contains three large Republican precincts."). Vance County was named for Zebulon Vance, a U.S. Senator at the time, and its racial roots led to it being labeled "Zeb's black baby:"

> In 1881, the state legislature carved out a new county from portions of Granville, Warren, and Franklin counties and named it "Vance." Predominantly African American in population and Republican in politics, Zeb's "black baby" stemmed from the Democrats' continuing efforts to both honor Vance and strengthen their party by gerrymandering the more densely black-populated areas into a new county to the advantage of white voters in the parent counties.

Steven E. Nash, The Political Commemoration of North Carolina's War Governor, in *North Carolinians in the Era of the Civil War and Reconstruction* 269, 277 (Paul D.

The second approach used by the Democrats was the elimination of "home rule" at the local level, which had to be accomplished through an amendment to the state constitution. The 1868 Constitution provided for the direct election of county commissioners and justices of the peace and, unsurprisingly, this led to the election of many black and Republican officials in areas where white Democrats did not predominate.[62] The Democrats, in a political maneuver that was repeated in other Southern states, wanted to change this process so that the General Assembly would have control over local officials.[63] This would allow for whatever statewide legislative majority existed in Raleigh—that is, Democratic—to appoint their own party members in the localities, despite the political (and racial) vagaries at the local level. This goal was accomplished through a constitutional convention which ratified an amendment that would allow the General Assembly to assume this power, if it so wished.[64] Home rule was, paradoxically, placed in the state legislature in Raleigh: "The purpose of this amendment, as was well understood, was to block control of local government in the eastern counties by blacks who were in the majority there."[65] Following ratification, the General Assembly, in Democratic hands, immediately enacted a statute giving itself this appointment power.[66] Thus, in both Democratic and Republican counties, local residents lost the ability to elect their own local officials, but the disconnect between population and the appointed officials was greatest in the majority-black areas in the eastern part of the state. Yet there was discontent among white Democrats in other parts of the state, especially in the west, as their voice over local officials was lost because of the party's interest in white political domination in the other parts of the state.

Despite these attempts to solidify Democratic Party control across the

---

Escott ed., 2008). As Nash notes, however, the Democrats did not win easily in the two preexisting counties—Granville and Warren—until the disenfranchisement of blacks. Id. at 291 n.23.

62. N.C. Const. of 1868, art. VII, §§ 1, 5.

63. See Woodward, *New South*, supra note 5, at 54 (in Louisiana, similar power given to governor to appoint local officials).

64. Orth and Newby, supra note 22, at 25–26.

65. Id. at 26. See also 3 Joseph G. de Roulhac Hamilton, *History of North Carolina: North Carolina Since 1860*, at 193 (1919) (claiming law "violated every principle of local self-government").

66. 1876–77 N.C. Sess. Laws 226, 227–28, ch. 141, §§ 4–5.

state, there remained more political competition and volatility in North Carolina than in virtually any other Southern state. A referendum put forward to voters in 1871 by the Redeemers to hold a new constitutional convention went down to defeat at the ballot box.[67] In 1872, the Republicans not only held onto the governorship, but they won back seats and cut into the Conservatives' majorities in the General Assembly, this being only one election cycle after the Redeemers had captured the legislature with the help of the Klan.[68] Similarly, the 1875 constitutional convention's elected delegates included 58 Democrats, 58 Republicans, and 3 independents who held the balance of power between the two parties.[69] Precisely because of the numbers of black and white Republicans in the eastern and western parts of the state, the Democratic Party did not dominate North Carolina politics to the degree it did elsewhere in the South. The state possessed the most robust two-party system in the South prior to 1900.[70] As Morgan Kousser calculated, between 1880 and 1896 in North Carolina, "the Democrats never won more than 54 percent of the vote in the races for governor."[71] And the Democratic Party had multiple tensions within its own constituencies. In 1882, there was a liberal wing of the party that split off, at least temporarily, over the Democrats' support for prohibition and, under a third-party banner, this splinter party was able to win one seat in the General Assembly and one of the state's congressional seats.[72] The Democratic Party lost its absolute majority in the state legislature in the 1886 election because another faction of the party split from what its members saw as the older, sclerotic leadership of the party, and these independent legislators held the balance of power during that session of the General Assembly.[73]

The greatest internal party tensions, however, were between the Demo-

---

67. Lefler and Newsome, supra note 34, at 499.
68. Link, supra note 9, at 234.
69. Id. at 235.
70. Jeffrey J. Crow, Cracking the Solid South: Populism and the Fusionist Interlude, in *The North Carolina Experience: An Interpretive and Documentary History* 333, 335 (Lindley S. Butler and Alan D. Watson eds., 1984).
71. J. Morgan Kousser, *The Shaping of Southern Politics: Suffrage Restriction and the Establishment of the One-Party South, 1880–1910*, at 183 (1974).
72. Lefler and Newsome, supra note 34, at 544. The break-away party was called the Liberal Anti-Prohibitionist Party. Id.
73. Link, supra note 9, at 261.

crats' support for railroad and industrial interests and, on the other hand, the struggling rural farmers. The rural farmers were the Democrats' natural base, but, at the same time, the party leaders courted corporate interests such as railroads and banks. Thus, the party did not put its full support behind the creation of a railroad regulatory commission that would have provided oversight of the high freight rates charged to farmers and the railroads' favoritism toward other shippers.[74] In the mid-1880s throughout the South, farmers started banding together in an organization called the Farmers' Alliance that sought to counter monopolistic railroads and a harsh credit system through both political advocacy and, at the local level, consumer cooperatives that would allow the farmers to band together "to launch a local enterprise that would allow them to deal with the Alliance rather than a merchant and the crop lien."[75] The Farmers' Alliance was led at the state level by Leonidas LaFayette Polk, a former N.C. Commissioner of Agriculture and publisher of the weekly *Progressive Farmer* paper. Polk was elected president of the national Alliance in 1887 and at subsequent conventions.[76] In North Carolina, the Alliance supported the Democrats in the late 1880s and tried to work with the established party but felt bitterly betrayed in the 1889 legislature when the Democrats in the General Assembly turned against the party's prior endorsement of a railroad commission and killed legislation to set up such an entity.[77]

The inability of the Democratic Party to fully cement its power in North Carolina and the continued strength of the Republican coalition of eastern blacks and mountain whites allowed for less election corruption and more voter participation relative to other states in the South,[78] but the Democrats were the party of white supremacy and the issue of race was a constant in elections, even after the Redeemers gained control of the legislature in 1870. Thus, "the race issue figured prominently" in the 1872 election.[79] In 1876, when Democrat Zebulon Vance won the gubernatorial race and fully "redeemed" North Carolina government, "the dominant

---

74. Lefler and Newsome, supra note 34, at 545–546.
75. Edward L. Ayers, *The Promise of the New South: Life After Reconstruction* 221 (1992).
76. Stuart Noblin, *Leonidas LaFayette Polk: Agrarian Crusader* 202–214 (1949).
77. Lefler and Newsome, supra note 34, at 546.
78. Kousser, supra note 71, at 183.
79. Link, supra note 9, at 234.

theme of the Democrats' campaign was white supremacy."[80] In the 1888 campaign, the Democrats "desperately invoked the race issue to escape defeat."[81] In the 1892 election, the Democratic Party (under Chairman Furnifold Simmons) emphasized "the fear of Republican-Negro rule."[82] The constant claim of the party was that to waiver in support for the Democrats would bring "Negro rule" and Republican mismanagement and, thus, a supposed return to the grievous days of Reconstruction.[83] The Southern, white memory of Reconstruction was constructed around "black domination, carpetbagger corruption, and federal tyranny" and, at the same time, the eventual "victory" of Southern whites over outsiders and blacks a decade after the initial loss in 1865.[84] The Democratic Party proclaimed that "there ought to be no negro officials in authority over

---

80. Escott, supra note 27, at 169. Escott called the 1876 election "the most racist" in peoples' memory. Id.

81. Anderson, supra note 54, at 145. Anderson argues that the 1888 campaign presaged the white supremacy campaigns of 1898 and 1900. Id.

82. Lefler and Newsome, supra note 34, at 548. See also Helen G. Edmonds, *The Negro and Fusion Politics in North Carolina: 1894–1901*, at 26 (1951) (noting that in 1892 the Democrats "prophesied the return of Reconstruction should the Republican party and the Negro return to power").

83. The dire economic circumstances for the South following the war were real, but the scapegoating of Reconstruction itself was misguided:

> Economic suffering was widespread, the result almost entirely of the war. Its injurious effects were mostly temporary, but some families or individuals were hit harder than others and recovered more slowly. Reconstruction policy had comparatively little to do with their plight, except that higher taxation may have sharpened their pain. The second form of suffering, more psychological and political in bearing, was that experienced by the master race, and especially its ruling elite, when they found themselves ejected from power and replaced by people they regarded as social and racial inferiors. They were mortified at the sight of black voters crowding to the polls and carrying elections or serving in the legislature and on county commissions. This was perhaps the supreme horror of Reconstruction, exaggerated tales of which were handed down from generation to generation as object lessons for the future.

Allen W. Trelease, Reconstruction: The Halfway Revolution, in *The North Carolina Experience: An Interpretive and Documentary History* 285, 293–294 (Lindley S. Butler and Alan D. Watson eds., 1984).

84. David W. Blight, *Race and Reunion: The Civil War in American Memory* 138–139 (2001). See also Woodward, *New South*, supra note 5, at 51 ("After the two objects of that revolution [i.e., Redemption] were achieved—the crushing of Negro power and the ousting of foreign control—party discipline was still dependent upon keeping

white men."[85] Yet, throughout this period, black officials continued to be elected to Congress and to the state legislature. There were 54 black members of the General Assembly between 1877 and 1890,[86] and there were never less than 5 black members in every General Assembly from 1868 to 1897.[87] There were also scores of black officials appointed at the local level because of mutually beneficial alliances between white Democrats and the local black communities. After the General Assembly removed the popular election of local officials in favor of appointment by the legislature, ostensibly to minimize officeholding by black Republicans, the General Assembly appointed 30 black justices of the peace to the great discontent of many whites who thought that they had agreed to subordinate their interests so that such black political power would not exist.[88]

The 1890s upended all of what had come before. It started with a crippling economic depression and the collapse of farm prices nationwide during the early years of the decade.[89] The farmers, already struggling economically and dissatisfied with the Democratic Party, realized that beyond unity and cooperation, an engaged Farmers' Alliance could become a force within politics. Although the Farmers' Alliance in North Carolina and the nation had not been directly involved in state or national politics,

---

vividly alive the memories of these menaces. They were the only reliable bases for white solidarity.").

85. To the People of North Carolina, in *Democratic State Executive Committee: Democracy vs. Radicalism, Handbook of N.C. Politics for 1888*, at 25, 27 (1888). The party went on to say that "the great controlling reason why the Democratic party fights the Republican party . . . is that the Democratic party is a white man's party, and recognizes its obligation to protect its members, in whatever part of the State they may be, from the curse of negro rule." Id. at 83.

86. Link, supra note 9, at 259.

87. Benjamin R. Justesen, "The Class of '83": Black Watershed in the North Carolina General Assembly, 86 *N.C. Historical Review* 282, 283–284 (2009) (includes figures on African Americans in General Assembly up through 1892 election); Allen W. Trelease, Fusion Legislatures of 1895 and 1897: A Roll-Call Analysis of the North Carolina House of Representatives, 57 *N.C. Historical Review* 280, 281 (1980) (includes figures on African Americans in General Assembly from 1894 and 1896 elections).

88. Logan, supra note 4, at 51. See also Woodward, *New South*, supra note 5, at 80 ("When the North Carolina General Assembly elected several 'colored magistrates in and for certain counties,' nine white Democratic members signed a protest against their election as 'inconsistent with the principles and purposes of the party' as proclaimed 'by its thousands of speakers' in the campaign of Redemption.").

89. Ayers, supra note 75, at 3.

by 1890, there were 100,000 members in North Carolina alone.[90] The Alliance was composed of both white and black wings and, while some members could be labeled planters, most were farmers who were struggling to simply keep from being swallowed by debt.[91] It was a group through which farmers met, operated cooperative stores among members, and exchanged ideas on their economic difficulties and the ways that these struggles were driven by corporate financial forces and lending policies that affected them as a "laboring class."[92] The Alliance initially sought to work through the Democrats—rather than with the Republicans or as an independent third party—both because the Democrats in the South held the power and because of the fear stoked by Democrats that to oppose them would split the white vote and pave the way for "Negro rule" and a return to (the strawman of) Reconstruction.[93] As Alliance leader and soon-to-be U.S. Senator Marion Butler put it, Democrats tried to maintain white loyalty to the party by throwing around claims about "fiat money, third party, [and] 'nigger in the wood-pile.'"[94] In the so-called Farmers' Legislature of 1891, the Alliance counted as allies both its own members in the legislature and Democrats there who supported their goals.[95] But when the Farmers' Alliance and Leonidas Polk became discontented with the Democrats' commitment to their cause and subsequently fielded their own candidates under the banner of the People's/Populist Party in 1892, the victorious Democrats turned on the Alliance and exacted revenge by enacting a law to prohibit its business activities such as the consumer cooperatives that the Alliance operated for its members.[96] That led the Alliance and the Populist Party to fully break with the Democrats, and the Populists subsequently worked with the Republican Party to field a "fusion" ticket in 1894 whereby the

---

90. Escott, supra note 27, at 242.

91. Link, supra note 9, at 262.

92. Escott, supra note 27, at 242–243. Escott concluded that "the mood of many Tar Heel agriculturalists grew angry and class conscious. Their bitter experience had convinced them that they were a class—they often described it as the laboring class—whose very existence was threatened by corporations, merchants, banks, and capitalists." Id. at 242.

93. Id. at 243.

94. Marion Butler, *Clinton Caucasian* (Jan. 14, 1892), quoted in Escott, supra note 27, at 245.

95. Escott, supra note 27, at 245.

96. Id. at 245–247.

two parties agreed to not compete and to support each others' candidates. Under the fusion banner in North Carolina, they achieved something in 1894 that happened in no other Southern state after 1876: they unseated the Democratic majority in the state legislature.[97]

Even though the changes were set in motion over a number of years, the 1890s political upheaval altered the status quo in North Carolina in unprecedented and profound ways. The fusion of the discontented Populists and the Republicans in 1894 led to the Democrats' loss of their majority in the legislature. Then, in 1896, the fusionists not only strengthened their majorities in the North Carolina legislature, but they added to their laurels with the election of Republican Daniel L. Russell as governor.[98] Following the 1894 election, there were 74 fusionists and 46 Democrats elected to the House and 42 fusionists and 8 Democrats elected to the state Senate.[99] Then, after the 1896 election, there were 94 fusionists and 26 Democrats elected to the state House and 43 fusionists and 7 Democrats elected to the Senate.[100] Moreover, the fusionists won five out of the eight congressional seats from North Carolina in 1896.[101]

The fusionists accomplished a great deal in the legislative sessions fol-

---

97. Id. at 247. The fusionists elected 74 legislators to the General Assembly in 1894 and the Democrats only 46 members. Id.

98. Lefler and Newsome, supra note 34, at 549–553.

99. Kousser, supra note 71, at 186. Kousser's breakdown of the fusionist victors is 38 Republicans and 36 Populists in the House and 18 Republicans and 24 Populists in the Senate. Id.

The numbers used by different scholars for the composition of the General Assembly sessions following the 1894 and 1896 elections are, in a word, complex. For example, for the 1895 House of Representatives, Trelease stated that it "was composed of 44 Republicans, 38 Populists, and 45 Democrats (of whom six were unseated after successful election contests by fusionist opponents)." Trelease, supra note 87, at 281. He included within those figures "replacements occasioned by death and contested elections." Id. So, by my reading, even if you subtract the six Democrats from the original count of 45 for a final Democratic contingent of 39, these numbers still add up to 121 members (44 G.O.P. + 38 Pop. + 39 Dems) when the House only had 120 seats. The numbers I have used in the text match the Democratic totals calculated by Richard Watson, but he does not attempt to separate out the non-Democratic numbers like Kousser and Trelease do. Richard L. Watson, Jr., Furnifold M. Simmons and the Politics of White Supremacy, in *Race, Class, and Politics in Southern History* 126, 130 (Jeffrey J. Crow et al. eds., 1989).

100. Kousser, supra note 71, at 186. The breakdown of the fusionist coalition is 54 Republicans and 40 Populists in the House and 18 Republicans and 25 Populists in the Senate. Id.

101. Watson, supra note 99, at 130.

lowing their 1894 victory, and the 1896 results hinted that the Populists and Republicans could do even more in subsequent years. After 1894, laws were passed to support the public schools, restore the democratic election of local officials by the people, and establish a less-restrictive voting law meant to increase participation at the ballot-box.[102]

The fusionists' wins in 1896 were the high-water mark for their political fortunes, however, both because of rising tensions within the coalition and a concomitant backlash from without. The internal political conflicts were evident even before Election Day 1896. For the presidential election that year, the Populists opposed Republican William McKinley because of his and the national Republican Party's continued backing of the gold standard. Because the North Carolina Populists supported increasing the money supply through the use of silver, the Populists in the state did not "fuse" with the G.O.P. with regard to the federal races. Instead, because of Democratic candidate William Jennings Bryan's support for coining silver (which many farmers championed), the Southern Populists were supporters of the Democratic ticket at the national level, and that support allowed the Democrat Bryan to carry North Carolina despite the fusionist victories that year.[103] The national Republican Party's support for the gold standard caused particular tensions within the North Carolina fusionist coalition because it was a policy supported by Republican Senator Jeter Pritchard, who was eventually re-elected by the fusionist General Assembly, but only after a bitter battle within the Populist membership.[104] Moreover, many white Populists remained sensitive to the racial politics of the time and to the charge that they were splitting the white vote and allowing the Republican Party to hold power as in the bad-old days of Re-

---

102. 1895 N.C. Sess. Laws 436, ch. 404 (money refunded to state by Congress to go to public schools); 1895 N.C. Sess. Laws 211, ch. 159, § 7 (appointment of voting registrars and judges of election from each political party), § 10 (voter registration not invalidated because of failure to specify age and place of residence of elector); 1895 N.C. Sess. Laws 185, ch. 135 (local self-government); 1895 N.C. Sess. Laws 113, ch. 116, § 3 (raising tax to eighteen cents per one hundred dollar property valuation for public schools).

103. Ayers, supra note 75, at 294–297.

104. Link, supra note 9, at 267–268. Some of the tensions were also within the Republican Party, given Daniel Russell's promise in his inaugural address to protect taxpayers from "the danger of misrule by propertyless and ignorant elements," an unmistakable reference to black Republican officeholders. Daniel L. Russell, quoted in Jeffrey J. Crow and Robert F. Durden, *Maverick Republican in the Old North State: A Political Biography of Daniel L. Russell* 82 (1977).

construction. The white Populists did not have a goal of abandoning the color line in politics, but the fusionist successes suggested that this was an ancillary possibility.[105]

For the Democrats after the 1896 election, their losses led them to resolve to take back power by whatever means necessary, and the primary issue which they used to return to political power was race. The problem for the North Carolina Democrats in the first half of the 1890s was that the party was out of step with the bulk of its potential voters—rural whites in the Piedmont and eastern parts of the state—who were hurting economically at the same time that the Democratic Party and its leaders embraced backing from the corporate and financial world. In 1895, Democratic Governor Elias Carr further angered Populists and many others by leasing the state-owned railroad to the Southern Railway Company (controlled by financier J.P. Morgan) for 99 years.[106] The Populist Party in North Carolina became the force that it did precisely because so many rural whites wanted representatives who supported their interests and not those of railroads and other corporations.[107] If the Democrats hoped to retake the state legislature and, eventually, the governor's mansion, they had to woo back those disaffected white voters, energize their own base, and yet not repudiate the business interests that were still allies. The one issue that would cut across those cleavages in a clean fashion was race.

While the Democrats used the supposed threat of Negro rule with success in previous elections, the White Supremacy Campaigns of 1898 and 1900 made the appeals to racism in the earlier elections seem quite tame by comparison. Whether the racial campaign of 1898 was the brainchild of Democratic Party chair Furnifold Simmons, as he claimed, or engineered by *News and Observer* editor and owner Josephus Daniels, is not as important as the simple recognition that this tactic was embraced and orchestrated by the Democratic Party in a methodical, unrelenting cam-

---

105. These tensions were evident in the fact that the Populists ended up having their own, albeit weak, candidate for governor in 1896 opposite the Republican candidate, Russell. Crow and Durden, supra note 104, at 65–68. See also Crow, supra note 70, at 338 ("Populists and Republicans alike were wary of Negro participation in politics, but they understood the practical realities of winning elections.").

106. Escott, supra note 27, at 247. See Crow, supra note 70, at 340 ("The leasing of the state's property to the symbol of northern finance seemed to confirm their worst fears about collusion between government and corporate enterprise.").

107. Ayers, supra note 75, at 280–281; Watson, supra note 99, at 130.

paign to draw a stark racial line for white citizens and to create an atmosphere where whites were forced—figuratively or literally—to choose a side.[108] To not support the Democratic Party came to mean that a white was a traitor to the race. During this era, virtually all Southern whites believed in the superiority of the white race by whatever metric they might use: intellectual, cultural, moral, and the like. This was a time when ideas such as Herbert Spencer's notion about the survival of the fittest and what is today termed Social Darwinism were blithely applied to race by commentators and even scientists in order to confirm whites' belief in their

---

108. Furnifold M. Simmons, Memoirs, in *F.M. Simmons, Statesman of the New South: Memoirs and Addresses* 3, 26 (J. Fred Rippy ed., 1936) ("[T]he keynote of the [1898] campaign was White Supremacy, and I believe I was chiefly responsible for the choice of the issue."). See also Watson, supra note 99, at 133 (declaring that Simmons was "the political leader perhaps most responsible for the return of the Democrats to power in North Carolina in 1898 and for the disfranchisement of black people in 1900").

Josephus Daniels, the editor and owner of the *News and Observer* in Raleigh, which was the state's largest circulation newspaper at the time, has also frequently been labeled as the person most responsible for the White Supremacy Campaigns and the disenfranchisement of blacks. Daniels was an important Democratic leader and, starting in 1896, was the state's "Democratic national committeeman." Anderson, supra note 54, at 339. His biographer, Lee Craig, has concluded that Daniels "led North Carolina's white supremacy movement and, more than any other individual, was responsible for the disfranchisement of the state's African American citizens." Lee A. Craig, *Josephus Daniels: His Life & Times* xiv (2013). Craig observed that after the Democratic losses of 1896, Daniels "tried to lure Populists back into the Democratic Party with race-baiting and Free Silver, or as he regularly put it in print, into the party of 'white men and white metal.'" Id. at 184. Craig wrote that in anticipation of the 1898 campaign, Daniels "had orchestrated the appointment of Furnifold Simmons" as chair of the Democratic Party, id. at 178, and that he and Simmons together coordinated the 1898 campaign. Id. at 180–186. See also Crow, supra note 70, at 340 ("[T]he cry of 'negro rule' led by Josephus Daniels's *Raleigh News and Observer* overwhelmed any public discussion of the economic issues involved in the campaign."). Whether Daniels' biographer places too much responsibility on his shoulders alone, other scholars have concluded that "[t]he genius of Furnifold Simmons and Josephus Daniels made it [i.e., race] the only issue in 1898." Eric Anderson, The Populists and Capitalist America: The Case of Edgecombe County, North Carolina, in *Race, Class, and Politics in Southern History* 106, 125 (Jeffrey J. Crow et al. eds., 1989).

While Simmons and Daniels may have been the initiators and organizers, other people such as Charles Brantley Aycock were willing and enthusiastic participants in the White Supremacy Campaigns. As Eric Anderson has pointed out, "Quite simply, Simmons, Daniels, Aycock, and [Claude] Kitchin (and other men to a lesser degree) rode the race issue into power." Anderson, supra note 54, at 340. See also Ayers, supra note 75, at 299.

absolute superiority compared to other races.[109] If the Democrats could thereby make the 1898 political campaign a referendum on racial loyalties and shift white voters' focus away from the issues that had caused the fissure with the Populists in particular, then the Democrats had a clear path back to power.[110] Race was a trump card in North Carolina politics,

---

109. Charles A. Lofgren, *The Plessy Case: A Legal-Historical Interpretation* 101–111 (1987). For a scholarly tract of the time, published by the American Economic Association, see Frederick L. Hoffman, *Race Traits and Tendencies of the American Negro* (1896).

110. There is an ongoing scholarly debate about the motivations for the White Supremacy Campaigns of 1898 and 1900 and whether they were primarily, if not exclusively, based upon racial animus and prejudice. Most scholars would acknowledge multiple motivations, of course, but the argument that racism was the primary motivation has been made with force. Anderson, supra note 54, at 252–255. See also Ayers, supra note 75, at 530 n.48 ("Anderson convincingly argues, contrary to other historians, that the 'white supremacy' campaign of North Carolina was just what it appeared to be, not a cover for some deeper, more 'realistic,' issues of class, party, or economic advantage."). In the early decades of the twentieth century, Joseph G. de Roulhac Hamilton made this argument in his own way:

> It nevertheless remained a fact that while the negroes in a solid body voted the republican ticket and formed a clear majority of that party they would in a sense control it, making it irresponsible, easily swayed by the necessity of holding the negro vote, and hence unfit to rule. It was also true that republican control in the state meant negro control in the east with all that is therein implied—sometimes violence, injustice, dishonesty; always inefficiency, incompetence, and partisanship, accompanied by a deadly blight upon all progress. Herein lay the justification of the chosen issue.

Hamilton, supra note 65, at 280.

Other scholars have argued that race was a smokescreen for class and economic interests and that the Democratic Party had given the business and industrial interests "the bridle by which to check progressive legislation. Democratic victory guaranteed to them a domination in politics which far exceeded their numerical strength." Edmonds, supra note 82, at 153. See also Escott, supra note 27, at 254–255 (arguing that behind "the entire white supremacy campaign was the old aristocratic notion that only certain people had a right to power").

My own view is that there is an almost perfect correlation between racist motivations and partisan political motivations in 1898, and that both were equally salient to the leaders of the White Supremacy Campaign. One piece of evidence for this conclusion is the Populist Party's offer to fuse with the Democrats in May 1898. Watson, supra note 99, at 152–153. If white supremacy was the primary motivating factor, I think that the Democrats would have accepted the Populists' offer to fuse, thus returning the multiracial Republican Party to minority status in the state (if not in every locality). While the Democrats would have had to share power with Populists in the General Assembly, elected black officials would have been concentrated in areas in the eastern part of the state and black appointees limited to those areas as well. While the Populists' fusion proposal

3. VILE AMBITIONS AND LOW INSTINCTS | 81

and the Populist Party was vulnerable because of the racial composition

spoke about free silver and railroad rates, Hamilton, supra note 65, at 280–282, a fusion of the Populists and the Democrats was the straightest line to reach white supremacy. As a "leading Democrat" was quoted in the *News and Observer* on the fusion proposal: "We (i.e., Democrats) cannot win without co-operation with the Populist party or the assistance of many who have heretofore voted with that party. If the first can be secured, it makes the success of 'the white man and the white metal' certain . . . ." Significance of the Action By Populist Convention, *News and Observer*, May 19, 1898, at 4. At the conference of Democratic leaders, the speaker who turned the leaders against fusion was Charles B. Aycock. Hamilton, supra note 65, at 281–282. Aycock's biographer concluded that Aycock "wanted more than white supremacy; he wanted white solidarity and Democratic supremacy. He wished *to force* the white Populists into the Democratic party, which could then maintain white supremacy and work for the welfare of all classes of the white society." Oliver H. Orr, Jr., *Charles Brantley Aycock* 113 (1961) (emphasis added). I think Orr's observation about Aycock is ultimately a concise summary of the motivations for the White Supremacy Campaigns. Simmons and Daniels and Aycock wanted to return the Democrats to power and do that by excluding and politically isolating the Populist Party, which had collapsed after 1896 everywhere else in the South. Woodward, *New South*, supra note 5, at 289. With that short-term goal accomplished, the Populists could then be assimilated back into the Democratic fold and the Democrats could, thus, gain a white-majority party by which white supremacy could be achieved once and for all. Apart from Democratic leaders, though, it may very well have been the case that the motivation of a majority of white voters in 1898 and 1900 was primarily racial animus and not a devotion to the return of the Democratic Party to power.

Another example demonstrating Democratic leaders' interests beyond racial animus is the 1901 impeachments of Chief Justice David M. Furches and Justice Robert M. Douglas of the N.C. Supreme Court over litigation involving the chief inspector of the oyster industry. Pursuant to an 1897 law passed by the fusionist legislature, 1897 N.C. Sess. Laws 61, 65, ch. 13, § 12, Governor Russell appointed Theophilus White as the chief inspector of the oyster industry for a four-year term. Then, the Democratic-controlled legislature in 1899 repealed the 1897 law and put in place a new seven-member commission to oversee the "shell-fish industry in North Carolina." 1899 N.C. Sess. Laws 111, ch. 19, § 1. Although the 1899 statute appeared to dislodge the Russell-appointed commissioner from his job, Theophilus White went to court and argued that he still held the office because his appointment under the original statute was for a four-year term. The N.C. Supreme Court held that the office, once created, was the property of White and that the legislature could not "as long as the office remains, deprive the officer of the material part of his duties and emoluments, and that the oath and salary are the incidents of an office." *White v. Hill*, 125 N.C. 194, 195 (1899). In subsequent litigation over the unpaid salary, White sought a writ of mandamus to order the State Auditor and State Treasurer to pay the salary owed to him pursuant to the previous Supreme Court decision. *White v. Ayer*, 126 N.C. 570, 578–579 (1900). The majority opinion in *White v. Ayer* was written by then-Justice Furches and a concurring opinion was written by Justice Douglas. Id. at 572 (Furches) and 584 (Douglas, concurring). Both of these justices were Republicans, White was a Populist and, thus, all three were under the fusionist umbrella. Although the money was not immediately paid, White went back to court and the writ

of its fusionist partner. The fact that blacks made up a sizable subset of the Republican Party was a strike against it in the eyes of the Populists. As a practical matter, in 1898, there were certainly more important issues than the bugbear of race for voters in their day-to-day lives,[111] but political campaigns repeatedly remind us that, historically, emotions and resentments often matter more than policies and decency. Bread-and-butter issues were subordinated by the Democrats for reasons of both immediate political advantage and the long-term goal of the elimination of blacks from politics. Thus, as historian Edward Ayers has concluded, "So it was that North Carolina, the state with the highest voter turnout . . . and the most evenly matched party system in the region throughout the 1880s and 1890s, underwent the most violent convulsion to restore unquestioned and unblemished white power."[112]

---

of mandamus was issued to the Auditor and Treasurer, and White was ultimately paid what he was due: $831.15. Theophilus Finds Relief, *News and Observer*, Oct. 19, 1900, at 6. When White's attorney asked the Supreme Court to issue the writ of mandamus so that the money would be paid, the *News and Observer* ominously noted that the Supreme Court was in a "bad hole" and, given that, "the Legislature meets in less than three months from now, [and] the situation is decidedly interesting." Supreme Court and "Offie" White: Both of Them in a Bad Hole Just Now, *News and Observer*, Oct. 13, 1900, at 5. It turned out that the Democratic-majority legislature seated in January 1901 was not about to forget the state Supreme Court's rulings in favor of the Populist White. In Article I of the impeachment, the House of Representatives stated that the "mandamus writs were unlawfully issued" because no statutory appropriation was made and that Furches and Douglas "did then and there commit, and were guilty of, a high crime and misdemeanor in office." Article I, Articles of Impeachment, in 2 *Public Documents of the State of North Carolina*, Document No. 2, at 3, 8–9 (1901). The chief supporter of impeachment in the House of Representatives was future-governor Locke Craig, who made rather extravagant claims about the need for impeachment of Republicans Furches and Douglas: "I say if there ever was a time in human history, if there ever was a period in this Government or any other Government when the high and extraordinary power given to this high court of impeachment should be invoked, it is here in the year 1901, and by the General Assembly elected by the people in 1900." Locke Craig, quoted in The Impeachment Resolution was Passed by a 2 to 1 Vote, *News and Observer*, Feb. 19, 1901, at 1. The House impeached both Furches and Douglas on all five articles of impeachment. Id. In the end, even the Democratically controlled Senate could not bring itself to convict Furches and Douglas on any of the articles of impeachment. The Judges are Acquitted, *The Morning Post*, Mar. 29, 1901, at 1. However, the entire episode shows the lengths to which the Democratic legislature would go in order to demonstrate its revived power and to punish heretics.

111. Crow, supra note 70, at 340.
112. Ayers, supra note 75, at 300.

3. VILE AMBITIONS AND LOW INSTINCTS | 83

As regards black officeholding, it remains one of the tragic ironies of this history that the relatively meager number of black officials in federal or state offices was used as a cudgel by Democrats to argue that there was Negro supremacy in North Carolina. It is absolutely true that with the fusionist tide in the state in 1894 and 1896 and the Republican victories at the federal level in 1896, there were large and unprecedented numbers of black elected and appointed officials in the state, especially relative to other Southern states. But black supremacy would imply power, yet the election of one black member of Congress from the majority-minority second congressional district in 1896[113] and the numbers in the General Assembly—5 black members following 1894 and 11 black members following 1896 (out of a total of 170 between the two houses)[114]—do not suggest supremacy or parity or even particularly robust political strength. Instead, it was the pronounced increase in the number of black officials at the local level and in less powerful positions that seemed to disturb the white population the most. There were hundreds of black officials, most in eastern North Carolina. While precise numbers do not exist, they included 34 postmasters appointed in the "Black Second" congressional district and probably several hundred magistrates and school committeemen across the state,[115] but these positions did not afford access to the great levers of power. In the positions where there was significant power, black officials were exceedingly rare: there were only three black county commissioners on the multi-person boards in the 90-odd counties then extant, and there were no black sheriffs or clerks of superior court in the state.[116] Yet the presence of blacks in positions that brought them into frequent contact with whites, such as in the post offices and with local magistrates, animated whites' fears of Negro supremacy more than the black officeholders who possessed more substantial political power. As Eric Anderson has concluded with regard to the numerous lower-level

---

113. Anderson, supra note 54, at 237.
114. Trelease, supra note 87, at 281 (1894 figure); Watson, supra note 99, at 132 (1896 figure). Justesen counts 12 black members elected in 1896, but does not specify names. Justesen, supra note 87, at 302 (citing John L. Cheney, Jr., *North Carolina Government, 1585–1979: A Narrative and Statistical History* 464–479 (1981)).
115. Benjamin R. Justesen, Black Tip, White Iceberg: Black Postmasters and the Rise of White Supremacy in North Carolina, 1897–1901, 82 *N.C. Historical Review* 193, 197–198 (2005). See also Anderson, supra note 54, at 245–247.
116. Anderson, supra note 54, at 247–249.

officials, it was "the proximity of power, rather than its magnitude, [that] fueled white supremacists' fears of black officeholding."[117] This claim of Negro rule in North Carolina was trafficked across the South, in order to alert whites of the need to stay vigilant. The newspapers in Atlanta, New Orleans, and Richmond broadcast the assertion that this "once proud State is virtually under the feet of the negroes."[118]

The Democrats focused the North Carolina campaigns of 1898 and 1900 on race through emotional appeals to the necessity of maintaining the eternal supremacy of the white race, and through violence and the intimidation of everyone not committed to the principle of white supremacy. The Democrats' battle plan in 1898 encompassed the deployment of speakers across the state, a constant focus by Democratic newspapers on racial issues, and what newspaper editor Josephus Daniels later approvingly termed "men who could ride," by which he meant the intimidation of white and black voters by white paramilitary groups.[119] The Democrats claimed that the election was about "whether in any part of North Carolina men of Anglo-Saxon blood should be subjected to the rule and mastery of the negro" and their answer was that "North Carolina is a WHITE MAN'S State, and WHITE MEN will rule it."[120]

The leading Democratic speakers went from town to town in the state and, in an age when open-air speeches and rallies were well attended and important, they spoke at length on the need for white supremacy in politics and all aspects of life in North Carolina. One of the first rallies was on May 12, 1898, in Laurinburg, where future governors Charles B. Aycock

---

117. Id. at 251.

118. Desperate Politics in North Carolina, *Daily Picayune* (New Orleans), Oct. 26, 1898, at 4. The *Atlanta Constitution* published a lengthy article making the outlandish claim that this alleged black supremacy was the first step in a grand plan of blacks to colonize North Carolina for themselves. Frank Weldon, Blacks Propose to Colonize and Control North Carolina: They Are at Work on a Startling Solution to the Race Problem, *Atlanta Constitution*, Oct. 2, 1898, at 5. As for the Richmond newspaper, see, e.g., North State Fight: The Coming Great Struggle for White Supremacy, *Richmond Dispatch*, Nov. 1, 1898, at 1.

119. Josephus Daniels, *Editor in Politics* 284 (1941). Daniels' complete statement was that the Democrats relied upon "men who could write, men who could speak, and men who could ride—*the last by no means the least important.*" Id. (emphasis added).

120. Chairman F.M. Simmons: Issues a Patriotic and Able Address, Summing Up the Issues, and Appealing Eloquently to the White Voters to Redeem the State, *News and Observer*, Nov. 3, 1898, at 1, 1–2 (emphasis in original).

and Locke Craig made speeches.[121] As reported, Aycock "emphasize[d] the necessity of unifying the white forces before we can hope for the restoration of white supremacy in North Carolina."[122]

One of the issues that Aycock used to stir the emotions of the crowds across the state was the supposed danger that social equality, framed in terms of Negro supremacy, posed to the sexual purity and virtue of white womanhood. It was a subject that Simmons specifically chose to emphasize.[123] Aycock spoke about it at the May rally in Laurinburg[124] and returned to the subject frequently, as when he concluded a Raleigh speech in October 1898 by saying: "I appeal to you in the name of white womanhood and motherhood of North Carolina to come to the rescue of your state now so seriously threatened."[125] At one of Aycock's most famous debates during the 1898 campaign, he even made favorable reference to the recent lynching of two blacks in the county: "Why, you white men of Cabarrus [County] don't even wait for the law when negroes have dishonored your helpless, innocent women."[126] The newspaper account reported that the "room went wild. Men sitting rose unconsciously to their feet! The thunder of the cheering rose and fell and rose again."[127] Democratic speakers frequently returned to this subject on the stump because of its emotional power. At a rally in Fayetteville where it was reported that there were over 7000 people in attendance, guest speaker Senator Ben Tillman of South Carolina made reference to a well-known editorial published in a

---

121. Grand Democratic Rally: Aycock and Craig Open the Ball Gloriously, White Man and Metal, *News and Observer*, May 13, 1898, at 2.

122. Id.

123. Glenda Elizabeth Gilmore, *Gender and Jim Crow: Women and the Politics of White Supremacy in North Carolina, 1896–1920*, at 82–83 (1996) ("[Simmons] chose to make protection of white women the centerpiece of the campaign. By emphasizing sexuality, the Democrats placed race over class and spun a yarn in which white women of all classes highly prized their chastity and black men of all classes barely controlled their sexuality.").

124. Grand Democratic Rally: Aycock and Craig Open the Ball Gloriously, White Man and Metal, *News and Observer*, May 13, 1898, at 2.

125. Charles B. Aycock, quoted in A Telling Speech, *Wilmington Messenger*, Oct. 23, 1898, at 5.

126. Charles B. Aycock, quoted in Aycock's Victory, *Charlotte Observer*, Sept. 13, 1898, at 8.

127. Id. Another paper's account was similar. The Concord Debate, *The North Carolinian* (Raleigh), Sept. 15, 1898, at 3 ("It seemed that the entire six hundred men became frantic. They waved and yelled and cheered.").

black Wilmington newspaper about inter-racial liaisons as "an insult to the women of North Carolina" and he further enflamed the white crowd by challenging them: "Why didn't you kill that nigger editor who wrote that?"[128] Professor Glenda Gilmore has highlighted how racial and sexual fears were intentionally tied together as, with regard to the white women, "the white supremacy campaign depicted them as virginal treasures under assault from 'Negro domination' in politics."[129]

The intimidation of those not sufficiently committed to white supremacy in the 1898 campaign ranged from the social and economic pressure exerted by the White Government Unions to the paramilitary Red Shirts

---

128. Benjamin R. Tillman, quoted in Glorious Day in Cumberland, *Wilmington Messenger*, Oct. 22, 1898, at 5.

The Wilmington editor to whom Tillman was referring was Alexander Manly, the mulatto grandson of the antebellum Governor Charles Manly. Interview with Milo Manly (Alexander Manly's son), Sept. 11, 1984, at minute 78, available online at Louie B. Nunn Center for Oral History, University of Kentucky Libraries, https://kentuckyoralhistory.org/ark:/16417/xt75tb0xs97g (last visited Nov. 11, 2019). The Wilmington newspaper that Manly owned and edited, *The Daily Record*, published an editorial on August 18, 1898, that argued against lynching and about the hypocrisy of white society toward interracial liaisons. Alex Manly on Lynching, 1898, in *The North Carolina Experience: An Interpretive and Documentary History* 347 (Lindley S. Butler and Alan D. Watson eds., 1984) (Manly editorial as reprinted in *Wilmington Messenger*, Oct. 20, 1898). The language of the editorial was frank on the taboo subject of interracial sex, especially for its time. The editorial argued that interracial relationships occurred because of attraction between the parties and only became a crime for black men when the couple was found out by the white community: "[O]ur experience among poor white people in the country teaches us that women of that race are not more particular in the matter of clandestine meetings with colored men, than are the white men with colored women." Id. at 348. The reaction of the white-owned newspapers across the state was immediate and hostile. See, e.g., A Negro Defamer of the White Women of North Carolina, *Wilmington Messenger*, Aug. 21, 1898, at 2 (the "intent" of the editorial "is to justify the black brutes who commit rape at the expense of the character of every white wife in the south"). The *Wilmington Messenger*'s response to Manly's editorial was republished under the same headline in four newspapers across the state in the next four days. See A Negro Defamer of the White Women of North Carolina, *Goldsboro Weekly Argus*, Aug. 25, 1898, at 3; A Negro Defamer of the White Women of North Carolina, *Messenger and Intelligencer* (Wadesboro, N.C.), Aug. 25, 1898, at 2; A Negro Defamer of the White Women of North Carolina, *Webster's Weekly* (Reidsville, N.C.), Aug. 25, 1898, at 2; A Negro Defamer of the White Women of North Carolina, *Morning Post* (Raleigh, N.C.), Aug. 23, 1898, at 4. The Raleigh *News and Observer* "printed and distributed 300,000 copies of Manly's editorial." Ayers, supra note 75, at 301. Needless to say, Manly's editorial set the state's white newspapers on fire.

129. Gilmore, supra note 123, at 104.

on horseback. Groups in the cities and towns such as the White Government Unions pressured whites to join their ranks "regardless of party affiliation."[130] The groups also attempted to strong-arm businesses into not hiring blacks who were competing for jobs with whites.[131] The Red Shirts originated in South Carolina with Ben Tillman in the 1870s, but similar groups of red-shirted horsemen appeared in North Carolina during the latter part of the 1898 campaign in the southern and "Black Belt" counties of the state.[132] The Red Shirts were more overt and visible than had been the Klan in the 1870s, as their mounted columns were a feature of the political parades that preceded the rallies and speeches, with huge numbers such as 400 Red Shirts at a November rally in Laurinburg and 1000 at a Lumberton rally.[133] The weapon of choice for the riders was the Winchester rifle.[134] Given the murders and even massacres that Red Shirts carried out in South Carolina (with Tillman participating),[135] their appearance in North Carolina was clearly to intimidate. They fired canons near fusionist political rallies.[136] While the Red Shirts in North Carolina did not murder with impunity as had the Klan in previous decades, they frequently resorted to violence such as whipping blacks and the destruction of their property.[137] The potential of Red Shirt violence was so great that campaign appearances by Governor Russell and U.S. Senators Marion Butler and Jeter Pritchard were canceled in the latter stages of the 1898 campaign.[138] The

---

130. H. Leon Prather, Sr., We Have Taken a City: A Centennial Essay, in *Democracy Betrayed: The Wilmington Race Riot of 1898 and Its Legacy* 15, 22 (Davis S. Cecelski and Timothy B. Tyson eds., 1998).

131. Id. at 23.

132. Stephen Kantrowitz, *Ben Tillman and the Reconstruction of White Supremacy* 67 (2000); H. Leon Prather, Sr., The Red Shirt Movement in North Carolina, 1898–1900, 62 *Journal of Negro History* 174 (1977). The Red Shirts first appeared in North Carolina at the October 22, 1898, rally in Fayetteville where Ben Tillman spoke. Prather, supra, at 175.

133. Prather, supra note 132, at 178.

134. Id. at 175.

135. Tillman participated in what came to be called the Hamburg Massacre in 1876, where at least seven blacks were murdered in Hamburg, S.C. Kantrowitz, supra note 132, at 64–69. Tillman's Red Shirt outfit was known as the Sweetwater Sabre Club. Id. at 67.

136. Prather, supra note 132, at 175.

137. Id. at 175–176. This is not to say that the Red Shirts were not murderous, because the killing of at least two blacks in the southeastern part of the state has been attributed to them. Crow and Durden, supra note 104, at 133.

138. Crow and Durden, supra note 104, at 130–134.

possible assassination of Governor Russell on Election Day was averted when Red Shirt leader (and future governor) Cameron Morrison tipped off Russell on the plan by a different faction of Red Shirts to grab him off of his train at a later stop.[139] The Red Shirts were a visible terrorist group in support of "the Democratic party and white supremacy."[140]

In this era before the advent of modern media, the Democrats' battle plan included a coordinated effort with Democratic newspapers, the most important being Josephus Daniels' *News and Observer* in Raleigh, to arouse whites' emotions on the (supposed) dangers of blacks' insolence, immorality, criminality, and Negro officeholding. The *News and Observer* was both "the state's best-known newspaper"[141] and "powerful,"[142] an unequaled voice in the politics of the state. While many other newspapers in the state emphasized the alleged insolence and criminality of blacks and Negro rule in North Carolina,[143] Daniels and the *News and Observer* were ruthless in stoking racial fears and exaggerating the truth, all to support Democratic white supremacy. The tortured logic of Daniels was summed up in an editorial entitled, "The Damned Nigger," where he wrote: "The real friends of the negroes are the white men who advocate White Supremacy, not to injure the negro, but to make good government that is best for the negro as well as the white man."[144] The headlines in the *News and Observer* certainly tell part of the story: "A Fusion Barbecue: The Nigger Gets His Rights at a Jubilee"[145] and "How 'Niggers in Office' Are to Be

---

139. Id. at 134.

140. Prather, supra note 132, at 175.

141. Craig, supra note 108, at 134.

142. Ayers, supra note 75, at 426. The *News and Observer* proclaimed in the banner on its front page every day: "Leads All North Carolina Dailies in News and Circulation." See, e.g., *News and Observer*, Oct. 18, 1898, at 1. However, reliable circulation figures do not exist until after 1900. Craig, supra note 108, at 145.

143. Negro Insolence, *Wilmington Morning Star*, Oct. 12, 1898, at 2; Inspected by a Negro: White School in Maysville Visited by a Negro Committeeman. Result of Russellism in Jones County, *Washington Progress* (Washington, N.C.), Sept. 21, 1898, at 1; Criminality of Negroes and Foreigners, *Goldsboro Headlight*, Jan. 20, 1898, at 1.

The jostling for space on sidewalks and for seats on railroads and streetcars between blacks and whites was a continuing focus of the Democratic papers. See, e.g., Still Another Outrage, *Charlotte Observer*, Sept. 8, 1898, at 7 ("Three well know and highly estimable young ladies were on their way to Oakdale cemetery and when they reached a point between the streets mentioned they were confronted by two negro women who refused to turn aside and give them even a portion of the walk.").

144. The Damned Nigger, *News and Observer*, Oct. 28, 1898, at 4.

145. A Fusion Barbecue: The Nigger Gets His Rights at a Jubilee, *News and Observer*, Oct. 25, 1898, at 6.

Secured,"[146] and a running tally of (alleged) Negro calumnies on the front page with titles such as "More Negro Scoundrelism: Black Beasts Attempt to Outrage the Young Daughter of a Respectable Farmer"[147] and "Worse and Worse: A White Insane Man Brought to the Asylum by a Negro Deputy Sheriff."[148] But, a proper accounting for Daniels and the *News and Observer* must record the way that they blared these types of headlines in large type and the way that Daniels used racially-stereotyped cartoons in conjunction with those headlines to grab white readers by their proverbial collars. The only way to truly get a sense for the tenor of Daniels' tactics is to see the pages from the paper. Thus, with regard to the "outrage" of the existence of a black supervisor at a road construction project that had white workers, the *News and Observer* gave it all of page 9 on September 11, 1898:

---

146. How "Niggers in Office" Are to Be Secured, *News and Observer*, Oct. 16, 1898, at 8.
147. More Negro Scoundrelism: Black Beasts Attempt to Outrage the Young Daughter of a Respectable Farmer, *News and Observer*, Sept. 23, 1898, at 1.
148. Worse and Worse: A White Insane Man Brought to the Asylum by a Negro Deputy Sheriff, *News and Observer*, Sept. 24, 1898, at 1.

And, with regard to the daily drumbeat of alleged crimes by blacks and the misguided Republicans, the front page of the paper continually dedicated space to such items as typified by the front page of October 18, 1898:

And while stories of Negro domination and alleged atrocities filled the text of the *News and Observer* and were a focus of Daniels' editorials, the *News and Observer*'s cartoonist was Norman Jennett, who drew exaggerated, stereotyped pictures of blacks and pressed the case for Negro incapacity and the danger of Negro rule.[149] In the cartoon shown on the next page, from the front page on October 9, 1898, the *News and Observer* itself is perched atop a rock in the middle of a turbulent sea, implying that Daniels' newspaper was a steadfast watchtower built upon "truth" and "principle" and that all of these institutions were steadied by the underpinning of white supremacy.

While the Democrats' rallies and barbecues were important, in these years before television and radio and the internet, it was the *News and Observer* that was the daily Democratic campaign outreach to white voters in a large portion of the state. Daniels was absolutely correct in his memoirs when he claimed that the *News and Observer* "was the printed voice of the campaign."[150]

---

149. Rachel Marie-Crane Williams, A War in Black and White: The Cartoons of Norman Ethre Jennett & the North Carolina Election of 1898, *Southern Cultures*, Summer 2013, at 7, 9 ("Between August and early November 1898, Jennett produced over seventy-five single-panel editorial cartoons for Daniels. . . . What made Jennett's cartoons significant was not his drawing ability and wit, but rather the way they provided a visual element to the prevailing propaganda.").

150. Daniels, supra note 119, at 293.

3. VILE AMBITIONS AND LOW INSTINCTS | 91

The Waves and Rain and Hail and Missiles of Fusion Orators are Hurled at It in Vain, Because It's Built Upon a Solid Foundation.

The political epicenter of the 1898 election was in many ways Wilmington which was, at the time, the state's largest city and a city with a majority-black population. With a population of 11,324 "Negro" and 8,731 "White" in the 1890 census, Wilmington was also a historically Republican-leaning city.[151] However, that voting strength was stymied for years by gerrymanders and the appointment powers of the Democratically controlled General Assemblies before 1895.[152] But, in 1898, following the fusion legislature's return of power to local electorates and an amendment to the Wilmington city charter which provided for the appointment

---

151. Bureau of the Census, *Report on Population of the United States at the Eleventh Census: 1890*, Part I, at 473 (1895).
152. Prather, supra note 130, at 18. Prather wrote:
> Since Redemption in the 1870s, the Democratic Party had conspired successfully to deny political power to Wilmington's black citizens. This could not be accomplished with much grace or subtlety in a black-majority city, for it meant, in effect, that the Democrats had to suffocate local democracy for the sake of holding power. . . . Democratic leaders vested control over city government not in Wilmington, but at the state level . . . .

Id.

by the governor of half of the city's aldermen,[153] the city's Board of Aldermen had six Republicans (three of whom where black) and four Democrats, as well as a Republican mayor, Silas Wright.[154] The White Supremacy Campaign focused upon Wilmington because of its size, the fact that it was a Republican stronghold, and the fact that it was Republican Governor Russell's home base.[155] Prior to election day, white Democrats had been organizing secret paramilitary forces for months in order to retake the city in every sense possible.[156] One important group was the White Government Union, a white supremacy club that used pressure and even threats of violence on the white men of Wilmington to force them to join the group.[157] The tenor of the times was exemplified by a well-attended October 6 Chamber of Commerce meeting which issued a resolution, the substance of which was succinctly stated in the next day's newspaper headline: "The Chamber of Commerce Declares Against Negro Domination."[158] With threats of violence mounting by the day, Wilmington's racial tensions were at a boiling point. White leaders demanded that Governor Russell withdraw the Republican slate of candidates for Wilmington and New Hanover County from the ballot because any chance of their success was unacceptable. Textile magnate James Sprunt wrote to Governor Russell on October 24: "[W]e declare to you our conviction that we are on the brink of a revolution which can only be averted by the suppression of

---

153. 1897 N.C. Sess. Laws 282, ch. 150, § 2 (Private). This statute was upheld in *Harriss v. Wright*, 121 N.C. 172 (1897).

154. Crow and Durden, supra note 104, at 97–98; Lefler and Newsome, supra note 34, at 559.

155. Crow and Durden, supra note 104, at 129. The racially charged editorial by Alex Manly in his Wilmington newspaper, *The Daily Record*, which was so well known that Ben Tillman used it to energize the crowd at the Fayetteville rally in October, supra note 128 and accompanying text, also made the city a target of the White Supremacy Campaign.

156. Crow and Durden, supra note 104, at 129. Crow and Durden wrote: "In Wilmington two paramilitary forces, the Red Shirts and the Rough Riders, terrorized fusionist sympathizers and blacks. The units often paraded through black localities, firing off their rifles, and a favorite tactic was to warn blacks that if they attempted to register to vote they would be discharged from their jobs." Id. at 133.

157. Prather, supra note 130, at 22–23. Prather quoted a white Wilmingtonian: "Many good people ... were marched from their homes, some by committees, and taken to headquarters and told to sign. Those that did not were notified that they must leave the city ... as there was plenty of rope in the city." Id. (internal quotation marks omitted).

158. Business and Politics: The Chamber of Commerce Declares Against Negro Domination, *Wilmington Messenger*, Oct. 7, 1898, at 4.

a republican ticket."[159] Russell had himself been warned that if he went to Wilmington, he would be killed.[160] Reluctantly, Russell removed the local Republican candidates from the ballot.[161] At a rally on the eve of Election Day, former member of Congress Alfred Moore Waddell urged the white men of the city to do their duty:

> This city, county and state shall be rid of negro domination, once and forever. You have the courage. You are brave. You are the sons of noble ancestry. You are Anglo-Saxons. You are arme[d] and prepared, and you will do your duty. Be ready at a moment's notice. Go to the polls tomorrow and if you find the negro outvoting [sic], tell him to leave the polls, and if he refuses kill him; shoot him down in his tracks. We shall win tomorrow if we have to do it with guns.[162]

Thus, in Wilmington, the proverbial table was set for the 1898 election and what was to follow.

The results of the 1898 election dramatically shifted power to the Democratic Party in North Carolina. Although the voting margins may not have been very large (the one statewide race saw the Democratic candidate receive only 52.8 percent of the vote),[163] Democratic turnout and Republicans' fear as well as political gerrymandering allowed the Democrats to achieve large majorities in the General Assembly. In the state Senate, Democrats won 40 seats to the fusionists' 10; by comparison, the Democrats held only 7 seats after the 1896 election.[164] Similarly, the Democrats garnered 94 seats in the House, with the fusionists only holding on to 26 seats in the 120-person chamber.[165] That was a jump from the 26 seats that the Democrats won in 1896.[166]

---

159. James Sprunt to Daniel L. Russell, Oct. 24, 1898, quoted in LeRae Sikes Umfleet, *A Day of Blood: The 1898 Wilmington Race Riot* 216–217 n.22 (2009).

160. Crow and Durden, supra note 104, at 130.

161. Id. at 132. On October 26, Russell issued an executive proclamation ordering "ill-disposed" persons to "desist from all unlawful practices and all turbulent conduct." Id. at 131 (quoting Russell).

162. Alfred Moore Waddell, quoted in Riot Feared in Wilmington: Both Whites and Blacks Armed, *Atlanta Constitution*, Nov. 8, 1898, at 1.

163. Kousser, supra note 71, at 188. The statewide race was for chief justice of the North Carolina Supreme Court. Id.

164. Id. at 186.

165. Id.

166. Id.

Although Election Day itself was not marred by widespread violence, the events two days later in Wilmington demonstrate that the racial animosity and militancy on the part of the white population had not ebbed. The bloodletting that occurred on November 10, 1898, has frequently been labeled a riot, but that word connotes a spontaneous combustion of events which is not what happened in Wilmington. What happened was well planned. The pot had been stirred for months prior to election day by the white-supremacist Democrats.[167] On the morning of November 9, the day after the election, the *Wilmington Morning Star* and the *Wilmington Messenger* newspapers carried announcements for a meeting of "white men" at the New Hanover County Courthouse that same morning at 11:00 a.m. for "business in furtherance of White Supremacy."[168] The crowded meeting began with the reading of a document that has come to be known as the "White Declaration of Independence" which called for, among other things, the end of political rule by "men of African origin," the "giving of nearly all the employment to negro laborers," as well as the demand that Alexander Manly's newspaper, *The Daily Record*, cease publication and that Manly be banished from the city.[169] Manly's newspaper published an editorial in August which had inflamed many whites, and Manly was the editor that Ben Tillman referred to at an earlier Fayetteville rally.[170] In addition to the focus on Manly and his newspaper, though, wording was then added at the November 9 meeting to require the resignations of Wilmington Mayor Silas P. Wright (white) and Chief

---

167. The preelection-day event reported in the Atlanta newspaper cited above and which quoted Alfred Moore Waddell was entitled, "Riot Feared in Wilmington." See supra note 162.

168. Attention White Men, *Wilmington Messenger*, Nov. 9, 1898, at 8. See also Mass Meeting, *Wilmington Morning Star*, Nov. 9, 1898, at 1 (meeting "to consider matters of very great importance to the maintenance of white supremacy").

169. Umfleet, supra note 159, at 73–77. The full text of the White Declaration of Independence is reprinted in Umfleet, supra note 159, at 76–77. The White Declaration of Independence was a document drawn up by a group of prominent white Wilmingtonians called the Secret Nine. Id. at 218 n.53. The Secret Nine worked behind the scenes to advance the causes of white supremacy and Democratic power in Wilmington. Id. at 47.

Umfleet was the Principal Researcher for the 1898 Wilmington Race Riot Commission, and her contribution was revised and published under her name as a book, *A Day of Blood*. The full report, 1898 Wilmington Race Riot Commission, *1898 Wilmington Race Riot Report* (2006) is available at http://digital.ncdcr.gov/cdm/compoundobject/collection/p249901coll22/id/5842/rec/16 (last visited Nov. 24, 2019).

170. See supra note 128 and accompanying text.

3. VILE AMBITIONS AND LOW INSTINCTS | 95

of Police John R. Melton (white) because of "their continuance in office being a constant menace to the peace and welfare of this community."[171] Alfred Moore Waddell was charged by the crowd to lead a committee of twenty-five other white men, "to carry out the purpose of the meeting."[172] Although the white Democratic leaders presented their demands to leaders of Wilmington's black community that same evening, the actions of the white militants the next morning quickly spun out of control.[173] A column of white militants led by Waddell marched to the building that housed Manly's *Daily Record* newspaper and broke down the door and set the entire building on fire.[174] Following that, armed white men began moving through the city and the fighting broke out in earnest. Although the number of dead will never be known with certainty, a report issued pursuant to a historical commission created in 2000 — the most thorough study of the Wilmington conflagration — lists 22 individual blacks known dead, as well as 9 blacks known to have been wounded but whose ultimate fate in the aftermath was unknown.[175] While one would assume that

---

171. Remarkable Meeting: The Negro Editor Banished from the City, *Wilmington Messenger*, Nov. 10, 1898, at 8, 5. The logic of some of the resolutions escapes modern readers: "That the negro has demonstrated by antagonizing our interest in every way, and especially by his ballot, that he is incapable of realizing that his interests are and should be identical with those of the [white] community." Id. at 8.

172. Id. at 5.

173. Umfleet, supra note 159, at 81–88.

174. Id. at 83–84.

175. Id. at 117–119. Umfleet's conservative numbers are based on the existence of multiple sources for each named or unknown individual killed or wounded. There were often conflicting accounts in contemporary newspaper articles, in correspondence, and in written and oral histories created decades after the event. Thus, these numbers of the dead and wounded are a known floor, but there were almost certainly additional blacks who died. Umfleet did not include in her list "the names of others, or the locations of shootings, that have only vague references [in written accounts]." Id. at 117. She identified 13 of the dead by name. Id. at 117–118.

The report of the 1898 Wilmington Race Riot Commission, with thirteen members, stated in its section entitled "Findings" that "other evidence indicates that the total number of deaths was as high as sixty." 1898 Wilmington Race Riot Commission, supra note 169, at 1. The body of the Commission's report, however, with Umfleet as the Principal Researcher, contained the list of 22 known dead and the statement that "no actual number of dead will ever be known." Id. at 176.

A new book, which the author describes as "a work of journalism ... [which relies] on a foundation laid by historians," provides a detailed narrative account of what occurred in Wilmington. David Zucchino, *Wilmington's Lie: The Murderous Coup of 1898 and the Rise of White Supremacy* 353 (2020).

any deaths of whites would have been recorded and widely reported, no such deaths ever came to light, and the number of whites wounded was reported to be three.[176] What is certain is that a coup d'etat occurred, as individuals from the twenty-five person committee headed by Waddell forced the resignations of the city aldermen, the Chief of Police, and the Mayor.[177] The existing aldermen (who, as a body, selected the city's mayor) were not up for reelection in 1898 and were to continue in office until at least the following year's election.[178] Nevertheless, with the open warfare taking place in the streets, the aldermen were "replaced" by men selected by Waddell and his cohorts, and those replacements chose Alfred Moore Waddell, unanimously, to be mayor.[179] The *News and Observer* stretched the meaning of the term "elected" when its caption on the front page of the next day's paper under a picture of Waddell read: "The New Mayor of Wilmington Who was Elected Yesterday."[180] In sum, for the only time in the United States, political officials who were duly elected and who held their offices according to law were ousted through extra-legal means by people who were leaders of an armed and murderous group action who, then, installed people of their own choosing into those same political offices.[181]

---

176. Umfleet, supra note 159, at 93.
177. Id. at 103–104.
178. Id. at 102.
179. Id. at 104.
180. *News and Observer*, Nov. 11, 1898, at 1.
181. While Alexander Manly fled the city, the white supremacist leaders in Wilmington also worked to banish blacks from the city who advocated for black political participation, black businessmen who had been a bit too successful for white tastes, as well as white Republicans who achieved positions of political power because of black votes. Umfleet, supra note 159, at 106. These individuals, who were perceived by the white-supremacist Democrats as antagonistic to their desire to rid Wilmington of black political and economic power, were often arrested and marched by white militia members to the train station where they were forced onto north-bound trains and told never to return to the state. Id. at 106–113.
  Even aside from the specific people banished from the city, though, the 1898 white takeover of Wilmington resulted in a quick decrease in the black population because of black individuals and families subsequently moving out of the city. As previously noted, according to the 1890 U.S. Census, Wilmington was a majority-black city. See supra note 151 and accompanying text. In 1890, Wilmington had an overall population of 20,056, with 11,324 "Negro" and 8,731 "White" residents. Bureau of the Census, *Report on Population of the United States at the Eleventh Census: 1890*, Part I, 259, 473 (1895). But

3. VILE AMBITIONS AND LOW INSTINCTS | 97

What followed the 1898 election and the Wilmington coup was an attempt to make permanent and (somewhat) legal the white Democrats' control of political power in the state. In the General Assembly session that began in January 1899, the Democrats immediately went to work to overturn what the fusionist legislatures had done and, then, they sought to create a system that would eliminate black political participation. The Democrats repealed the fusionists' voting laws on January 26.[182] Simmons and the Democrats then reneged on a pledge made during the 1898 campaign to not disenfranchise anyone by proposing (with passage in the two legislative houses on February 18 and 19) an amendment to the state constitution to be submitted to voters that was to limit voter registration to those "who shall be able to read and write any section of the Constitution in the English language."[183] Not content to let this amendment's fate be decided by the voters in a fair manner, Furnifold Simmons then orchestrated the passage of a new election law on March 6 that, among other things, erased the voting rolls and forced all voters to reregister, gave the registrars (indirectly appointed by the legislature) discretion over whom to reject through the voter registration process, provided that ballots placed in the wrong ballot box out of the six separate ballot boxes would not count, and moved the date of the state election from November (when the federal election would take place) to August so as to avoid any possible

---

in the 1900 census, two years after the 1898 coup d'etat, Wilmington was no longer a majority-black city and it had lost black population in absolute terms. While the population of Wilmington in 1900 had grown slightly over the preceding ten years to 20,976, that was in the face of a decrease in the Negro population to 10,407, while the White population had grown to 10,556. 1 Bureau of the Census, *Twelfth Census of the United States Taken in the Year 1900, Population: Part I*, at 633 (1901).

182. 1899 N.C. Sess. Laws 106, ch. 16 (1899).

183. Amendment of 1900 to N.C. Const. of 1868, art. VI, § 4 (final version proposed at 1900 N.C. Sess. Laws 54, ch. 2). As to the dates of passage, see Watson, supra note 99, at 134.

federal oversight of the voting.[184] This statute was termed the "Simmons Election Law."[185]

With that election law and the proposed amendment to the constitution to be voted upon, the 1900 election was a second and continuing episode of the White Supremacy Campaign. The primary difference from 1898 was that instead of clamoring for the abstract notion of denying blacks political power, the white-supremacist Democrats claimed that the specific remedy of black disenfranchisement was needed. Much was the same in 1900 in terms of the people and the tactics. Thus, one study has concluded that "under the leadership of Furnifold Simmons... the Democratic campaign matched in ferocity the election of 1898."[186] The *News and Observer* reprised the same themes in 1900, with headlines such as "Adams is a Negro Lover,"[187] "Negro Rule in Eastern Counties: Here Are a Few Samples of Ebon Supremacy,"[188] and the page one insolence article, "A Shameful Scene: Negro Cursed and Abused an Old Man."[189] Josephus Daniels' editorials again used racist hyperbole to stir the pot: "Every evil

---

184. 1899 N.C. Sess. Laws 658, ch. 507, § 1 (date of election) and § 11 (new registration of all voters and discretion of registrars) and § 29 (disallow ballots placed in wrong box). During this era, there was not one ballot but, instead, multiple ballots for different offices and, in turn, a separate ballot box for each ballot. Thus, the correct ballot had to be matched with its corresponding ballot box or it would not count. This was a system that obviously and intentionally worked against those who could not read well (i.e., blacks), and while voting officials could be asked for help, a precinct official (often a Democrat) could invalidate the vote of someone that was not of the same political stripe by offering misinformation as to the appropriate ballot box. See Kousser, supra note 71, at 50 ("Boxes were constantly shifted to prevent a literate voter from arranging the tickets of an uneducated friend in the correct order before he entered the voting place. Illiterates could ask the election judges to read the names on the boxes, but since all election officials were [Democrats] ... it is doubtful that Republicans got much assistance in voting.").

185. Watson, supra note 99, at 151.

186. Crow and Durden, supra note 104, at 148. See also Watson, supra note 99, at 143 ("Simmons was the principal campaigner for the Democrats in ... 1900.").

187. Adams is a Negro Lover, *News and Observer*, July 29, 1900, at 1. Spencer B. Adams was the Republican nominee for Governor in 1900. Crow and Durden, supra note 104, at 156.

188. Negro Rule in Eastern Counties: Here Are a Few Samples of Ebon Supremacy, *News and Observer*, May 4, 1900, at 3.

189. A Shameful Scene: Negro Cursed and Abused an Old Man, *News and Observer*, July 21, 1900, at 1.

3. VILE AMBITIONS AND LOW INSTINCTS | 99

that the South has suffered has come from the negro."[190] A similar tone is contained in this introductory sentence to an editorial about second district U.S. Representative George White: "It is bad enough that North Carolina should have the only nigger Congressman."[191] The only other difference between the two elections, aside from the disenfranchisement amendment, was that Charles Brantley Aycock was running for the office of governor in 1900. At the political rallies where he appeared, Aycock was accompanied by huge columns of mounted Red Shirts.[192] Aycock, in accepting the Democratic nomination, accurately summed up the Democratic Party's position: "When we say that the negro is unfit to rule we carry it one step further and convey the correct idea when we declare that he is unfit to vote."[193] Arguing for a political system controlled at every point by whites, Aycock taunted the Republicans and Populists: "We have taught them much in the past two years in the University of White Supremacy, we will graduate them in August next with a diploma that will entitle them to form a genuine white man's party."[194] The election results reaffirmed the goal of white supremacy with Aycock's victory and the passage of the constitutional amendment.[195]

Looking back over this history, the White Supremacy Campaigns were the culmination of almost 40 years of unceasing attempts to undermine

---

190. Why the South is Behind, *News and Observer*, June 1, 1900, at 4. See also As To the "Nigger" Party, *News and Observer*, June 22, 1899, at 4.

191. The Colored Member, *News and Observer*, Feb. 2, 1900, at 4.

192. See, e.g., Red Shirt's [sic] Day in Duplin County: Aycock Met by a Measured Mile of Mounted Red Shirts, *News and Observer*, July 27, 1900, at 6.

193. Charles B. Aycock, Address Accepting the Democratic Nomination for Governor, April 11, 1900, in *The Life and Speeches of Charles Brantley Aycock* 211, 216–217 (R.D.W. Connor and Clarence Poe eds., 1912). See also id. at 220–221 ("The Democratic party takes the true, bold ground that a white man is superior to a negro and that the law of man will follow the law of God in recognition of it.").

194. Id. at 218. On this score, Aycock proved prophetic. In 1902, the North Carolina Republican Party banished blacks from the state convention and reinvented itself as a "Lily-white" party. Woodward, *New South*, supra note 5, at 463. As John Haley has recognized, the leading black Republicans "did not easily understand that disfranchisement had destroyed the base of the Republican party in North Carolina. Without the masses of black voters, the party had no use for a few educated blacks. In terms of real politics the Republicans' only chance to construct a viable party rested on their ability to attract white voters...." John Haley, *Charles N. Hunter and Race Relations in North Carolina* 143 (1987).

195. Watson, supra note 99, at 139.

black political power and weaken blacks' economic power and social status. The rhetoric of the 1898 and 1900 political campaigns and the violence and threats of violence of those years made race and racial loyalty a test for whites in the state. The White Supremacy Campaigns were intended to shape the mindset of whites, and to brand blacks as sexually, socially, and politically dangerous, and the campaigns succeeded on all fronts. It was a type of contagion that swept the state. Even the beneficiaries of the White Supremacy Campaigns recognized the degree to which they had upended and shifted white attitudes. A white Democrat wrote on the eve of the 1898 election that with the racial animosity unleashed by his party, he prayed for the safety of the black population "and hope that enough good strong men may be found to protect them from both the vile ambitions and low instincts of men of our race. The problem is an awful one...."[196] In a reply letter, Henry G. Connor, who would be selected as Speaker of the House in the subsequent General Assembly session, observed that the "politicians have stirred the minds and feelings of the people more deeply than they intended."[197] In 1903, the tensions were still evident, as Trinity College (now Duke University) Professor John Spencer Bassett concluded that the "torrent of [political] passion" is "awaking a demon in the South. There is today more hatred of whites for blacks ... than ever before."[198] The White Supremacy Campaigns had political consequences, for sure, but it is also clear that the torrent of racial rhetoric shifted the attitudes of whites about blacks in profound ways. There was racism in North Carolina prior to the White Supremacy Campaigns, and there is no effort here

---

196. George Howard to Henry G. Connor, Oct. 29, 1898, quoted in Ayers, supra note 75, at 300–301.

197. Henry G. Connor to George Howard, Nov. 25, 1898, reprinted in *The North Carolina Experience: An Interpretive and Documentary History* at 349 (Lindley S. Butler and Alan D. Watson eds., 1984).

198. John Spencer Bassett, Stirring Up the Fires of Race Antipathy, 2 *South Atlantic Quarterly* 297, 304 (1903). The entire passage reads: "This political agitation is awaking a demon in the South. There is today more hatred of whites for blacks and of blacks for whites than ever before. Each race seems to be caught in a torrent of passion, which, I fear, is leading the country to an end which I dare not name." Id. Although Bassett's essay did not mention any instances of blacks' hatred for whites, his reference to hatred by both whites and blacks was almost certainly employed because of the racial sensitivities of his white audience. This essay still inflamed whites such as Josephus Daniels, and it almost led to the loss of his job. See Joel Williamson, *The Crucible of Race: Black-White Relations in the American South Since Emancipation* 261–271 (1984).

to quantify the level of racism after 1900. This book is primarily focused on laws and the application of law. But the racial paroxysm in North Carolina in 1898–1900 had consequences, and it was not a flood of new discriminatory state statutes. One of the conclusions of the present study is that, in the years to come, the White Supremacy Campaigns did impact the application of laws to such a degree that new types of discriminatory statutes were not necessary.

4
De Jure Discrimination in North Carolina

This study focuses upon the ways that the laws of North Carolina established *de jure* discrimination and, also, opened the door for the discriminatory application of these statutes against African Americans and American Indians. Of course, constitutions and statutes do not correspond precisely with the depth of racial animus or the breadth of discrimination in a state. Nevertheless, the laws enacted by a popularly elected legislature are perhaps the most important criterion by which to judge the way that a democratic society treats its citizens as a whole and relative to one another. As William Wiecek has observed, "Statutory law is a distillation of some of society's most cherished values, or at least the values of the class that wields the hegemonic power that produces laws."[1] The session laws cataloged here are a measure of the baseline racial animus of the political majority—that is, whites—during the period under consideration because of the very nature of the legislative process. It is much easier to prevent or derail the enactment of a proposed law than it is to pass a law. Political scientists speak in terms of "veto points"[2] and

---

1. William W. Wiecek, The Statutory Law of Slavery and Race in the Thirteen Mainland Colonies of British America, 34 *William and Mary Quarterly* 258, 280 (1977).

2. See, e.g., Kenneth A. Shepsle, Dysfuctional Congress?, 89 *Boston University Law Review* 371, 380 (2009).

"gridlock intervals,"[3] and legal scholars term them "vetogates,"[4] but the phenomena they are describing are the many hurdles that any proposed bill must navigate in order to be enacted in most legislative bodies. Those hurdles are bicameralism, committees, subcommittees, party leaders who control which bills are brought to the floor, floor debates, the tactical use of amendments, individual legislators with other agendas, conference committees and, at each step, the requirement for at least a majority of votes to keep a bill alive. Unanimity is not a requirement for lawmaking. However, for a proposed law to survive the legislative gauntlet and be enacted is an important indicator of where a majority can reach agreement on the political questions of the day.

At the same time, "law in action"[5] is of great importance because session laws have to be applied by local officials and there can be a great disparity between the language on a page and the end result for individuals. For any law, there are different degrees of discretion, judgment, and legal clarity. To use the most obvious example from the U.S. Constitution, there is a wide gulf of specificity between the requirement that members of the Senate shall "have attained to the Age of thirty Years"[6] and the mandate that no person shall "be deprived of life, liberty, or property, without due process of law."[7] The same basic principle applies to the laws of North Carolina.

While this book is focused on the laws enacted by North Carolina's legislature, a word should be said here at the outset about the city ordinances in the state that drew racial lines.[8] There were race-conscious provisions in city ordinances, but there were not many of them, at least

---

3. Keith Krehbiel, Institutional and Partisan Sources of Gridlock: A Theory of Divided and Unified Government, 8 *Journal of Theoretical Politics* 7, 17–23 (1996). See generally Keith Krehbiel, *Pivotal Politics: A Theory of U.S. Lawmaking* 51–75 (1998).

4. See, e.g., William N. Eskridge, Jr., Vetogates, *Chevron*, Preemption, 83 *Notre Dame Law Review* 1441 (2008).

5. Roscoe Pound, Law in Books and Law in Action, 44 *American Law Review* 12 (1910).

6. U.S. Const., art. I, sec. 3.

7. U.S. Const., amend. V.

8. The extant North Carolina city codes from the nineteenth and early-twentieth centuries are not numerous. The Wilson Library at the University of North Carolina at Chapel Hill has the most extensive collection but, even acknowledging that the city codes were not published with the regularity that they are today, there appear to be gaps in the historical record. The most likely explanation is that many printed codes were

in the late-nineteenth and early-twentieth centuries. The City of Raleigh had only one explicit race-conscious ordinance during the nineteenth and early twentieth centuries, and it concerned the city cemetery. The provision antedated the Civil War: "[The Grave Yard] is divided into four Squares. The two Northern Squares are for the use of the citizens and their friends. Strangers are to be interred in the South-Westerly Square, and negroes and persons of color in the South-Easterly Square."[9] By 1876, the Raleigh ordinances had been modified so as to recognize the existence of racially separate cemeteries: "The City Graveyard, between Hargett and Newbern [sic] Streets, east of East street, hereafter shall be used exclusively for the burial of white persons and the Colored Cemetery on the Fayetteville Road, shall be used exclusively for the burial of colored persons."[10] The City of Charlotte, on the other hand, was more circumspect. Its code had no explicit references to race, but the section on cemeteries noted that there was to be "a Keeper of Elmwood Cemetery and a Keeper of Pinewood Cemetery," the unstated reality being that Elmwood was a cemetery solely for whites and Pinewood was a cemetery for blacks.[11] For saloons, the City of Winston adopted an ordinance that prohibited any dealer selling near beer from obstructing the view of the establishment through the use of blinds, painted windows, and partitions "except such partitions as may be necessary to separate the white people from the colored people."[12] After the turn of the century, explicit residential segregation ordinances were enacted in a few municipalities. The very first one in the state was adopted in Mooresville on May 1, 1912, and it prohibited "any colored person or family" from moving "within

---

discarded once they were superseded by new revised versions and were not saved for posterity.

9. *Laws for the Governance of the City of Raleigh* 56 (1838).

10. *Charter of the City of Raleigh* 96, 96–97, ch. 15, § 1 (1876). This provision remained the only race-conscious ordinance when the ordinances were consolidated and reenacted in 1900. See *Ordinances of the City of Raleigh* 78, ch. 18, § 1 (1900).

11. *The Code of the City of Charlotte* 152, ch. 6, § 32 (1902). See also Thomas W. Hanchett, *Sorting Out the New South: Race, Class, and Urban Development in Charlotte, 1875–1975*, at 252 (1998) (referring to the "fence dividing white Elmwood Cemetery from black Pinewood Cemetery").

12. *The Charter and Ordinances of the City of Winston, North Carolina* 130, ch. 21, § 391 (1910). I would note the obvious point that the premise of this ordinance—that at least some saloons were serving both black and white patrons, on different sides of a partition—adds a necessary complexity to any ideas about a strict world of Jim Crow.

the boundaries hereinafter set out."[13] Subsequently, the City of Winston enacted one in July 1912 (one year prior to its merger as Winston-Salem) and the City of Greensboro enacted a virtually identical one in February 1914, both of which mandated that no person of a different race could move into a residence where the majority of residents on the street were of a different color. The Greensboro version of the ordinance stated that "it shall be unlawful for any negro, to occupy as a residence ... any house upon any street ... on which a greater number of houses are occupied as residences by white people than are occupied as residences by negroes."[14] While it is thus evident that there were a few city ordinances from 1865 to 1920 that embodied explicit racial segregation and discrimination, the provisions set out here constitute a compilation of the relevant provisions in these city codes. In sum, it is clear that city ordinances in North Caro-

---

13. Ordinance No. 62, May 1, 1912, in minute book, Mooresville Board of Town Commissioners 107 (1912) (copy on file with author).

14. *Supplement to the Code of the City of Greensboro, North Carolina* 20, 21, § 2 (1916). The Winston version used "colored person" instead of negro, stating that "it shall be unlawful for any colored person to occupy as a residence ... any house upon any street ... on which a greater number of houses are occupied as residences by white people than are occupied as residences by colored people." Section 2 of Ordinance, quoted in Segregation in Whole City: Not Constitutional to Apply Only to Individual Sections, *Winston-Salem Journal*, July 6, 1912, at 1. The Winston ordinance was struck down by the N.C. Supreme Court two years later. *State v. Darnell*, 166 N.C. 300 (1914). Because of the short period of time between the Winston ordinance's adoption and its invalidation by the N.C. Supreme Court, I do not believe that the ordinance ever appeared in a published version of the city code. For a history of *Darnell* and Chief Justice Walter Clark's opinion for the N.C. Supreme Court, see John W. Wertheimer, *Law and Society in the South: A History of North Carolina Court Cases* 43–60 (2009).

The history of Winston's residential segregation ordinance is more complex, however. The Winston Board of Aldermen had adopted a segregation ordinance one month prior to the July 1912 version, in June 1912. Segregate Negroes in East Winston, *Winston-Salem Journal*, June 14, 1912, at 1. However, that version of the ordinance set out specific city streets which were to be off limits to colored persons, as in: "That it shall be unlawful for any colored person to own or occupy any dwelling fronting on East Fourth street, between Depot street and the city limits on the east." Section 1 of Ordinance, quoted in id. The Board of Alderman chose to repeal and replace the June 1912 ordinance because of legal advice that racial segregation on specific streets was constitutionally suspect. Segregation in Whole City: Not Constitutional to Apply Only to Individual Sections, *Winston-Salem Journal*, July 6, 1912, at 1 (stating that June ordinance "has been declared unconstitutional by the leading legal talent of the city").

4. *DE JURE* DISCRIMINATION IN NORTH CAROLINA | 107

lina did not play a large role in *de jure* Jim Crow up through the first two decades of the twentieth century.

The primary focus of this study is, therefore, the laws of the State of North Carolina and this chapter will address both the laws enacted by the state legislature and the ways that the legal texts do not tell the full story of *de jure* discrimination. First, I will set out my research methodology and discuss the most significant legal enactments up to 1920 that are contained in Table 1 of this book. Second, I will analyze three areas where *de jure* racial discrimination was most acute: the funding of schools, the access to the voting booth, and the composition of juries. These subjects are exemplars of the fact that the statutory language was not the measure of the discrimination created by law. Providing an overview of the legislative output is valuable because it demonstrates the subjects and timing of *de jure* discrimination in North Carolina over the period under review. But the scope of discrimination through the application of the statutes provides another metric, especially with regard to the funding of schools, the ability to vote, and the ability to participate on a jury.[15] These three areas demonstrate the ways that law was a fulcrum by which racial inequality was increased, especially after the White Supremacy Campaigns of 1898 and 1900, to discriminate against the African American citizens of North Carolina.

It is important, here at the outset, to spell out the methodology used in gathering, classifying, and sorting the various statutes in this study. The methodology obviously reflects judgments made during the research, and it is important to set out what was done and why.

The two tables appended to this study list race-conscious statutes from all of the sessions of the North Carolina legislature from 1865 to 1920. Table 1 catalogs statutes that discriminated based on race, and Table 2 lists statutes that, in my estimation, advanced the interests of African Americans and Native Americans. What I mean by race-conscious statutes is that the law, simply put, was intended to move the proverbial needle one

---

15. In addressing the application of these statutes, I am not referring to the modern distinction between facial and as-applied challenges to laws. The vast majority of the statutes compiled in Table 1 would be invalidated on their face today. See Richard H. Fallon, Jr., Fact and Fiction about Facial Challenges, 99 *California Law Review* 915, 945 (2011) (the Supreme Court "generally welcomes facial challenges under virtually all judicially enforceable constitutional provisions").

way or the other with regard to racial minorities. Thus, in Table 1, I have included not only statutes that drew racial lines on their face, such as the one outlawing marriages between a white person and either a "Negro" or an "Indian,"[16] but ones such as the post-Civil War statute that created a cause of action for the enticement of a servant away from "his master or employer" by another employer, a law that was textually race-neutral but was intended to maintain control over the former slaves.[17] For many of these statutes, there is a knowledge about the background and statutory intentions and discriminatory applications that informs these judgments. In addition, the tables are chronological and they list statutes that were distinct and novel. No attempt was made to create a separate entry for every statute that discriminated based on race (Table 1) or that advanced racial equality (Table 2) and, thus, subsequent session laws that used the same language and approach as a previous law did not merit a separate listing, although some of these laws are noted in a column in the tables entitled "Subsequent Statute(s)." Thus, once an entry was made in the table, I did not separately list subsequent laws that took the same approach or that were virtually identical to the original statute listed. I came to the

---

16. 1871–72 N.C. Sess. Laws 328, ch. 193, § 2.

17. 1866 N.C. Sess. Laws 122, ch. 58 ("That if . . . any person shall entice, persuade and procure any servant . . . to unlawfully leave the service of his master or employer . . . [then] such person and servant may be sued, singly or jointly, by the master, and on recovery, he shall have judgment for the actual double value of the damages assessed."). Enticement statutes and vagrancy laws, while facially neutral as to race, were enacted and enforced in a way for white landowners to maintain a vice grip on black labor:
> What gave life to the system was the intent of the men who wrote its laws and the spirit in which these measures were enforced. Most of the laws discussed here made no mention of race, but southerners knew that they were intended to maintain white control of the labor system, and local enforcement authorities implemented them with this in mind.

William Cohen, Negro Involuntary Servitude in the South, 1865–1940: A Preliminary Analysis, 42 *Journal of Southern History* 31, 34 (1976). Enticement statutes had existed since colonial times but, by the mid-1800s, criminal enforcement was "virtually nonexistent and civil cases were rare." Id. at 35. However, the statutes enacted after 1865 were aimed at the freedmen: "Enticement statutes established the proprietary claims of employers to 'their' Negroes by making it a crime to hire away a laborer under contract to another man." Id. at 33. See also Eric Foner, *Reconstruction* 199 (1988) ("Henceforth, the state would enforce labor agreements and plantation discipline, punish those who refused to contract, and prevent whites from competing among themselves for black workers.").

4. DE JURE DISCRIMINATION IN NORTH CAROLINA | 109

conclusion that this compilation of laws should emphasize the subjects and methods of racial discrimination that aroused legislative attention and action rather than the sheer volume of enactments. The "Subsequent Statute(s)" column includes amendments to the cataloged statute itself and, frequently, other laws that either addressed the same subject or took the same approach as the original statute listed.

The tables contain the state statutes that I found through my research methods. However, I excluded from these lists appropriations statutes, criminal statutes, resolutions of one or both houses of the General Assembly, and rules governing the legislature itself.[18] I identified statutes using searches in the Session Laws Library database for North Carolina on HeinOnline, a subscription research service.[19] This approach brought

---

18. These types of legislative action were important—appropriations and criminal statutes in particular—but they were either too numerous (appropriations), were often hortatory (joint resolutions), or did not follow the statutory enactment process (one-house resolutions). As to the disparate enforcement and impact of criminal laws in the South, there is a vast literature. See, e.g., Edward L. Ayers, *Vengeance and Justice: Crime and Punishment in the 19th-Century American South* 197 (1984) ("Before the Civil War, virtually all the prisoners [in Southern penitentiaries] had been white; now [after 1865] about nine out of ten were black.")

For appropriations statutes, compare appropriations in a single legislative session for the completion of white and colored asylums. Compare 1876–77 N.C. Sess. Laws 400, 401, ch. 204, § 5 ($60,000 for two years for the Western Asylum for whites) with 1876–77 N.C. Sess. Laws 547, ch. 278, § 1 ($20,000 for two years for "asylum for the colored insane"). For a sample joint resolution, see Resolution Concerning the Relations Between the White and Colored People of the State, 1876–77 N.C. Sess. Laws 589, 589–590 ("*The General Assembly of North Carolina do resolve,* That while we regard with repugnance the absurd attempts, by means of 'civil rights' bills, to eradicate certain race distinctions, implanted by nature and sustained by the habits of forty centuries . . . .") (emphasis in original). For legislative actions as to the functioning of the General Assembly itself, an example is the creation of three distinct galleries in the Senate: one for "white ladies and gentlemen," one for "colored ladies and gentlemen," and the one in between those for "any that choose to occupy it." *Journal of the Senate of the General Assembly* 41 (1868).

To provide one example of how discriminatory legislative appropriations worked over time, I examine the topic of state appropriations to private orphanages in Chapter 5.

19. HeinOnline contains all of the pages, scanned and in pdf format, from all of the volumes of the North Carolina session laws, and HeinOnline has a search function to identify words in these scanned pages. I ran searches on HeinOnline using the following words: race, racial, Negro, Negroes, black, color, colored, mulatto, mulattoes, Indian, Indians. Having said this, it is natural that the scans of some pages were imperfect and, where such flawed scans existed, searches were unable to identify word matches because of a problem with the original document as scanned.

up a huge number of initial results, but it was imperfect because any law that contained race-neutral language—but which was intended to discriminate—would not be found through such a search. To the degree that I knew about methods of discrimination in statutes that did not depend upon an overt mention of race (e.g., enticement, apprenticeship, gerrymandering), I was frequently able to identify relevant statutes and they are included here. While there is no guarantee that an otherwise relevant statute has been overlooked, I believe that Tables 1 and 2 are a thorough catalog of the Jim Crow laws in North Carolina for the period under review. In both tables, I provide a description of the purpose of the statutes, in addition to a quotation of the relevant statutory text.[20]

What, then, constitutes a distinct and novel statute and what distinguishes the laws in Tables 1 and 2? These are, without question, the most subjective aspects of the enactments collected in this book. As to what I understood to be new or unique about a statute, I sought to be generous and inclusive. Statutes on cemeteries are a good example. I list the first law which mandated that a town (Morganton) was to provide racially segregated cemeteries,[21] but I also list the first statute which expanded that requirement to an entire county,[22] and I also list the first statute which mandated that only a "white keeper" could tend the white graveyard and a "colored keeper" was to tend the colored graveyard.[23] In my estimation, each of these statutes expanded the realm of discrimination.

---

20. In describing the purpose of a given statute, I tried to be succinct and, at the same time, somewhat blunt about what an act's language required or permitted. To give a maximalist reading of these statutes certainly gives rise to a danger of misinterpretation or editorializing but, knowing the history of the ways in which whites used fairly innocuous language to benefit themselves and to hinder African Americans, it seemed fair to emphasize the possibilities of these laws. Thus, for example, in the 1885 law regarding public schools in Raleigh, 1885 N.C. Sess. Laws 218, 221, ch. 141, § 6 (money to be apportioned between white and colored schools "without discrimination in favor of or to the prejudice of either race, due regard being paid to the cost of keeping up the public schools for both races"), my description in the "purpose" column placed less emphasis on the statute's language pointing toward a fair allocation of funds between the races and more on the almost total discretion given to the school committee because of the "due regard" phrasing about the different needs of different schools.

21. 1885 N.C. Sess. Laws 1050, 1068, ch. 119, § 9 (Private).

22. 1895 N.C. Sess. Laws 198, 199, ch. 150, § 5. This statute pertained to Duplin County.

23. 1895 N.C. Sess. Laws 90, 92, ch. 75, § 7 (Private).

4. DE JURE DISCRIMINATION IN NORTH CAROLINA | 111

As for the dividing line between the statutes listed in Table 1 and Table 2, the line of demarcation between discriminatory and equality-advancing is not as wide or as clear as one might think. Following the lead of Howard Rabinowitz, whose historical scholarship highlighted the fact that racial segregation was not viewed as a per se evil in the decades immediately after the Civil War, I list statutes that created new segregated institutions for blacks or that opened doors for black participation in Table 2.[24] As Rabinowitz pointed out, racially segregated schools and asylums were an advancement for blacks because, during this period, the only other realistic option was continued exclusion, and not integration. Thus, for example, I list the first legislative steps toward the creation of a separate program for "colored pupils" at the Institution for the Deaf and Dumb and Blind in Table 2 rather than Table 1.[25] Admittedly, many judgment calls have been made. The creation of institutions and asylums and other entities specifically for blacks was a half-step in the right direction and was an approach that acknowledged, at least to some degree, the needs of the black community which had been otherwise downplayed or ignored.[26] Leon Litwack, likewise, acknowledged this historical reality: "The

---

24. See Howard N. Rabinowitz, *Race Relations in the Urban South, 1865–1890* (1978). For an overview of the history recounted by Rabinowitz, see Chapter 2.

25. 1872–73 N.C. Sess. Laws 212, ch. 134, § 1. I should point out that my decision to exclude appropriations from my catalog of statutes leads to an undercount of the creation of black institutions in Table 2. This fact arises because, often, what became black schools and colleges were initially founded by freedmen in the years after the Civil War and the General Assembly began by appropriating money to these schools. One example of this approach arises with the Howard School in Fayetteville, N.C., which was founded shortly after the war. When the legislature recognized the need for a colored normal school (i.e., a school that trains future school teachers), it did not create one but made a $2,000 appropriation to the Howard School in 1877 that was reauthorized in 1879. 1876–77 N.C. Sess. Laws 437, 438, ch. 234, § 2; 1879 N.C. Sess. Laws 61, ch. 54, § 2. Thus, because these statutes were appropriations and there was not a session law that founded a colored normal school, no such entry for the Howard School or what is later known as the State Colored Normal School (and which is today known as Fayetteville State University) can be found in Table 2. The first direct mention of a state (colored) normal school at Fayetteville in the session laws is in 1881. 1881 N.C. Sess. Laws 290, 293, ch. 141, § 5.

26. As a historical matter, this view was generally shared by a majority of blacks on the theory that segregated institutions could be equal:

> The interest in Negro orphanages or cemeteries suggests that blacks were less concerned with encouraging integration than with ending exclusion. For the most part Negro leaders left unchallenged the existence of

determination of blacks to improve their position during and after Reconstruction revolved largely around efforts to secure accommodations that equaled those afforded whites."[27] But, as we all know, these segregated institutions eventually became discriminatory because of the intent behind the racial separation and the vast disparities in funding by (white) legislative majorities. The ongoing creation of new racially segregated schools was not intended to advance equality, for example. In an attempt to acknowledge these complexities, I have occasionally modified a strict adherence to this "segregated institutions were good" rule and placed a statute mandating segregation in Table 1. An example of this approach can be found with regard to the laws involving public schools: while I list the 1868 Constitution's provision tasking the General Assembly with opening public schools "to all the children of the state" in Table 2,[28] I list the 1869 law requiring separate schools for the "youth of each race" in Table 1 because that was a retrenchment from the previous year.[29] Thus, by necessity, the dividing line between Tables 1 and 2 is not a sharp one because of the complexity of the subject matter.

With regard to the discriminatory statutes listed in Table 1, their enactment established a base line of racial exclusion and discrimination. During the Jim Crow era, the differences between *de facto* and *de jure* discrimination remained substantial, because the affronts and exclusion that existed outside of the statute books were always greater than those covered by the laws. What is found in the statute books, however, was enforceable law. Enactments gave form to the racial prejudices of the age, whether they codified existing practice or reached out to address a new subject of legislative concern.

Here, then, is a list of some of the most notable enactments found in Table 1, not necessarily the most important ones, but also the statutes that typify the range of subjects addressed by the laws:

---

segregation in welfare facilities. This attitude did not indicate passivity, however. Where blacks were barred, they requested the establishment of Negro departments or separate institutions.

Rabinowitz, supra note 24, at 144.

27. Leon F. Litwack, Jim Crow Blues, *OAH Magazine of History*, Jan. 2004, at 7, 8.
28. N.C. Const. of 1868, art. IX, § 2.
29. 1868–69 N.C. Sess. Laws 458, 471, ch. 134, § 50.

4. *DE JURE* DISCRIMINATION IN NORTH CAROLINA

LEGISLATIVE SESSION	PURPOSE
1868	State militia companies segregated[30]
1868–69	Required townships to establish segregated schools[31]
1871–72	County schools to be segregated[32]
1871–72	Outlawed marriages between white and a person of another race[33]
1872–73	Reenacted requirement in code revisal that county jails be racially segregated[34]
1872–73	Buildings at proposed New Hanover County juvenile detention facility to be constructed so as to segregate races[35]
1880	School tax revenues in towns of Salisbury and Goldsboro to be segregated by race; revenues from white persons only for support of white schools and revenues from colored persons only for support of colored schools[36]
1883	School law allowed local assessments and disbursements to be segregated by race for entire state[37]

---

30. 1868 N.C. Sess. Laws 35, ch. 22, § 7.
31. 1868–69 N.C. Sess. Laws 458, 471, ch. 134, § 50.
32. 1871–72 N.C. Sess. Laws 308, 312, ch. 189, § 20.
33. 1871–72 N.C. Sess. Laws 328, ch. 193, § 2.
34. 1872–73 N.C. Sess. Laws 92, ch. 74 (adopting Battle's Revisal as law, which reenacted law on segregation of county jails (Battle's Revisal of the Public Statutes of North Carolina ch. 31, § 2 (1873))).
35. 1872–73 N.C. Sess. Laws 267, 274, ch. 163, § 14.
36. 1880 N.C. Sess. Laws 67, 68–71, ch. 27, §§ 3 and 8.
37. 1883 N.C. Sess. Laws 225, 226, ch. 148, § 4. These provisions were subsequently held to be unconstitutional. See *Riggsbee v. Town of Durham*, 94 N.C. 800 (1886); *Puitt v. Commissioners of Gaston County*, 94 N.C. 709 (1886).

LEGISLATIVE SESSION	PURPOSE
1883	Trustees of segregated schools in Town of Washington to be of the same race as school(s) for which they are trustees[38]
1885	Defined who is a Croatan Indian and instituted separate schools[39]
1885	In language that would be used repeatedly for decades, Raleigh school committee given discretion to fund schools with "due regard being paid to the cost of keeping up the public schools for both races"[40]
1885	Statute incorporating Town of Morganton required town to racially segregate cemeteries[41]
1887	Marriages between Croatan Indian and Negro void[42]
1889	Negroes excluded from schools for Croatan Indians[43]
1889	No white child to be apprenticed to a person of color and no colored child to be apprenticed to a white person (if suitable colored person available)[44]
1891	Railroad commissioners could require railroads to segregate trains, stations, and waiting rooms[45]

38. 1883 N.C. Sess. Laws 587, 588, ch. 412, § 4.
39. 1885 N.C. Sess. Laws 92, ch. 51, §§ 1–2.
40. 1885 N.C. Sess. Laws 218, 221, ch. 141, § 6.
41. 1885 N.C. Sess. Laws 1050, 1068, ch. 119, § 59 (Private).
42. 1887 N.C. Sess. Laws 499, ch. 254, § 1.
43. 1889 N.C. Sess. Laws 72, ch. 60, § 1.
44. 1889 N.C. Sess. Laws 138, 141, ch. 169, § 17.
45. 1891 N.C. Sess. Laws 275, 286, ch. 320, § 23.

LEGISLATIVE SESSION	PURPOSE
1895	Duplin County to establish segregated burial grounds in townships[46]
1897	New Hanover County allowed to create "home" for orphaned or homeless colored children who were to be worked on farm and who, if they ran away, would be guilty of misdemeanor[47]
1897	School committee of Town of Washington to have six white members and three colored members[48]
1899	Railroads and steamboats to be segregated by race[49]
1899	Colored militia troops must be under command of white officers[50]
1899	White and colored schools in Town of Chadbourn to be at least 500 yards apart[51]
1899	Restrictive election law required reregistration of all voters and imposed hurdles for illiterate voters with 5 ballots and 5 distinct ballot boxes[52]
1900	Constitutional amendment to impose literacy test and poll tax[53]
1901	State library to segregate colored patrons[54]

46. 1895 N.C. Sess. Laws 198, 199, ch. 150, § 5.
47. 1897 N.C. Sess. Laws 486, ch. 315.
48. 1897 N.C. Sess. Laws 522, 523, ch. 343, § 8.
49. 1899 N.C. Sess. Laws 539, ch. 384, § 1.
50. 1899 N.C. Sess. Laws 543, 543–44, ch. 390, § 1.
51. 1899 N.C. Sess. Laws 655, 657, ch. 504, § 10.
52. 1899 N.C. Sess. Laws 658, 661, ch. 507, § 11.
53. 1899 N.C. Sess. Laws 341, ch. 218.
54. 1901 N.C. Sess. Laws 702, ch. 503, § 2.

LEGISLATIVE SESSION	PURPOSE
1901	Charlotte school commissioners to segregate rooms and books for colored teachers and students[55]
1903	No white cadavers to go to school for colored persons[56]
1905	Separate Charlotte parks commissions created by race; four parks created for white citizens and "goal" for colored commission to create a park for colored citizens[57]
1907	Road crews in Wake County to be segregated by race[58]
1907	Streetcars to be segregated by race[59]
1911	Segregation of Indians of Robeson County (formerly referred to in statutes as Croatan Indians) in state hospital for insane, Robeson jail, and Robeson home for aged and infirm[60]
1913	Manufacturers and other employers required to provide racially separate toilet facilities[61]
1915	Hospitals that admit colored patients required to have colored nurses to attend to colored patients[62]
1915	Town of Benson allowed to impose residential segregation by race[63]

55. 1901 N.C. Sess. Laws 476, ch. 176, § 4 (Private).
56. 1903 N.C. Sess. Laws 1055, 1056, ch. 666, § 2.
57. 1905 N.C. Sess. Laws 83, 87–88, ch. 32, §§ 25–27 (Private).
58. 1907 N.C. Sess. Laws 531, 544, ch. 365, § 47.
59. 1907 N.C. Sess. Laws 1238, ch. 850.
60. 1911 N.C. Sess. Laws 354, 354–355, ch. 215, §§ 2, 4–6.
61. 1913 N.C. Sess. Laws 127, ch. 83, § 1.
62. 1915 N.C. Sess. Laws 365, ch. 284, § 1.
63. 1915 N.C. Sess. Laws 124, 137, ch. 63, § 47 (Private).

4. *DE JURE* DISCRIMINATION IN NORTH CAROLINA | 117

While all of the statutes in this sampling are not necessarily of great import, the range of subjects touched by these enactments was certainly broad, and the impact of the laws can be found from one end of the state to the other.

As seen in Table 1 and the sample list here, there were numerous laws in North Carolina enacted before the 1890s that segregated and discriminated against African Americans and Native Americans. Even excepting the Black Code enacted in 1866 from this listing because of their questionable legal validity with the start of Congressional Reconstruction in March 1867, there were many other statutes and constitutional amendments over the next several decades that were hostile to every race and color other than white.[64] C. Vann Woodward may have been correct in

---

64. I have included the enactments known as the Black Code in Table 1. The so-called Black Code was written by a committee selected by the 1865–66 Holden Convention. The Black Code in North Carolina was of dubious legal validity from the outset because of the uncertain status of the state's government in the immediate aftermath of the Civil War. A provisional government for North Carolina was put in place by a May 29, 1865, proclamation by President Andrew Johnson. Proclamation of May 29, 1865, in 6 *A Compilation of the Messages and Papers of the Presidents: 1789-1897*, at 312 (James D. Richardson ed., 1897). However, the actions of the Southern governments—such as whether to repudiate the debts incurred during the war as well as the enactment of the various Black Codes—ultimately doomed the provisional governments. The advent of Military Reconstruction cast doubt on the validity of the enactments of the provisional governments. See Reconstruction Act of March 2, 1867, ch. 153, 14 Stat. 428 (1867) (establishing that "no legal State governments . . . now exist in the rebel States"). North Carolina's Black Code was not repealed explicitly or *in toto*, but Military Reconstruction and North Carolina's ratification of a new constitution in April 1868 certainly invalidated any existing North Carolina statutes that conflicted with the federal Constitution—at least as understood at that time. See General Orders No. 1, Second Military District, March 21, 1867, § III (Gen. Daniel E. Sickles) ("Local laws and municipal regulations not inconsistent with the Constitution and laws of the United States or the proclamations of the President, or with such regulations as are or may be prescribed in the orders of the commanding general, are hereby declared to be in force . . . ."), reprinted in *Indexes to the Executive Documents of the Senate of the United States for the First Session Fortieth Congress, and for the Special Session, 1867*, at 60, 61 (1868). See also N.C. Const. of 1868, art. IV, § 24 ("The laws of North Carolina, not repugnant to this Constitution, or to the Constitution and laws of the United States, shall be in force until lawfully altered."). One statute that was enacted with the rest of the N.C. Black Code and which clearly survived as valid law is the 1866 enticement statute listed in Table 1. 1866 N.C. Sess. Laws 122, ch. 58. This session law remained on the books as part of the codifications and was cited in Battle's 1873 revisal and Womack's 1905 revisal. See Battle's Revisal of the Public Statutes of North Carolina ch. 70, § 1 (1873); Revisal of 1905 of North Carolina § 3365 (1905). See

The Strange Career of Jim Crow that the racial animus and discrimination in the South of 1870 or 1880 were not, as often assumed, indistinguishable from that in 1900 or 1910. But did Woodward and his scholarly disciples overstate the historical case for an interlude between the harsh Black Codes and the muscular white supremacy in the South around 1900? In his study, Woodward asserted that "[u]p to 1900 the only law of this type adopted by the majority of Southern states was that applying to passengers aboard trains."[65] As can be seen in the list above and more completely in Table 1, that claim was not accurate as to North Carolina.

Table 1 and the sampling here also demonstrate that the aftermath of the White Supremacy Campaigns of 1898 and 1900 did not bring about a huge surge of new and consequential Jim Crow laws in North Carolina. Racial discrimination increased after 1898–1900, but it does not appear that this increase was because of the enactment of numerous statutes impacting blacks residents across the state. In the legislative session following the 1898 political campaign, the General Assembly passed the law requiring segregation on railroads and steamboats and proposed the constitutional amendment imposing a poll tax and requiring that anyone seeking to vote "shall be able to read and write any section of the Constitution in the English language."[66] Those enactments were obviously consequential, and they impacted virtually all of North Carolina's citizens after the 1898 election. But from 1900, there is not another statute of similar import until the passage, in 1907, of the law requiring racial segregation on streetcars.[67] There were statutes enacted during that period that drew lines based on race, but requiring segregation at the State Library in Raleigh and mandating separate parks and libraries in Charlotte for blacks did not impact large numbers of the state's residents.[68] The only

---

also *State v. Hairston*, 63 N.C. 451, 452 (1869) (upholding North Carolina statutes outlawing interracial marriage—citing both the 1855 Revised Code and the provision of the 1866 Black Code—because "the intermarriage of whites and blacks is against public policy and is unlawful").

65. C. Vann Woodward, *The Strange Career of Jim Crow* 97 (3d rev. ed. 1974).

66. 1899 N.C. Sess. Laws 539, ch. 384, § 1 (statute on segregation of railroads and steamboats); 1899 N.C. Sess. Laws 341, ch. 218 (proposed constitutional amendment).

67. 1907 N.C. Sess. Laws 1238, ch. 850.

68. 1901 N.C. Sess. Laws 702, ch. 503, § 2 (state library); 1901 N.C. Sess. Laws 476, ch. 176, § 4 (Private) (Charlotte school commissioners to make arrangements for library usage by colored students); 1905 N.C. Sess. Laws 83, 87–88, ch. 32, §§ 25–27 (Private) (goal for Charlotte of establishing park for "Colored People").

other statute enacted between the 1900 election and the 1907 streetcar law that even merits consideration in terms of its importance is the 1903 law on schools, which stated that "no child with negro blood in his veins, however remote the strain, shall attend a school for the white race; and no such child shall be considered a white child."[69] While that language might sound momentous, it only minimally changed the substance of the existing law.[70]

---

69. 1903 N.C. Sess. Laws 751, 756, ch. 435, § 22 (1903).

70. The 1901 school law reaffirmed the existing standard that a person was a "Negro" or "Indian" if that person was of Negro or Indian descent "to the third generation, inclusive." 1 The Code of North Carolina § 1810, at 688 (1883), applied to schools by 1901 N.C. Sess. Laws 45, 64, ch. 4, § 68 (stating that the rule to follow was "laid down in section 1810 of The Code"). The 1901 statute's reference to the formulation for marriages had been repeated in school laws in preceding years. See 1899 N.C. Sess. Laws 903, 921, ch. 732, § 71; 1889 N.C. Sess. Laws 163, 170, ch. 199, § 42. However, prior to the 1889 law and a statute passed the same year which defined "Negro" to exclude such children from schools established for the Croatans of Robeson County, 1889 N.C. Sess. Laws 72, ch. 60, § 1 ("all children of the negro race to the fourth generation"), there were no school-specific laws that referenced any definition of race. There were, of course, other statutes that did set out what constituted a person of "Negro descent" and it was even written into the state constitution. Amendment of 1875, ch. 30, to N.C. Const. of 1868, art. XIV, § 8 ("a person of negro descent to the third generation inclusive").

The way that these race-definition provisions were confusingly interpreted was that "third generation inclusive" was essentially the equivalent of "fourth generation." *Hare v. Board of Education of Gates County*, 113 N.C. 10, 15 (1893) (noting that in the statute defining Croatan Indians, "the exclusion extends to the fourth generation, omitting the word 'inclusive,' which is synonymous with 'the third generation inclusive'"). The *Hare* decision is particularly instructive on how this definition based on ancestry worked. A person of "Negro" descent tied to "third generation inclusive" was interpreted to mean that if one of person A's grandparents was at least three-quarters white (all other grandparents being "white"), then A would be considered "white" under the § 1810 provision. Id. at 14–15. And, as made clear in *Hare*, that was another way of saying that if one of person A's great-grandparents was at least one-half white (all other great-grandparents being "white"), then A would be considered "white" under the law. Id. The *Hare* Court wrote: "The words used in section 1810, 'to the third generation inclusive,' must therefore be construed to prohibit intermarriage of whites with persons who are not beyond the third or in the fourth generation from the pure negro ancestor." Id. at 15. Thus, if just one great-grandparent was a "pure negro," then the descendant would not be "white" under the statutory definition. See Gilbert Thomas Stephenson, *Race Distinctions in American Law* 17–19 (1910); Peter Wallenstein, Race, Marriage, and the Law of Freedom: Alabama and Virginia, 1860s–1960s, 70 *Chicago-Kent Law Review* 371, 406 (1994) (describing third-generation inclusive as a "one-eighth fraction").

The 1903 change barring any child "with negro blood in his veins" may have impacted some nominal number of students, but it was not a significant change from the previous

It is certainly true that the constitutional amendment imposing a poll tax and requiring potential voters to be able to read the Constitution was a momentous change but, as will be seen in greater detail in this chapter, the impact of that amendment cannot be fully explained by its text.[71] Between 1890 and 1908, seven states of the former Confederacy, including North Carolina, adopted literacy test requirements for potential voters.[72] These literacy qualifications were intended to disenfranchise large numbers of blacks and lower-class whites.[73] But what happened in North Carolina set it apart. In Mississippi, with a more lenient provision that allowed illiterates to register if they could simply prove an understanding of the constitution, 2 percent of blacks in Mississippi still voted in the next presidential election after the state's constitutional convention.[74] And in Virginia, where voters had to prove literacy by filling out (unaided) a "very complex blank registration form," 10 percent of blacks voted in the gubernatorial election following the enactment of that constitutional

---

standard of "third generation inclusive." Nevertheless, I have included the 1903 statutory provision in Table 1 because it was a change in the law.

Another reason to think that the 1903 statutory change was not considered momentous is that the statute's provision on race merited little attention in the state's newspapers. In several articles at the time of legislative debate and passage, the provision was not even mentioned in a summary of the law's important changes. See, e.g., New School Law Passed by Senate, *Morning Post* (Raleigh, N.C.), Mar. 4, 1903, at 5 (although it should be noted that the entire text of the bill was appended to the article). Other articles may have noted the existence of Section 22, but the extent of explication was that it would "settle all controversy about the color line." The Senate Amends Public School Law, *News and Observer*, Mar. 4, 1903, at 1. Other articles reprinted the text of Section 22 without any commentary on its import. Legislature: Proceedings of the State Senate and House Yesterday, *Wilmington Messenger*, Mar. 4, 1903, at 1; General Assembly, *Daily Free Press* (Kinston, N.C.), Mar. 4, 1903, at 1.

71. I prefer the word disenfranchise to disfranchise and believe that disenfranchise is generally the preferred variant today. For example, in *Black's Law Dictionary*, the entries for "disfranchise" and "disfranchisement" direct the reader to see "disenfranchise" and "disenfranchisement," respectively. *Black's Law Dictionary* 568 (10th ed. 2009).

72. J. Morgan Kousser, *The Shaping of Southern Politics: Suffrage Restriction and the Establishment of the One-Party South, 1880–1910*, at 57–58 (1974) (hereinafter *Southern Politics*).

73. See *Charlotte Daily Observer*, June 6, 1900, at 4 ("The struggle of the white people of North Carolina to rid themselves of the danger of the rule of negroes and the lower class of whites is being watched with interest outside the State."), quoted in Kousser, *Southern Politics*, supra note 72, at 191.

74. Kousser, *Southern Politics*, supra note 72, at 143–145.

requirement.⁷⁵ Those were not large numbers of black voters, but they were at least measurable percentages. In North Carolina, however, with its literacy provision, the percentage of blacks who voted in the next gubernatorial election after the approval of the constitutional amendment was calculated to be effectively zero.⁷⁶

To the modern reader, one oddity about some of the statutes listed in Tables 1 and 2 and in the sample list above is that many laws were drafted so as to be limited in application to one town or county and, thus, there were few laws of general applicability. One such example is the law requiring the racial segregation of cemeteries in the Town of Morganton.⁷⁷ Perhaps one possible reason for a limited scope in an initial statute is that localities might be allowed to try something new, much like Justice Brandeis's notion of a state in a federal union as a "laboratory" of democracy in which to "try novel social and economic experiments."⁷⁸ But, by the time that other towns and counties subsequently approached the General Assembly to request the passage of a law mandating racially segregated cemeteries in their own communities, one would think that the legislature would pass a general law allowing all localities in the state to segregate in this fashion. This did not occur because, as in this example, there were later statutes that granted particular localities the power to segregate the cemeteries in those specific counties and towns.⁷⁹

This localized approach to legislation was not unique to North Carolina. One scholar has observed that throughout the nineteenth century, "state legislatures mostly enacted local, private, and special legislation, and very little general legislation."⁸⁰ In line with that conclusion, Albert

---

75. Id. at 174, 180.

76. Id. at 194. A more recent study calculated a raw voter turnout estimate for blacks of one percent in the 1912 North Carolina election. Kent Redding and David R. James, Estimating Levels of Modeling Determinants of Black and White Voter Turnout in the South, 1880 to 1912, 34 *Historical Methods* 141, 148 (2001). However, the authors of this study on research methodologies declared that their results should "be considered preliminary" until further research is completed. Id. at 156.

77. 1885 N.C. Sess. Laws 1050, 1068, ch. 119, § 59 (Private).

78. *New State Ice Co. v. Liebmann*, 285 U.S. 262, 311 (1932).

79. See, e.g., 1897 N.C. Sess. Laws 133, 134, ch. 83, § 6 (Private) (City of Winston authorized to purchase cemeteries, one for whites and one for colored citizens); 1901 N.C. Sess. Laws 650, 653, ch. 248, § 55 (Private) (same for Town of Carthage).

80. Robert M. Ireland, The Problem of Local, Private, and Special Legislation in the Nineteenth-Century United States, 46 *American Journal of Legal History* 271, 271 (2004). It

Coates' study on the distribution of session laws in North Carolina found that between 1868 and 1917, "at least 49 percent of the laws" enacted were "private, local or special acts."[81] The lack of legislative attention to generally applicable statutes in North Carolina was recognized and criticized around the turn of the century: "We regret the tendency in our course of legislation to reduce the force of acts from public laws to public local statutes."[82] The imbalance became clear after the General Assembly enacted a law in 1909 which mandated, starting with the next legislative session in 1911, that statutes be divided into three categories: public, public-local, and private.[83] In the 1911 session, there were 215 public laws and 1,245 laws in the other two categories.[84] Prior to the start of that legislative session, Governor W.W. Kitchin criticized the underemphasis on public lawmaking: "The General Assembly is for general legislation. Special legislation is contrary to the genius of our institutions and local relief should be administered by the localities interested under general laws."[85] Relief was sought with the proposal of a state constitutional amendment by the legislature in 1915 and its subsequent ratification. This amendment to Article II of the state constitution prohibited the General Assembly from enacting "local, private or special act[s]" in fourteen specified areas.[86] One of

---

is true that the distinctions between and definitions of general/public statutes as well as private/local/special statutes are difficult to state with precision. In 1894, one commentator wrote that "a general Act must be one which is designed neither for one or more particular persons, nor to operate exclusively in any particular part or parts of the States; yet such an Act is not necessarily universal, *i.e.*, capable of operating upon all persons or all things within the State legislated for." Charles Chauncey Binney, *Restrictions Upon Local and Special Legislation in State Constitutions* 22 (1894). For a discussion of pronouncements in North Carolina on the distinctions between private, special, and general laws, see Albert Coates, The Problem of Private, Local, and Special Legislation and City and County Home Rule in North Carolina, *Popular Government*, Feb.–Mar. 1949, at 6, 8–12.

81. Coates, supra note 80, at 7.

82. The North Carolina General Assembly, 2 *North Carolina Journal of Law* 150, 153 (1905). A "public local statute" in North Carolina during this era was elsewhere described as a statute "having reference entirely to the counties [or cities, towns] named." Ill Considered Legislation, 1 *North Carolina Journal of Law* 255, 255 (1904).

83. 1909 N.C. Sess. Laws 832, ch. 473, § 1.

84. Coates, supra note 80, at 7.

85. Gov. W.W. Kitchin, quoted in Joseph F. Ferrell, Local Legislation in the North Carolina General Assembly, 45 *North Carolina Law Review* 340, 350 (1967) (quoting 1911 Biennial Message of Gov. W.W. Kitchin to the General Assembly 22–25 (1911)).

86. 1915 N.C. Sess. Laws 148, ch. 99, § 1.

the specific areas was with regard to cemeteries.[87] The hope was that this amendment would help "to concentrate the minds of legislators on statewide concerns."[88] This hope was not immediately realized but, gradually, the General Assembly broadened its legislative focus.[89]

In the foregoing list of statutes and in Table 1, there are no laws affecting either transportation or public accommodations until the 1890s, but it is undeniable that discrimination through statutory enactments was commonplace in North Carolina in the decades after the Civil War. There are certainly contemporaneous descriptions, especially among whites, that there was no discrimination against blacks under the laws of North Carolina, but such claims were fanciful.[90]

Beyond *de jure* discrimination, though, there is admittedly evidence in the historical record of places of public accommodation serving white and black patrons in a manner approaching social equality, especially in the aftermath of the war and after the passage of the 1875 federal civil rights

---

87. Id.

88. John V. Orth and Paul Martin Newby, *The North Carolina State Constitution* 30 (2d ed. 2013).

89. Coates, supra note 80, at 12–13. As an example of a law applicable across the state, North Carolina enacted a more general statute as to the segregation of cemeteries in 1947. It mandated that cemeteries which had been "heretofore used exclusively for the burial of members" of a certain race were to "remain and be established as a burial ground" for that race. 1947 N.C. Sess. Laws 1115, 1115–1116, ch. 821, § 2 (codified at N.C. Gen. Stat. § 65-38 (Michie 1950)).

90. The following description of the law in North Carolina, in an 1875 grand jury charge by a federal district judge, was one such depiction that strains credulity:

> I will briefly restate the principles of law which we have been considering as they exist in this state, independent of the [federal] civil rights bill. The law only requires innkeepers, common carriers, etc., to furnish accommodations to colored men, equal to those provided for white men, when the same price is paid. Innkeepers may have separate rooms and accommodations for colored men, but they must be equal in quality and convenience to those furnished white men. Railroad companies may have first class coaches for colored men, and first class coaches for white men. If white men are protected from the intrusion of colored men, colored men must likewise be protected from the intrusion of white men, as the legal rights of both classes are the same.

Charge to Grand Jury—The Civil Rights Act, 30 F. Cas. 999, 1001 (Cir. Ct., W.D.N.C. April 1875). This jury charge was quoted in slightly different form in Charles A. Lofgren, *The Plessy Case: A Legal-Historical Interpretation* 134 (1987).

act.[91] These encroachments on the norms of strict racial segregation were rarities, however, but they received significant attention because even relatively small transgressions of these norms merited newspaper coverage. For example, in 1875, the black lawyer and future member of Congress James O'Hara was admitted to the saloon on the steamer "Cotton Plant" on a trip from Tarboro to Greenville after he pointed out to the captain that the civil rights act was now law.[92] One newspaper story noted that white and black delegates to the 1874 state Republican convention in Fayetteville "ignored all differences of race, color and previous condition of servitude by eating together at the same time at the same table."[93] While those examples predate the 1883 invalidation of the federal civil rights law by the U.S. Supreme Court,[94] the hotel owned by the Atlantic Coast Line Railroad at the stop in Weldon, N.C., was unique in that it allowed both white and black customers to sit in the same dining room into the 1890s.[95] The Weldon dining room was a genuine anomaly, especially in the 1890s, and it drew condemnation from the (white) newspapers in both North Carolina and Virginia.[96]

---

91. Civil Rights Act of 1875, ch. 114, 18 Stat. 335 (1875).

92. *The Raleigh News*, Mar. 13, 1875, at 3, cited in Frenise A. Logan, *The Negro in North Carolina, 1876–1894*, at 177 (1964).

93. Civil Rights at the Fayetteville Convention, *Wilmington Journal*, May 29, 1874, at 2.

94. *Civil Rights Cases*, 109 U.S. 3 (1883).

95. There are news stories, often critical, of this practice from 1885 to 1891. See, e.g., An Insult, Deep and Stinging, *The Commonwealth* (Scotland Neck, N.C.), Apr. 30, 1885, at 2 (stating that it is an insult to the South that "white folks and negroes at this hotel are treated alike and at the same tables, in the same dining room"); Mr. Emerson's Letter, *Roanoke News* (Weldon, N.C.), Apr. 2, 1891, at 14 (supervisor of Atlantic Coast Line Railway responds to criticism of his "indiscriminate seating of white and colored passengers" in the dining room by saying that he was following rules set out by Vice President and General Manager of the Atlantic Coast Line). This rampant social equality was noted in newspapers outside of North Carolina. The periodic reports about the lack of exclusion or segregation at the hotel would prompt the railway officials to respond. See Was Not Social Equality, *Richmond Dispatch*, Apr. 12, 1892, at 7 (railway superintendent defended seating of white and black patrons at same time because of delay to chartered train from Florida); The Weldon Hotel Matter, *News and Observer*, Oct. 1, 1886, at 1 (manager of Atlantic Coast Line Hotel stated that he "guarded against outraging the sentiments of Southern white people" by having "colored people ... behind a screen").

96. See, e.g., Social Equality at Weldon, *Times* (Richmond, Va.), Apr. 11, 1891, at 4 (commenting on the violation of a Southern principle that was as clear in Richmond "as it is in the city of Weldon, and one which the Southern people, irrespective of localities

The reality is that exclusion of and discrimination against blacks were commonplace after the Civil War, often enforced by customs and social norms imposed by whites. One example of the enforcement of those norms occurred in Wilmington in 1873 when "three colored men" bought tickets and were seated in the orchestra section of the Opera House theater. This event was noted in the next day's write-up in the *Daily Journal* and was described as a "novel and disagreeable feature of the occasion."[97] The newspaper brought this to the attention of the Opera House lessee, "who was much mortified at the occurrence, [and who] assures us that it shall not happen again."[98] Two days later, another "party of young colored men" tried "to force their way into the parquette at the Opera House."[99] True to his word, the lessee ejected the men and did it so forcefully that he was charged with assault and battery.[100]

Other examples of exclusion and discrimination abound. White churches were one of the first institutions in the South to exclude the former slaves after 1865 and, at the same time, blacks withdrew to form their own church communities.[101] But, immediately after the war, the Episcopal Diocese of North Carolina resolved in 1865 that "separate houses of Wor-

---

are fully determined to enforce, namely, that any approach to social equality with the negro will not be tolerated").

97. Skiff & Gaylord's Minstrels, *Daily Journal* (Wilmington, N.C.), Oct. 7, 1873, at 4.
98. Id.
99. More Trouble at the Opera House, *Wilmington Morning Star*, Oct. 9, 1873, at 1. Subsequent to the first incident at the Opera House, the *Wilmington Morning Star* reported that the three individuals intended their attendance "as an experiment to test the feeling of the white people of Wilmington in regard to the promiscuous occupancy of the theatre by the two races." The Colored Question, *Wilmington Morning Star*, Oct. 8, 1873, at 1.
100. The Theatre Question, *Daily Journal*, Oct. 10, 1873, at 4. Interestingly, the lessee sought and obtained warrants against the black men for forcible trespass. The case was heard by Judge (and future Governor) Daniel Russell. For a full account of Russell's decision, see Jeffrey J. Crow and Robert F. Durden, *Maverick Republican in the Old North State: A Political Biography of Daniel L. Russell* 26–27 (1977).
101. Foner, supra note 17, at 89 ("Two causes combined to produce the independent black church: the refusal of whites to offer blacks an equal place within their congregations and the black quest for self-determination."). Prior to the war, select slaves often attended church with their owners, generally in separate sections of the church. Id. at 88 (stating that in the antebellum Southern churches, slaves possessed "a kind of associate membership. Subject to the same rules and discipline as whites, they were required to sit in the back of the church or in the gallery during service, and excluded from Sabbath schools and a role in church governance.").

ship should be provided as soon as practicable ... [and] that there should be separate Sunday Schools—separate congregations."[102] The North Carolina Baptist State Convention followed suit in 1867 and adopted a report "suggesting" that "our colored brethren be encouraged to form separate Churches and Associations."[103] Separation was occasionally enforced by white passengers on trains by the ejectment of black passengers[104] and on other occasions by the railway companies' segregation of cars, as one newspaper ad made clear: "Excursion to Asheville for white and colored next Friday, over Western road. Return Saturday. Refreshment car separates the races."[105] In employment, white and colored miners might work the same shift "but when practicable they are always kept apart and worked as separate squads."[106] The racial divide was particularly evident in the tobacco factories and textile mills in the state, with the textile mills and their mill villages the almost exclusive domain of whites.[107] In some courtrooms in the state, for swearing-in witnesses, there were separate Bibles for blacks and whites.[108]

Many public spaces were segregated. Even without an extant state law

---

102. Proceedings of the 49th Annual Council of the Protestant Episcopal Church for the Diocese of North Carolina, *Daily Standard*, Sept. 18, 1865, at 3.

103. Baptist State Convention of North Carolina, *Biblical Recorder*, June 5, 1867, at 1, 2.

104. *Britton v. Atlanta & Charlotte Air-Line Ry. Co.*, 88 N.C. 536, 537 (1883). The court held that the plaintiff had an "established right to the seat which she occupied upon entering the defendant's train. She held it by the same tenure that every other passenger upon the train held his seat, and no one had the right either to call upon her to surrender it or to eject her from it by force." Id. at 545–546.

105. Ad, *Charlotte Observer*, Aug. 7, 1895, at 1.

106. The Kind We Need, *Weekly Star* (Wilmington, N.C.), Apr. 28, 1893, at 2.

107. Historian Edward Ayers recognized the divide:

> The textile labor force was also unique in its racial composition. Whereas the workers in virtually every other major industry in the South were nearly balanced between the races, the machine rooms of the cotton mills rapidly became the preserve of whites only. Mill owners would not allow blacks to work alongside the white women and girls who made up the bulk of the work force. Black men were permitted to work only at outside loading and unloading and in the suffocating rooms where they opened bales for processing. Black women found no work at all.

Edward L. Ayers, *The Promise of the New South: Life After Reconstruction* 114 (1992).

108. No Bible Kissing Votes the Senate, *News and Observer*, Feb. 5, 1903, at 1 ("[Senator Wellborn] told of Granville county and said they had 'White Supremacy' Bibles there, one set for the white and one for the colored.").

or city ordinance mandating segregation, the train station in Raleigh separated passengers by race: "Here in Raleigh, where the Union Station has a separate room for the negroes, there has been continual opposition and complaint on the part of the negroes [to the segregation of rail cars]."[109] Similarly, even without a state or city law on the subject, trolley parks in the City of Winston (soon to be Winston-Salem) were established for each race, the Nissen Park for whites and Washington Park for blacks.[110] Greensboro had a segregated courthouse with "a gallery exclusively for colored people."[111] Again, enacted laws and ordinances were never the full measure of discrimination and there was more exclusion and discrimination against blacks than the statutes or ordinances alone would suggest.[112]

---

109. Race Problem on Railroads: The Plan in North Carolina for Running Separate Coaches, *N.Y. Times*, Dec. 18, 1898, at 11. This article makes note of the important fact that the railroads generally opposed the Jim Crow laws because it often required that each train have an additional car for black passengers and that railroad employees had to enforce the law, which frequently meant making judgments about a person's racial purity. This 1898 newspaper article stated that, previously, "the influence of the railroads has been sufficient to prevent the introduction of the 'Jim Crow' cars, as they are called by the negroes. The argument of the railroads was that separate coaches would add greatly to the expense of the railroads, and this prevailed ... until now." Id.

110. The Nissen Park, *Union Republican* (Winston, N.C.), July 5, 1900, at 6. In a letter to the editor of the paper, Lieutenant Governor Charles A. Reynolds, who had been "closely connected to the enterprise," argued against any danger that the new Nissen Park "might be marred on some holiday occasion by the presence of colored people." Letter to the Editor by C.A. Reynolds, *Union Republican* (Winston, N.C.), July 5, 1900, at 6. Reynolds stated that the best plan for the city was to make the new Nissen Park "for the whites and to fit up the old Park and call it the Washington Park for the blacks." Id.

111. *Durham Sun*, Aug. 28, 1903, at 2.

112. I believe that Rabinowitz somewhat overstated the case when he wrote: "Not only was segregation the norm in many areas from at least 1865 on, it was often, as in the case of schools, admittedly enforced by law." Howard N. Rabinowitz, More than the Woodward Thesis: Assessing *The Strange Career of Jim Crow*, 75 *Journal of American History* 843, 847 (1988). From 1865, in North Carolina, there were no laws mandating segregation in public accommodations or churches or parks or employment. Segregation may have been, to a greater or lesser extent, the cultural norm in the South and in North Carolina for three decades after the Civil War, but it was a norm policed and enforced by white society and occasionally by law. It is true that, as Rabinowitz documented in his 1978 book, racial segregation was created by law with the addition of heretofore nonexistent black orphanages and asylums and schools for the "deaf, dumb, and blind." Rabinowitz, supra note 24, at 128–151. But, again, I accept the creation of institutions for blacks alone—segregated though they may have been—soon after 1865 as a better option than the continued exclusion of an entire race.

From the selected laws here and the complete list in Table 1, though, it seems clear that a steady stream of statutes was enacted in North Carolina after the Civil War that sought to segregate and discriminate against minorities and, in addition, that there was not a pronounced increase in important statutes immediately after the White Supremacy Campaigns. There does not seem to have been a true postbellum interlude in North Carolina when the state legislature did not concern itself with matters of race, contrary to what C. Vann Woodward suggested in his book on Jim Crow. The statutes cataloged here suggest that the status of blacks in North Carolina in the decades after 1865 was never far removed from the minds of the white members of the General Assembly. At the same time, after the political campaigns of 1898 and 1900 and with the exception of the streetcar law of 1907, what laws were enacted in the decade after 1900 were relatively miniscule in their reach. For example, while a 1901 statute required segregation at the state library, by the late 1930s, there were still only two tables in the stacks for black library patrons.[113] It is only after 1910, and still with not much greater frequency, that Jim Crow laws with broader discriminatory aims began to appear in the state's session laws. Nevertheless, even during this legislative interlude after 1900, racial discrimination was increasing under the laws of the state. The application and use of law, and not the volume of enacted statutory texts, is being driven by racial animus against blacks in the aftermath of the White Supremacy Campaigns, as will be seen in the areas of education, voting, and jury participation. Buffeted by the prevailing winds of the moment, *de jure* discrimination worsens after 1898–1900 through the operation of the law.

A. Education Law: Discretion to Discriminate

The education of blacks may have no longer been a criminal offense in North Carolina by 1920, but it was not a priority for the majority-white population, either. Prior to the Civil War, it was a crime for anyone to teach "any slave within this State to read or write . . . [or] give or sell to

---

113. John Hope Franklin, *Mirror to America: The Autobiography of John Hope Franklin* 84 (2005). With regard to the North Carolina state archives, no accommodations for black patrons were made even by the late 1930s, when John Hope Franklin showed up to conduct research for his Ph.D. dissertation, and special arrangements had to made for him. Id. at 83.

such slave or slaves any books or pamphlets"[114] and that law, when put into a code, was broadened by the codifiers to outlaw teaching any "slave or free negro" to read or write.[115] After the war, the new 1868 North Carolina Constitution set out to establish a system of public schools "free of charge to all the children of the State,"[116] without any mention of race. But distinctions were quickly drawn, with the passage of an 1869 law that townships should establish "a separate school or separate schools for the instruction of children and youth of each race resident therein."[117] That principle was added to the state constitution with the 1875 amendment which wrote into the state's fundamental law that "the children of the white race and the children of the colored race shall be taught in separate public schools."[118] The 1875 amendment went on to promise equality among the schools: "[T]here shall be no discrimination made in favor of, or to the prejudice of, either race."[119] Yet it would be hard to prove that any other provision of North Carolina's fundamental law has ever turned out to be a greater fiction than this one, because the majority of state legislators and local school officials worked diligently over the ensuing decades to cripple and beggar the schools for black children. This impoverishment was not a mere unintended byproduct of the support for the white schools but was, instead, based on intentional actions by these legislative majorities to harm the black schools. The attitude of the white South was the frequent refrain that "to educate a Negro is to spoil a good field hand."[120] The black schools were intentionally hamstrung, and the white schools were

---

114. 1830–31 N.C. Sess. Laws 11, ch. 6.
115. Revised Code of North Carolina ch. 107, § 31 (1855) (prohibiting any slave "to teach, or attempt to teach, any other slave or free negro to read or write, the use of figures excepted"). See also Revised Code of North Carolina ch. 34, § 82 (1855) ("Any free person who shall teach, or attempt to teach any slave to read or write . . . shall be deemed guilty of a misdemeanor, and . . . if a white man or woman, shall be fined not less than one hundred [dollars] . . . and if a free person of color, shall be fined, imprisoned, or whipped not exceeding thirty-nine, nor less than twenty lashes.").
116. N.C. Const. of 1868, art. IX, § 2.
117. 1868–69 N.C. Sess. Laws 458, 471, ch. 134, § 50.
118. Amendment of 1875, ch. 26, to N.C. Const. of 1868, art. IX, § 2.
119. Id.
120. See, e.g., An Important Lesson from a Northern Source, *Charlotte Democrat*, Nov. 19, 1886, at 3 ("It is a common saying now in the South, 'Educate the negro and you spoil a good corn-field hand.'"); Our State Contemporaries, *Wilmington Morning Star*, Nov. 2, 1886, at 3 ("When you educate a negro you educate a candidate for the peniten-

the beneficiaries. This conclusion was supported by the 1914 observation of the (white) State Agent of Negro Rural Schools, N.C. Newbold, who reported on the condition of the state's Negro schools:

> The average negro schoolhouse is really a disgrace to an independent, civilized people. To one who does not know our history, these schoolhouses, though mute, would tell in unmistakable terms a story of injustice, inhumanity and neglect on the part of our white people. Such a condition would appear to an observer uninformed of our past as intolerable, indefensible, unbusinesslike, and, above all, unchristian.[121]

The situation described by Newbold in 1914 was decades in the making, but it accelerated greatly in the years immediately after 1900 because of increasingly inequitable funding of black schools relative to the white schools under the same basic statutory funding framework that had existed prior to the White Supremacy Campaigns.

Aside from racial inequities, up through 1900, public schools in North Carolina suffered from a general lack of funding and support, even when compared to the other states of the former Confederacy. The statistics are shocking to modern eyes. In 1900, the average number days of school attendance in North Carolina was 21.9, the lowest number for any state in the nation.[122] In 1900, it was reported that there were only 4 four-year high schools in the state.[123] In 1900, the average public expenditure per pupil per year was $4.34 in North Carolina, compared to a national average of

---

tiary and spoil a good field hand.") (quoting Ben Tillman); *The Home* (Pittsboro, NC), Jan. 24, 1889, at 2 ("It is said that when you 'educate a negro you spoil a field hand.'").

121. N.C. Newbold, First Biennial Report of State Agent of Negro Rural Schools, in *Biennial Report of the Superintendent of Public Instruction of North Carolina for the Scholastic Years 1912–1913 and 1913–1914*, at Part III, 122, 124 (1915).

122. 1 *Report of the [U.S.] Commissioner of Education for the Year 1899–1900*, at lxix (1901) [hereinafter 1 *Report for 1899–1900*], cited by Louis R. Harlan, *Separate and Unequal: Public School Campaigns and Racism in the Southern Seaboard States, 1901–1915*, at 9–10 (1958). The states closest to North Carolina were Arkansas (32.4), Alabama (35.7), and South Carolina (35.8). 1 *Report for 1899–1900*, at lxix.

123. 2 *Report of the [U.S.] Commissioner of Education for the Year 1899–1900*, at 2289–2290 (1901), cited by Harlan, supra note 122, at 28. Compare this number to Georgia with seven, Virginia with twenty-eight, and South Carolina with thirty. Harlan, supra note 122, at 28.

4. DE JURE DISCRIMINATION IN NORTH CAROLINA | 131

$20.29 and to $37.76 spent per child in Massachusetts.[124] In that same year, the value of public school property per child in North Carolina was $1.64, compared to a national average of $24.20.[125] As a result, North Carolina in 1900 had the highest proportion of *white* illiterates in the nation, except for New Mexico.[126] This situation was a dramatic change for the state, because North Carolina had one of the best public school systems in the South on the eve of the Civil War.[127] Even apart from racial inequities, the 1900 figures demonstrate negligent leadership over several decades by the state's elected political officials and it added up to short school terms and dilapidated schoolhouses and uneducated students.

There were certainly efforts at both the state and local levels to better fund the state's public schools in the first two decades after the Civil War, but two decisions of the N.C. Supreme Court placed restraints on these attempts. The 1868 Constitution embraced the idea of public schools open "at least four months every year,"[128] but it also placed limitations on any capitation tax (i.e., poll tax) by the General Assembly, as well as capitation and property taxes by the state and counties through a formula tying one to the other,[129] and it fixed a maximum capitation tax, state and county combined, of two dollars per male inhabitant.[130] The taxation limitations were written into the constitution out of a distrust of

---

124. 1 *Report for 1899–1900*, at lxxix, cited by Harlan, supra note 122, at 10. It should be noted that the North Carolina figures were from 1897–98, presumably the most recent data available. Compare North Carolina's $4.34 with South Carolina's $4.44, Georgia's $6.64, and Virginia's $9.70. 1 *Report for 1899–1900*, at lxxix.

125. Harlan, supra note 122, at 10. Compare North Carolina's $1.64 with $5.33 per child in Virginia. Id. These numbers were not generated by the U.S. Commissioner of Education but were calculated by Harlan by dividing the estimated value of all public school property, 1 *Report for 1899–1900*, at lxxiii, by the school population, id. at lxiii.

126. *Bureau of the Census, Abstract of the Twelfth Census of the United States, 1900*, at 75 (1904), cited by Harlan, supra note 122, at 11 n.17.

127. William Eskridge King, *The Era of Progressive Reform in Southern Education: The Growth of Public Schools in North Carolina, 1885–1910*, at vii (1969) (unpublished Ph.D. dissertation, Duke University).

128. N.C. Const. of 1868, art. IX, sec. 3.

129. N.C. Const. of 1868, art. V, sec. 1 (stating that any capitation tax by the General Assembly "shall be equal on each [male inhabitant], to the tax on property valued at three hundred dollars in cash"); N.C. Const. of 1868, art. V, sec. 7 (stating that taxes levied by the county commissioners "for county purposes, shall be levied in like manner with the State taxes").

130. N.C. Const. of 1868, art. V, sec. 1.

legislatures and future legislative action.[131] The intractable problem was that while the education section of the constitution made county commissioners "liable to indictment" if the public schools were not kept open for four months,[132] the amount of state and local money combined was not enough to achieve that goal, even from the time that the 1868 Constitution was ratified. For example, two years later, in preparation for the 1870 school year, the county commissioners of Craven County levied a tax on the property in one township for the benefit of that township's schools in order to keep those schools open for the requisite four-month period. However, in the following year, the N.C. Supreme Court invalidated the tax in *Lane v. Stanley*.[133] Despite the constitutional mandate to keep the public schools open for four months and the placement of this responsibility on the county commissioners, the court held that the county commissioners could not impose taxes on individual townships apart from a general county-wide school tax, even though there was a statute that appeared to give the commissioners just such a power.[134] A decade and a

---

131. C. Vann Woodward, *Origins of the New South: 1877–1913*, at 65 (1951).
132. N.C. Const. of 1868, art. IX, sec. 3.
133. 65 N.C. 153 (1871).
134. Id. at 158. In the case at issue, the School Committee of a particular township made an estimate of the funds needed to keep the schools open for four months and the School Committee of that township forwarded that estimate to the Township Trustees, the corporate body for N.C. townships at the time. Id. at 153; 1868–69 N.C. Sess. Laws 478, ch. 185, § 2. The Trustees submitted the estimate to a vote of the township, it was rejected by a majority of the township's voters, and the Township Trustees then submitted the estimate to the Commissioners of Craven County. 65 N.C. at 153–154. The county commissioners, in turn, levied a tax upon the township for the estimated expenses, which was the action challenged in the lawsuit. Id. The state's laws here were a convoluted mess. The state constitution stated that county commissioners had a duty to ensure that public schools were open for four months, N.C. Const. of 1868, art. IX, sec. 3, while an 1869 statute set out that it was the School Committee of each township which had the duty to establish and maintain schools "for at least four months in every year." 1868–69 N.C. Sess. Laws 458, 460, ch. 184, § 15. That same statute then seems to say that it was the responsibility of the township itself, as a corporate entity, to maintain the schools: "In case any Township, at annual meeting, shall fail to provide for schools to be taught at least four months for that year, and to provide fuel, and to make any other provisions necessary for the efficiency and success of the schools . . . ." Id. § 25. Thus, between the 1868 Constitution (county commissioners) and the 1869 statute establishing a system of public instruction (School Committee of township and/or township), it is an understatement to say that the entity responsible for keeping the schools open for four months was unclear.

half later, with the continuing inability to keep the schools open for the constitutionally mandated four months, the N.C. Supreme Court again relied on the constitutional tax limitation to strike down a revenue measure, this time a state statute, which granted county commissioners the power to levy a special tax in order to keep the schools open. In *Barksdale v. Commissioners of Sampson County*,[135] the court concluded that the 1885 state law could not be upheld even in light of the provision in the state constitution which allowed taxes beyond the two-dollar limit for "a special purpose ... with the approval of the General Assembly."[136] The court

---

The 1869 statute went on to set out a process whereby if a township did not maintain schools for four months, the School Committee of the township was to forward to the county commissioners an estimate of the amount needed to keep the schools open for that period "and a tax equal to the amount of such estimate shall be levied on the Township by the County Commissioners at the same time that the County taxes are levied." 1868–69 N.C. Sess. Laws 458, 464, ch. 184, § 25 (the chapter number is misprinted on page 458 of the volume as "CXXXIV" instead of "CLXXXIV" but was clearly intended to be "184" as that number is used in the headers of subsequent pages). That provision certainly makes it sound like it was to be an automatic process once the township failed to provide the necessary funds. In *Lane*, it was the Township Trustees and not the School Committee that forwarded the estimate to the county commissioners, *Lane*, 65 N.C. at 153–154, but that minor detail is not relied upon by the court. Nonetheless, and contrary to that statutory language, the Supreme Court held that the county commissioners did not possess "the power to lay township taxes, as distinguished from the general county tax for School purposes." Id. at 158. The court did not rely—or even mention—the constitutional limit on capitation taxes. Rather, the court turned to an entirely different provision of the constitution to infer that, despite all of this language to the contrary, it was really the state General Assembly which was responsible for providing "by taxation and otherwise for a general and uniform system of Public Schools." Id. at 157 (quoting N.C. Const. of 1868, art. IX, sec. 2).

In addition to holding that county commissioners could not impose taxes on townships for school funding, the court concluded that Township Trustees lacked power to tax their own townships for school funds. The court maintained that the statute creating the entities known as townships did not include the power to tax for public schools when it gave the Township Trustees the ability to tax for "the necessary expenses of the Township." Id. at 155–156. See also 1868–69 N.C. Sess. Laws 478, 481, ch. 185, § 19. The obvious implication here is that the court believed that public schools were not a necessary expense. Although this assertion was dicta, since the only tax at issue here was the one imposed by the county commissioners, the court stated that Township Trustees do not "have any taxing power for school purposes." *Lane*, 65 N.C. at 156.

135. 93 N.C. 472 (1885).

136. N.C. Const. of 1868, art. V, sec. 6 (as amended by 1873 constitutional amendment) (stating that taxes levied by the county commissioners "for county purposes, shall

brushed aside the fact that the statute pronounced it just such a "special tax."[137] The court acknowledged that the constitutional tax limitation has "crippled the action of the General Assembly in its course of legislation,"[138] but the hidebound majority held that "the repugnance of the provisions under consideration is manifest."[139] The decisions in *Lane* and *Barksdale* worked to financially cripple the state's public schools for decades.

With regard to matters of race, though, the segregation of schools was not an end in itself for the Democrats in power following Redemption but, rather, it was also the means by which money and resources could be preserved for the white schools at the expense of the black schools. An early and overt method of discrimination was begun in conjunction with the statutes authorizing the graded schools that were opening in towns across the state. State legislation authorized individual towns to submit to voters the question of whether taxes should be levied for graded schools and, eventually, the General Assembly drafted some of these statutes to divide the tax money by race. These city graded schools were, in effect, an end run around the constitutional tax limitations on the counties, but

---

be levied in like manner with the State taxes").

The section cited here in 1885 as Article V, section 6 was, in actuality, numbered as section 7 of the 1868 Constitution. However, an 1873 constitutional amendment deleted Article V, section 4 and, thus, it was understood that the subsequent sections of Article V changed their numbers, as well. That is, section 5 became section 4, section 6 became section 5, and so on. See *Collie v. Commissioners of Franklin County*, 145 N.C. 170, 172 (1907) (citing the passage here as "Section 6" of Article V); *Barksdale*, 93 N.C. at 475 (citing passage here as "sec. 6 of article V"). See Orth and Newby, supra note 88, at 25 (referring to North Carolina "practice of incorporating amendments into the text of the constitution, rather than merely appending them").

137. 1885 N.C. Sess. Laws 266, 273, ch. 174, § 23. The statutory section set out: "If the tax levied by the State for the support of the public schools shall be insufficient to maintain one or more schools in each school district for the period of four months, then the board of commissioners of each county shall levy annually a *special tax* to supply the deficiency for the support and maintenance of said schools for the said period of four months or more." Id. (emphasis added).

138. 93 N.C. at 476.

139. Id. at 477. *Barksdale* was finally overruled in 1907. *Collie v. Commissioners of Franklin County*, 145 N.C. 170 (1907). Then, in addition, a new constitutional amendment was approved in 1920 "eliminating the mandatory equation between poll and property taxes and replacing it with maximum rates on each." Orth and Newby, supra note 88, at 30.

the rural schools were left behind.[140] Prior to the 1880s, North Carolina's education system relied solely on common schools, the one-room schoolhouses where children of a broad range of ages and of vast differences in academic achievement were educated all together by a single teacher in a single room, without tests or true distinctions among students in terms of levels of knowledge. But in the 1880s, the movement for graded schools reached North Carolina, and cities and towns increasingly wanted graded schools where students were grouped by academic level and where students progressed based on demonstrated mastery of distinct levels of learning.[141]

Although graded-school legislation for several towns had been enacted and graded schools were in existence,[142] it was the 1881 statute for the Goldsboro graded school which inaugurated the overt segregation of tax dollars based on race. This statute provided that if Goldsboro voters agreed to an annual tax for graded schools, the special taxes from "white persons shall be expended in keeping up a graded public school in said township for white persons" and the special taxes from "colored persons shall be expended in keeping up a graded school in said township for

---

140. H. Leon Prather, Sr., *Resurgent Politics and Educational Progressivism in the New South: North Carolina, 1890–1913*, at 34–35 (1979). See id. at 35 ("The entire financial responsibility for the [city] schools' operation, aside from the four month school fund, was borne by the cites and towns that founded them.").

141. James L. Leloudis, *Schooling the New South: Pedagogy, Self, and Society in North Carolina, 1880–1920*, at 22–23 (1996). It should be noted that, on a parallel track, the state was opening "normal" schools during the period, as well. Normal schools were to educate individuals to be teachers and, while strictly segregated and not equally funded, there was an acknowledgment of the need for colored normal schools with the limited number of educated blacks who were qualified to be teachers in the decades after the Civil War. Id. at 74–75.

142. There were authorizing acts for graded schools in Charlotte, 1874–75 N.C. Sess. Laws 673, ch. 138, and Fayetteville, 1876–77 N.C. Sess. Laws 556, ch. 285. Strangely, while the Charlotte authorizing legislation was enacted on March 22, 1875, there was a "Report" from the supposed first session of the white "Graded School in Charlotte" which stated that the session commenced on October 28, 1873. *The Charlotte Observer*, July 23, 1874, at 1. The first graded school in operation in North Carolina was in Greensboro following legislative authorization in 1870, 1869–70 N.C. Sess. Laws 201, 220, ch. 122, § 74 (Private), but that school closed its doors in June 1880. *Greensboro North State*, June 10, 1880, at 3. On the early graded schools, see M.C.S. Noble, *A History of the Public Schools of North Carolina* 399–408 (1930).

colored persons."¹⁴³ This law, approved by the city's voters, thus segregated the tax dollars raised in Goldsboro.¹⁴⁴ The obvious and inescapable fact was that a little over fifteen years after the end of slavery, the property of the colored population was worth only a fraction of that of whites and, therefore, the tax money available for the colored schools under such a system would be a pittance.¹⁴⁵ This statute and subsequent ones were enacted for many towns in the eastern part of the state, such as Goldsboro, where the black population was a majority, or close to it. The Goldsboro statute was the beginning of a new tactic to benefit white schools at the expense of the colored schools, and similar laws walling off tax dollars for graded schools based on race were passed by the General Assembly for eastern towns such as NewBerne,¹⁴⁶ Wilson,¹⁴⁷ and Kinston.¹⁴⁸

At the same time that those town-specific statutes were enacted, the

---

143. 1881 N.C. Sess. Laws 360, ch. 189, § 3.

This statute was not the first one to allow the segregation of tax dollars by race, but it was the first such law approved at the polls. The previous year, a similar law was passed for both Salisbury and Goldsboro, and this statute is the one listed in Table 1. 1880 N.C. Sess. Laws 67, ch. 27. It appears that no vote pursuant to this law authorizing a tax was ever held in Salisbury. But the histories as to Goldsboro are inaccurate. Frenise Logan wrote that when the question of the tax was put to a vote, "the poor whites and 'ignorant' Negroes of Goldsboro united to defeat it." Logan, supra note 92, at 155. M.C.S. Noble wrote: "No vote was ever held under this act." Noble, supra note 142, at 404. In fact, however, Goldsboro did vote and the numbers were 330 "for school" and 191 "no school." The Graded School, *Goldsboro Messenger*, May 6, 1880, at 2. The reason that a new law was passed for Goldsboro the following year, in 1881, was that the 1880 statute specified that "a majority of all the qualified voters of the Township" had to vote for the law and low turnout in 1880 tripped up its passage. The Graded School, *Goldsboro Messenger*, May 2, 1881, at 1.

144. 1881 N.C. Sess. Laws 360, 361–362, ch. 189, §§ 6–7. The 1881 General Assembly also passed a graded school law for Durham which segregated the tax dollars raised specifically for the graded school, but the Durham statute did not divide the funds from the general school tax dollars by race. 1881 N.C. Sess. Laws 433, ch. 231.

145. Although comparative statistics as to wealth in the latter half of the nineteenth century lack breadth and, thus, precision, Loren Schweninger calculated that by 1870 in the Upper South (which included North Carolina), the percentage of families which held at least $2,000 worth of real property was 22 percent for white families and one half of one percent for black families. Loren Schweninger, Prosperous Blacks in the South, 1790–1880, 95 *American Historical Review* 31, 54 (1990).

146. 1883 N.C. Sess. Laws 170, 171, ch. 117, § 3 (for "the city of NewBerne [sic]").

147. 1883 N.C. Sess. Laws 318, 319, ch. 192, § 4.

148. 1883 N.C. Sess. Laws 391, 392, ch. 236, § 3.

General Assembly decided to broaden the principle to every school district across the state in 1883. That year, the legislature enacted the so-called Dortch Act which allowed for a local school district assessment for schools, with the money raised segregated by race.[149] The statute provided that a mere ten voters, white or black, could petition for a vote on the assessment, and the ensuing vote would be limited to the voters of that race. If approved, the assessment on the taxable property and polls of whites would be used solely in support of white schools and, again if approved by black voters, the assessment "from the taxable property and polls of colored persons shall be expended in aiding to keep up the public school in said district for colored children."[150] Ostensibly, the law allowed each race to determine whether to improve its schools by raising additional dollars, but the intent was to allow whites to improve the schools for their race alone. As one newspaper commented, "[T]he white people, or many of them, feel that if any more taxes are to be wrung from them, it ought to be appropriated to the whites, and if the colored race desire more facilities for schooling, let them be taxed to furnish the means."[151]

The Dortch Act was short-lived, however, because the N.C. Supreme Court struck it down as unconstitutional two years later in *Puitt v. Commissioners of Gaston County*.[152] The Court based its ruling on the fact that the tax was not uniform, as required by the state constitution. By allowing one group to tax only itself, the Court held that the assessment was not uniform because it rested "wholly upon race."[153] But, perhaps surprisingly for the era, the Court recognized the true intent and impact of the law:

> Nor can we shut our eyes to the fact, that the bulk of property, yielding the fruits of taxation belongs to the white people of the State, and very little is held by the emancipated race; and yet the needs of the latter for free tuition, in proportion to its numbers are as great or greater than the needs of the former. The act, then,

---

149. 1883 N.C. Sess. Laws 225, ch. 148.
150. Id. at 226, § 4.
151. Mr. Dortch's Educational Bill, *Charlotte Democrat*, Feb. 9, 1883, at 3.
152. 94 N.C. 709 (1886). Although the opinion is found in Volume 94 for the February Term 1886, the opinion was handed down in December 1885. Supreme Court, *News and Observer*, Dec. 25, 1885, at 4.
153. 94 N.C. at 715.

in directing an appropriation of what taxes are collected from each class, to the improved education of the children of that class, does necessarily discriminate "in favor of the one and to the prejudice" of the other race.[154]

The words quoted in the last sentence were from the 1875 constitutional amendment to Article IX, section 2 of the state constitution.[155] The Court thus based its decision not only on the lack of uniformity, but on the discrimination worked by the law as between the races, a somewhat remarkable rationale for any American court in 1885. In response to the decision, some jurisdictions, such as Person County, simply ignored the decision and continued to segregate funds by race, while Goldsboro and several other towns closed their free public graded schools for a time rather than fund the schools out of one pot of money.[156]

In that same year, in 1885, the General Assembly enacted a new general school law that also sought to tilt funding in favor of white schools at the expense of black schools. Nevertheless, this statute was significant in many respects and it has been called "the foundation of the education system in North Carolina."[157] The law was enacted on March 11, 1885, which was prior to the invalidation of the Dortch Act and, thus, it was an attempt to pile on and add even further to the racial disparity in funding through the method for the disbursement of state school funds.[158] The law had two components of importance for the funding of black schools. First, it ensured that the county boards of education would be composed of people politically aligned with the Democratic-controlled General Assembly. Section 1 of the statute set out that the justices of the peace and the county commissioners would jointly elect the county board of education.[159] This

---

154. Id. at 715–716.
155. Amendment of 1875, ch. 26, to N.C. Const. of 1868, art. IX, § 2 ("And the children of the white race and the children of the colored race shall be taught in separate public schools, but there shall be no discrimination made in favor of, or to the prejudice of, either race.").
156. Leloudis, supra note 141, at 122 (on Person County's continued segregation of funds); Prather, supra note 140, at 76 (on fate of Goldsboro, Durham, and Kinston schools).
157. King, supra note 127, at 8.
158. 1885 N.C. Sess. Laws 266, ch. 174.
159. Id. § 1.

method ensured Democratic dominance—even in heavily black (and, thus, Republican) towns in the eastern part of the state—because of the 1876 law which gave the redeemed Democratic General Assembly the power to appoint justices of the peace who, in turn, elected the county commissioners.[160] With this political-party control over the members of boards of education, the statute's second important component was the formula it set out for the distribution of the state school funds. It directed those local boards of education to use the money to pay for the general school expenses set out by law (such as the school superintendent's salary) and then, for all remaining funds, two thirds of those were to go to the individual schools based upon "the whole number of children" while the other one third was effectively to be spent at the discretion of the board of education.[161] The latter provision stated: "[T]he remaining one-third shall be apportioned in such manner as to equalize school facilities to all the districts of the county, as far as may be practicable and just to all concerned, without discrimination in favor of or to the prejudice of either race."[162] It was the funding discretion available under this provision, and not the nondiscrimination language, that was important in practice. The discretion allowed for funding disparities, especially in the heavily black-populated towns in the eastern part of the state.[163] The Raleigh *News and Observer* recognized that the "provision is expected to afford relief in the east by allowing the allotment of something like a just part of their own money to the whites who are discriminated against by the present *per capita* apportionment."[164] As James Leloudis has concluded, the disbursement of money was "limited only by the school boards' imaginative definitions of equity."[165]

This discretion over the disbursement of the state school funds was coupled with the discretion given to the local boards and committees over the expenditure of local city funds. Starting with yet another 1885 law, and using language that would be used in similar statutes for decades,

---

160. 1876–77 N.C. Sess. Laws 226, 227–228, ch. 141, §§ 4–5.
161. 1885 N.C. Sess. Laws 266, 268–269, ch. 174, § 6.
162. Id.
163. King, supra note 127, at 11 ("In other words, despite the law's wording, the minority of white children in the eastern counties were to be favored at the expense of the Negro children.").
164. The School Bill, *News and Observer*, Feb. 7, 1885, at 2.
165. Leloudis, supra note 141, at 122.

the General Assembly gave the school committee for the City of Raleigh the power to apportion money with "due regard being paid to the cost of keeping up the public schools for both races."[166]

Given this discretionary language over the distribution of money at the state and local levels, the surprising fact is that, up to 1900 and taken as a whole, there was not as wide a disparity in funding between white and black schools as the modern reader might suspect. Yes, there were local instances where black students were grievously harmed because of funding differences. In Duplin County, even though the local board was ostensibly following the 1885 law, the black schools did not even receive the meager six cents per student to which they were entitled under the two-thirds *per capita* distribution.[167] But, up to 1900, the statewide numbers taken as a whole show an unexpectedly small gap between the disbursements to white and black schools. Using per-pupil expenditures in North Carolina, Morgan Kousser concluded that "[w]hites and blacks shared scholastic poverty relatively equally until 1900."[168] Similarly, looking at various data on expenditures and apportionment of county school funds, Frenise Logan found that the differences before 1900 "were comparatively slight."[169]

It is what happened after 1900, though — that is, after the White Supremacy Campaigns — which demonstrates how the tides shifted dramatically against black students and in favor of the white schools. From the outset of the 1901 legislative session, there was a legislative push for an amendment to the state constitution that would have resurrected the idea of segregating tax dollars for schools based on race.[170] None of these

---

166. 1885 N.C. Sess. Laws 218, 221, ch. 141, § 6. To quote in greater detail, the provision set out that money should be apportioned "as shall be just to the white and colored races, without discrimination in favor of or to the prejudice of either race, due regard being paid to the cost of keeping up the public schools for both races." Id. For a sampling of the subsequent uses of this language in the following decades, see the statutes listed with this 1885 law for Raleigh in Table 1.

167. Leloudis, supra note 141, at 122–123.

168. J. Morgan Kousser, Progressivism — For Middle-Class Whites Only: North Carolina Education, 1880–1910, 46 *Journal of Southern History* 169, 179 (1980) (hereinafter "North Carolina Education").

169. Logan, supra note 92, at 140. See also Prather, supra note 140, at 43 ("Evidence indicates that the discrepancy between Negro and white public school opportunities in the state was not so wide in 1900 as it was later.").

170. Two School Funds: To Submit a Constitutional Amendment, *Farmer and Mechanic* (Raleigh, N.C.), Mar. 5, 1901, at 8 (Senate Judiciary Committee voted unani-

4. DE JURE DISCRIMINATION IN NORTH CAROLINA | 141

amendments passed, despite strong legislative support, largely because of the opposition of Governor Charles B. Aycock, who went so far as to threaten to resign if such an amendment were passed.[171] More consequential than the legislative debates, however, was the fact that between 1900 and 1910, the inequity and disparity in the funding of the white and black schools grew exponentially.

With regard to the disbursements of school funds, the statutory language starting in 1897 actually appeared to rein in the discretion over spending by the school boards. The school board's discretion over the final one third of the school funds was eliminated in 1897 and in subsequent

---

mously in favor of amendment). The proposed amendment reported out of the committee stated that nothing in the constitutional text "herein shall prohibit the people of any race . . . from levying a special tax for educational purposes of that race, if a majority of the qualified voters of that race" shall approve such a tax at the polls. Id. (quoting proposed amendment).

171. Oliver H. Orr, Jr., *Charles Brantley Aycock* 208–209 (1961).

Morgan Kousser has argued that Aycock's motive in opposing the proposed amendment was not about fairness for the black population but was, rather, Aycock's concern that it would endanger the recently adopted constitutional amendment imposing a literacy test through possible federal judicial scrutiny. Kousser, North Carolina Education, supra note 168, at 185–186. Kousser relies on Aycock's arguments to the General Assembly about this possibility. Id. at 185. Supporting his point as to motives, Kousser notes that Aycock was aware "that the white subsidy to black schools was very small," id. at 186 n.31, the implication being that Aycock knew and privately approved of the lack of financial support to the black schools.

Even apart from the reality that individuals can have multiple motives, I think that Kousser is not fair to Aycock here. Aycock did not have to step in front of the proverbial legislative train that was pushing for the passage of this proposed amendment. To oppose a clear majority of his fellow Democrats and to threaten to resign if the amendment passed the General Assembly made little political sense, especially over the issue of race in 1901. That posture is not one that a politician would take lightly. But, moreover, I think that Kousser misreads Aycock as to his knowledge about tax expenditures as between white and black schools. A subsequent event is instructive. In 1909, when school administrator Charles Coon was harshly criticized by the *News and Observer* and other newspapers as having tarnished the white citizens of North Carolina after a conference paper Coon wrote demonstrated, through calculations, how black tax dollars were being siphoned away from black schools so that the black schools did not even receive the tax receipts from black taxpayers, Aycock came to Coon's defense. Aycock personally visited Josephus Daniels of the *News and Observer* and criticized Daniels because Aycock knew that Coon's statistics were correct and that not all black tax dollars were even going to the black public schools. John H. Haley, *Charles N. Hunter and Race Relations in North Carolina* 184 (1987). The episode suggests that Aycock was, indeed, concerned about the inequities in the state's school finance system between the schools for the different races.

years in favor of a distribution "to give each school in their district, white and colored, the same length of school term, as nearly as may be each year."[172] Given that the 1897 law was passed by the fusionist legislature, that directive certainly reads as if greater fairness was the goal and that was certainly the understanding of many individuals at the time. Charles B. Aycock, who supported the 1897 law and was governor when the similar 1901 law was passed, argued that this new method of apportionment was more equitable than the previous method.[173]

This statutory language which appeared to be equitable proved to be of limited import, however, because the difference as to the funding of white and black schools grew markedly after 1900. The discrimination was "almost universal, flagrant, and increasing."[174] Although the years used and the particular statistics generated by scholars do not always align and allow for precise comparisons, the various calculations of historians are in basic agreement. Morgan Kousser's calculations of statewide *per capita* expenditures by race over the relevant five-year periods shows the shift toward inequality:

YEAR	BLACK	WHITE
1896–1900	$1.14	$1.22
1906–1910	$1.49	$3.70[175]

---

172. 1897 N.C. Sess. Laws 149, 151, ch. 108, § 11. Under the fusionist 1897 school statute, the county board of education was to disburse funds to the various school districts on a *per capita* basis, id. § 10, and it was the district school committee that was "to give each school in their district, white and colored, the same length of school term, as nearly as may be each year." Id. § 11.

Under the short-lived 1899 school law, the local school officials were to "distribute and apportion the school money of their townships so as to give each school in their township for each race the same length of school term as nearly as may be each year." 1899 N.C. Sess. Laws 903, 909, ch. 732, § 25. The 1901 school law language gave the duties to the county board of education to disburse the school fund to "the various townships in said county per capita" and "to distribute and apportion the school money of each township so as to give to each school in said township for each race the same length of school term, as nearly as may be each year." 1901 N.C. Sess. Laws 45, 53, ch. 4, § 24.

173. Orr, supra note 171, at 210. See also Harlan, supra note 122, at 64 ("Aycock alone among leading Democrats had supported the local tax campaign to the bitter end.").

174. Harlan, supra note 122, at 269.

175. Kousser, North Carolina Education, supra note 168, at 178.

4. DE JURE DISCRIMINATION IN NORTH CAROLINA | 143

Similarly, Robert Margo's calculations (using 1950 dollars) of per pupil expenditures for circa 1890 and circa 1910 show a relative parity between the races that gives way to a wide racial divergence:

YEAR	BLACK	WHITE
c. 1890	$7.75	$7.67
c. 1910	$9.28	$17.25[176]

Other statistics on the gap between white schools and black schools during this period tell a similar story. James Leloudis calculated that in 1899, black teachers in the state earned an average of $68 per year while white teachers earned an average of $88 per year, but that by 1913, the relative amounts had changed dramatically: "Blacks received $127 a year—about half of the $252 paid to whites."[177] As Louis Harlan argued, "The system of segregation, far from being a burden, was a convenient means of economizing at the expense of Negro children."[178]

At the time it was occurring, this discrimination in expenditures was well known by many in state government, including Superintendent of Public Instruction James Y. Joyner. Indeed, the inequity was a conscious choice by white school leaders, and Joyner advocated for it behind the scenes. In a 1903 letter to the superintendent of the schools in Greene County, Joyner wrote:

> The negro schools can be run for much less expense and should be. In most places it does not take more than one fourth as much to run the negro schools as it does to run the white schools for about the same number of children. The salaries paid teachers are very properly much smaller, the houses are cheaper, the number of teachers smaller.... [I]f quietly managed, the negroes will give no trouble about it.[179]

---

176. Robert A. Margo, *Race and Schooling in the South, 1880–1950: An Economic History* 21 (1990).
177. Leloudis, supra note 141, at 187.
178. Harlan, supra note 122, at 15.
179. James Y. Joyner to Supt. J.E. Debnam, Feb. 3, 1903, quoted in Kousser, North Carolina Education, supra note 168, at 186.

The last sentence of this quotation, stating that "negroes will give no trouble" or challenge the discriminatory funding system, is a reminder that this letter is a product of its time, being only three years after the 1900 campaign. This attitude permeated the state's educational system. The text of the law had not changed appreciably, but white attitudes after the White Supremacy Campaigns of 1898 and 1900 had changed, and this shift resulted in dramatically different treatment for black residents of the state within a decade.[180]

---

180. It should be noted that a similar trend occurred with regard to the balance of payments as between tax revenues and the subsequent disbursement of those funds because by 1910, black schools were essentially operating under the segregated funding regime that was contemplated by the short-lived Dortch Act and the subsequent unsuccessful constitutional amendment. It is clear that white tax dollars were helping to subsidize black schools up until 1900. Kousser, North Carolina Education, supra note 168, at 183. The General Assembly wanted to allow for increased support of the schools through local taxation, though, and that approach ultimately carried the day and was upheld by the N.C. Supreme Court in *Collie v. Commissioners of Franklin County*, 145 N.C. 170 (1907). The shift in what Morgan Kousser termed the "black balance of payments"—the amount that black schools received compared to the black population's tax burden—is striking and counterintuitive to modern readers because virtually no white tax dollars were going to black schools by 1910. And it was just as striking and counterintuitive when Charles Coon, the superintendent of the Wilson County Schools, first pointed out this discrepancy in 1909 in a paper presented at an education conference in Atlanta. Charles Coon, Public Taxation and Negro Schools, in *Proceedings of the Twelfth Conference for Education in the South* 157 (1909). Using estimates, what Coon showed was that by using current tax rates and the appropriate percentages of figures such as the assessed value of black property, state appropriations, poll taxes and the like, the black schools did not even receive the amount that blacks had paid into the various state and local school funds. Coon calculated that North Carolina was spending $402,658 on the black schools, including both state and local funds, id. at 159, but that blacks had paid approximately $429,197 into these school funds, a difference of over $26,000. Id. at 162–163. Coon's conclusions that whites were not funding black schools have largely been confirmed. In a study using county-by-county data, Morgan Kousser demonstrated that after 1900, the decrease in the proportion of the disbursements to black schools was so dramatic that "the black balance of payments may well have been reduced to little or nothing by 1910." Kousser, North Carolina Education, supra note 168, at 194. Focusing on the economic incidence of property taxes in North Carolina—that is, on property owners shifting the tax onto renters of property and onto workers—Jonathan Pritchett likewise calculated that if as little as 30 percent of the property tax burden had been shifted from owners to renters and workers, "the tax burden on blacks would have exceeded public expenditures for [black schools]." Jonathan B. Pritchett, The Burden of Negro Schooling: Tax Incidence and Racial Redistribution in Postbellum North Carolina, 49 *Journal of Economic History* 966, 973 (1989).

In sum, one reason for the relative dearth of consequential Jim Crow statutes immediately after 1900 can be seen with regard to the funding of schools, because the funding disparities between black and white schools increased dramatically without new statutory language to accomplish this goal. Relative racial parity during the last decade of the nineteenth century gave way to the racial disparity in funding after the turn of the century. Discrimination by government was accomplished under the existing statutory framework.

B. Voting and Disenfranchisement

Of all of the states in the South up to 1900, North Carolina was perhaps the most distinctive in terms of its politics, political parties, and access to the franchise. Compared to the recurrent violence, intimidation, and fraud in the other Southern states, North Carolina had fewer problems on these fronts prior to 1898. Morgan Kousser concluded that the state's "political system was perhaps the most democratic in the late nineteenth-century South."[181] Part of the reason for this difference was the continued strength of the Republican Party in the state, even after the end of Reconstruction, and the emergence of the Populist Party in the 1890s. North Carolina was the only Southern state where the Democrats lost power between the end of Reconstruction and the turn of the century, when the "fusion" of Republicans and Populists won control of both houses of the General Assembly from 1895 to 1899 and, with Republican Daniel Russell's 1896 electoral victory, the governorship from 1897 to 1901. But another reason for the uniqueness of North Carolina was the level of participation by blacks in the voting booth and through elective office up until the late 1890s. Despite the intermittent enactment of election laws by Democratic legislatures aimed at curtailing participation by blacks and, concomitantly, Republican or Populist whites, the level of participation by blacks did not drop precipitously until the White Supremacy Campaigns of 1898 and 1900. The passage of the earlier election laws to diminish the number of black voters but the relatively high levels of continued black registration and voting in the late 1880s and early 1890s suggest that the implementa-

---

181. Kousser, *Southern Politics*, supra note 72, at 183. This is not to say that North Carolina's elections were free of fraud and vote tampering. On that subject, see Eric Anderson, *Race and Politics in North Carolina, 1872–1901*, at 71–72, 160–161 (1981).

tion of these laws by the local officials was not as racially discriminatory as it could have been and, thus, that the virulent racism which came later had not taken hold among white election officials. The other side of the coin is that the fair implementation of the literacy requirement imposed by the 1900 constitutional amendment should not have decimated black registration and voting in the way it did given the black literacy rates of the time and, therefore, it was the shift in the racial temperament among the white population that led to such discriminatory enforcement of the voting requirements. Illiterate and poor whites were certainly affected by the literacy requirement and not necessarily saved by the amendment's grandfather clause, but there is little doubt that the discriminatory overenforcement against blacks was of a different character and of greater harm. With respect to voting, the application of the laws was of far greater importance than the legal text and the application, in turn, was a function of the societal and cultural winds at the turn of the century.

While some number of free blacks voted up to 1835 in North Carolina, after the Civil War, the first step toward the registration of black voters was the federal Reconstruction Act of March 2, 1867.[182] Following the dictates of this law, the initial registration of the former slaves in 1867 was conducted by the federal military authorities, who established 170 registration precincts in North Carolina. By October, 71,657 freedmen were registered to vote for delegates to the constitutional convention.[183] The subsequent election resulted in 15 black delegates to the 1868 convention.[184]

The 1868 North Carolina Constitution drafted at the convention established that suffrage for males did not depend upon race and, for almost three decades, blacks were active participants in the state's political sys-

---

182. 14 Stat. 428, 429, ch. 153, § 5 (1867) (conditioning readmission of rebel states to union on the formation of a constitution "framed by a convention of delegates elected by the male citizens of said State, twenty-one years old and upward, of whatever race, color, or previous condition"). On voting by free blacks up until 1835, see John Hope Franklin, *The Free Negro in North Carolina: 1790–1860*, at 105–109 (1943).

183. Report of Major General Canby, Commanding Second Military District, Oct. 24, 1867, in Report of the Secretary of War, Part I, in House of Representatives Ex. Doc. No. 1, 40th Cong., 2d Sess. at 299, 301 (1867).

184. Logan, supra note 92, at 8.

4. DE JURE DISCRIMINATION IN NORTH CAROLINA | 147

tem.[185] There were 20 freedmen elected to the General Assembly in the fall elections of 1868.[186] Indeed, there were never less than five black members of every General Assembly held between 1868 and 1897,[187] and there were even four blacks elected to the state House of Representatives in the notorious 1898 campaign.[188] Four blacks from North Carolina were elected to the U.S. Congress in the nineteenth century from the gerrymandered Second District, the last one being George Henry White, who served until 1901.[189] He would be the last African American member of Congress from North Carolina for 90 years. There were also significant numbers of black officials at the local level in the decades after the Civil War. Importantly, this local office-holding continued to some degree even after the enactment of the 1877 statute that eliminated the election of county commissioners and gave the Democratic-controlled legislature the power to appoint—directly or indirectly—local officials.[190] While these numbers are impressive relative to the other Southern states during this period, the claim of "Negro domination" made by the Democrats in the 1898 campaign was an absolute canard because five (1895) and nine (1897) members of the General Assembly have to be compared to the 170 total seats in the two legislative chambers. That is not "Negro rule" or even a significant

---

185. N.C. Const. of 1868, art. VI, sec. 1 ("Every male person ... twenty one years old or upward, who shall have resided in this State twelve months next preceeding [sic] the election, and thirty days in the county, in which he offers to vote, shall be deemed an elector.").

186. Elizabeth Balanoff, Negro Legislators in the North Carolina General Assembly, July, 1868—February, 1872, 49 *North Carolina Historical Review* 22, 22 (1972).

187. Benjamin R. Justesen, "The Class of '83": Black Watershed in the North Carolina General Assembly, 86 *North Carolina Historical Review* 282, 283–284 (2009) (includes figures on African Americans in General Assembly up through 1892 election); Allen W. Trelease, Fusion Legislatures of 1895 and 1897: A Roll-Call Analysis of the North Carolina House of Representatives, 57 *North Carolina Historical Review* 280, 281 (1980) (includes figures on blacks in General Assembly from 1894 and 1896 elections).

188. Helen G. Edmonds, *The Negro and Fusion Politics in North Carolina: 1894–1901*, at 100 (1951).

189. See generally Anderson, supra note 181.

190. 1876–77 N.C. Sess. Laws 226, 227–28, ch. 141, §§ 4–5 (statute which gave the General Assembly the power to appoint local justices of the peace who, in turn, elected county commissioners). See Logan, supra note 92, at 51 (describing the anger of "mountain whites," who acceded to the loss of local self-government in order to prevent "Negro rule" in the eastern counties, when Democratic legislature selected "thirty Negro justices of the peace for some of the eastern counties").

and meaningful political bloc. There were many hundreds of local officials—from federal postmasters to local magistrates—but nothing that would equate to Negro domination in eastern North Carolina. These statistics on office holding, however, are a testament to the presence of some number of blacks in voting booths up to the end of the nineteenth century.

It is unfortunately one of the historic features of American democracy that political parties often attempt to protect their majorities by controlling who votes, and that was the case when the redeemer Democrats returned to power after 1870 in North Carolina. One of the primary methods for controlling who votes was the discretion given to registrars and election judges.[191] Under an 1877 statute, registrars and "four judges or inspectors of election" were to be selected by the justices of the peace for each county (who were appointed by the Democratic General Assembly in Raleigh) and the registrars and judges were to decide all challenges to voters listed in the registration books, and the challenges could be made by any registered voter.[192] And, on election day, the election judges "shall in no case receive the vote of any person unless they shall be satisfied that such person is in all respects qualified and entitled to vote."[193] All of these features of the statute provided a potential means by which some people in the state—i.e., blacks in the east—could be prevented from entering the polling place.

The first significant attempt to curtail black voting in North Carolina after the Civil War came with the passage of the election law of 1889 by the Democratic legislature.[194] This statute had several provisions that were intended to make voting more difficult, such as requiring a "separate and distinct" voting place for federal offices "at such distance from the polling place for State and county officers as the judges of the election may designate."[195] Another section of the law, though, seemed to be aimed at Republican voters in general and blacks in particular: "No registration shall be valid unless it specifies as near as may be the age, occupation, place of

---

191. Kousser, *Southern Politics*, supra note 72, at 48 (recognizing "the amount of discretion granted to the registrars").
192. 1876–77 N.C. Sess. Laws 516, 517–518, ch. 275, §§ 5, 8–9.
193. Id. § 63.
194. 1889 N.C. Sess. Laws 289, ch. 287.
195. Id. § 8.

birth and place of residence of the elector...."[196] For many former slaves, their exact age was unknown. And, in an era when many streets and rural roads were not denominated or numbered, the lack of specificity about one's place of residence was a potential hurdle for many blacks in the face of a hostile registrar.[197] It was also the case that blacks, overall, were more likely to be laborers and less likely to be owners of real property, and that combination meant that blacks moved more than whites and was another reason why requiring specificity about a "place of residence" was a hurdle for blacks.

The 1889 statute, undoubtedly, prevented some blacks from registering to vote, but the levels of black participation at the polls remained relatively high in North Carolina until the cultural tide turned in the White Supremacy Campaigns of 1898 and 1900. In the most detailed study of nineteenth-century voting in the South, Morgan Kousser calculated the following estimates for voting by black males in North Carolina in the following years:

YEAR (AND POLITICAL CONTEST)	ESTIMATE OF VOTING BY BLACK MALES
1880 (presidential)	83 percent[198]
1880 (gubernatorial)	86 percent[199]
1884 (gubernatorial)	98 percent[200]
1888 (gubernatorial)	68 percent[201]
1892 (gubernatorial)	64 percent[202]
1896 (gubernatorial)	87 percent[203]

196. Id. § 3.
197. Kousser, *Southern Politics*, supra note 72, at 48; Woodward, supra note 131, at 55–57.
198. Kousser, *Southern Politics*, supra note 72, at 15.
199. Id. at 28.
200. Id. at 183.
201. Id.
202. Id.
203. Id. at 42.

There was a sizeable drop in black participation in 1888, but that was prior to the passage of the 1889 law, and the 1892 percentage was not significantly different from the 1888 estimate. It would appear that the 1889 law itself had minimal impact upon the estimated levels of black voting.

What is apparent from these estimates, however, is that there was an increase in black participation in 1896 following the repeal of the 1889 law by the fusion legislature.[204] With an estimated 87 percent of black males voting in the 1896 governor's race, there was a sizeable increase in black participation over previous elections. It came on the heels of the 1895 enactment of an electoral law which was intended to make elections honest and to keep the voting booth open irrespective of race or political party. Kousser concluded that this 1895 law "was probably the fairest and most democratic election law in the post-Reconstruction South."[205] The statute made many changes, but five with the largest impact on black access to the polls stand out: (1) clerks in each county were to appoint persons approved by each political party as registrars and judges of election so that there would be multiple registrars and judges from the different parties present to oversee registration and voting;[206] (2) the inability of a voter to specify age and place of residence would not prevent the registration of that voter unless the person declined to answer the questions;[207] (3) the presence of a name in the precinct's registration book gave that person the presumption of being properly registered;[208] (4) ballots—which, during this era, were provided by political parties and candidates and not

---

204. 1895 N.C. Sess. Laws 211, ch.159.
205. Kousser, *Southern Politics*, supra note 72, at 187.
206. 1895 N.C. Sess. Laws 211, 212, ch. 159, § 7 ("[T]he clerks in their several counties shall appoint, upon the written recommendation or approval of the chairman of the state executive committee of each political party of the state, one citizen and qualified voter from each of said political parties of and for each election precinct . . . as registrars of election in their respective precincts. And . . . the clerk shall appoint, upon the recommendation of the respective chairman aforesaid, one citizen and qualified voter of each party . . . as judges of election . . . .").
207. 1895 N.C. Sess. Laws 211, 216, ch. 159, § 10 ("[B]ut no registration shall be invalidated because of a failure to specify the age and place of residence, etc., unless it shall appear that, upon the registrar properly questioning the elector, he declined to answer the questions pertaining to these matters.").
208. 1895 N.C. Sess. Laws 211, 216, ch. 159, § 12 ("[T]he entry of the name, age, residence, and date of registration of any person by the registrar, upon the registration book of the precinct, shall be presumptive evidence of the regularity of such registration . . . .").

4. *DE JURE* DISCRIMINATION IN NORTH CAROLINA | 151

by election officials—could be of different colors and could contain party symbols in order to ease voting for the large segment of the population for whom reading and writing were difficult;[209] and (5) while there would be two separate ballots for different offices and two separate ballot boxes for each of these ballots, the fact that a ballot was deposited in the wrong box did not prevent that vote from being counted.[210] Most of these provisions worked to benefit illiterate voters and, thus, many black voters. The first change in this list helped to make the registration and voting processes fair, because the presence of representatives from all political parties would ensure the equitable application of the laws.

What occurred in North Carolina after the 1896 election is a lesson about the limits of law in the face of violence, fraud, and a cultural shift by the majority-white population to an overt and unabashed enmity toward blacks. If physical violence and intimidation keep voters from going to the polls on election day, the application of the law becomes irrelevant. Continued intimidation and outright fraud, as in the 1900 election, demonstrate how extralegal means produced the political disempowerment of an entire race. And, after the enactment of the constitutional amendment, the discriminatory enforcement of the literacy test effectively disenfranchised blacks for over half a century in North Carolina.

Even with the fair election laws on the books in 1898, the suppression of some black votes in such a closely divided election through violence and intimidation led to a Democratic victory and the capture of both houses of the legislature. Many Populists returned to the Democratic fold, and the combination of a solid white front and the intimidation of blacks was enough to shift the political balance. Morgan Kousser was unable to calculate estimates of voting participation for 1898 by race or political party,[211] but the Democrat in the one statewide race, for a seat on the

---

209. 1895 N.C. Sess. Laws 211, 218, § 18 ("All ballots shall be printed or written, or partly printed and partly written, on paper, which may be of any color, and may, or may not, have thereon a device.").

210. 1895 N.C. Sess. Laws 211, 218–19, ch. 159, §§ 18–20. Section 20 stated: "Any ballot found in the wrong box shall be presumed to have been deposited there by mistake of the officers of election, and unless such presumption shall be rebutted, the ballot shall be counted."

211. Kousser made his estimates using county-by-county voting figures for statewide elections. In 1898, there was only one statewide race, for a seat on the N.C. Supreme

N.C. Supreme Court, only garnered 52.8 percent of the vote while overall turnout was calculated to be 84.2 percent of the registered adult males.[212]

The Democrats took advantage of the recapture of the General Assembly in the subsequent 1899 legislative session and pushed to finish off what they had started during the political campaign: the evisceration of blacks' political power and enforced racial subjugation. The Democrats enacted a segregation law for railroads and steamboats,[213] proposed an amendment to the state constitution imposing a literacy requirement for voting that would be sent to the state's voters[214] and, to ensure the success of the amendment and the Democratic Party at the next election, passed a new restrictive election law.[215] The election law replaced *in toto* the existing statutes, and it was intended to make it harder for blacks, in particular, to register and then cast ballots that would count. The most important changes were: (1) local election officials were to be appointed by a state board of election whose members were selected by the (Democratic) General Assembly;[216] (2) the existing voter rolls were to be purged and an entirely new registration was mandated;[217] (3) registration itself was made more difficult by allowing the registrar to require the potential voter "to prove his identity or age and residence by the testimony of *at least* two electors under oath" and to ask "any other questions which may be regarded by the registrar as material upon the question of the identify and qualification of the said applicant;"[218] and (4) voting for the various offices was to be by five separate ballots, with ballots of the same size and with no party symbols or designations, and there were to be five separate ballot boxes into which the ballots were to go but if a ballot was found in the wrong box, it was not to be counted.[219]

With the requirement that all voters reregister before the next election, the Populist Party created a campaign in 1900 to assist black voters in the

---

Court, but Kousser was unable to obtain the county-by-county vote totals for this race. Kousser, *Southern Politics*, supra note 72, at 194 n.19.

212. Id. at 188.
213. 1899 N.C. Sess. Laws 539, ch. 384.
214. 1899 N.C. Sess. Laws 341, ch. 218.
215. 1899 N.C. Sess. Laws 658, ch. 507.
216. Id. at 659, §§ 4–5.
217. Id. at 661, § 11.
218. Id. (emphasis added).
219. Id. at 668–670, §§ 26–29.

4. DE JURE DISCRIMINATION IN NORTH CAROLINA | 153

eastern part of the state. These efforts included information packets for voters about registration rules as well as draft affidavits for use if blacks were denied the ability to register by an election official.[220] In the eastern part of the state, there was intimidation and even violence. A Populist supporter from Greene County wrote to U.S. Senator Marion Butler that the "only Populist who had taken a stand against Democratic tactics had been shot and seriously wounded in a fight with a Democrat."[221] However, an indicator of the impact of the Populists' campaign to monitor the re-registration of voters was that "at least forty five" registrars were arrested prior to the 1900 election for failing to abide by the registration laws.[222]

The returns for the 1900 election show reduced levels of black voting, but what is particularly evident is that the virulent racism within the Democratic Party led to blatant fraud in some counties. According to Kousser's analysis of the county-by-county votes in the race for governor and on the constitutional amendment, the only measurable black voting on those two matters was for the Democratic candidate for governor, Charles B. Aycock, and in support of the proposed constitutional amendment that would impose a literacy test. Kousser's calculations reveal the outright fraud: (1) the estimated percentage of the black vote was zero for both the Populist-Republican gubernatorial candidate as well as in opposition to the constitutional amendment[223] and (2) the estimated percentage of the black vote for the Democratic Party gubernatorial candidate was 67 percent and for the constitutional amendment that would disenfranchise many blacks was 73 percent.[224] That is, using estimates for adult black males, the county-by-county vote totals suggest that blacks voted overwhelmingly to disenfranchise themselves. Helen Edmonds, in her book on fusion politics, reprinted the county vote totals from 1900: Out of 2,969 total votes on the amendment in New Hanover County, home to Wilmington and a majority-black population, there were only 2 votes against the amendment, while in Scotland County, in the southeastern part of the

---

220. Crow and Durden, supra note 100, at 152.
221. Id. at 153.
222. Id. (citing 3 Joseph G. de Roulhac Hamilton, *History of North Carolina: North Carolina Since 1860*, at 313 (1919)).
223. Kousser, *Southern Politics*, supra note 72, at 194.
224. Id.

state, out of 1,810 votes, there were only 7 votes against the amendment.[225] The idea that blacks supported their own disenfranchisement and that virtually none opposed it was "simple fraud."[226] Although it is evident that some local Democratic election officials aided and abetted this farce, these results did not come about because of the application of any law. Even if the 1899 election law was intended to be a hindrance to minority voting, the vote totals from 1900 are only evidence of illegality.

The operation of the constitutional amendment was a different matter. The intent behind the literacy test and required poll tax was to severely restrict black voting. Strangely enough, though, the political leaders of the time never anticipated that the amendment would result in the removal of virtually all blacks from the voting rolls. The amendment's literacy provision required that the person seeking to register to vote "be able to read and write any section of the Constitution in the English language."[227] The U.S. Census Bureau may not have employed rigorous standards, but it calculated the illiteracy rate of voting-age colored males in North Carolina to be 53.1 percent in 1900[228] and the illiteracy rate of voting-age Negro males to be 38.6 percent in 1910.[229] Even if those figures are not precisely accurate, the numbers make clear that the percentage of literate blacks in North Carolina was well above zero.

Legislators of both parties believed that some number of blacks would still be able to register under the literacy provision. The Democratic Party leader, Furnifold Simmons, believed that around 30,000 blacks would still

---

225. Edmonds, supra note 188, at 233.
226. Id. at 193.
227. Amendment of 1900 to N.C. Const. of 1868, art. VI, sec. 4.
228. 1 Bureau of the Census, *Census Reports, Twelfth Census of the United States, Taken in the Year 1900: Population*, Part I, at ccv (1901). "Colored" here included persons "of negro descent, Chinese, Japanese, and Indians." Id. The Report also calculated that the number of voting-age colored males in North Carolina was 128,315, of which 128,315 were "Negro." Id. at cxcix.
229. 1 Bureau of the Census, *Thirteenth Census of the United States Taken in the Year 1910: Population* at 1258 (1913). In the 1910 census, "Negro" was separated out from "Indian, Chinese, and Japanese" but who, as a combined group, had an illiteracy rate of 51.4 percent. Id. The 1910 Census also calculated that the number of voting-age Negro males in North Carolina was 146,752, while the combined number of voting-age "Indians, Chinese, and Japanese" was 1,771. Id. at 1044.

4. DE JURE DISCRIMINATION IN NORTH CAROLINA | 155

be able to vote.[230] The Democratic Speaker of the N.C. House, Henry G. Connor, anticipated that at least 25,000 blacks would still be able to register.[231] Republican U.S. Senator Jeter Pritchard was more optimistic about his party's membership, because he thought that 60,000 blacks would be able to satisfy the standard and register.[232] But, in applying the literacy provision, those predictions turned out to be wrong. Michael Perman has noted the conundrum here: "The disenfranchisers had fully intended to cut the eligible voting population. What they had not anticipated, however, was the extent to which the electorate would be reduced."[233]

What those estimates on black registration by Simmons and Connor and Pritchard assume is that the registrars would be administering the literacy test fairly. Even among the disenfranchisers, there seems to have been an implicit belief that literate blacks would be allowed to register. Consider the problem of registration and the administration of the literacy test as set out by Morgan Kousser:

> [E]ven if the supervisors managed to guarantee impartial administrative practices in registration—a difficult task, since registration took place at myriads of different places and times—a large portion of the Negroes and lower-class whites would be disfranchised by the literacy and poll tax qualifications.[234]

Although Kousser's statement here is correct, the flip side of that claim is accurate as well. That is, if fairness by the registrars was hard to guarantee because of the diverse locations and large number of election officials, the uniform unfairness that actually occurred is an oddity, too. There were

---

230. Richard L. Watson, Jr., Furnifold M. Simmons and the Politics of White Supremacy, in *Race, Class, and Politics in Southern History* 126, 137 (Jeffrey J. Crow et al. eds., 1989) (Simmons concluded that 25,000 to 30,000 blacks would be able to vote because literate, while more than 2,000 might vote pursuant to the amendment's grandfather clause because they were lineal descendants of free Negroes who voted in North Carolina or other states prior to 1867). U.S. Senator Marion Butler, a Populist, believed that about 50,000 literate blacks would still be qualified to vote under the amendment. Id. at 138.

231. Gregory P. Downs, University Men, Social Science, and White Supremacy in North Carolina, 75 *Journal of Southern History* 267, 294 (2009).

232. Failure to Wrong the South, *Wilmington Messenger*, Jan. 10, 1901, at 2.

233. Michael Perman, *Struggle for Mastery: Disfranchisement in the South, 1888–1910*, at 313 (2001).

234. Kousser, *Southern Politics*, supra note 72, at 33.

certainly blacks who did not even attempt to register once the pattern was set, but there would have been an initial wave of literate black citizens who appeared before the registrars and were denied the ability to register for no valid reason. The refusal to register black males in North Carolina occurred at essentially one point in time and uniformly, as well, from one end of the state to the other. And what happened in North Carolina is an oddity relative to what happened in the other Southern states.

It is the disjuncture between the legal text and the operation of the law, as well as the chasm between the assumptions of the politicians and the results on the ground, which show the impact of the racial contagion spawned by the White Supremacy Campaigns. After the constitutional amendment went into effect, the percentage of blacks registered to vote in North Carolina was estimated to be 4.6 percent in both 1902 and 1904.[235] But, in the next statewide election, the estimated percentage of black votes in the 1904 governor's race was effectively zero.[236] The amendment to the state constitution, which simply required that the person seeking to register to vote "be able to read and write any section of the Constitution in the English language,"[237] was applied so as to take away the vote from the entire black male population. There was no connection between the literacy rates of blacks between 1900 and 1920 and the virtually complete removal of these citizens from the voting booths of North Carolina.

The gap between the constitutional text and the operation of that text is also wider in North Carolina relative to the other Southern states that disenfranchised black voters. Compare the effective black voting percentage in North Carolina's next statewide election after the amendment went into effect, zero, with others in the region. Although the precise language of the disenfranchising amendments differed, there was at least measurable black voting in other Southern states in the elections following adoption of their amendments: in Mississippi, 2 percent of blacks voted in the next presidential election, 10 percent voted in Virginia in the gubernatorial election, and Louisiana saw voting by Republicans (composed of a large percentage of blacks) in 1900 of 3.6 percent in the governor's race and 4.4 percent in the presidential race.[238]

---

235. Kousser, *Southern Politics*, supra note 72, at 61.
236. Id. at 194.
237. Amendment of 1900 to N.C. Const. of 1868, art. VI, sec. 4.
238. Kousser, *Southern Politics*, supra note 72, at 143–145, 163, 174, 180.

The decimation of black voting in North Carolina, from one end of the state to the other, set it apart. The ballot box stuffing and fraudulent returns of previous decades were simply replaced with another type of disregard and disrespect for the law, one in which law was applied through the lens of the white culture's views on race and what was necessary to maintain its racial supremacy. And those views on race were certainly brought to a fever pitch by the White Supremacy Campaigns of 1898 and 1900.

C. Black Participation on Juries

Service on juries is an important part of citizens' participation in government, both in terms of the application of law to cases and in educating citizens about what law(s) should exist. It was clear in the eighteenth and nineteenth centuries that the jury was "an essential democratic institution because it was a means by which citizens could engage in self-government."[239] The presence of blacks on jury lists and in the jury box in North Carolina varied from county to county but, as was the case in education and with voting rights, their participation in the jury system declined precipitously after 1900 and not because of any statutory change. There is consensus that, starting around 1895, blacks' access to the jury box "was sharply curtailed across the South, despite dogged efforts by activists and frequent legal challenges."[240] For North Carolina, the questions are whether that drop occurred immediately after 1900 and how thoroughgoing the exclusion from the jury box was. The answers to these questions are less clear because no rigorous, systematic studies of minority participation on juries exist. While I think that there was a decided shift after 1900, I have found anecdotal evidence of at least some inclusion of blacks on jury venires in a limited number of counties in the two decades after 1900, so the exclusion from the jury box was not as complete as it was from the voting booth.

In North Carolina, the statutes both before and after the Civil War which set out the method for establishing a jury list were race neutral on their face. The 1855 revisal stated that jury lists were to be composed of

---

239. Vikram David Amar, Jury Service as Political Participation Akin to Voting, 80 *Cornell Law Review* 203, 218 (1995).

240. Thomas Ward Frampton, The Jim Crow Jury, 71 *Vanderbilt Law Review* 1593, 1595 (2018).

landowners who "are well qualified to act as jurors."[241] Absent an individual whose racial lineage was hidden, it is almost certainly the case that no free Negroes, even freeholders, were on the antebellum jury lists because the judges had quite a bit of discretion as to which freeholders were "well qualified"[242] per the statute. Another law in the *Revised Code* mandated that "Negroes, Indians, and persons of mixed blood . . . whether bond or free" could not be witnesses in court except "against each other,"[243] which likewise suggests that free Negroes would not have been considered "well qualified" to sit in the jury box.

With the end of the Civil War, change—of a sort—came to North Carolina. When Chief Justice Salmon P. Chase began riding circuit in the former Confederate states, he issued an order that federal juries were to be chosen without regard to race. Chase ordered that in the District of North Carolina, for the selection of grand and petit jurors, there was to be "no distinction, on account of color or race, among citizens otherwise qualified to serve."[244] Change was brought to the North Carolina state courts by the command of the Second Military District. On May 30, 1867, General Orders No. 32 was issued by General Daniel E. Sickles and, in section two, it mandated that jury lists in North and South Carolina were to include "[a]ll citizens assessed for taxes and who shall have paid taxes for the current year."[245] Governor Jonathan Worth, in a letter to the

---

241. Revised Code of North Carolina ch. 31, § 25 (1855).

242. Here, in terms of jury participation being somewhat analogous to voting, it is worth remembering that free blacks were denied the ability to vote for members of the senate or the house of commons with the ratification of the 1835 amendments to the state constitution. See Amend. 1835, art. I, sec. 3. Aside from the jury lists, it has been suggested that the first blacks empaneled on a jury were in a Massachusetts trial in 1860. Leon F. Litwack, *North of Slavery: The Negro in the Free States, 1790–1860*, at 94 (1961).

243. Revised Code of North Carolina ch. 107, § 71 (1855). Testimony by "a negro, Indian, and of all persons of mixed blood" could be used by the state when the criminal defendant was "a negro, Indian, or person of mixed blood." Id.

244. Chief Justice Salmon P. Chase, quoted in North Carolina, in 7 *American Annual Cyclopedia* at 546, 548 (1869). Although it is not clear when, precisely, Chase issued this order, he began sitting in Raleigh on June 6, 1867, and this was the first instance of a Supreme Court Justice on circuit in the South since the end of the Civil War. See Summary of Events, 1 *American Law Review* 743, 745 (1867).

245. General Orders No. 32, Headquarters Second Military District, May 30, 1867, reprinted in Report of the Secretary of War, Part I, in Message of the President of the United States to the Two Houses of Congress, 40th Cong., 3d Sess., at 342 (H.R. Exec. Doc. No. 1, 1868).

military authorities, noted that North Carolina's laws as to jurors—the 1855 revisal language still on the books—made no distinctions based on color and "the negro being made a citizen, has all the rights and privileges as to serving on juries which belong to the white citizen."[246] What Worth objected to, though, was the fact that the military order neglected to include the "freehold qualification"[247] of land ownership under existing North Carolina law. Worth realized that General Orders No. 32 would have included all males who paid a poll tax in the previous year. His criticism went unheeded, though. Another military order was soon issued that modified the previous language to require that potential jurors would

---

246. Extract of Letter from Governor Jonathan Worth to Commanding General, Second Military District (September 10, 1867), reprinted in Report of the Secretary of War, Part I, in Message of the President of the United States to the Two Houses of Congress, 40th Cong., 3d Sess., at 343 (H.R. Exec. Doc. No. 1, 1868).

Governor Worth was correct that the existing statute made no distinctions based on race, but his assertion that the freedmen's new status as citizens qualified them for jury duty under the law was incorrect, at least as a historical claim. Although the law in antebellum North Carolina was not clear, free blacks in North Carolina were citizens—at least to some degree. In 1838, the North Carolina Supreme Court concluded: "Slaves manumitted here become free-men—and, therefore, if born within North Carolina are citizens of North Carolina—and all free persons born within the State are born citizens of the State." *State v. Manuel*, 20 N.C. 144, 151 (1838). The Court reasoned that even though free Negroes could no longer vote after the 1835 amendment to the state constitution, the right to vote was not a component of citizenship because (white) women and minors were not able to vote. Id. at 152. In a later decision, however, the Court muddied the waters by concluding that free Negroes were not citizens "in the largest sense of the term" because they were subject to various legal disabilities that did not pertain to white citizens. *State v. Newsom*, 27 N.C. 250, 254 (1844).

It is true, however, that one court in North Carolina—subsequent to the issuance of General Orders No. 32 in May 1867, but before it was fully implemented—ordered the inclusion of colored men on jury lists pursuant to North Carolina law. In Superior Court in Martin County, Judge Daniel G. Fowle maintained that with the abolition of slavery, all qualified men were entitled to be included on jury lists. A new venire was selected under this order and "three colored men" were on the panel for the session of court. An Important Decision in North Carolina—Colored Jurymen, *Norfolk Journal* (Tri-Weekly edition) (Norfolk, Va.), Aug. 29, 1867, at 1. Fowle was later elected governor in 1888.

247. Extract of Letter from Governor Jonathan Worth to Commanding General, Second Military District (September 10, 1867), reprinted in Report of the Secretary of War, Part I, in Message of the President of the United States to the Two Houses of Congress, 40th Cong., 3d Sess., at 343 (H.R. Exec. Doc. No. 1, 1868).

need to be "qualified . . . as voters," but which made clear that any state freehold requirement "is hereby abrogated."[248]

More legislation at the state and national level soon followed. After the ratification of the 1868 state constitution, the North Carolina legislature enacted a new statute for the creation of jury lists.[249] The 1868 law made several changes. It put the county commissioners in charge of creating the jury lists, and it set out three requirements for inclusion on a jury list: the person must have "paid tax for the proceeding year and . . . [be] of good moral character and of sufficient intelligence."[250] Although subsequent statutory changes were made with regard to how frequently the jury lists were to be created,[251] this race-neutral statutory language from 1868 was retained without change until the middle of the twentieth century.[252] On the federal side, the Civil Rights Act of 1875 provided that no citizen should be disqualified from service on a grand or petit jury "on account of race, color, or previous condition of servitude."[253]

As is well known, these statutes did not ensure that minorities were on jury lists or in the jury box. North Carolina law on how jury lists were to be constituted was facially neutral as to race. However, the statutory requirements of good moral character and sufficient intelligence were separate invitations for county officials to discriminate. At least with regard to North Carolina, there is little support for the general claim by some scholars that all-white juries appeared "[a]lmost immediately after the

---

248. General Orders No. 89, Headquarters Second Military District, Sept. 13, 1867, reprinted in Report of the Secretary of War, Part I, in Message of the President of the United States to the Two Houses of Congress, 40th Cong., 3d Sess, at 344 (H.R. Exec. Doc. No. 1, 1868) (issued by Gen. E.R.S. Canby).

249. 1868 N.C. Sess. Laws 9, ch. 9 (Special Sess.).

250. Id. § 1.

251. 1899 N.C. Sess. Laws 901, ch. 729, § 1 ("every two years").

252. The requirement that the individual have paid taxes was eliminated in 1947, 1947 N.C. Sess. Laws 1433, ch. 1007, § 1, and the requirements that the individual be of good moral character and of sufficient intelligence were removed in 1967 in favor of citizens who are "physically and mentally competent" and who have not been convicted or pleaded nolo contendere to a felony. 1967 N.C. Sess. Laws 255, ch. 218, § 1. These provisions are currently codified at N.C. Gen. Stat. § 9-2.

253. Act of March 1, 1875, ch. 114, § 4, 18 Stat. 335, 336 (1875). This language has survived and remains the law today. 12 U.S.C. § 243.

Civil War,"²⁵⁴ but the degree to which blacks were included on the jury lists cannot be fixed with certainty. Eric Foner concluded, though, that during Reconstruction "politics and government were the most integrated institutions in Southern life. Blacks and whites sat together on juries, school boards, and city councils . . . . Thus, if Reconstruction did not create an integrated society, it did establish a standard of equal citizenship . . . ."²⁵⁵

The evidence as to the inclusion of blacks on the jury lists in North Carolina creates a picture of variety, not only during Reconstruction but at least into the first decade of the twentieth century. At any given time, there were often radical differences in the inclusion of blacks on jury lists because of variations in the different counties. And those differences in the counties were caused by some mix of factors such as the size of the nonwhite population in the county, the vitality of the two-party system in the county, the judges on the bench, and whether there was a history of black officeholding.

A thorough and systematic analysis of the inclusion of people of color on juries across North Carolina from the end of the Civil War through the era of Jim Crow is beyond the scope of the present study, but certain evidence exists that, while anecdotal, provides at least a partial picture of the racial composition of jury lists. Relying on my own research in primary sources—mainly local newspapers—and what can be found in published court opinions and in other scholarly literature, snapshots of evidence exist. But these observations are limited to their time and place. It is impossible to make any general conclusions about what occurred in North Carolina, as a whole, until further study is conducted.

What can be said is that freedmen began to appear on North Carolina juries by 1867. The number of black jurors—American Indian jury participation was nonexistent until much later—was almost certainly never in proportion to the percentages of blacks eligible for jury service in the various counties. In August 1867, "three colored men" served on a jury in Superior Court in Martin County²⁵⁶ and "two negroes" served on a jury in

---

254. James Forman, Jr., Juries and Race in the Nineteenth Century, 113 *Yale Law Journal* 895, 909 (2004).

255. Foner, supra note 17, at 372.

256. An Important Decision in North Carolina—Colored Jurymen, *Norfolk Journal* (Tri-Weekly edition) (Norfolk, Va.), Aug. 30, 1867, at 1.

Catawba County.[257] A newspaper item from Wilmington in the following year noted that three Negroes had been drawn from the jury list to be part of the venire for the next term.[258] These events, it should be remembered, occurred at a time when military courts such as military commissions and post courts tried many cases in North Carolina, and the level of activity for the civilian courts was somewhat reduced. At the same time, the complete absence of blacks from jury lists in some counties was not unusual in the immediate postbellum years. In an 1869 trial in Alamance County, the chairman of the county commissioners was examined as to why there were no Negroes on the jury lists, and he testified that of the Negro residents who had paid their taxes, "none of them were morally and mentally competent to act as jurors."[259]

During this period, the reaction by the white population to freedmen on juries was one of strong but not virulent opposition to the practice. Although C. Vann Woodward quotes Kemp Battle's amazement at "how quietly our people take negro juries, or rather negroes on juries" in North Carolina,[260] there is plenty of evidence to the contrary. After the issuance of General Orders No. 32, the Tarboro newspaper argued that under this order, "a large portion of our best and most intelligent citizens are deprived of the right and privilege of serving as jurors, while at the same time every ignorant and unlearned negro is invested with such privilege."[261] The *Wilmington Journal* asserted that the new, inclusive jury lists

---

257. *The Western Democrat* (Charlotte, N.C.), Aug. 27, 1867, at 3.
258. Negro Jurors, *Wilmington Morning Star*, Mar. 17, 1868, at 3.
259. *The Charlotte Democrat*, June 22, 1869, at 2.
260. Kemp Battle, quoted in Woodward, supra note 65, at 26. The Republican newspaper formerly owned by Gov. W.W. Holden, *The Daily Standard*, put forward its own view on the matter:

> There seems now to be no objection urged against the colored juror—he tries cases, and sits as a grand inquest, to decide on the merits of bills of indictment, and *we know*, that they do exercise good judgment in their decisions, not biased by any sympathetic appeals—they are as quick to do justice, and as quick to show mercy, when the ends of justice are not subverted thereby, as any class of people we have.

The Colored Man as Juror, *Daily Standard* (Raleigh, N.C.), Dec. 29, 1869, at 2 (emphasis in original).
261. A Difference of Opinion, *Tarborough Southerner* (Tarboro, N.C.), Sept. 26, 1867, at 2. See also Negro Juries, *Wilmington Journal*, Oct. 18, 1867, at 2 (criticizing "juries formed of the ignorant masses").

would prevent white people from moving to the state because "so long as the immigrant feels that . . . the negro will sit beside him in the jury box . . . he will stifle any desire he many have to invest in, and cultivate, the rich fields now lying idle."[262]

In the 1870s and 1880s, there are indications that the inclusion of blacks on jury lists was more widespread, at least in some North Carolina counties. Moreover, there is some evidence which suggests that the proportion of blacks on these lists had increased, even if not in proportion to their numbers in the counties. Several jury lists from Warren County are instructive, given that the local newspaper was relatively diligent in printing the jury lists for the court terms and, in the style of the day, identifying which individuals were "Col." or colored. As for the size of the black population: in the 1870 and 1880 censuses, the percentage of colored persons in Warren County constituted 70 percent and 72 percent, respectively.[263] In August 1876, the venire pulled from the jury list contained the names of 28 white men and 26 colored men.[264] In January 1878, the venire listed 28 white men and 7 colored men.[265] But seven months later, the venire contained no colored jurors and 54 white men.[266] That obvious drop was an outlier and not the end of jury service by blacks in Warren County, however, because a venire in the 1880s contained 41 white men and 13 colored men.[267] Jury lists in Wake County in the 1870s were well populated with black men because several important trials had juries that were composed either entirely of "colored men"[268] or with a clear majority of colored persons.[269] But the picture from other counties is one of exclusion.

---

262. Immigration, *Wilmington Journal*, Jan. 17, 1868, at 4.
263. U.S. Bureau of the Census, *Statistics of the Population of the United States at the Tenth Census* 404 (1882) (listing Warren County as having 6,386 white and 16,233 colored persons in 1880) and 1 U.S. Bureau of the Census, *Statistics of the Population of the United States* 53–54 (1872) (listing Warren County as having 5,276 white and 12,492 "free colored" in 1870).
264. Jurors for August Court, *Warrenton Gazette* (Warrenton, N.C.), Aug. 10, 1876, at 3.
265. Jurors for Superior Court, *Warrenton Gazette* (Warrenton, N.C.), Jan. 18, 1878, at 3.
266. *Warrenton Gazette* (Warrenton, N.C.), Aug. 16, 1878, at 3.
267. *Warrenton Gazette* (Warrenton, N.C.), Feb. 8, 1889, at 3.
268. Trial of William Stinson, *Daily Standard* (Raleigh, N.C.), Oct. 7, 1870, at 3.
269. The Finale of the Hicks Outrage, *Raleigh Weekly News*, Jan 16, 1873, at 3 (describing jury "ten-twelfths of which was colored men").

In Carteret County, Eric Anderson found that "no Negro had ever served on a jury as late as 1877."[270] The chairman of an 1880 conference of colored men argued for change given that "in many of the countries [sic], colored men are not permitted to act as jurors."[271]

The portrait of the next three decades, from 1890 to 1920, is a more complicated one as to whether the application of the state's race-neutral law on the creation of jury lists was biased with regard to blacks. It is this era, in particular, that calls out for further scholarly study on the makeup of the jury lists. The existing historical perspective is that jury service by blacks in North Carolina increased markedly in the mid-1890s during the fusion era,[272] but that the state soon came back into line with the rest of the region so that "[f]or the first three decades of the twentieth century, essentially no blacks sat on Southern juries."[273] The differences between counties assume even greater importance here, because at least some blacks did serve on juries in a limited number of North Carolina counties for at least the first decade of the twentieth century. However, the numbers were low and were decreasing and, as before, they were not close to being in proportion to the black populations of the counties.

The evidence of minority jury service after 1890 is undeniably complex and dynamic because, at some point in the next twenty years, jury lists did become effectively white. Pinpointing when that shift occurred and whether it was sharp or gradual cannot be stated with precision. In this era, as before, there are corners of the state where no blacks were on the jury lists or in the jury boxes, as when a committee of colored individuals complained to the Buncombe County Commissioners in 1897 that "colored citizens are not considered in drawing jurors."[274] In the decade after 1900, Gilbert Thomas Stephenson researched Negro jury participation by sending letters to the clerks of court in every Southern county where

---

270. Anderson, supra note 181, at 318.
271. An Address of the Conference of Representative Colored Men that Assembled in the Senate Chamber, in the City of Raleigh, Jan. 15 & 16, 1880, *The Signal* (Raleigh, N.C.), Jan. 21, 1880, at 3.
272. Anderson, supra note 181, at 319.
273. Michael J. Klarman, *From Jim Crow to Civil Rights: The Supreme Court and the Struggle for Racial Equality* 40 (2004).
274. Board of Commissioners, *Asheville Citizen-Times* (Asheville, N.C.), Sept. 8, 1897, at 4.

4. DE JURE DISCRIMINATION IN NORTH CAROLINA | 165

Negroes constituted at least half of the population of the county.[275] Although Stephenson did not receive replies to all of his letters, he received responses from six North Carolina counties. While he did not identify the counties by name in his book, they can be identified with certainty because he did include the 1900 population figures by race, and those numbers align with particular counties in the U.S. Census.[276] The responses from Halifax, New Hanover, and Scotland counties said that Negroes did not serve on juries in their counties at all,[277] and one of these stated that the Negroes "have not since we, the white people, got the government in our hands."[278] The responses from Caswell and Warren counties said that "very few" and "some" Negroes serve on juries,[279] while the response from Hertford County said that Negroes "occasionally" serve.[280] Even in Caswell County, where some minimal level of black inclusion existed, the county official asserted that those low numbers were because "they are an illiterate race and moral character not what it should be."[281]

---

275. Stephenson, supra note 70, at 253.
276. Id. at 265–67. "County No. 1" was identified as having 6,800 white people and 8,000 Negroes. Id. at 265. These figures correspond to Caswell County, which the U.S. Census listed as having 6,829 white inhabitants and 8,199 Negro inhabitants in 1900. 1 U.S. Bureau of the Census, *Twelfth Census of the United States, Taken in the Year 1900: Population*, Part 1, at 550 (1901) (hereinafter "Twelfth Census"). "County No. 2" was identified as having 11,000 whites and 19,000 Negroes. Stephenson, supra note 70, at 265. These figures correspond to Halifax County, which had 11,060 white inhabitants and 19,733 Negro inhabitants. Twelfth Census, supra, at 550. "County No. 3" was identified as having 5,800 whites and 8,300 Negroes. Stephenson, supra note 70, at 265. These figures correspond to Hertford County, which had 5,895 white inhabitants and 8,391 Negro inhabitants. Twelfth Census, supra, at 550. "County No. 4" was identified as having 12,600 whites and 13,100 Negroes. Stephenson, supra note 70, at 266. These figures correspond to New Hanover County, which had 12,663 white inhabitants and 13,109 Negro inhabitants. Twelfth Census, supra, at 551. "County No. 5" was identified as having 5,700 whites and 6,700 Negroes. Stephenson, supra note 70, at 266. These figures correspond to Scotland County, which had 5,709 white inhabitants and 6,710 Negro inhabitants. Twelfth Census, supra, at 551. "County No. 6" was identified as having 6,000 white people and 13,000 Negroes. Stephenson, supra note 70, at 266. These figures correspond to Warren County, which had 6,082 white inhabitants and 13,069 Negro inhabitants. Twelfth Census, supra, at 551.
277. Stephenson, supra note 70, at 265–66.
278. Id. at 265 (quoting letter from Halifax County).
279. Id. at 265, 266 (quoting letters from Caswell and Warren counties).
280. Id. at 265 (quoting letter from Hertford County).
281. Id. at 265 (quoting letter from Caswell County).

Thus, there is at least some evidence of the inclusion of Negroes on jury lists and venires, but it is impossible to say whether these numbers add up to any genuine level of inclusion until more research is done. In a few areas of the state, Negroes can be found on lists of venires published in local newspapers at least through 1910. Even in these counties, though, the levels of participation are significantly lower than they were a decade earlier. Vance County is one example. In May 1898 and April 1899, the jury venires for Superior Court listed 18 and 6 "colored," respectively.[282] By September 1909 and September 1910, however, the number of Negroes on the venires was down to two and one, respectively.[283] Warren County, surveyed by Stephenson, is another example of a county where the inclusion of blacks continued. In the published list of jurors drawn by the county commissioners in May 1901, five Negroes were on the venire.[284] Colored members of the venire can be found in Warren County for many years, in ever-smaller numbers; for the February 1907 court, there were four colored members of the venire and for the September 1918 court, there was one colored person included.[285] It is impossible to say whether these counties were typical or outliers in terms of continued inclusion of black citizens, but my suspicion is that they would be outliers. It can be said that, after 1910, the service of blacks on a state or federal jury was such a rarity that it generally resulted in a newspaper story.[286]

From the 1920s to the 1960s, evidence of the exclusion of blacks from jury lists in North Carolina is widespread. After the U.S. Supreme Court's 1935 decision in the second Scottsboro case, *Norris v. Alabama*,[287] in which the Court held that the systematic exclusion of blacks from grand and trial juries in Alabama violated the Fourteenth Amendment, counties in North Carolina took notice. Again, the mere inclusion of blacks on jury lists at

---

282. Jurors Drawn, *Henderson Gold Leaf* (Henderson, N.C.), Apr. 6, 1899, at 3; List of Jurors, *Henderson Gold Leaf*, May 12, 1898, at 3.

283. Jurors Drawn, *Henderson Gold Leaf*, Sept. 8, 1910, at 3; Jurors for Next Court, *Henderson Gold Leaf*, Sept. 16, 1909, at 5.

284. Criminal Court Jurors, *The Warren Record* (Warrenton, N.C.), May 10, 1901, at 1.

285. List of Jurors for September Court, *The Warren Record* (Warrenton, N.C.), Aug. 9, 1918, at 1; Jurors for February Court, *The Warren Record*, Jan. 11, 1907, at 5.

286. Negroes Serve on Jury in the Federal Court, *News and Observer*, Oct. 17, 1919, at 19 (noting that this was "[f]or the first time in many years").

287. 294 U.S. 587 (1935).

this time merited front-page news stories in local newspapers. The Statesville newspaper had a large headline which read: "Juries in Iredell May Have Negroes After July First."[288] But Negro inclusion on jury lists soon vanished, yet again. In 1948, the U.S. Supreme Court reversed five convictions from Forsyth County because of the systematic exclusion of blacks from juries.[289] The lack of black inclusion on juries was not recognized by most whites; even the report of the North Carolina Advisory Committee to the U.S. Commission on Civil Rights, a committee whose work was celebrated because of its thoroughness and fairness, made the rather over-optimistic claim in 1962 that "[i]n recent years, in most counties, Negroes have regularly been included in jury panels."[290]

While the foregoing evidence demonstrates some minimal inclusion of blacks on jury venires at least to 1910, it is undeniable that the discriminatory application of the same state law after 1900 made jury participation by blacks a rarity and that the numbers dwindled to, effectively, zero for several decades. The few instances that can be found of blacks on jury lists by the second decade of the twentieth century may not be out of line with the similar participation by a handful of blacks in voting booths after 1900, but they may not add up to any real, measurable level of inclusion. Any other conclusions will have to await further historical research.

The statutes cataloged here and in Table 1 reveal that there were many discriminatory, race-conscious statutes enacted by North Carolina after 1865, but what occurred in the years immediately after the White Supremacy Campaigns demonstrates the gap that existed between statutory text and the operation of law. The funding of schools through the state and the counties changed dramatically to the detriment of the black schools, even though the statutory funding formula did not change. The application of a literacy test, the text of which was not obviously discriminatory as to

---

288. Juries in Iredell May Have Negroes After July First, *Statesville Record and Landmark* (Statesville, N.C.), June 18, 1935, at 1. See also Negro Serves on Recorder's Court Jury, *The Bee* (Danville, Va.), Aug. 30, 1935, at 1 (story from Leaksville, N.C.).

289. *Brunson v. North Carolina*, 333 U.S. 851 (1948) (per curiam).

290. Equal Protection of the Laws in North Carolina, Report of the North Carolina Advisory Committee to the United States Commission on Civil Rights, 1959–1962, at 56 (1962).

race, resulted in the absolute decimation of black voter rolls. The numbers of blacks on jury venires declined too, although there were apparently some low levels of participation in a few counties. It is worth noting the apparent variation between the counties as to the juror rolls, but the discriminatory uniformity across the counties as to the voter rolls. While whites' racial animus was certainly evident from 1865 through 1920 and beyond, it is hard to escape the conclusion that the shift in the operation of law after 1900 was directly related to the racial paroxysm arising from the White Supremacy Campaigns. The fears, resentments, and hostility unleashed in 1898 and 1900 affected whites throughout North Carolina, and the operation of law was impacted by the shift in racial enmity, as well. Law and the application of law are not shielded from the attitudes and prejudices of the society.

5
State Institutions and Legislative Appropriations

Even though the laws compiled in Tables 1 and 2 provide a catalog of the General Assembly's enactments on race, as with the operation of the laws examined in the previous chapter, those statutes do not provide a full accounting of the many ways that *de jure* discrimination was practiced by the State of North Carolina. Such a gap often exists because the operation and application of the law frequently deviate from the statutory text. Even aside from racial discrimination, there is commonly a fissure between positive law and the interpretation and application of legal text. Law is a human institution and only operates in the world through imperfect human beings. There is often some distance between a law's text and its operation because "the law" may not be clear or its application to particular circumstances may be uncertain. As Edward Levi wrote, "In an important sense legal rules are never clear, and, if a rule had to be clear before it could be imposed, society would be impossible."[1] This chapter is intended to acknowledge these gaps, point out the rich material available for further study, and highlight the multiple ways that *de jure* racial discrimination existed in North Carolina. Two main lacunae are addressed here. First, with regard to state public welfare institutions, racial exclusion and discrimination took many forms and the statutory law sometimes diverged from actual practice. Second, some *de jure* discrimination in North Carolina was achieved through legislative appropriations which, as a type

---

1. Edward H. Levi, *An Introduction to Legal Reasoning* 1 (1949).

of statute, were not included in the catalog of laws compiled for this study. The differences in funding based on race are another important way in which discrimination and inequality were furthered by the state. The following review is not intended to give a complete accounting of these gaps but is, instead, meant to offer a glimpse of the multiple forms of *de jure* discrimination, note how they compare with C. Vann Woodward's thesis in *The Strange Career of Jim Crow*, and to suggest that further, valuable research remains to be done.

It should be noted here at the outset that North Carolina lagged behind other states in creating institutions to address public welfare needs. That was true both before and after the Civil War. An example demonstrates the point. The 1868 Constitution set out to establish a state institution, the Board of Public Charities, to superintend these matters: "Beneficent provision for the poor, the unfortunate and orphan, being one of the first duties of a civilized and christian [sic] State, the General Assembly, shall at its first session, appoint and define the duties of a Board of Public Charities."[2] However, with the Board's creation, its members discovered that not only was there no great concern for the disadvantaged in the state in the years after 1865, but that the most influential people were "opposed to the Board's very existence" and it essentially ceased to function for a number of years starting in 1872.[3] Nevertheless, the General Assembly did create individual institutions and appropriate money and these actions reveal a part of the story of Jim Crow in the state.

A. Asylums for the Insane[4]

North Carolina, a provincial backwater relative to other states until after 1835, had long been unable to summon the will for internal improvements or the creation of state institutions and, as a result, it had no institution

---

2. N.C. Const. of 1868, art. XI, sec. 7.

3. John Hope Franklin, Public Welfare in the South During the Reconstruction Era, 1865-80, 44 *Social Service Review* 379, 385 (1970).

4. Again, as with the racial terminology used in this book, the historical nomenclature of the era under study—words such as "insane" and "lunatics" and "dumb"—will be retained in this chapter to maintain the continuity and context of the statutes and labels of the era.

5. INSTITUTIONS AND APPROPRIATIONS | 171

for the mentally ill until the 1850s.[5] The humanitarian case for the state to care for the mentally ill was made to the legislature by social activist Dorothea Dix in the late 1840s, and the first statutes were enacted in 1849.[6] A lack of legislative funding, however, delayed the opening for several years.[7] Thus, the asylum in Raleigh only began receiving patients in March 1856.[8] While the statutory language was race neutral as to the patients to be admitted to the asylum both before and immediately after the Civil War, blacks were only admitted to the Raleigh institution during Reconstruction and were otherwise excluded until the creation of a separate institution in Goldsboro that did not open its doors until 1880.

The first North Carolina session laws establishing a state mental hospital, passed in the 1840s and 1850s, did not mention race. With regard to the persons to be admitted, the initial statute simply provided that the "admission of insane patients from the several counties of the State shall be in the ratio of their insane population."[9] Presumably, the statute did not mention race because, in antebellum North Carolina, it was understood that the asylum would be for white patients and not for free blacks or slaves. The compilers of the *Revised Code* of 1855, however, added their own flourish as to race and, thus, the code provision was modified to say that patients were to be admitted "as far as practicable, apportion[ed] ... according to the *white* population of each county."[10] Technically, this was

---

5. See Larry E. Tise and Jeffrey J. Crow, A New Description of North Carolina, in *New Voyages to Carolina: Reinterpreting North Carolina History* 354, 371 (Larry E. Tise and Jeffrey J. Crow eds., 2017) (concluding, with respect to this era, that "North Carolina lacked a will, a governmental structure, or a pool of leadership to move programs that would benefit the state as a whole"). North Carolina was the last of the original thirteen states to have an institution for the mentally ill. Lynne M. Getz, "A Strong Man of Large Human Sympathy": Dr. Patrick L. Murphy and the Challenges of Nineteenth-Century Asylum Psychiatry in North Carolina, 86 *North Carolina Historical Review* 32, 32 (2009).
6. 1848–49 N.C. Sess. Laws 3, ch. 1; 1848–49 N.C. Sess. Laws 13, ch. 2.
7. Margaret Callender McCulloch, Founding the North Carolina Asylum for the Insane, 13 *North Carolina Historical Review* 185, 193 (1936) ("[After legislative approval in 1849, interest] in the asylum tended to subside. Perhaps even more important in causing the delay was the fact that the funds had to be raised gradually by taxation and so were not immediately available.").
8. Insane Asylum (public notice), *Weekly Standard* (Raleigh, N.C.), Mar. 5, 1856, at 3 ("Notice is hereby given, that apartments are now ready for the reception of 40 patients, in the Asylum.").
9. 1848–49 N.C. Sess. Laws 3, 7, ch. 1, § 11.
10. Revised Code of North Carolina ch. 6, § 14 (1855) (emphasis added).

not a prohibition on blacks as patients, but the limitation was certainly implied and, at this time, it was absolute.[11]

Following the end of the Civil War, however, there was a brief period during Reconstruction when black patients were admitted to the Raleigh asylum, irrespective of any implication or intent behind the legal text then in force. In the November 1, 1866, report for the institution, it was stated that there were "two colored insane" who were patients.[12] It appears that these patients were there at the behest of the Freedmen's Bureau.[13] Subsequently, in the November 1, 1868, report for the asylum, Superintendent Eugene Grissom recorded three colored male patients and six colored female patients in the Raleigh asylum as of that date.[14] Given the needs of the mentally ill of all races, there was not enough space in the Raleigh facility to meet the needs within the state.[15]

It is unclear whether the black patients during this period were segregated within the building because the written accounts conflict. The superintendent in 1866, E.C. Fisher, commented in his report that he was unhappy about the fact that a ward had to be set aside in order to maintain a separate space for the black patients: "Objectionable as this plan is on many accounts, it seems to be the only one which can be devised to meet the demands upon the Institution by the colored insane; and at the

---

11. An 1857 report on the asylum which set out detailed listings of the patients admitted since the institution's inception confirms this reading, because the report does not see the need to specify the race of the patients, and this was an era when it was typical for reports and newspapers to note the inclusion of colored individuals. *Reports of the Board of Directors and Superintendent of the Asylum for the Insane of North Carolina* (1857).

12. Report of the Physician and Superintendent of the Insane Asylum of North Carolina, for the Year Ending Nov. 1, 1866 (Executive Doc. No. 3), in *Executive and Legislative Documents Laid Before the General Assembly of North Carolina, Session 1866'-7*, at 7 (1867).

13. Id. at 10 ("Since it had been made known to authorities of the Freedmen's Bureau, of a readiness on the part of the Board of Supervisors to admit colored insane into the Institution ....").

14. Report of the Physician and Superintendent of the Insane Asylum of North Carolina (Doc. No. 11), in *Executive and Legislative Documents Laid Before the General Assembly of North Carolina, Session 1868–69*, at 2 (1869).

15. Dr. M.K. Hogan, an Army medical officer attached to the Freedmen's Bureau, believed that the freedmen had a particularly difficult time in being admitted to the Raleigh asylum. Reggie L. Pearson, "There Are Many Sick, Feeble, and Suffering Freedmen": The Freedmen's Bureau Health-Care Activities during Reconstruction in North Carolina, 1865–1868, 79 *North Carolina Historical Review* 141, 173–175 (2002).

5. INSTITUTIONS AND APPROPRIATIONS | 173

same time preserve the necessary separation between the two races."[16] Eugene Grissom's report two years hence, however, reported that separate wards with individual rooms had not been provided to the black patients: "Owing to want of room, my predecessor found it impossible to assign separate apartments to our colored insane, an arrangement I think highly desirable, and should be made as soon as facilities will permit."[17]

The North Carolina Constitution of 1868 did not draw racial lines and, similarly, the new comprehensive statute on the asylum in 1869 did not mention race or segregation, but those silences did not mean admission across racial lines.[18] The Constitution made the care of the insane an affirmative duty of the state.[19] The 1869 statute set out that the institution was "for the accommodation, maintenance, support and care of the insane of this State."[20]

By 1869 and with the end of Congressional Reconstruction in North Carolina, however, any evidence of non-white patients at the Raleigh institution disappears. Thus, there is a gap between the statutory text and the availability of care for freedmen and women because, starting with the reports for that year, there is no further mention of any black patients at the Raleigh asylum. Even though the new statute spoke in general terms, the Raleigh asylum was for the white insane only, and the asylum apparently excluded other mentally ill persons from proper care based on race.[21] All the while, a Wilmington newspaper reported that the "number

---

16. Report of the Physician and Superintendent of the Insane Asylum of North Carolina, for the Year Ending Nov. 1, 1866 (Executive Doc. No. 3), supra note 12, at 10.

17. Report of the Physician and Superintendent of the Insane Asylum of North Carolina (Doc. No. 11), supra note 14, at 17. This report described the asylum in the following manner: "There are in the building twelve wards—six male and six female—each containing twenty rooms." Id. at 15.

18. See 1868–69 N.C. Sess. Laws 139, 149, ch. 67, § 29 ("shall be apportioned among the Counties of the State, as near as may be, according to their respective population"). Battle's 1872 codification did not refer to race, either. See Battle's Revisal of the Public Statutes of North Carolina ch. 6, § 19 (where the questions about the patients' age, marital status, cause of insanity, etc., do not include a query about race).

19. N.C. Const. of 1868, art. XI, sec. 10 (stating that the General Assembly "shall provide that *all* . . . the insane of the State, shall be cared for at the charge of the State") (emphasis added).

20. 1868–69 N.C. Sess. Laws 139, ch. 67.

21. I have found no support for Howard Rabinowitz's claim that, in the late 1860s, the "North Carolina legislature set aside separate quarters for Negroes at the state insane asylum in Raleigh." Howard N. Rabinowitz, *Race Relations in the Urban South,*

of colored lunatics is largely on the increase."²² The only governmental institutions that were available to house mentally ill blacks were the county jail and, in some communities, the poor house.²³

One champion for the care of the black insane was Governor Curtis Brogden. In his annual message to the General Assembly in November 1876, he argued for the creation of a facility for blacks that would provide the same level of care as was provided to white patients at the Raleigh facility. He wrote if whites composed two-thirds of the state's population and that two facilities were to exist for their care (a new institution was underway in Morganton for whites in the western part of the state), then "surely the colored race, composing one-third of the population, ought in justice to have one Asylum for the support of the colored insane."²⁴

1865–1890, at 132 (1978). The newspaper article he cites for that proposition, from 1875, states that the General Assembly passed a law appropriating money for a colored insane asylum in Wilmington and that "[t]he colored insane from this [Raleigh] asylum will be removed to Wilmington." Insane Asylum at Wilmington, *Raleigh Sentinel*, Mar. 18, 1875, at 1. However, this newspaper article does not state that the legislature set aside quarters for Negroes in the late 1860s and I have found no evidence in the session laws that such separate quarters were to be created at the Raleigh asylum. As for the newspaper article's statement about colored insane at the Raleigh asylum, it is repeating the language from the statute: *"Provided,* That no more colored insane shall be received in the asylum at Raleigh, and that all the colored inmates now in the asylum at Raleigh, North Carolina, be removed to Wilmington...." 1874–75 N.C. Sess. Laws 338, ch. 250, § 1. Even so, I am somewhat dubious that such patients were admitted, except perhaps on a temporary basis, by the mid-1870s. In the reports of the asylum from 1869 onward, there is no mention of black patients in the Raleigh institution at a time when those racial designations were almost universally made in newspapers and reports. The October 1, 1874, report makes no note of any black individuals at the Raleigh facility, although it does separate out the races in a request made of sheriffs to provide a count of white and black insane in their counties. Report of the Board of Directors and Superintendent of the Insane Asylum of North Carolina, For the Official Year Ending October 1st, 1874 (Doc. No. 7), in *Executive and Legislative Documents Laid Before the General Assembly of North Carolina, Session 1874–75*, at 5–15 (1875). In addition, in a section of the 1874 report on the necessity of "additional provision" for the insane of the state, there is no mention whatsoever of the needs of the black mentally ill. Id. at 23–28.

22. A Supposed Lunatic, *Wilmington Morning Star*, Aug. 30, 1876, at 1.

23. *Wilmington Morning Star*, July 8, 1876, at 1 ("Henry Graham, the well known colored lunatic ... was yesterday sent to the hospital for the insane at the county Poor House.").

24. Governor's Message (Doc. No. 1), in *Executive and Legislative Documents Laid Before the General Assembly of North Carolina, Session 1876–77*, at 11 (1877).

5. INSTITUTIONS AND APPROPRIATIONS | 175

Moreover, Brogden urged the legislature to create an institution "under the same rules, regulations and treatment as white patients."[25]

The eventual and permanent provision of mental health facilities for black citizens was a long time in coming, though. In 1877, money that had been set aside for the purpose was finally appropriated "for the establishment of an asylum for the colored insane, at some point in the state."[26] The facility, eventually located in Goldsboro, was finally able to accept patients in August 1880.[27] Given that appropriations such as the one in 1877 are not included in Table 1 of this book, the statute listed in the table is the 1883 law to incorporate the Goldsboro asylum "exclusively for the accommodation, maintenance, care and treatment of the colored insane of the state."[28] These laws were a step in the right direction, but care for the white mentally ill had been expanding at the same time. As previously noted, in 1875, the General Assembly passed a law for the creation of another asylum in Morganton for "the cure, comfort and care of her insane" but, as one might suspect, "her insane" only referred to North Carolina's white insane.[29]

The care of mentally ill Croatan Indians—today, the tribe known as the Lumbees—was apparently not achieved until the twentieth century. An 1899 statute mandated that the state hospital in Raleigh was to take in "insane and inebriate Croatan Indians . . . in a department separate and distinct from the white insane and inebriates" at that hospital.[30] However, it appears that this legal directive had little effect and that new legisla-

---

25. Id. at 10.

26. 1876–77 N.C. Sess. Laws 547, ch. 278, § 1. Note that since this is an appropriation law, it is not listed in Table 1.

27. Report of the Chairman of the Board of Directors of the Asylum for the Colored Insane (Document No. 12), in *North Carolina Executive and Legislative Documents, Session 1881*, at 2 (1881).

28. 1883 N.C. Sess. Laws 237, 238, ch. 156, §§ 1, 3. I do include in Table 1 the 1875 law which designated the "Marine Hospital building at Wilmington" for the colored asylum and set aside money for it. 1874–75 N.C. Sess. Laws 338, ch. 250, § 1. It should be noted that in 1899, the legislature consolidated the insanity laws but did not change anything with regard to the racial segregation of the institutions. See 1899 N.C. Sess. Laws 3, ch. 1, § 3.

29. 1874–75 N.C. Sess. Laws 336, ch. 249. Because of building delays, the Morganton asylum did not receive patients until May 1883. *Carolina Mountaineer* (Morganton, N.C.), May 19, 1883, at 3.

30. 1899 N.C. Sess. Laws 492, ch. 355, § 1.

tion was required to reaffirm the principle. A February 1919 newspaper article on the "Indians of Robeson [County]" stated that they "have been excluded heretofore from the hospitals for the insane, while the negroes have a hospital for their insane."[31] Thus, in the same year, the General Assembly passed a law which established that they "shall be cared for and receive same treatment as other patients in said hospital receive."[32]

The desire of the State of North Carolina to separate the mentally ill by race was a product of its time and a reflection of the white majority's prejudices. Indeed, many of the leading physicians in the mental health field at this time believed that racial segregation was advantageous from a therapeutic point of view. Dr. T.S. Kirkbride, a physician at the Pennsylvania Hospital for the Insane in Philadelphia, set out the tenet that was to govern the treatment of the mentally ill for decades: "The idea of mixing up all colors and classes, as is seen in one or two institutions of the United States, is not what is wanted in our hospitals for the insane . . . ."[33] With the possible exception of a couple of years immediately after the Civil War, North Carolina segregated the mentally ill by race. The state continued to do so until the state hospitals were finally desegregated in the summer of 1965.[34]

B. Institutions for the Deaf, Dumb, and Blind

At the urging of Governor John Motley Morehead, the North Carolina legislature appropriated five thousand dollars in 1845 for "the maintenance and education of such poor and destitute deaf mutes and blind per-

---

31. Work of the Legislature, *The Robesonian* (Lumberton, N.C.), Feb. 20, 1919, at 1.
32. 1919 N.C. Sess. Laws 416, ch. 211, § 1.
33. Dr. T.S. Kirkbride, quoted in Proceedings of the Tenth Annual Meeting of the Association of Medical Superintendents of American Institutions for the Insane, 12 *American Journal of Insanity* 39, 43 (1855).
34. Mental Patients Being Transferred Today to Home District Hospitals, *Charlotte Observer*, July 7, 1965, at 3 ("District lines were redrawn to compose a desegregated system from the white hospitals and the previously all-Negro Cherry Hospital in Goldsboro.").

5. INSTITUTIONS AND APPROPRIATIONS | 177

sons."[35] The school opened in May 1845 in Raleigh.[36] Apparently unaware that the original statute explicitly included "blind persons," the legislature passed a new law in 1852 stating that the prior law was to be "amended to include the blind in all the provisions."[37] Given that this was a period when teaching either a free black or a slave to read was a criminal offense, this institution was solely for white children despite the race-neutral statutory language.[38] The compilers of the 1855 *Revised Code* chose to make the racial exclusion explicit, and rendered the description of the students to be admitted as "all *white* deaf mutes and blind persons, residents of the State, not physically or mentally imbecile."[39] For a period after the Civil War, however, the operation of the law did not strictly correspond to the racial restriction found in the code.

Within the state's laws, there was a conflict. The 1868 North Carolina Constitution set out that the General Assembly was to provide for "*all* the deaf mutes, the blind . . . of the State."[40] However, the *Revised Code* provision, with its racial restriction, was still on the books and not automatically superseded by the new state constitution.[41] This tension between the constitutional and statutory language went unresolved for years because, aside from a few 1870s legislative appropriations, the next revisal of the state's laws in 1873 retained the antebellum language that the institution

---

35. 1844–45 N.C. Sess. Laws 59, ch. 37, § 1. See also 1846–47 N.C. Sess. Laws 114, ch. 48, § 1 (to provide buildings for "such deaf mutes and blind persons as now are, or may hereafter become, pupils or inmates of the institution").

36. Hugh Talmage Lefler and Albert Ray Newsome, *North Carolina: The History of a Southern State* 369–370 (3d ed. 1973).

37. 1852 N.C. Sess. Laws 102, 103, ch. 48, § 1.

38. Revised Code of North Carolina ch. 107, § 31 (1855) (prohibiting any slave "to teach, or attempt to teach, any other slave or free negro to read or write, the use of figures excepted"). See also Revised Code of North Carolina ch. 34, § 82 (1855) ("Any free person who shall teach, or attempt to teach any slave to read or write . . . shall be deemed guilty of a misdemeanor, and . . . if a white man or woman, shall be fined not less than one hundred [dollars] . . . and if a free person of color, shall be fined, imprisoned, or whipped not exceeding thirty-nine, nor less than twenty lashes.").

39. Revised Code of North Carolina ch. 6, § 8 (1855) (emphasis added).

40. N.C. Const. of 1868, art. XI, sec. 10 (emphasis added).

41. The *Revised Code* was indeed law because it was passed by the legislature. The *Revised Code* was enacted in sections, as the codifiers completed their task. The last sections were passed in February 1855. Afternoon Session, *Raleigh Register*, Feb. 7, 1855, at 2 (report on the legislature that "this is the last of the Revisal, and provides for publication and distribution of the Revised Code").

was to admit as pupils "all white deaf mutes and blind persons" and cited, as authority, the 1855 *Revised Code*.[42]

The institution for the deaf and blind did not admit black students immediately after the end of the war, but its principal did request the Freedmen's Bureau's help in setting up a school for them. When the institution reopened in January 1866, there were 41 deaf and 21 blind students.[43] All of them were white. The next year, in October 1867, Principal W.J. Palmer asked for assistance from the Freedmen's Bureau in making provision for nonwhite students because segregation would be necessary and "in our present crowded condition, no arrangement can be made for their accommodation."[44] Palmer said that if the Bureau could appropriate money for the purchase of a building and provide food for the students, then the state institution would provide teachers for the colored deaf and blind.[45] Ultimately, in a return dated December 4, 1867, the Freedmen's Bureau informed Principal Palmer that it could not expend the money for the purchase of a building, but that it could offer to help repair a building, if purchased, and provide rations to the students.[46] The North Carolina institution did not have the money for such an endeavor and, thus, Palmer submitted the report to the General Assembly in the hope of an appropriation so that "provision will be made for the establishment of a separate school for the education of the colored deaf and dumb and blind."[47]

---

42. Battle's Revisal of the Public Statutes of North Carolina ch. 6, § 7 (1873).

43. Reports of the President of the Board of Directors, Principal, Auditor and Treasurer of the North Carolina Institution for the Deaf and Dumb and the Blind (Document No. 5), in *Executive and Legislative Documents Laid Before the General Assembly of North Carolina, Session 1866'-7*, at 4 (1867).

44. Letter of W.J. Palmer to Gen. Nelson A. Miles, Oct. 7, 1867, reprinted in Reports of the President of the Board of Directors, Principal and Treasurer of the North Carolina Institution for the Deaf and Dumb and Blind (Document No. 3), in *Executive and Legislative Documents Laid Before the General Assembly of North Carolina, Session 1868–69*, at 9 (1869).

45. Id. at 10.

46. Endorsement from Freedmen's Bureau, Dec. 2, 1867, reprinted in Reports of the President of the Board of Directors, Principal and Treasurer of the North Carolina Institution for the Deaf and Dumb and Blind (Document No. 3), in *Executive and Legislative Documents Laid Before the General Assembly of North Carolina, Session 1868–69*, at 12–13 (1869).

47. Reports of the President of the Board of Directors, Principal and Treasurer of the North Carolina Institution for the Deaf and Dumb and Blind (Document No. 3), in *Executive and Legislative Documents Laid Before the General Assembly of North Carolina, Session 1868–'69*, at 13 (1869).

A little over a year later, in January 1869, a separate school for the state's black students finally did open its doors.[48] At this time, as previously noted, aside from the 1868 constitutional provision, there was no law creating the colored branch of the school and the later 1873 codification still spoke of the admission of "white deaf mutes and blind persons."[49] There was not even a statutory appropriation that referenced money for a colored branch of the institution.[50] A separate school came into being, nonetheless, with the rental of a building in Raleigh from the American Missionary Association.[51] By July 1, 1869, there were 28 colored students, of whom "twenty-one were deaf and dumb and seven blind."[52]

The state's laws gradually came to take account of black students and their needs. The first statute to explicitly reference the "colored pupils" of the Institution for the Deaf and Dumb and Blind was passed in 1873 to donate a lot in Raleigh where a school for them could be built.[53] An appropriation enacted the following year was "for the completion of the building for the colored department."[54] It was only in 1881, however, that the state finally acknowledged by statute that the Institution for the Deaf

---

48. There is no consensus on the specific date the school opened its doors. See, e.g., Edward McKee Goodwin, *The North Carolina Institution for the Deaf and Dumb and the Blind* 6 (1893) ("The colored department opened on the 4th of January, 1869, with 26 pupils."); Otis A. Betts, *The North Carolina School for the Deaf at Morganton: 1894–1944*, at 25 (1945) (noting the "convenient and well arranged building for the colored department in the southern section of the city of Raleigh and there the school work began January 7, 1869"); *New Berne Times*, Jan. 2, 1869, at 2 ("The colored department of the North Carolina Institution for the deaf and dumb and blind, was opened yesterday.").

49. Battle's Revisal of the Public Statutes of North Carolina ch. 6, § 7 (1873).

50. Subsequent to the Freedmen's Bureau denial of funds in December 1867, there were three appropriations statutes that could have been relevant to the establishment of a school for black students, but none made reference to any such institution. See 1869–70 N.C. Sess. Laws 54, ch. 15; 1868–69 N.C. Sess. Laws 56, ch. 13; 1868 N.C. Sess. Laws 41, ch. 28.

51. See *Thirty-Eighth Annual Report of the American Missionary Association* 68 (1884) ("In 1869 this house [what had been the Washington School] was rented to the State of North Carolina for the use of her colored deaf and dumb and blind children.").

52. Report of the President of the Board of Directors and Principal of the North Carolina Institution for the Deaf, Dumb and the Blind (Document No. 9), in *Executive and Legislative Documents Laid Before the General Assembly of North Carolina, Session 1869–'70*, at 4 (1870).

53. 1872–73 N.C. Sess. Laws 212, ch. 134, § 1 (donation "for the purpose of establishing thereon buildings for the accommodation of the colored pupils of said institution").

54. 1873–74 N.C. Sess. Laws 85, 86, ch. 59, § 2.

and Dumb and Blind was composed of separate departments for both white and colored children.[55]

Although a detailed assessment of the department for the black students is beyond the scope of the present study, a preliminary review suggests that it achieved some degree of parity with the white branch of the institution. James O'Hara, a political leader in the black community, testified before a U.S. Senate committee in 1880 about the North Carolina colored department: "They have the same kind of provisions, meats, vegetables, and fruits; the same bedding and furniture, carpets, pianos, etc., all the same in both institutions, without distinction at all."[56] In an 1893 history of the entire institution, Edward McKee Goodwin wrote: "The Institution for the Colored is a commodious, well arranged building, more suitable for its purpose than the buildings for the white department."[57]

Beyond the buildings and material goods up to the end of the nineteenth century, however, one suspects that there were substantive differences based on race. One reason for this suspicion is that, in 1891, the General Assembly subdivided the white department to allow for the admission of far more students; thus, the school for the blind was kept in Raleigh, but a new facility "for the white deaf and dumb children" was to be built on a one-hundred acre tract in Morganton.[58] The entire colored department remained in the one building in Raleigh. In addition, there was no provision for the teaching of deaf and blind American Indian children by the state until a 1935 statute.[59] The novelty of providing for the American Indian children apparently made a person's application to be a teacher of those students at the Pembroke Indian School a newsworthy event.[60]

---

55. 1881 N.C. Sess. Laws 410, ch. 211, § 1 (stating that the institution on Caswell Square in Raleigh "and on lot located in the eastern part of the city ... and on which the institution for the colored children is located, shall be, and the same is, and shall remain a corporation under the name and style of 'The North Carolina Institution for the Education of the Deaf and Dumb and Blind'").

56. James O'Hara, Testimony in U.S. Senate, 46th Cong., 2d Sess., quoted in Rabinowitz, supra note 21, at 146.

57. Goodwin, supra note 48, at 6.

58. 1891 N.C. Sess. Laws 468, ch. 399.

59. 1935 N.C. Sess. Laws 736, ch. 435, § 1 (stating "no provisions being now made for the teaching of said children").

60. Seeks Job of Teaching Deaf Indian Children, *Charlotte News*, Sept. 24, 1935, at 10 (stating that, pursuant to new law, a teacher had applied for "the position of teacher

5. INSTITUTIONS AND APPROPRIATIONS | 181

It is perhaps not surprising that the administrators in the institution for the deaf and blind recognized the unmet needs of the black citizenry before the state's legislators did, but it is at least somewhat surprising that there was an extended period when the statutes did not correspond to what was happening within this public welfare institution. The statutes on the books and in the *Revised Code* at the end of the Civil War prescribed that the institution was for whites. Even so, the institution for the deaf and blind accepted black pupils starting in January 1869. While those black students were attending the school, it took four years and, thus, two election cycles before the General Assembly even acknowledged the possibility of a black department when it enacted a statute to donate property as a site for a future building. And while money was subsequently appropriated for construction of the building, it was twelve years after black students first attended the school before a statute affirmatively recognized that there was a separate department for black students. While the Institute's reports to the governor and legislature over the years would have informed the elected officials that black students were enrolled and that a building was rented for that purpose, the distance between the statutes and what was happening within the school over those twelve years suggests that members of the General Assembly were not overly concerned with the gap between the state's statutes and the law in action.

C. Appropriations to Private Orphanages

The statutes catalogued in the tables appended to this study are an important part of any assessment of Jim Crow in North Carolina but, because of what was not included in the tables, even the chronicled statutes do not tell the whole story of unequal treatment within the state's session laws. One significant gap is with regard to the appropriations laws that were not included in the tabulation.[61] Nevertheless, the power of the purse is central to the legislative power under American constitutional government at both the state and federal level. It is obvious that different levels of funding for racially separate institutions resulted in, and compounded, discrimination over time. This section sinks one shaft into the state's appropriations stat-

---

of deaf, dumb and blind Indian children at the Pembroke Indian school in Robeson county").

61. For a description of what was and was not included in the tables, see Chapter 4.

utes to show how those disparities took shape over several decades and to suggest that valuable spadework remains to be done in this field.

Although most orphanages founded during nineteenth-century America were "usually private and often sectarian institutions,"[62] North Carolina sought to make it a state responsibility after the Civil War. After the end of the war, the Republican-led state government wanted to expand the reach of state government and one of its aspirations was for state orphanages. The 1868 constitution proclaimed that "provision for the poor, the unfortunate and orphan . . . [is] one of the first duties of a civilized and christian [sic] State."[63] Thus, the constitution pronounced that the state should adopt measures "for the establishment of one or more orphan Houses, where destitute orphans may be cared for, educated and taught, some business or trade."[64] Like many other mandates in the 1868 document, though, this one never came to fruition. North Carolina never established an orphanage.[65] Private groups and churches stepped into the void, however, and opened up what were termed orphan asylums and orphanages.[66] During the time period under review, all orphanages in North Carolina were restricted by race and many did not survive for long.[67]

Instead of founding and operating orphanages, the state provided subsidies to two private orphanages located in Oxford, North Carolina:

---

62. Matthew A. Crenson, *Building the Invisible Orphanage: A Prehistory of the American Welfare System* 41 (1998).

63. N.C. Const. of 1868, art. XI, sec. 7.

64. N.C. Const. of 1868, art. XI, sec. 8.

65. Arthur E. Fink, Changing Philosophies and Practices in North Carolina Orphanages, 48 *North Carolina Historical Review* 333, 339 (1971).

66. Matthew Crenson elucidated the philosophical tie between the nineteenth-century asylum and orphanages:

> The institutional rationale and operating practices of the orphanage were grounded in the regime of the asylum. It assumed the malleability of individual character and its susceptibility to environmental influences, but the creation of the asylum was an admission that reformers lacked the means to manage the social environment itself. Only by creating artificial environments outside the ambit of society could they structure the social experiences that shaped characters.

Crenson, supra note 62, at 19.

67. See, e.g., 1883 N.C. Sess. Laws 851, ch. 110, § 1 (Private) (incorporating "Colored Orphan Home of Eastern North Carolina" in Goldsboro); 1866–67 N.C. Sess. Laws 304, ch. 48 (Private) (incorporating "North Carolina Orphan Asylum" in Charlotte for whites).

the Oxford Orphan Asylum (for white children) and the Colored Orphan Asylum of North Carolina.[68] The former was founded by the Grand Lodge of Masons and it opened its doors in the first months of 1873 on the grounds of the former St. John's College.[69] The latter asylum was initially launched in 1883 as the Grant Colored Orphan Asylum by the Wake Baptist Association and the American Baptist Publication Society, but it was unable to admit any children until January 1887.[70] In that same year, 1887, the colored institution was incorporated by statute and renamed the Colored Orphan Asylum.[71]

Although neither of the orphanages in Oxford was founded or operated by the State of North Carolina, the General Assembly became involved in supporting these institutions—but at different times and with very different levels of support. Governor Tod Caldwell, in his 1873 message to the General Assembly, urged the legislature to support the "Orphan House at Oxford," the white institution, because the state constitution "sympathises [sic] with unfortunate humanity by requiring some suitable provision."[72] Several years later, in 1879, the General Assembly passed a law to provide $3,000 annually to the "Orphan Asylum at Oxford."[73] That funding level

---

68. The Oxford Orphan Asylum was not actually incorporated until 1897. 1897 N.C. Sess. Laws 240, ch. 132 (Private). Aside from the subsidies provided to these two orphanages, I have not found an appropriation for any other orphanage in the session laws for the years under study.

69. *Raleigh News*, Mar. 8, 1873, at 1. See also An Orphan Asylum for North Carolina, *Raleigh News*, Dec. 10, 1872, at 2 (reporting that the Grand Lodge of Masons adopted a resolution "donating the magnificent building of St. John's College at Oxford, as an Asylum to the indigent orphan children of the State, and making an annual appropriation for its support").

70. *News and Observer*, Jan. 13, 1887, at 3 (summarizing news from Oxford newspaper that the "colored orphan asylum near town, is now open and in charge of Miss Bessie Hocking, a Canadian lady. Several girls have already been admitted."). On the movement to create the orphanage, see J.A. Whitted, *A History of the Negro Baptists of North Carolina* 27, 91 (1908); *Biblical Recorder* (Raleigh), Aug. 29, 1883, at 3.

71. The Colored Orphan Asylum was incorporated in 1887. 1887 N.C. Sess. Laws 863, ch. 47 (Private). Although there were numerous denominational orphanages for whites, there was only one other enduring orphanage in the state for black children, the Memorial Industrial School in Winston-Salem. Formal Opening of Colored Orphan's Home, *Twin-City Daily Sentinel* (Winston-Salem), Aug. 4, 1906, at 1.

72. Governor Tod R. Caldwell, Governor's Message (Nov. 17, 1873), quoted in Fink, supra note 65, at 337.

73. 1879 N.C. Sess. Laws 546 (resolution of Mar. 14, 1879).

was increased in two years to $5,000 a year[74] and then, in 1885, to $10,000 per year for the institution.[75] In less than six years, the support had more than tripled. In 1913, the appropriation to this private institution was set at $20,000.[76]

On the other hand, the Colored Orphan Asylum in Oxford did not receive any state support until 1891. At that time, the General Assembly made an appropriation of $1,000 per year.[77] In 1893, that appropriation was increased to $1,500 annually,[78] in 1895 it was raised to $3,000 per year,[79] and it was increased to $5,000 in 1897.[80] After that, the annual appropriation was raised slightly 14 years later[81] and again six years later, in 1917,[82] until in 1919 the annual appropriation was set at $10,000.[83] There were also a few specific appropriations to the colored orphanage in the first two decades after 1900, and these totaled $24,600.[84] These totals for the colored orphanage were welcome given that it was described in one of the statutes as "overcrowded" and with the buildings "in very bad condition."[85] But compare these state appropriations for the white and colored orphanages in the following chart, which tracks the funding up through 1920:

---

74. 1881 N.C. Sess. Laws 633 (resolution of Feb. 25, 1881).
75. 1885 N.C. Sess. Laws 515 (resolution of March 9, 1885).
76. 1913 N.C. Sess. Laws 180, ch. 106, § 5. This appropriation level was maintained in future years and was made explicit in the statutes in future legislative sessions. See 1915 N.C. Sess. Laws 143, 146, ch. 98, § 16; 1917 N.C. Sess. Laws 344, 345, ch. 193, § 16; 1919 N.C. Sess. Laws 321, 323, ch. 145, § 16 (but omitting "orphan" from text by calling it "Oxford Asylum").
77. 1891 N.C. Sess. Laws 584, ch. 530, § 1.
78. 1893 N.C. Sess. Laws 468, ch. 513, § 1.
79. 1895 N.C. Sess. Laws 260, ch. 174, § 1.
80. 1897 N.C. Sess. Laws 206, ch. 115, § 2 (Private).
81. 1911 N.C. Sess. Laws 283, 284, ch. 121, § 3.
82. 1917 N.C. Sess. Laws 344, 345, ch. 193, § 17 ($8,000).
83. 1919 N.C. Sess. Laws 321, 323, ch. 145, § 17.
84. See 1919 N.C. Sess. Laws 321, 323, ch. 145, § 17 ($2,000 over two years for indebtedness); 1917 N.C. Sess. Laws 344, 345, ch. 193, § 17 ($5,000 for indebtedness); 1915 N.C. Sess. Laws 143, 146, ch. 98, § 17 ($2,500 for indebtedness); 1913 N.C. Sess. Laws 180, 182, ch. 106 ($4,000 for "permanent improvements"); 1911 N.C. Sess. Laws 337, ch. 191, § 1 ($2,000 for completion of building); 1909 N.C. Sess. Laws 1132. ch. 747, § 1 ($5,000 for dormitory); 1907 N.C. Sess. Laws 390, 393, ch. 262, § 14 ($1,250 in 1907 and 1908); 1901 N.C. Sess. Laws 988, ch. 762, § 1 ($1,600).
85. 1909 N.C. Sess. Laws 1132, ch. 747, preamble.

5. INSTITUTIONS AND APPROPRIATIONS | 185

	ORPHANAGE, WHITE	ORPHANAGE, COLORED
1879	$3,000	n/a[86]
1880	$3,000	n/a
1881	$5,000	n/a
1882	$5,000	n/a
1883	$5,000	n/a
1884	$5,000	n/a
1885	$10,000	n/a
1886	$10,000	n/a
1887	$10,000	$0
1888	$10,000	$0
1889	$10,000	$0
1890	$10,000	$0
1891	$10,000	$1,000
1892	$10,000	$1,000
1893	$10,000	$1,500
1894	$10,000	$1,500
1895	$10,000	$3,000
1896	$10,000	$3,000
1897	$10,000	$5,000
1898	$10,000	$5,000
1899	$10,000	$5,000
1900	$10,000	$5,000
1901	$10,000	$5,000
1902	$10,000	$5,000

continued

86. The "n/a" here references the fact that the Colored Orphan Asylum was not open for the admission of children until 1887.

continued from previous page

	ORPHANAGE, WHITE	ORPHANAGE, COLORED
1903	$10,000	$5,000
1904	$10,000	$5,000
1905	$10,000	$5,000
1906	$10,000	$5,000
1907	$10,000	$5,000
1908	$10,000	$5,000
1909	$10,000	$5,000
1910	$10,000	$5,000
1911	$10,000	$6,000
1912	$10,000	$6,000
1913	$20,000	$6,000
1914	$20,000	$6,000
1915	$20,000	$6,000
1916	$20,000	$6,000
1917	$20,000	$8,000
1918	$20,000	$8,000
1919	$20,000	$10,000
1920	$20,000	$10,000
Special	$0	$24,600
Totals	$466,000	$177,600

In looking at these totals, it is certainly true that these appropriations were not required, because neither one of these institutions was an arm of the state. The subsidies were, in essence, charitable donations to private institutions. But, at the same time, these appropriations are an indication of the ways that state-created inequality reached down through law in ways that were not within the ambit of what is generally understood to be Jim

Crow, strictly speaking. Yet racial funding disparities such as these subsidies helped to sustain the Jim Crow system.[87]

Surprisingly, the state's subsidies to racially restrictive private orphanages continued until the 1980s. The white orphanage in Oxford, which became known as the Oxford Orphanage and is now the Masonic Home for Children, did not admit any African American children until 1995.[88] The State of North Carolina only ceased public financial support of the whites-only Oxford Orphanage in 1981.[89]

In the decades after the Civil War, public welfare institutions as well as a few private charities provided care and services to black children and adults, yet there were disparities in the statute books and on the ground. The statutes involving the state insane asylums and schools for the deaf and blind as well as legislative appropriations for the private orphanages reveal a much more complex world of Jim Crow than that suggested by C. Vann Woodward and subsequent scholarship. The fact that services were provided to black deaf and blind children before there was even a statute authorizing their inclusion indicates that there was not a rigid legal system of Jim Crow because, in this example, it took twelve years to address in law what already existed in fact. Similarly, the codification of a colored insane asylum in 1883 came after appropriations were made and after the Goldsboro institution was already admitting patients.[90] At the same time, though, even if there was not a rigid system of legalized

---

87. The importance of equitable funding was recognized in 1947 by the President's Committee on Civil Rights when it recommended that "public funds, which belong to the whole people, will be used for the benefit of the entire population." President's Committee on Civil Rights, *To Secure These Rights* 170 (1947).

88. Jennifer Toth, *Orphans of the Living: Stories of America's Children in Foster Care* 30 (1997). See also Orphanages: Racial Lines Divide Many, *N.Y. Times*, Nov. 28, 1986, at A25 (quoting Masonic administrator at the white Oxford Orphanage saying that, as a private institution, "[w]e're not in violation of any laws of the United States, or the State of North Carolina").

89. Director of Home Resigns, *Nashville Graphic* (Nashville, N.C.), July 9, 1981, at 2 ("The General Assembly this session adopted a state budget in which funding to . . . the Oxford Orphanage was cut off. An appropriations committee studied the grant-in-aid funds . . . after Rep. Kenneth B. Spaulding, D-Durham, introduced legislation calling for an investigation of the propriety of state financing for the all-white home."). The state had also been providing funding, at this time, to the all-white Free Will Baptist Children's Home and that funding was ceased, as well. Id.

90. The same statutorily flexible approach clearly did not obtain for American Indians, before or after 1890.

Jim Crow, the fact that there were pre-1890 statutes mandating separate white and black public welfare institutions does reinforce my observation that there were numerous Jim Crow laws prior to the shift identified by Woodward. Especially in instances where there was the physical proximity of residential treatment facilities and residential schools, the existence of racial segregation statutes is not surprising. But the question as to when legalized Jim Crow began is ultimately less important than how law fostered racial segregation, discrimination, and subordination. At the same time, the state's funding subsidies helped to maintain racial barriers in private settings, primarily for white benefactors and children and not for black orphans. Subsidies by the General Assembly to such private institutions furthered racial separation for many decades, and valuable research remains to be done on the ways that money labeled "charitable" evaded scrutiny and abetted discrimination in the state.

6

Conclusion

In 1899, the North Carolina legislature enacted a statute mandating racial segregation on railroads and steamboats. The law set out that these common carriers were to "provide separate but equal accommodations for the white and colored races."[1] However, the statute exempted from its coverage "negro servants in attendance to their employers."[2] That is, with the employer being white clearly implied, blacks could sit in the white car or section only if they were servants of a white passenger. If blacks and whites were generally to be separated from one another, why allow for this exception? The answer, of course, is that this statute was about racial subordination rather than separate-but-supposedly-equal accommodations. A "negro servant" was allowed in the white compartment because that person was not an equal of the other passengers.

From 1865 to 1920 and beyond, racial discrimination and subordination by private persons ran the gamut from petty slights to grisly lynchings, but discrimination and subordination by government and governmental actors have left an undeniable footprint on America's history and they cast a long shadow over the present day. In North Carolina, the statutes enforcing racial segregation and discrimination began well before the 1890s and what has been thought of as the start of the Jim Crow era. State militia

---

1. 1899 N.C. Sess. Laws 539, ch. 384, § 1.
2. Id.

companies were required to be segregated in 1868.[3] The General Assembly reaffirmed that county jails were to be segregated based on race.[4] With the enactment of multiple statutes in the early 1870s, the freedmen's political power was weakened through political gerrymanders, both in the "packing" of one U.S. congressional district and the resulting dilution of black votes in neighboring districts, as well as in the Republican stronghold of New Hanover County, where a new, whiter county was cut out from the northern half of the existing one.[5] The legislature then eliminated one state House seat from New Hanover, to boot.[6] The Democratically controlled General Assembly passed a law which minimized black officeholding at the local level, especially in the eastern part of the state, by no longer allowing for the election of the important office of justice of the peace in favor of the JOPs' appointment by the Democrats in power in Raleigh.[7] The state not only segregated the public schools but, then, attempted to segregate the money for those schools by race.[8] An 1885 statute defined who was a Croatan Indian and also established separate schools for the Croatan children.[9] In the same year, the state law incorporating the Town of Morganton required segregated cemeteries.[10] These state statutes were a part of Jim Crow in North Carolina prior to 1890.

Statutes are not enacted or implemented in a societal vacuum, however, and the racial contagion which swept the state in 1898–1900 provides a compelling example of how law and a society interact. The White Supremacy Campaigns of those years sought to divide the state along racial lines, and the Democrats forced whites to choose which side they were

---

3. 1868 N.C. Sess. Laws 35, ch. 22, § 7.
4. 1872-73 N.C. Sess. Laws 92, ch. 74 (adopting Battle's Revisal as law, which continued segregation of county jails from Revised Code (Battle's Revisal of the Public Laws of North Carolina 286, ch. 31, § 2)).
5. The Second Congressional District was created by 1871-72 N.C. Sess. Laws 259, ch. 171. The statute creating the new Pender County is at 1874-75 N.C. Sess. Laws 96 [sic], ch. 91.
6. 1874-75 N.C. Sess. Laws 154, ch. 136, § 4.
7. 1876-77 N.C. Sess. Laws 226, 227-28, ch. 141, § 4.
8. The initial school segregation statutes are at 1868-69 N.C. Sess. Laws 458, 471, ch. 134, § 50 (townships) and at 1871-72 N.C. Sess. Laws 308, 312, ch. 189, § 20 (counties). The Dortch Act, segregating school funds by race, is at 1883 N.C. Sess. Laws 225, 226, ch. 148, § 4.
9. 1885 N.C. Sess. Laws 92, ch. 51, §§ 1-2.
10. 1885 N.C. Sess. Laws 1050, 1068, ch. 119, § 59 (Private).

on. But law provided no buffer or refuge from the racial enmity. In fact, the operation of the law changed to the detriment of the black population, not because of but, rather, in defiance of the legal text. An amendment to the state constitution that imposed a literacy test for voter registration was applied in a way that essentially wiped out black voting, summarily and in every corner of the state, irrespective of African American literacy rates.[11] The implementation of that amendment removed blacks' political power for generations. The funding of black and white public schools, which had been largely equalized over the previous fifteen years, shifted markedly in the first decade of the twentieth century in favor of the white schools and to the detriment of the black schools even though there was no significant change in the statutory text.[12] Those educational disparities for African Americans rippled out and resulted in restricted employment opportunities over lifetimes and, thus, reduced economic earning power. And while there may have been some vanishingly small number of blacks in jury pools in certain counties, the research suggests that blacks were largely excluded from jury participation in North Carolina after 1900, again without any change in the statute books.[13] The lack of African Americans in the jury box worked to the detriment of the black community and black criminal defendants for decades. The racial incitement of the White Supremacy Campaigns created a chasm between legal text and the application and operation of the law, as local officials tilted the playing field decisively against the state's African American population. Yet even with the virtual disenfranchisement of African Americans in 1900, the following decade saw the enactment of relatively few statutes reinforcing Jim Crow. The cultural shift in the attitudes of the white majority following the 1898–1900 White Supremacy Campaigns was much more important than legal text as to whether blacks had access to the voting booth or the jury box or to an adequate education.

To comprehend the ways that law influences society and society influences law, a broad lens is required, and this study has hopefully demonstrated the value of a detailed historical excavation. Law can be instrumental, and statutes do not necessarily broadcast the political and social

---

11. See Chapter 4, section B.
12. See Chapter 4, section A.
13. See Chapter 4, section C.

interests behind enactments.[14] Thus, even though a Jim Crow statute could be straightforward, as with the segregation of cemeteries, racial discrimination by and through law has often been uniquely hidden and camouflaged in American history. The reason for this masking of discrimination is because of the potential scrutiny by federal judges, even under the hollow "reasonableness" judicial standard of *Plessy* for the Jim Crow era, pursuant to the Fourteenth and Fifteenth Amendments.[15] Intentional racial discrimination has frequently been achieved in post-1865 America by enveloping that goal within more publicly palatable aims precisely because they are desirable: stable property values, similarly sized residential lots, neighborhood schools, beneficence to private orphanages, literate voters, perceptive jurors, reduced numbers of vagrants, training of apprentices, and the catch-all "public peace and good order."[16] Indeed, "separate but equal" was a phrase that could appease the American public for decades with the claim that it did not discriminate against blacks, and that if blacks chose to view it as a badge of inferiority, that was their problem and "solely because the colored race chooses to put that construction upon it."[17]

The text of a law does not tell you all you need to know about how that law operates in the world. To fully comprehend law in action, one must gather the empirical evidence and arrange the collected fragments to assess what happened after the law was enacted. That is, in the light of the statutory text, it is necessary to examine how the law was implemented by government actors, interpreted by judges, and received by stakeholders and the public at large. Roscoe Pound concluded that "defective administration, perhaps more than any other cause, is immediately responsible for

---

14. A classic example of this point is provided by Lawrence Friedman, who noted that the Sunday closing laws of the late nineteenth century were strongly supported by labor unions, not because of "morality," but because the unions wanted a shorter work week for their members: "[Labor Unions] wanted a shorter work week, and Sunday laws were a useful tool toward this end. Ministers and preachers acted as willing accomplices; labor and religion formed an odd but understandable coalition." Lawrence M. Friedman, *A History of American Law* 447 (3d ed. 2005).

15. *Plessy v. Ferguson*, 163 U.S. 537, 550 (1896) ("So far, then, as a conflict with the Fourteenth Amendment is concerned, the case reduces itself to the question whether the statute of Louisiana is a reasonable regulation....").

16. Id.

17. Id. at 551.

making law in action different from law in the books."[18] But, with regard to racial discrimination in the era of Jim Crow, the legislators who drafted the laws knew precisely what they were doing. As made apparent in this study, statutes that were racially neutral on their face were intentionally crafted so that (white) governmental officials had room to maneuver in order to hinder African Americans and benefit whites.

In the context of intentional discrimination based upon race, in the Jim Crow era and beyond, it is thus necessary to uncover the ways that laws and actions pursuant to those laws disadvantaged African Americans. The ways that law discriminated have not been obvious. Thus, this process of historical excavation is important in order to show, for example, the intentions and effects of federal home loan guarantees and local zoning ordinances which, in combination, worked to segregate the Detroit metropolitan area and other cities across this country. And, as I also demonstrate in this study, it is similarly important to uncover the ways that *de jure* racial discrimination operated in the decades after 1865, because facially neutral statutes involving literacy tests and public school funding and jury participation were weaponized in North Carolina to injure African Americans. One important function of this history is that we can see with a magnifying glass how the state and local government in North Carolina worked to intentionally disadvantage a population based upon race. I have sought to provide an accounting for what happened, under law, in North Carolina from 1865 to 1920. Legal history may not be neat or entirely comprehensible but, as Robert Gordon has recognized, "we need to know what it looks like, and how it looms, for good or ill, over our present."[19]

Even if the American public is largely unaware of it, not only did the end of slavery not put African Americans on a level playing field with regard to law but, as I have shown for North Carolina, the inequity was made greater in the decades following the Civil War. It is a canard that African Americans were equal before the law from the time of emancipation or that Reconstruction was an attempt to Africanize the South or that there was Negro domination in North Carolina in the 1890s. James Baldwin famously wrote that the difference between the racial segregation

---

18. Roscoe Pound, Law in Books and Law in Action, 44 *American Law Review* 12, 34 (1910).
19. Robert W. Gordon, *Taming the Past: Essays on Law in History and History in Law* 11 (2017).

in the North and in the South was that, in the South, it was "official."[20] Baldwin's observation was true, but the more that we understand about law and governmental policies that impacted blacks and whites differently, the more we see how pervasive *de jure* racial discrimination has been throughout the entire country and well beyond the era of Jim Crow. Residential segregation in metropolitan Detroit and throughout America did not occur simply because of individuals' private preferences. And current disparities between the races as to economic and educational attainment did not arise only recently and out of thin air. With this study, I did not set out to write some type of forensic legal history in order to provide answers to modern American debates about affirmative action or reparations or mass incarceration but, instead, I have provided an accounting as to *de jure* racial discrimination in one state over one period of time. This history is a part of how we, as Americans, got to where we are now. It is not the entire story, but it is an important part of that history. Law was central to Jim Crow in North Carolina and elsewhere. In order to fully understand the shadow that Jim Crow continues to cast over us today, it is necessary to know how ostensibly democratic government at all levels and in all places used law to advance white interests while disadvantaging the interests of African Americans and other minorities.

---

20. James Baldwin, Nobody Knows My Name: A Letter from the South, in *James Baldwin: Collected Essays* 197, 203 (Toni Morrison ed., 1998).

TABLE 1

North Carolina Constitutional and Statutory Provisions that Discriminated Based on Race, 1865 to 1920

Law	Political Party Controling General Assembly or Convention/Governor [1]	Purpose
1866 N.C. Sess. Laws 99, ch. 40, § 1.	Conservatives, Ex-Whigs/Jonathan Worth (Conservative, Ex-Whig)	Defined who is a "Negro."
1866 N.C. Sess. Laws 99, ch. 40, § 2.	Conservatives, Ex-Whigs/Jonathan Worth (Conservative, Ex-Whig)	Placed freedmen on same legal footing as free persons of color prior to Civil War, such free blacks having limited rights (i.e., not equal to whites).
1866 N.C. Sess. Laws 99, 100, ch. 40, § 4.	Conservatives, Ex-Whigs/Jonathan Worth (Conservative, Ex-Whig)	Former masters have preference over others when former slaves are apprenticed.
1866 N.C. Sess. Laws 99, 101, ch. 40, § 7.	Conservatives, Ex-Whigs/Jonathan Worth (Conservative, Ex-Whig)	Contracts, when one of the parties is a person of color, void unless contract is in writing and witnessed by a white person.
1866 N.C Sess. Laws 99, 101, ch. 40, § 8.	Conservatives, Ex-Whigs/Jonathan Worth (Conservative, Ex-Whig)	Outlawed marriage between whites and persons of color.

1. Although governors are listed in this table, note that North Carolina did not allow for a gubernatorial veto of legislation at any time during the period under consideration.

Text	Previous Law	Subsequent Statute(s)
"That negroes and their issue, even where one ancestor in each succeeding generation to the fourth inclusive, is white, shall be deemed persons of color."		
"That all persons of color . . . shall be entitled to the same privileges and subject to the same burthen and disabilities as . . . were attached to, free persons of color, prior to ordinance of emancipation . . . ."		See also 1866 N.C. Sess. Laws 99, 103, ch. 40, § 15 (repealing many existing statutory differences between "slaves" and "free negroes").
"That in the binding out of apprentices of color, the former master of such apprentices . . . shall be entitled to have such apprentices bound to them in preference to other persons."		
"That all contracts between any persons whatever, whereof one or more of them shall be a person of color, for the sale or purchase of any horse, mule, ass, jennet, neat cattle, hog, sheep or goat, whatever may be the value of such articles, and all contracts . . . of the value of ten dollars or more, shall be void as to all persons whatever, unless the same be put in writing and signed by the vendors or debtors, and witnessed by a white person who can read and write."		
"That marriage between white persons and persons of color shall be void . . . ."	Revised Code of North Carolina ch. 68, § 7 (1855) ("[All marriages] between a white person and a free negro, or free person of color, to the third generation, shall be void.").	

Law	Political Party Controling General Assembly or Convention/Governor	Purpose
1866 N.C. Sess. Laws 99, 101, ch. 40, § 8.	Conservatives, Ex-Whigs/ Jonathan Worth (Conservative, Ex-Whig)	Penalized ministers and clerks of court if they married or issued license for interracial marriage by (a) making act a misdemeanor and (b) making them subject to suit by any person for penalty of $500.
1866 N.C. Sess. Laws 99, 102, ch. 40, § 9.	Conservatives, Ex-Whigs/ Jonathan Worth (Conservative, Ex-Whig)	Restricted ability of colored persons to offer evidence in cases of law and equity to only when rights of colored person are at issue, when property of person of color at issue, or by consent of parties of record.
1866 N.C. Sess. Laws 99, 102, ch. 40, § 10.	Conservatives, Ex-Whigs/ Jonathan Worth (Conservative, Ex-Whig)	Directed judges to remind sworn witnesses of color that they should tell the truth.
1866 N.C. Sess. Laws 99, 102, ch. 40, § 11.	Conservatives, Ex-Whigs/ Jonathan Worth (Conservative, Ex-Whig)	Attempted rape of a white female by person of color punishable by death.

Text	Previous Law	Subsequent Statute(s)
"[E]very person authorized to solemnize the rites of matrimony, who shall knowingly solemnize the same between . . . persons [of different races]; and every clerk of a court who shall knowingly issue license for their marriage, shall be deemed guilty of a misdemeanor, and, moreover, shall pay a penalty of five hundred dollars to any person sueing [sic] for the same."		
"That persons of color, not otherwise incompetent, shall be capable of bearing evidence in all controversies at law and in equity, where the rights of persons or property of persons of color, shall be put in issue, and would be concluded by the judgment or decree of court; and also in pleas of the State, where the violence, fraud or injury alleged shall be charged to have been done by or to persons of color. In all other civil and criminal cases such evidence shall be deemed inadmissible, unless by consent of the parties of record: Provided, That this section shall not go into effect until jurisdiction in matters relating to freedmen shall be fully committed to the courts of this State . . . ."		See *State v. Underwood*, 63 N.C. 98 (1869) (which invalidated similar provision contained in 1855 Revised Code which set out that persons of color were incapable of being witnesses, except against each other; the court did not reference 1866 statute).
"That whenever a person of color shall be examined as a witness, the court shall warn the witness to declare the truth."		
"That any person of color, convicted by due course of law, of an assault with intent to commit rape upon the body of a white female, shall suffer death."		

Law	Political Party Controling General Assembly or Convention/Governor	Purpose
1866 N.C. Sess. Laws 111, ch. 42.	Conservatives, Ex-Whigs/ Jonathan Worth (Conservative, Ex-Whig)	New vagrancy laws aimed at freedmen who traveled without proof of employment.
1866 N.C. Sess. Laws 122, ch. 58.	Conservatives, Ex-Whigs/ Jonathan Worth (Conservative, Ex-Whig)	Anti-enticement law aimed at controlling laborers (especially freedmen) by penalizing any employer who lured workers under contract to another employer.
1866–67 N.C. Sess. Laws 87, 88, ch. 66, § 1.	Conservatives, Ex-Whigs/ Jonathan Worth (Conservative, Ex-Whig)	Landlords entitled to double damages if tenant (often black) who held over lost appeal of legal dispute.
1866–67 N.C. Sess. Laws 89, 89–90, ch. 67, § 1.	Conservatives, Ex-Whigs/ Jonathan Worth (Conservative, Ex-Whig)	Landlords entitled to pledged portion of tenant's crop if landlord believes that tenant intended to use or sell crop, effectively binding tenant (often black) to landlord.

Text	Previous Law	Subsequent Statute(s)
"That if any person who may be able to labor has no apparent means of subsistence ... or [is] sauntering about without employment ... such person shall be deemed a vagrant, and guilty of a misdemeanor.... [U]pon conviction, the court may fine or imprison him, or both, or sentence him to the workhouse for such time as the court may think fit."		Battle's Revisal of the Public Statutes of North Carolina ch. 32, § 139 (1873) (codifying 1866 law). See also 1873–74 N.C. Sess. Laws 259, 260–61, ch. 176, § 12 (amending earlier law); 1905 N.C. Sess. Laws 412, ch. 391 (amending entire vagrancy law).
"That if ... any person shall entice, persuade and procure any servant by indenture, or any servant who shall have contracted in writing ... to unlawfully leave the service of his master or employer...."		1866–67 N.C. Sess. Laws 197, ch. 124 (amended 1866 statute by adding other penalties). See Battle's Revisal of the Public Statutes of North Carolina ch. 70, § 1 (1873) (codifying 1866 and 1866–67 laws). See also 1901 N.C. Sess. Laws 913, ch. 682 (making person liable for civil damages if that person hired or employed a person who had an employment contract and left employment before end of contract, but only in 13 counties).
"[I]f the defendant shall appeal ... if, upon trial of the cause in the Superior Court, the finding shall be in favor of the Landlord, the jury shall assess the damage to which the Landlord shall be entitled at double the value of the rent or occupation of the premises sued for ...."		
"[That whenever a lessee agrees] to deliver to his landlord a certain share of the crop ... [that portion of the crop] shall be deemed the property of such landlord ... [if] his lessee or under-tenant has refused or failed to deliver it, and that he has reason to believe, that his lessee or under-tenant intends to use, sell or destroy it ...."		

Law	Political Party Controling General Assembly or Convention/Governor	Purpose
1866–67 N.C. Sess. Laws 95, 97–98, ch. 72, § 1.	Conservatives, Ex-Whigs/ Jonathan Worth (Conservative, Ex-Whig)	Poll taxes to be paid by employer, with amount withheld from employee's pay, and if employee moved, the employer was entitled to double tax on employee from any subsequent employer.
1866–67 N.C. Sess. Laws 92, ch. 69, § 3.	Conservatives, Ex-Whigs/ Jonathan Worth (Conservative, Ex-Whig)	Required clerks to keep separate books recording marriages of white and colored persons, presumably to track lineal descendants of persons defined as Negroes.
1868–69 N.C. Sess. Laws 458, 471, ch. 134, § 50.	Republicans/William Woods Holden (Republican)	Established racially separate schools for each race residing in a township (presumably including Native Americans, id. at 466, § 32)
1869–70 N.C. Sess. Laws 48, ch. 7, § 1.	Republicans/William Woods Holden (Republican)	Bound apprentices, overwhelmingly black, to "some discreet person" selected by a probate judge up until the age of 21, if male, and 18, if female.
1869–70 N.C. Sess. Laws 271, 280, ch. 225, § 21.[2]	Republicans/William Woods Holden (Republican)	Clerk of county commissioners to maintain racially separate poll tax lists.

2. This section was part of a statute authorizing the valuation and collection of taxes by the state and counties. Although the revenue statute was phrased generally and did not contain a sunset provision, the General Assembly passed new versions of this statute in subsequent years with the same section requiring racially separate poll tax lists. Only the provision in the original statute is listed in the above table. For subsequent versions, see 1870–71 N.C. Sess. Laws 294,

Text	Previous Law	Subsequent Statute(s)
"It shall be the duty of all persons and corporations to list and pay the tax of such persons liable to the same, as are in their employment, on the 1st day of April of each year, as laborers, and the amount of said tax may be retained out of any moneys due such employees.... [A]ny person or persons subject to such poll-tax, removing himself or themselves from one county into another.... [upon failure to keep certificate showing employer duly listed] shall be subject to double tax, retained from his or their wages by the first person employing him or them...."		
"[I]t shall be the duty of the Clerk to copy such evidence of marriage ... keeping such registry of white and colored persons in separate books...."		
"The school authorities of each and every Township shall establish a separate school or separate schools for the instruction of children and youth of each race resident therein ... and such school or schools shall be supported, regulated, and instructed in the same manner and to the same extent as any other public school or schools of the same grade."		See infra 1871-72 N.C. Sess. Laws 308, 312, ch. 189, § 20.
"Every male apprentice shall be bound to some discreet person approved by the judge of probate until the age of twenty-one years, and every female apprentice until the age of eighteen years."		
"[The clerk of the commissioners shall send list to state auditor of] the number of white and colored polls separately."		See footnote 2.

303, ch. 195, § 22; 1871-72 N.C. Sess. Laws 55, 64-65, ch. 49, § 22; 1872-73 N.C. Sess. Laws 158, 168-69, ch. 115, § 22; 1873-74 N.C. Sess. Laws 173, 184, ch. 133, § 22; 1874-75 N.C. Sess. Laws 213, 225, ch. 184, § 23; 1876-77 N.C. Sess. Laws 255, 267, ch. 155, § 23; 1879 N.C. Sess. Laws 103, 118, ch. 71, § 29.

Law	Political Party Controling General Assembly or Convention/Governor	Purpose
1871-72 N.C. Sess. Laws 308, 312, ch. 189, § 20.	Conservatives/ Tod Robinson Caldwell (Republican)	Required racially separate schools in counties but school districts for each race could be the same.
1871-72 N.C. Sess. Laws 328, ch. 193, § 2.	Conservatives/ Tod Robinson Caldwell (Republican)	Statute (a) outlawed marriages between a white person and either a Negro or an Indian or a person of Negro or Indian descent, and (b) marriage (voidable) between white person and a person of color should still be declared void even if child resulted from cohabitation.
1871-72 N.C. Sess. Laws 328, 331-32, ch. 193, §§ 9-10.	Conservatives/ Tod Robinson Caldwell (Republican)	Set out penalty for any register of deeds who did not record in a book of marriages certain information of each marriage license issued or marriage license returned, such as race of husband and wife, presumably to track lineal descendants of persons defined as Negroes.
1871-72 N.C. Sess. Laws 328, 339, ch. 193, § 34.	Conservatives/ Tod Robinson Caldwell (Republican)	Any offspring of a (voidable) marriage between a white person and a person of color (as defined in § 2) could not be legitimated to the father.

Text	Previous Law	Subsequent Statute(s)
"The schools of the two races shall be separate; the districts may be the same or not, according to the convenience of the parties concerned."		See 1872–73 N.C. Sess. Laws 119, 124, ch. 90, § 20 (reenacted with virtually identical language) and Amendment of 1875, ch. 26, to N.C. Const. of 1868, art. IX, § 2, listed infra. Identical language enacted in: 1881 N.C. Sess. Laws 371, 377, ch. 200, § 21.
"All marriages between a white person and a negro or Indian, or between a white person and a person of negro or Indian descent, to the third generation inclusive . . . shall be void."		See Amendment of 1875, ch. 30, to N.C. Const. of 1868, art. XIV, § 8, infra. See also 1899 N.C. Sess. Laws 729, ch. 541 (specifying how marriage licenses shall record "race and color").
"[N]o marriage followed by cohabitation and the birth of issue shall be declared void after the death of either of the parties for any of the causes stated in this section, except for that one of the parties was a white person and the other a negro or Indian, or of negro or Indian descent to the third generation inclusive."		
"Any register of deeds who shall fail to record, in the manner above prescribed, the substance of any marriage license issued by him, or who shall fail to record, in the manner above prescribed, the substance of any return . . . shall forfeit and pay two hundred dollars to any person who shall sue for the same."		
"[I]t shall not be lawful for the issue of any such marriage [between a white person and a person of color per § 2] to be legitimated to the supposed father."		

Law	Political Party Controling General Assembly or Convention/Governor	Purpose
1872–73 N.C. Sess. Laws 92, ch. 74.	Conservatives/ Tod Robinson Caldwell (Republican)	Continued legal segregation of county jails by General Assembly's adoption of Battle's Revisal.[3]
1872–73 N.C. Sess. Laws 92, ch. 74.	Conservatives/ Tod Robinson Caldwell (Republican)	Contracts with Cherokee Indians for $10 or more void unless put into writing and witnessed by two other persons.[4]
1872–73 N.C. Sess. Laws 119, 128, ch. 90, § 30.	Conservatives/ Tod Robinson Caldwell (Republican)	County boards of education to apportion money to townships based on number of children in townships, but with discretion to apportion unequally based on race.
1872–73 N.C. Sess. Laws 267, 274, ch. 163, § 14.	Conservatives/ Tod Robinson Caldwell (Republican)	New Hanover County given power to create juvenile detention facility, but law required any buildings to be constructed so as to keep races segregated.
1874–75 N.C. Sess. Laws 92, ch. 89, § 1.	Conservatives/ Curtis Hooks Brogden (Republican)	Prohibited white child from being apprenticed to any person of color.

3. The code revisal was adopted by the General Assembly as law: "[A]ll the provisions contained in the chapters revised and reported by the commissioner and to be known as 'Battle's Revisal,' shall take effect and go into operation on the first day of January, in the year one thousand eight hundred and seventy-four." 1872–73 N.C. Sess. Laws 92, ch. 74, § 1.

4. Again, this provision of Battle's Revisal was adopted as law by 1872–73 N.C. Sess. Laws 92, ch. 74, § 1.

Text	Previous Law	Subsequent Statute(s)
"The common jails of the several counties shall be provided with at least four separate comfortable apartments, one for the confinement of white male criminals, one for white female criminals, one for debtors, and one other for persons of color." (Battle's Revisal of the Public Statutes of North Carolina ch. 31, § 2 (1873)).		
"All contracts and agreements of every description made . . . with any Cherokee Indian, or any person of Cherokee Indian blood, within the second degree, for an amount equal to ten dollars or more, shall be void, unless some note or memorandum thereof be made in writing, and signed by such Indian or person of Indian blood . . . in the presence of two witnesses, who shall also subscribe the same." (Battle's Revisal of the Public Statutes of North Carolina ch. 50, § 9 (1873)).		
"[County board of education to] apportion among the several townships in the county, according to the number of children in each . . . specifying how much thereof is apportioned to the children of each race . . . ."		See also 1872–73 N.C. Sess. Laws 119, 128, ch. 90, § 30 (identical language); 1876–77 N.C. Sess. Laws 323, 331–32, ch. 162, § 31 (identical language).
"The buildings of the House of Correction and Refuge shall be so constructed that the children of the white race shall be kept separate and apart, and the children of the colored race shall be kept separate and apart from the other race."		
"*Provided*, That no white child shall be bound to a colored master or mistress."		See 1889 N.C. Sess. Laws 138, ch. 169, § 1 (indigent white child cannot be bound to colored person).

Law	Political Party Controling General Assembly or Convention/Governor	Purpose
1874–75 N.C. Sess. Laws 96 [sic], ch. 91.[5]	Conservatives/ Curtis Hooks Brogden (Republican)	Created Pender County from part of New Hanover County, a Republican stronghold, in order to pack Republican (and black) political power into New Hanover and allow for Conservative/Democratic power in new Pender County.
1874–75 N.C. Sess. Laws 154, ch. 136, § 4.	Conservatives/ Curtis Hooks Brogden (Republican)	Reduced number of state House seats representing heavily black and Republican New Hanover County (newly shrunk).
1874–75 N.C. Sess. Laws 462, ch. 43, § 4 (Private).	Conservatives/ Curtis Hooks Brogden (Republican)	Redrew political wards in Wilmington, a Republican and black political stronghold, so that majority white areas of city with 21 percent of city's population elected 6 aldermen, while black majority areas with 79 percent of population elected just 3 aldermen.
1874–75 N.C. Sess. Laws 529, 531–32, ch. 80, § 4. (Private).	Conservatives/ Curtis Hooks Brogden (Republican)	Voting registrars for City of Raleigh to keep separate lists of white and colored voters.

5. While the chapter number of this statute is correct, the page number at the top of the page in the published volume is clearly wrong: the page should actually be 93, as it is between pages 92 and 94 in the published session laws. I have retained the misprint in the table with "sic" to note the problem.

Text	Previous Law	Subsequent Statute(s)
"That all that part of the County of New Hanover included within the following bounds . . . is hereby created into a separate and distinct county by the name of Pender with all the rights, priviliges [sic] and immunities incident and belonging to the other counties in this State."		See 1874–75 N.C. Sess. Laws 154, ch. 136, § 4 (law from same session that reduced the number of state representatives from New Hanover County).
"[At next election] for members of the House of Representatives, the county of New Hanover shall elect two members and the county of Pender shall elect one member . . . ."		
"That the city of Wilmington shall be divided into three divisions or wards, denominated first, second and third wards respectively . . . . The third ward shall include all that portion of the city not included within the bounds of the first and second wards."		*State ex rel. Van Bokkelen v. Canaday*, 73 N.C. 198 (1875) (striking down 1875 statute cited here because it unconstitutionally changed residency requirements for voting by Wilmington residents). See also 1876–77 N.C. Sess. Laws 376, ch. 192, § 1 (new law subsequent to 1875 N.C. Supreme Court decision that again packed most blacks into two out of the five total wards).[6] Cf. 1874–75 N.C. Sess. Laws 723, ch. 168 (Private) (similar racial packing of political wards in Tarboro). Later, the 1897 fusionist legislature revised the Wilmington charter to eliminate the 1876 changes which had given the Democrats advantages in Wilmington elections. 1897 N.C. Sess. Laws 282, ch. 150 (Private).
"[Registrars to maintain registration books] keeping the names of the white voters separate and apart from those of colored voters . . . ."		See also 1883 N.C. Sess. Laws 967, 970, ch. 142, § 6 (Private) (identical language used for Town of Smithfield).

---

6. It should be noted that the Roman numerals for this chapter number (192) are printed as "CLXLII" instead of the "CXCII" to which modern readers would be more accustomed.

Law	Political Party Controling General Assembly or Convention/Governor	Purpose
Amendment of 1875, ch. 24, to N.C. Const. of 1868, art. VI, sec. 1.[7]	Equal number of Republican and Conservative delegates, with three independents (Convention)	Increased county residency requirement for voting registration from 30 to 90 days to dilute political power of blacks because blacks moved more than whites to find employment.
Amendment of 1875, ch. 24, to N.C. Const. of 1868, art. VI, sec. 1.	Equal number of Republican and Conservative delegates, with three independents (Convention)	Felons disenfranchised to reduce numbers of black voters.
Amendment of 1875, ch. 25, to N.C. Const. of 1868, art. VII.	Equal number of Republican and Conservative delegates, with three independents (Convention)	Granted General Assembly the power to modify or abrogate Article VII of 1868 Constitution which would allow General Assembly to change method of selection of county officers from elective to appointive (by General Assembly).
Amendment of 1875, ch. 26, to N.C. Const. of 1868, art. IX, sec. 2.	Equal number of Republican and Conservative delegates, with three independents (Convention)	Required racially separate public schools.
Amendment of 1875, ch. 30, to N.C. Const. of 1868, art. XIV, sec. 8.	Equal number of Republican and Conservative delegates, with three independents (Convention)	Prohibited marriage between a white and a Negro or a person of Negro descent to the third generation inclusive.

---

7. The amendments proposed by the constitutional convention of 1875—and the chapter numbers—are found in *Amendments to the Constitution of North Carolina, Proposed by the Constitutional Convention of 1875* (Raleigh: Josiah Turner, 1875).

Text	Previous Law	Subsequent Statute(s)
"Every male person, born [or naturalized] ... twenty-one years old or upward, who shall have resided ... ninety days in the county in which he offers to vote, shall be deemed an elector...."	N.C. Const. of 1868, art. VI, sec. 1. ("Every male person born [or naturalized] ... twenty-one years old or upward, who shall have resided ... thirty days in the county, in which he offers to vote, shall be deemed an elector.").	1876–77 N.C. Sess. Laws 516, 520, ch. 275, § 11 (extending 90-day residency requirement to township elections).
"But no person, who, upon conviction or confession in open Court, shall be adjudged guilty of felony, or of any other crime infamous by the laws of this State, and hereafter committed, shall be deemed an elector...."	People convicted of infamous crimes lost right to vote. *Shipp v. M'Craw*, 7 N.C. 463, 466 (1819) (Henderson, J., concurring) (stating that "for those who are punished for infamous crimes are degraded from their rank as citizens, they lose their privileges as freemen"). Conviction for an infamous crime allowed judge to impose "one or more public whippings." Revised Code of North Carolina ch. 34, § 27 (1855).	See Amendment of 1900 to N.C. Const. of 1868, art. VI, sec. 2, (final version proposed at 1900 N.C. Sess. Laws 54, 55, ch. 2, § 1 (person guilty of crime punished through confinement at state prison prohibited from voting).
"The General Assembly shall have full power by statute to modify, change or abrogate any and all of the provisions of this article and substitute others in their place...."	N.C. Const. of 1868, art. VII, sec. 5 ("In each township there shall be biennially elected, by the qualified voters thereof, a Clerk and two Justices of the Peace....").	1876–77 N.C. Sess. Laws 226, 227–28, ch. 141, §§ 4–5 (statute providing for "election" of local Justices of Peace by General Assembly pursuant to amendment).
"And the children of the white race and the children of the colored race shall be taught in separate public schools...."	See 1876–77 N.C. Sess. Laws 323, 327, ch. 162, § 22 ("The schools of the two races shall be separate; the districts the same or not, according to the convenience of the parties concerned.").	
"All marriages between a white person and a negro, or between a white person and a person of negro descent to the third generation inclusive, are hereby forever prohibited."		

Law	Political Party Controlling General Assembly or Convention/Governor	Purpose
1876–77 N.C. Sess. Laws 226, 227–28, ch. 141, §§ 4–5.	Democrats/Zebulon Baird Vance (Democrat)	Pursuant to constitutional amendment, General Assembly took back power from counties and townships and gave itself power to appoint justices of the peace and gave the JOPs the power to elect the county commissioners, thus weakening African American political power and office-holding in eastern N.C. counties where African Americans were majority of population.
1876–77 N.C. Sess. Laws 516, 517–518 ch. 275, § 6.	Democrats/Zebulon Baird Vance (Democrat)	Board of justices of the peace for each county empowered to wipe voting rolls clean and to require all voters to register again.[9]
1876–77 N.C. Sess. Laws 556–57, ch. 285, §§ 1, 4.	Democrats/Zebulon Baird Vance (Democrat)	Extended to Cross Creek township in Cumberland County the ability to hold an election to allow for extra taxes for schools as long as a majority of petitioners were white.

---

8. By Amendment of 1875, ch. 25, to N.C. Const. of 1868, art. VII, the N.C. Constitution allowed the General Assembly to "have full power by statute to modify, change, or abrogate any and all of the provisions of this Article, and substitute others in their place." N.C. Const. of 1868, art. VII, sec. 14. This provision allowing statutory revision of constitution contributed to a view of the 1868 Constitution as "a sort of super-statute . . . rather than a repository of fundamental principles and an outline of institutional structures." John V. Orth and Paul Martin Newby, *The North Carolina State Constitution* 25 (2d ed. 2013).

9. Although this was at the option of the boards of the individual counties, it appears that there was a good deal of coordination, because a new state-wide registration may have taken place in 1890 pursuant to this statutory provision.

Text	Previous Law	Subsequent Statute(s)
"The justices of the peace shall be elected by the general assembly." * * * "The justices of the peace for each county . . . shall proceed to the election of not less than three nor more than five persons, to be chosen from the body of the county (including the justices of the peace) who shall be styled the board of commissioners for the county . . . ."	N.C. Const. of 1868, art. VII, § 1 stated that county commissioners were to be elected by the qualified voters of the counties and, in turn, the justices of the peace were to be elected by the same voters. Id. at § 5. This act (1876–77 N.C. Sess. Laws 226, ch. 141) overturned those constitutional provisions.[8]	
"[T]he board of justices of the peace for such county may, upon giving thirty days' notice in each township, if they shall think proper, direct that there shall be an entirely new registration of voters before any election, instead of the revision of the registration lists . . . ."		1899 N.C. Sess. Laws 658, 661, ch. 507, § 11 (mandated new registration state-wide).
"Provided, The provisions of this act shall extend to Cross Creek township, in the county of Cumberland, provided the application for the election shall be made by two hundred of the qualified voters of said township who shall be freeholders therein, and at least one-half of such petitioners shall be of the white race."		

See, e.g., New Registration (Public Notice), *Tarborough Southerner* (Tarboro, N.C.), Nov. 13, 1890, at 3 (Edgecombe County); Notice! (Public Notice), *Concord Times* (Concord, N.C.), Oct. 17, 1890, at 1 (Cabarrus County); Registration, *Newton Enterprise* (Newton, N.C.), Oct. 10, 1890, at 3 (Catawba County); Locals, *Murfreesboro Index* (Murfreesboro, N.C.), Oct. 10, 1890, at 3 (Hertford County); Registration Notice! (Public Notice), *Daily Journal* (New Bern, N.C.), Sept. 11, 1890, at 2 (Craven County); New Registration Ordered (Public Notice), *Charlotte Democrat*, Aug. 29, 1890, at 3 (Mecklenburg County); Notice. A New Registration! (Public Notice), *Washington Progress* (Washington, N.C.), Aug. 19, 1890, at 3 (Beaufort County); A New Registration, *Oxford Public Ledger* (Oxford, N.C.), Aug. 15, 1890, at 4 (Granville County); New Registration! (Public Notice), *Southport Leader* (Southport, N.C.), Aug. 14, 1890, at 4 (Brunswick County).

Law	Political Party Controling General Assembly or Convention/Governor	Purpose
1880 N.C. Sess. Laws 67, 68–71, ch. 27, §§ 3 and 8.	Democrats/Thomas Jordan Jarvis (Democrat)	Vote allowed in Salisbury and Goldsboro on tax to support graded schools, with tax dollars from whites going only to white schools and tax dollars from colored persons going to colored schools.
1881 N.C. Sess. Laws 371, 377–378, 381, 385, ch. 200, §§ 22, 32, 45.	Democrats/Thomas Jordan Jarvis (Democrat)	State school law (1) gave county boards of education absolute discretion over division of school funds as between white and colored schools and prohibited use of funds apportioned to either race to be used for education of other race, (2) created some incentives to allow for unequal pay between white and colored teachers by requiring county treasurers and county superintendents of public instruction to report—each one, independently and separately—to the State Superintendent of Public Instruction on the salaries of white and colored teachers.

Text	Previous Law	Subsequent Statute(s)
"The special taxes thus levied and collected [in Salisbury] from the taxable property and polls of white persons shall be expended in keeping up a graded public school for white persons . . . and the special taxes thus levied and collected from the taxable property and polls of colored persons shall be expended in keeping up a graded public school for colored persons . . . ."		Virtually identical law for Goldsboro passed again in next legislative session. 1881 N.C. Sess. Laws 360, 361, ch. 189, § 3. See also 1883 N.C. Sess. Laws 225, 226, ch. 148, § 4, below, which extended policy statewide.

* * *

"The taxes raised [in Goldsboro] from the property and polls of white persons shall be appropriated exclusively to a graded school for white persons, and the taxes raised from the property and polls of colored persons shall be appropriated exclusively to a graded school for colored persons."

Text	Previous Law	Subsequent Statute(s)
"The county board of education shall . . . apportion among the several districts in the county . . . all school funds . . . specifying how much thereof is apportioned to the children of each race. . . . Provided, however, That in no case shall the school fund thus apportioned to either race by [sic] expended for the education of the other race . . . ."		See 1883 N.C. Sess. Laws 225, 228, ch. 148, § 12 (requiring county treasurers to report).

* * *

"The county treasurer of each county shall report to the state superintendent of public instruction . . . designating the sums paid to teachers for the white and colored children respectively . . . ."

* * *

"It shall be the duty of the county superintendent of public instruction of each county . . . to report to the state superintendent of public instruction . . . the average salary, respectively, of the white and colored teachers . . . ."

Law	Political Party Controling General Assembly or Convention/Governor	Purpose
1883 N.C. Sess. Laws 225, 226, ch. 148, § 4.	Democrats/Thomas Jordan Jarvis (Democrat)	General law required all school districts to segregate tax revenues by race and expend money based on race.
1883 N.C. Sess. Laws 252, 252–53, ch. 157, §§ 1, 3.	Democrats/Thomas Jordan Jarvis (Democrat)	Whites-only graded and normal schools established in Fayetteville, but vote as to annual tax limited to white residents, with no colored graded school or opportunity for black residents to vote on similar tax.
1883 N.C. Sess. Laws 357, 357–58, ch. 220, §§ 1–7.	Democrats/Thomas Jordan Jarvis (Democrat)	Members of Board of Trustees for white graded school in Edenton were to be white, but no reciprocal guarantee for trustees of colored graded school.
1883 N.C. Sess. Laws 851, 852, ch. 110, § 6 (Private).	Democrats/Thomas Jordan Jarvis (Democrat)	No white children to be admitted to private orphanage for colored children.

Text	Previous Law	Subsequent Statute(s)
"That the assessment thus levied and collected from the taxable property and polls of white persons, shall be expended in aiding to keep up the public school in said district for white children . . . and the assessment thus levied and collected from the taxable property and polls of colored persons shall be expended in aiding to keep up the public school in said district for colored children . . . ."		See also, e.g., 1883 N.C. Sess. Laws 170, 171, ch. 117, § 3 (repeating this requirement for graded schools in NewBerne [sic]).[10] These laws were held to be unconstitutional. *Riggsbee v. Town of Durham*, 94 N.C. 800 (1886); *Puitt v. Commissioners of Gaston County*, 94 N.C. 709 (1886).
"[Trustees of Fayetteville schools formed] for maintaining and carrying on a public graded and normal school for whites in Cross Creek township" and vote "by the white voters . . . [for annual tax] upon the property and polls of the white citizens and owners of property . . . ."		See, e.g., 1885 N.C. Sess. Laws 346, ch. 181, § 1 (whites-only graded school in Cabarrus County). See also 1893 N.C. Sess. Laws 146, ch. 189, § 1 (amended 1883 law so that law as to Fayetteville schools would allow for white and colored schools as well as votes on taxes).
"[Trustees of white graded school, designated in statute, are authorized] to elect seven men from among the white citizens of the school district . . . to constitute . . . the board of trustees of said graded school for the white race . . . ." (§ 2)		
* * *		
"That [named trustees] be and they are hereby constituted a board of trustees for the graded school for the colored race . . . ." (§ 7)		
"Provided, that the said institution shall be for children of the colored race only."		

10. The 1883 Session began a large wave of statutes passed to establish graded schools in cities, townships, and counties across the state. By my count, in 1883, there were six such acts beyond the ones listed in the above table, and more were to come in subsequent legislative sessions. Invariably, these acts all contained a similar section on the segregation of tax dollars for schools by race. I have not listed any act establishing a school district for 1883 or any subsequent legislative session in the above table unless the statute contained some novel race-conscious feature.

Law	Political Party Controling General Assembly or Convention/Governor	Purpose
1885 N.C. Sess. Laws 56, 56, 58–59, ch. 7, §§ 1, 9.	Democrats/Alfred Moore Scales (Democrat)	Act established Edenton graded school solely for white children and, in turn, repealed act from 1883 that established graded schools for white and colored children.
1885 N.C. Sess. Laws 81, ch. 35, § 1.	Democrats/Alfred Moore Scales (Democrat)	Authorized school committee for colored school district to transfer "surplus" funds "at their discretion" to Fayetteville graded school for whites; no authorization for any surplus funds to move in other direction.
1885 N.C. Sess. Laws 92, ch. 51, §§ 1–2.	Democrats/Alfred Moore Scales (Democrat)	Defined who is a Croatan Indian (today's Lumbee Indians) and instituted separate schools.

Text	Previous Law	Subsequent Statute(s)
"That a graded school is hereby incorporated to be known as the Edenton Graded School . . . for the white race . . . and said school shall be free to all the white children . . . ."		
* * *		
"That the act of the general assembly ratified March third, one thousand eight hundred and eighty-three, entitled 'An act to establish graded schools at Edenton, Chowan County, North Carolina', and all other laws in conflict with this act be hereby repealed . . . ."		
"That the school committee for district number one, colored, in Cross Creek township, Cumberland County, are hereby authorized, at their discretion, to transfer to the trustees of the Fayetteville graded school for whites in the said township, any surplus funds that may have accumulated, or may hereafter accumulate, to the credit of said district, after defraying all expenses incident to a ten months' school in the same annually."		
"[T]he Indians now living in Robeson county" and descendants "shall hereafter be designated and known as the Croatan Indians." (§ 1) * * * "That said Indians and their descendants shall have separate schools for their children, school committees of their own race and color . . . ." (§ 2)		Children of the Eastern Band of Cherokee Indians may not have been similarly excluded from white schools. See 1911 N.C. Sess. Laws 445, ch. 339, § 2 (referencing Indians recognized as citizens "and whose children are admitted to attendance in public schools for white children").[11]

11. This 1911 statute was clearly referencing the Eastern Band of Cherokee Indians in the western part of the state and the Cherokee children had (in the 1880s and 1890s) been educated by Quakers, pursuant to a contract between the U.S. Government, the Cherokees, and the Society of Friends. Sharlotte Neely, The Quaker Era of Cherokee Indian Education, 1880–1892, 2 *Appalachian Journal* 314, 315 (1975). However, it should be noted that, in 1913, the N.C. General Assembly changed the name of the "Indians of Robeson County" (the tribe which had previously been labeled "Croatan") to "Cherokee Indians of Robeson County." 1913 N.C. Sess. Laws 215, ch. 123, § 1.

Law	Political Party Controling General Assembly or Convention/Governor	Purpose
1885 N.C. Sess. Laws 161, 162–163, ch. 111, §§ 2–3, 5.	Democrats/Alfred Moore Scales (Democrat)	In Brevard, (1) special tax raised from white persons to create graded school for white children and special tax from colored persons just for "education" of colored children and not graded school; (2) town board of education could supplement funds going to white graded school with any public moneys "applicable" to education of white children.
1885 N.C. Sess. Laws 218, 221, ch. 141, § 6.	Democrats/Alfred Moore Scales (Democrat)	Raleigh school committee given discretion over funding of white and colored schools because of different "costs" for white and colored schools.
1885 N.C. Sess. Laws 780, ch. 31, §§ 1–3 (Private).	Democrats/Alfred Moore Scales (Democrat)	Revenues from privilege or license tax in City of Winston could be used by school commissioners in any way they saw fit relative to white and colored schools.

Text	Previous Law	Subsequent Statute(s)
"The special tax thus collected from the taxable property and polls of white persons shall be applied and expended exclusively to the purpose of a graded public school which shall be free to all white persons...."		
* * *		
"And the special tax collected from the property and polls of colored persons shall be expended exclusively for the education of colored children...."		
* * *		
"[A]nd the said board shall receive and apply to the purpose of said graded school all public moneys from whatsoever source arising, which are or may hereafter be applicable to the common school education of white children within the school age...."		
"[The Raleigh school committee shall apportion money] as shall be just to the white and colored races, without discrimination in favor of or to the prejudice of either race, due regard being paid to the cost of keeping up the public schools for both races."[12]		
"That the Winston commissioners of graded schools shall be and are hereby authorized to receive and use the moneys herein provided for and to apply the same in such a way as they may deem best for the benefit of the graded schools, white and colored, of said town...."		See 1891 N.C. Sess. Laws 1345, 1357, ch. 307, § 52 (Private) (again giving Winston commissioners discretion to apportion money "in such a way as they may deem best for the benefit of the graded schools, white and colored").

12. This "due regard" phrasing was repeated in many school statutes over the years. See, e.g., 1887 N.C. Sess. Laws 152, 156, ch. 86, § 9 (Durham schools); 1887 N.C. Sess. Laws 691, 694, ch. 397, § 9 (Asheville schools); 1887 N.C. Sess. Laws 755, 759, ch. 424, § 8 (Reidsville schools); 1889 N.C. Sess. Laws 50, ch. 20, § 1 (Salisbury schools); 1891 N.C. Sess. Laws 457, 459, ch. 386, § 8 (Statesville schools); 1895 N.C. Sess. Laws 3, 6, ch. 2, § 11 (Private) (Mount Airy schools).

Law	Political Party Controling General Assembly or Convention/Governor	Purpose
1885 N.C. Sess. Laws 976, ch. 87, § 2 (Private).	Democrats/Alfred Moore Scales (Democrat)	Authorized Durham town commissioners to issue bonds for purchase of land and buildings for white children.
1885 N.C. Sess. Laws 1050, 1068, ch. 119, § 59 (Private).	Democrats/Alfred Moore Scales (Democrat)	Statute to incorporate Town of Morganton mandated that town racially segregate cemeteries.
1887 N.C. Sess. Laws 368, 368–69, ch. 160, § 1.	Democrats and Republicans split with independents holding influence/Alfred Moore Scales (Democrat)	Allowed white residents in Rowan County to use public school funds to attend private segregated school.
1887 N.C. Sess. Laws 499, ch. 254, § 1.	Democrats and Republicans split with independents holding influence /Alfred Moore Scales (Democrat)	Marriages between Croatan Indian and a Negro or a person of Negro descent void.

Text	Previous Law	Subsequent Statute(s)
"[T]he proceeds arising from the sale of said bonds shall be expended by the Durham graded school committee in the purchase and erection of suitable grounds and buildings for the Durham graded or public schools for white children...."		
"The commissioners shall provide separate cemeteries for the white and the colored people...."		See also 1897 N.C. Sess. Laws 133, 134, ch. 83, § 6 (Private) (City of Winston authorized to purchase cemeteries, one for whites and one for colored citizens); 1901 N.C. Sess. Laws 650, 653, ch. 248, § 55 (Private) (same for Town of Carthage); 1905 N.C. Sess. Laws 221, 238–39, ch. 82 (Private) (revised charter for City of Winston repeated language used in 1897); 1909 N.C. Sess. Laws 460, ch. 203, § 7 (Private) (same for Town of Laurinburg); 1911 N.C. Sess. Laws 499, 512, ch. 219, § 31 (Private) (same for Town of Smithfield).
"That all the citizens of the white race entitled by law to the benefit of the public school fund, living and resident within one and a half miles of Thyatira church, in Rowan County, be and they are hereby allowed and permitted to use and enjoy that portion of the public school fund apportioned to them by law for the payment of tuition and other expenses in attendance at Thyatira academy...."		See, e.g., 1889 N.C. Sess. Laws 626, 627, ch. 71, § 3 (Private) (allowed whites to use pro rata share of public school funds to attend private segregated high school in Pender County).
"That all marriages between an Indian and a Negro or between an Indian and a person of Negro descent to the third generation inclusive shall be utterly void: Provided, this act shall only apply to the Croatan Indians."		

Law	Political Party Controling General Assembly or Convention/Governor	Purpose
1887 N.C. Sess. Laws 713, ch. 407, § 1.	Democrats and Republicans split with independents holding influence /Alfred Moore Scales (Democrat)	Allowed white residents in part of Sampson County to use public school funds to attend schools in Johnston County.
1887 N.C. Sess. Laws 870, 871, ch. 52, § 6 (Private).	Democrats and Republicans split with independents holding influence /Alfred Moore Scales (Democrat)	Prevented any person of color from owning stock in private seminary for white females.
1889 N.C. Sess. Laws 72, ch. 60, § 1.	Democrats/Daniel Gould Fowle (Democrat)	Excluded Negroes from schools for Croatan Indians in Robeson County.
1889 N.C. Sess. Laws 138, 141, ch. 169, § 17.	Democrats/Daniel Gould Fowle (Democrat)	No white child to be apprenticed to a person of color and no colored child to be apprenticed to white if colored person available.
1889 N.C. Sess. Laws 163, 170, ch. 199, § 42.	Democrats/Daniel Gould Fowle (Democrat)	Defined what children were barred from white schools.

Text	Previous Law	Subsequent Statute(s)
"That all the citizens of the white race entitled by law to the benefit of the public school fund, living and resident [in a certain area of Sampson County] . . . be allowed and permitted to use and enjoy that portion of the public school fund apportioned to them by law in the future, for the payment of tuition and other expenses incurred in attendance . . . [at any] convenient school district in said Johnston county."		
"The purpose of this institution is for the education of females of the white race, and no person of color shall own stock therein, and any stock transferred to a person of color shall be forfeited to said corporation."		
"[1885 Act that created schools for Croatans to be amended by adding] 'and there shall be excluded from such separate schools for the said Croatan Indians all children of the negro race to the fourth generation.'"		See 1889 N.C. Sess. Laws 436, ch. 458, § 1 (Croatan Indians in Richmond County may establish separate schools from which Negroes would be excluded).
"But no white child [whether indigent or not] shall be bound to a colored person, and no colored child shall be bound to any white person if a competent and suitable colored person can be found in the county."	See 1874–75 N.C. Sess. Laws 92, ch. 89, § 1, supra.	
"That in determining the right of any child to attend the white or colored schools, the rule laid down in section 1810 of The Code, regulating marriages, shall be followed." (The code provision distinguished between "a white person and a person of negro or Indian descent, to the third generation, inclusive." 1 Code of North Carolina § 1810 (1883)).		See also 1899 N.C. Sess. Laws 903, 921, ch. 732, § 71 (same); 1901 N.C. Sess. Laws 45, 64, ch. 4, § 68 (same).

Law	Political Party Controling General Assembly or Convention/Governor	Purpose
1889 N.C. Sess. Laws 171, 172, ch. 200, § 5.	Democrats/Daniel Gould Fowle (Democrat)	Abolished white normal schools and created institutes in individual counties for white teachers;[13] at the end of a session of county institute, there was teacher certificate testing for white and colored teachers, even though colored teachers had not attended institute.
1889 N.C. Sess. Laws 289, ch. 287, § 3.	Democrats/Daniel Gould Fowle (Democrat)	Statute created hurdle for many potential black voters by requiring specificity about age and residence that many former slaves and illiterates lacked.
1889 N.C. Sess. Laws 423, ch. 444.	Democrats/Daniel Gould Fowle (Democrat)	Statute made it a crime (beyond existing civil remedies) to obtain an advance of money or provisions in exchange for labor, and then to fail to do work; similar to contract enforcement statutes in other states.
1889 N.C. Sess. Laws 550, ch. 7, § 1 (Private).	Democrats/Daniel Gould Fowle (Democrat)	Limited Biddle University to colored students.

---

13. Although not made explicit in the statute, the county institutes were solely for white teachers. M.C.S. Noble, *A History of the Public Schools of North Carolina* 429 n.1 (1930).

Text	Previous Law	Subsequent Statute(s)
"At the close or during the sessions of every institute, the conductor thereof . . . shall hold written examinations of all public school teachers, white and colored, who may apply . . . ."		
"No registration shall be valid unless it specifies as near as may be the age, occupation, place of birth and place of residence of the elector . . . ."		1895 N.C. Sess. Laws 211, ch. 159, §§ 7, 10 (liberalized election law both in terms of registration of voters and with regard to election mechanics). See also 1899 N.C. Sess. Laws 658, ch. 507 (re-imposed voting restrictions).
"That if any person, with intent to cheat or defraud another, shall obtain any advances in money, provisions, goods, wares or merchandise . . . that the person making the same will commence or begin any work or labor of any description . . . and said person so making said promise or agreement shall unlawfully and willfully fail to commence or begin said work, without a lawful excuse, the person so offending shall be guilty of a misdemeanor . . . ."		1891 N.C. Sess. Laws 98, ch. 106 (amending 1889 law by increasing penalties); 1905 N.C. Sess. Laws 422, ch. 411 (amending 1889 and 1891 laws to make the advance and the failure to comply presumptive evidence of intent to cheat or defraud). See also 1905 N.C. Sess. Laws 333, ch. 297 (made express that obtaining an advance to plant a crop and abandoning crop before repaying advance is similarly a misdemeanor); 1905 N.C. Sess. Laws 334, ch. 299 (making it a crime to obtain advance to plant crop only to fail to cultivate crop or abandon crop before repayment). Chapter 297 of the 1905 laws was subsequently held to be unconstitutional, in violation of N.C. Constitution prohibition on imprisonment absent fraud because statute failed to make fraud an element of crime. *State v. Williams*, 150 N.C. 802 (1909).
"[1887 Act amended] by striking out the words 'and others,' between the words '[colored] race' and 'for' . . . ."		

Law	Political Party Controling General Assembly or Convention/Governor	Purpose
1891 N.C. Sess. Laws 275, 286, ch. 320, § 23.	Democrats/Daniel Gould Fowle (Democrat)	Railroad commissioners empowered to require railroads to segregate trains, stations, and waiting rooms.
1893 N.C. Sess. Laws 99, ch. 123, § 1.	Democrats/Elias Carr (Democrat, but ex-Alliance)	Required ferry company to keep record of race of persons bringing livestock for transport.
1893 N.C. Sess. Laws 486, 487, ch. 316, § 4 (Private).	Democrats/Elias Carr (Democrat, but ex-Alliance)	Williamston to hold vote on issuance of bonds of up to $1200 for purchase of private academy in order to make it a public school for whites; any money left over from bond could be used on schoolhouse for colored children.
1895 N.C. Sess. Laws 198, 199, ch. 150, § 5.	Fusion/Elias Carr (Democrat, but ex-Alliance)	Duplin County Commissioners, upon petition, to establish segregated burial grounds in townships.
1895 N.C. Sess. Laws 90, 92, ch. 75, § 7 (Private).	Fusion/Elias Carr (Democrat, but ex-Alliance)	Town of Kinston could provide graveyards, one for white race and one for colored race; keepers of graveyards must be of same race as the cemetery.
1895 N.C. Sess. Laws 588, 629, ch. 352, § 100 (Private).	Fusion/Elias Carr (Democrat, but ex-Alliance)	Board of Aldermen in Asheville to decide who qualified as "white" and as "other" for admission to different schools.

Text	Previous Law	Subsequent Statute(s)
"That said commissioners shall have power, whenever they deem it expedient and practicable, to require any railroad corporation operating a railroad or part of a railroad in this state to provide separate and equal accommodations for the white and colored races on the passenger trains and also at the passenger stations or waiting rooms in this state...."		See 1899 N.C. Sess. Laws 291, 300, ch. 164, § 11 (N.C. Corporation Commission has power to require railroads to segregate trains, stations, waiting rooms).
"[The Brunswick Bridge and Ferry company shall keep a book of all livestock to be transported on ferry at Wilmington] and shall take and record the name and color of the person or persons bringing the same for transportation."		
"That any balance arising from the bonds issued under this act the said commissioners are authorized and empowered to apply in enlarging, improving or building a school-house for the colored children in the school district...."		
"That separate grounds, as provided in this act, shall be established for the white and colored races."		
"[Kinston] may provide graveyards—at least one for the white race and one for the colored race ... [and] a white keeper for that of the white race, and a colored keeper for that of the colored race...."		
"[O]nly white children shall be admitted to the white schools and other children to the other schools, and said board of aldermen shall be the exclusive judges of whether or not any applicant ... is entitled to enter or attend the same under the provisions of this section."		

Law	Political Party Controling General Assembly or Convention/Governor	Purpose
1897 N.C. Sess. Laws 149, 151, ch. 108, § 11.	Fusion/Daniel L. Russell (Republican)	General law mandated that money be distributed by districts so that white and colored schools could have equal terms, but money should also be apportioned among schools based on qualifications of teachers and grade of work.
1897 N.C. Sess. Laws 433, 434, ch. 255, § 2.	Fusion/Daniel L. Russell (Republican)	Established school for colored teachers but mandated that school's location and buildings would have to be donated by local citizens.
1897 N.C. Sess. Laws 486, ch. 315.	Fusion/Daniel L. Russell (Republican)	Created "New Hanover Society for the Prevention of Crime" which was to operate a "home" (really, a juvenile detention facility) for orphaned or homeless colored children under the age of 14 with little education for the children; also, any child who ran away from this facility was guilty of misdemeanor.
1897 N.C. Sess. Laws 522, 523, ch. 343, § 8.	Fusion/Daniel L. Russell (Republican)	Public school committee of Town of Washington to be composed of six white members and three colored members.
1897 N.C. Sess. Laws 543, 546, ch. 361, § 13.	Fusion/Daniel L. Russell (Republican)	Allowed establishment of white graded school in Hayesville by vote for local tax, colored voters prohibited from voting on measure. (Note: There were similar laws on establishment of graded schools that put issue to white voters, but no previous law approached issue by prohibiting black voters.).
1899 N.C. 539, ch. 384, § 1.	Democrats/Daniel L. Russell (Republican)	Railroads and steamboats to be segregated by race.

Text	Previous Law	Subsequent Statute(s)
"[I]n making such apportionment the said committee shall have proper regard for the grade of work to be done and the qualifications of the teachers required in each school, white and colored, within their district."		
"That the institution shall be located . . . at some suitable place where the citizens thereof will furnish the necessary buildings or money sufficient to erect them."		
"That the said home shall be supported as near as may be by the labor of the inmates." (§ 8)		
"That the children shall be by their keepers or matrons taught a limited amount of reading, writing, spelling and arithmetic." (§ 9)		
"That the public school committee . . . shall consist of nine members, six of whom shall be of the white race and three of whom shall be of the colored race."		
"[T]he colored race shall not be allowed to vote as to levying tax, &c., for the Hayesville graded school for white children."		But see 1899 N.C. Sess. Laws 246, ch. 124, § 2 (Private) (vacancy of any corporator of Butler Institute in Jamesville, Martin County, to be filled "at general meeting of the colored citizens" of Jamesville and vicinity).
"That all railroad companies and steamboat companies engaged as common carriers in the transportation of passengers . . . other than street railways shall provide separate but equal accommodations for the white and colored races on all passenger trains and steamboats carrying passengers."		

Law	Political Party Controling General Assembly or Convention/Governor	Purpose
1899 N.C. Sess. Laws 543, 543-44, ch. 390, § 1.	Democrats/Daniel L. Russell (Republican)	For state militia, if colored troops called up, the troops must be under command of white officers; also, no colored troops to be called up if white troops available.
1899 N.C. Sess. Laws 655, 657, ch. 504, § 10.	Democrats/Daniel L. Russell (Republican)	White and colored schools in district near Chadbourn to be at least 500 yards apart.
1899 N.C. Sess. Laws 658, 661, ch. 507, § 11.	Democrats/Daniel L. Russell (Republican)	Voting rolls wiped clean for entire state so that anyone wishing to vote had to re-register.
1899 N.C. Sess. Laws 658, 663, ch. 507, § 12.	Democrats/Daniel L. Russell (Republican)	Indians now to be listed separately on voting rolls.
1899 N.C. Sess. Laws 903, 908, ch. 732, § 19.	Democrats/Daniel L. Russell (Republican)	Teachers institutes in counties to be racially segregated.
1899 N.C. Sess. Laws 571, 573, ch. 208, § 14 (Private).	Democrats/Daniel L. Russell (Republican)	No colored persons to be buried in Town of Siler City.

Text	Previous Law	Subsequent Statute(s)
"*Provided*, that no organization of colored troops shall be permitted while white troops are available and that when permitted to be organized colored troops shall be under command of white officers.		
"*Provided*, however, that said schools shall not be located nearer each other than five hundred yards."		
"That before the next general election . . . there shall be an entirely new registration of all persons who shall be entitled to register in every voting precinct in the state, and only such persons as are registered shall be entitled to vote in any election held under this act."	1876–77 N.C. Sess. Laws 516, 517–518 ch. 275, § 6 (boards of commissioners for individual counties could require new registration).	1900 N.C. Sess. Laws 54, 56, ch. 2, § 2 (new registration for 1900 vote on constitutional amendment).
"If the applicant for registration is an Indian, his name shall appear in a separate column from the column for the names of the white and colored persons."		
"Provided, that the teachers institutes shall be held for the white race and the colored race separate and apart from each other."	See 1889 N.C. Sess. Laws 171, 172, ch. 200, § 5, supra.	
"That the cemetery for the burial of white people shall be known by the name of Oak Hill Cemetery. No colored person shall be buried within the above-named cemetery. No colored person or anyone else shall be buried inside the limits of the town corporation outside the cemetery."		

Law	Political Party Controling General Assembly or Convention/Governor	Purpose
Amendment of 1900 to N.C. Const. of 1868, art. VI, final version proposed at 1900 N.C. Sess. Laws 54, ch. 2; and first version passed by General Assembly at 1899 N.C. Sess. Laws 341, ch. 218.	Democrats/Daniel L. Russell (Republican)	Intended to disenfranchise large numbers of black citizens by means of (1) a literacy test and (2) the prior year's payment of poll tax, but most black citizens could not benefit from Grandfather Clause which allowed illiterate whites to vote.
1901 N.C. Sess. Laws 690, 693–94, ch. 497, §§ 5, 8–9.	Democrats/Charles B. Aycock (Democrat)	Board of Trustees of Greenville graded schools given (1) absolute discretion over how school money to be disbursed among schools of two races and (2) if not enough students of a race to create graded school, then Trustees could either give pro rata proportion of tax revenue from colored population to the parents of colored children or Trustees could give pro rata proportion of tax revenue from that race to neighboring district (with, presumably, students of that race to attend school in neighboring district).
1901 N.C. Sess. Laws 702, ch. 503, § 2.	Democrats/Charles B. Aycock (Democrat)	State Librarian to create separate place for colored patrons.

Text	Previous Law	Subsequent Statute(s)
"Every person presenting himself for registration shall be able to read and write any section of the Constitution in the English language; and before he shall be entitled to vote, he shall have paid on or before the first day of May, of the year in which he proposes to vote, his poll tax for the previous year...."		See also 1901 N.C. Sess. Laws 756, ch. 550 (set out oaths for those claiming exemption under Grandfather Clause, and how those names were to be recorded at state and local levels).
* * *		
"But no male person, who was, on January 1, 1867, or at any time prior thereto, entitled to vote under the laws of any State... and no lineal descendant of any such person shall be denied the right to register and vote at any election in this State by reason of his failure to possess the educational qualifications herein prescribed...."		
"*Provided further*, that if there shall be so few children of either race in the district that the Board of Trustees shall deem it inadvisable to organize a school for that race, then they shall have power to arrange for the children of the race which shall be so represented to receive their pro rata proportion of the funds so raised by the special tax... or they may give such pro rata proportion to the public schools for that race adjoining the district described herein...."		See also 1901 N.C. Sess. Laws 642, 644, ch. 243, § 9 (Private) (Board of Trustees of Mount Olive schools given absolute discretion over spending); 1903 N.C. Sess. Laws 164, 166, ch. 97, § 5 (Private) (school trustees to establish two schools and spend money so as "practically the same advantages shall be offered" to children of each race).
* * *		
"[S]aid public moneys shall be... [expended by the Board of Trustees] in the interest of the said graded schools as they may deem best."		
"That the State Librarian be and is hereby authorized to fit up a separate place for the use of the colored people who may come to the Library for the purpose of reading books or periodicals."		

Law	Political Party Controling General Assembly or Convention/Governor	Purpose
1901 N.C. Sess. Laws 476, ch. 176, § 4 (Private).	Democrats/Charles B. Aycock (Democrat)	School Commissioners of Charlotte to make arrangements for a library to be used by colored teachers and students by providing separate books and separate rooms.
1903 N.C. Sess. Laws 736, 737, ch. 421, § 3.	Democrats/Charles B. Aycock (Democrat)	White principal in school district to be principal of colored school as well.
1903 N.C. Sess. Laws 751, 756, ch. 435, § 22.	Democrats/Charles B. Aycock (Democrat)	General school law provided definition of Negro child.
1903 N.C. Sess. Laws 1055, 1056, ch. 666, § 2.	Democrats/Charles B. Aycock (Democrat)	No white cadavers to go to any school for colored persons.
1903 N.C. Sess. Laws 29, 32–33, ch. 16, §§ 2, 23–27 (Private).	Democrats/Charles B. Aycock (Democrat)	Incorporated Carnegie Library in Charlotte for white persons only, mandated that a public library for colored persons be established, and stated that yearly appropriations from the city to these two libraries were to be divided in a fair way "all things being considered."

Text	Previous Law	Subsequent Statute(s)
"That the School Commissioners . . . shall establish and maintain a library . . . and shall arrange for separate books and publications for the white and colored races and provide separate rooms for the use of each of said races, said rooms to be located in such part or parts of said city as the School Commissioners may designate."		See also 1901 N.C. Sess. Laws 1052, 1053, ch. 432 (Private) (authorized Charlotte to put to vote appropriation to establish library, with separate books and rooms, for all citizens of Charlotte); 1913 N.C. Sess. Laws 51, ch. 29 (Private) (Extra Sess.) (Greensboro "may establish or cause to be established" a library for use of colored race).
"[The principal for the white school] shall also be principal of the colored school."		
"All white children shall be taught in the public schools provided for the white race, and all colored shall be taught in the public schools provided for the colored race; but no child with negro blood in his veins, however remote the strain, shall attend a school for the white race . . . ."		
"[T]hat the body of no white person shall be delivered to any school for the colored race . . . ."		
"[Purpose of corporation is to] establish and maintain a free library for the use . . . of the white citizens of the city of Charlotte." (§ 2)		
* * *		
"That the white library shall be used exclusively for white people and the colored library for the colored people." (§ 25)		
* * *		
"[T]hat the said sum of twenty-five hundred dollars shall be distributed between the trustees of the two libraries in such proportion as is just and equitable, all things being considered." (§ 27)		

Law	Political Party Controling General Assembly or Convention/Governor	Purpose
1905 N.C. Sess. Laws 227, 228, ch. 213, § 5.	Democrats/Robert B. Glenn (Democrat)	Compulsory school attendance law for special Indian school did not apply to anyone with less than one-eighth Indian blood.
1905 N.C. Sess. Laws 83, 87–88, ch. 32, §§ 25–27 (Private).	Democrats/Robert B. Glenn (Democrat)	Created Charlotte Park and Tree Commission with 4 parks for white citizens and a Charlotte Park and Tree Commission for Colored People with goal of establishing park or parks for colored people; mandated segregation in parks but penalties only for colored residents who entered white parks and refused to leave; colored park employees allowed in white parks.
1907 N.C. Sess. Laws 531, 544, ch. 365, § 47.	Democrats/Robert B. Glenn (Democrat)	Road crews (non-exempted citizens who worked on road upkeep) in Wake County to be segregated by race.
1907 N.C. Sess. Laws 597, ch. 406, § 1.	Democrats/Robert B. Glenn (Democrat)	Federal funds received for N.C. colleges of agricultural and mechanical arts to be apportioned between white and colored institutions based on ratio of state population from census (black population less than half of white in N.C. in 1900).
1907 N.C. Sess. Laws 1238, ch. 850.	Democrats/Robert B. Glenn (Democrat)	Mandated segregation of white and colored passengers on streetcars, with white passengers in front and colored passengers in rear of streetcar.

Text	Previous Law	Subsequent Statute(s)
"That nothing in this act shall apply to any child, parent or guardian with less than one-eighth Indian blood."		See 1908 N.C. Sess. Laws 77, ch. 59 (Extra Sess.) (amended to make law apply only to those with less than 1/16 Indian blood); 1909 N.C. Sess. Law 1224, ch. 834 (repealed 1908 session law with regard to ratio of Indian blood).
"[I]t shall be unlawful for any person other than white persons to go in said parks now owned by said corporation . . . [Provided] that colored persons employed to work for this corporation shall be allowed in said parks; that any person of color who shall be notified to leave said park or parks, or be notified not to come in said park or parks, and shall refuse to do so . . . shall be guilty of a trespass . . . ." (§ 25)		
* * *		
"[Corporation named the Charlotte Public Park Commission for Colored People established and the Charlotte Board of Aldermen] shall provide a suitable place for a park or parks . . . ." (§ 26)		
"[W]hites and blacks shall be worked in separate squads."		
"The appropriations made or which may hereafter be made by the Congress . . . shall be divided between the white and colored institutions in this State in the ratio of the white population to the colored . . . ."		
"That all street, inter-urban and suburban railway companies . . . shall provide and set apart so much of the front portion of each car . . . as shall be necessary, for occupation by the white passengers therein, and shall likewise provide and set apart so much of the rear part of said car as shall be necessary, for occupation by the colored passengers therein . . . ."		

Law	Political Party Controlling General Assembly or Convention/Governor	Purpose
1909 N.C. Sess. Laws 1110, ch. 720, § 1.	Democrats/William Walton Kitchin (Democrat)	White children in Scotland County to have separate schools from children with Negro or Indian blood.
1909 N.C. Sess. Laws 1194, ch. 817, § 2.	Democrats/William Walton Kitchin (Democrat)	Established reformatory for "Criminal Negro Youth" under the age of fourteen to "keep, restrain and control them."
1909 N.C. Sess. Laws 1215, ch. 832, § 1.	Democrats/William Walton Kitchin (Democrat)	Mandated racial segregation in state prisons.
1909 N.C. Sess. Laws 872, ch. 387 (Private).	Democrats/William Walton Kitchin (Democrat)	Allowed the disinterment and removal of bodies from "old Methodist Church lot" cemetery provided that bodies of white and colored dead be moved to separate cemeteries.

Text	Previous Law	Subsequent Statute(s)
"That the children of the white race in Scotland County shall be taught in public schools provided for them exclusively; and no child of negro blood, however remote the strain, or of Indian blood to the eighth degree, inclusive, shall attend a public school provided for the white race...."		
"Whereas it appears to this General Assembly that there are in this State many negro youths between the ages of seven and fourteen years who violate the criminal law.... [Reformatory to be established to] receive therein such delinquent and criminal children under the age of fourteen years... and shall have the sole right and authority to keep, restrain and control them during their minority or until such time as they shall deem proper for their discharge...."		See also 1911 N.C. Sess. Laws 286, ch. 122 (establishing a separate "Reform and Manual Training School for Colored Youths" with same language as 1909 law).
"That white and colored prisoners shall not be confined or shackled together in the same room... either in the State penitentiary or at any State or county convict camp during the eating and sleeping hours, and at all other times the separation of the two races shall be as complete as practicable."		Same provision reenacted when state prisons were made a department of state government. 1925 N.C. Sess. Laws 376, 386, ch. 163, § 1 (to revise Consolidated Statutes § 7740).
"[T]he bodies of white people there buried shall be decently buried in the Pine View Cemetery, and the bodies of colored people there buried shall be decently buried in Unity Cemetery."		See also 1913 N.C. Sess. Laws 15, ch. 9 (Private) (Extra Sess.) (allowed New Bern to remove dead bodies of colored persons from Cedar Grove Cemetery and reinter bodies at Greenwood Cemetery); 1915 N.C. Sess. Laws 214, ch. 105 (Private) (allowed private citizen to disinter and move colored dead on private property—not his own—to colored cemetery in Smithfield).

Law	Political Party Controling General Assembly or Convention/Governor	Purpose
1911 N.C. Sess. Laws 77, ch. 41, § 1.	Democrats/William Walton Kitchin (Democrat)	Railroad companies required to have two windows in depots for sale of fares or exchange of mileage/coupon books, but only in waiting room of race using the most mileage/coupon books.
1911 N.C. Sess. Laws 324, 325, ch. 168, § 3.	Democrats/William Walton Kitchin (Democrat)	Indian Normal School of Robeson County empowered to prevent Negroes from attending school.
1911 N.C. Sess. Laws 354, 354–355, ch. 215, §§ 2, 4–6.	Democrats/William Walton Kitchin (Democrat)	Mandated separate quarters for "Indians of Robeson County" (formerly referred to as Croatan Indians) in state hospital for insane, Robeson County jail, and Robeson County home for aged and infirm.
1913 N.C. Sess. Laws 127, ch. 83, § 1.	Democrats/Locke Craig (Democrat)	Manufacturers and other businesses required to provide separate toilets for white and colored employees.
1913 N.C. Sess. Laws 251, ch. 98, § 2 (Private).	Democrats/Locke Craig (Democrat)	Incorporated Chadbourn Memorial Association to establish cemetery near town, but only for white residents of town.

Text	Previous Law	Subsequent Statute(s)
"That all railroad companies . . . are hereby required to provide and keep at all depots . . . two windows, opening in the waiting-room for passengers of the race using the greatest amount of mileage or coupon books . . . ."		
"That the board of Trustees of said Indian Normal School of Robeson County shall have the power . . . to prevent negroes from attending said school . . . ."		
"That the [State Hospital for the Insane is] . . . directed to provide and set apart as said hospital . . . suitable apartments and wards for the accommodation of any of said Indians of Robeson County . . . ." (§ 5)		
* * *		
"That the sheriff . . . [and other] authorities of Robeson County shall provide in the common jail . . . and in the Home for the Aged and Infirm . . . separate cells, wards, or apartments for the said Indians of Robeson County." (§ 6)		
"That all persons and corporations employing males and females . . . shall provide and keep in a cleanly condition [sic] separate and distinct toilet rooms for such employees . . . so as to separate the white and colored males and females of both sexes . . . ."		
"[Association] may sell or dispose of land and suitable burial lots to be used exclusively for . . . the dead of said town and all such other people . . . [provided that] no negro or any person of African descent shall be buried on any lot belonging to said association."		See also 1915 N.C. Sess. Laws 364, ch. 163, § 1 (Private) (gave Stewartsville Cemetery Association sole power to determine "color of the person" buried); 1915 N.C. Sess. Laws 794, ch. 280 (Private) (created Cross Creek Cemetery Commission to provide burial ground "for the white race of the city of Fayetteville").

Law	Political Party Controling General Assembly or Convention/Governor	Purpose
1913 N.C. Sess. Laws 1222, ch. 575, § 1 (Public Local).	Democrats/Locke Craig (Democrat)	Committee appointed for Indian schools in Robeson County to have final determination of the race of those seeking admission to schools.
1915 N.C. Sess. Laws 305, ch. 236, § 1(a).	Democrats/Locke Craig (Democrat)	General school law amended to exclude children with "Croatan Indian blood" from white schools.
1915 N.C. Sess. Laws 365, ch. 284, § 1.	Democrats/Locke Craig (Democrat)	Hospitals which admitted colored patients required to employ colored nurses to attend to colored patients.
1915 N.C. Sess. Laws 124, 137, ch. 63, § 47 (Private).	Democrats/Locke Craig (Democrat)	Town of Benson allowed to impose residential segregation by race in town.
1917 N.C. Sess. Laws 521, ch. 401 (Public Local).	Democrats/ Thomas Walter Bickett (Democrat)	Mecklenburg County authorized to create reformatory for boys and girls and to segregate by race.

Text	Previous Law	Subsequent Statute(s)
"To protect the public schools established in Robeson County for the education of the Indian race only . . . all questions as to the race of those applying for admission into said Indian public school shall be submitted [to committee]."		
"[Children excluded with] what is generally known as Croatan Indian blood [from white schools]."		
"That in every public and private hospital, sanitarium, and institution . . . where colored patients are admitted for treatment and where nurses are employed it shall be mandatory upon the management . . . to employ colored nurses to care for and wait upon said colored patients."		
"[The] board of commissioners may also regulate and prescribe certain streets, blocks, and lots thereon on which negroes may reside, and certain streets, blocks, and lots on which white people may reside within the town."		
"[T]here shall be maintained thereon a building for boys with separate accommodations for white and colored boys, and a building for girls with separate accommodations for white and colored girls."		See also 1917 N.C. Sess. Laws 740, ch. 631 (Public Local) (County Industrial Home for Girls and Women in Buncombe County to be segregated by race); 1917 N.C. Sess. Laws 809, ch. 714 (Public Local) (Craven County reformatory for boys and girls to be segregated by race); 1919 N.C. Sess. Laws 760, 763–764, ch. 549, § 11 (reformatory in Buncombe County for criminal youth to be segregated and quarters for colored children to not "be nearer than one-half mile to the school established for white children").

TABLE 2

North Carolina Constitutional and
Statutory Provisions that Affirmed Legal Equality
and/or Benefited Racial Minorities,
1865 to 1920

Law	Political Party Controling General Assembly or Convention/Governor [1]	Purpose
1866 N.C. Sess. Laws 18, ch. 12.	Conservatives, Ex-Whigs/ Jonathan Worth (Conservative, Ex-Whig)	To establish a seminary for colored race (unsuccessful).
1866 N.C. Sess. Laws 99, 99–100, ch. 40, § 3.	Conservatives, Ex-Whigs/ Jonathan Worth (Conservative, Ex-Whig)	Freedmen entitled to right to trial by jury and to same ability to prosecute and defend suits at law and equity as white persons.
1866 N.C. Sess. Laws 99, 100, ch. 40, § 5.	Conservatives, Ex-Whigs/ Jonathan Worth (Conservative, Ex-Whig)	Declared that male and female former slaves who cohabited are married.
1866 N.C. Sess. Laws 99, 102–103, ch. 40, §§ 13–14.	Conservatives, Ex-Whigs/ Jonathan Worth (Conservative, Ex-Whig)	Created racially separate courts of wardens of the poor and these separate courts were to have same powers.

1. Again, although governors are listed in this table, note that North Carolina did not allow for a gubernatorial veto of legislation at any time during the period under consideration.

Text	Previous Law	Subsequent Statute(s)

"[T]here is at this time no College or literary institution where those of the colored race, who aspire to be teachers and ministers of the gospel, can receive a suitable education" and thus necessary to create "the Freedmen's College of North Carolina."

"[P]ersons of color shall be entitled to all the privileges of white persons in the mode of prosecuting, defending, continuing, removing and transferring their suits at law and equity; and, likewise, to the same mode of trial by jury, and all the privileges appertaining thereto."

"That in all cases where men and women, both or one of whom were lately slaves and are now emancipated, now cohabit together in the relation of husband and wife, the parties shall be deemed to have been lawfully married as man and wife at the time of the commencement of such cohabitation . . . ."

"That at the time now provided for the election of wardens of the poor, the justices of the court of pleas and quarter sessions of each county . . . may, in their discretion, elect two distinct and independent court [sic] of wardens; one of whom shall act as the wardens of the white poor, and the other as the wardens of the colored poor." (Sec. 13)

* * *

"[T]he wardens severally, and each court shall have all the powers and authorities now conferred on them . . . ." (Sec. 14)

Law	Political Party Controling General Assembly or Convention/Governor	Purpose
1866 N.C. Sess. Laws 99, 103–104, ch. 40, § 15.	Conservatives, Ex-Whigs/ Jonathan Worth (Conservative, Ex-Whig)	Repealed prior law so that Negroes could possess guns and other weapons.
1866–67 N.C. Sess. Laws 10, ch. 6, §§ 1, 3.	Conservatives, Ex-Whigs/ Jonathan Worth (Conservative, Ex-Whig)	Removed racial references in apprentice law from Revised Code of North Carolina ch. 5, §§ 1, 5 (1855).
N.C. Const. of 1868, art. I, sec. 33.	Republicans (Convention)	Slavery and involuntary servitude outlawed except as punishment for crime.
N.C. Const. of 1868, art. VI, sec. 1.	Republicans (Convention)	Equal voting rights for all adult males.

Text	Previous Law	Subsequent Statute(s)
"That the following laws and parts of laws are hereby repealed.... [Including the following] acts passed since the enactment of the Revised Code... an act ratified on the same day, chapter thirty-four, entitled 'an act to amend chapter one hundred and seven, section sixty-six, of the Revised Code, relating to free negroes having arms'...."	1860–1861 N.C. Sess. Laws 68, ch. 34 (prohibited free Negroes from possessing guns or other weapons and repealed provision from 1855 Revised Code that allowed free Negroes to carry arms if they were granted license by county court). See also Revised Code of North Carolina ch. 107, § 66 (1855) ("If any free negro shall wear or carry... any shot-gun, musket, rifle, pistol, sword, dagger, or bowie-knife, unless he shall have obtained a license... within one year next preceding... he shall be guilty of a misdemeanor.").	N.C. Const. of 1868, art. I, sec. 24 ("A well regulated militia being necessary to the security of a free State, the right of the people to keep and bear arms shall not be infringed....").
"That the 1st section of the 5th chapter of the Revised Code... be amended by striking out the words 'also the children of free negroes ....'" (§1)		
* * *		
"That the 5th section of said chapter be, and the same is hereby repealed, and that all other laws and parts of laws discriminating between whites and blacks in the apprenticing of children, be, and they are hereby repealed."		
"Slavery and involuntary servitude, otherwise than for crime... shall be, and are hereby forever prohibited within this State."		
"Every male person... twenty one years old or upward, who shall have resided in this State twelve months next preceeding [sic] the election, and thirty days in the county, in which he offers to vote, shall be deemed an elector."		

Law	Political Party Controling General Assembly or Convention/Governor	Purpose
N.C. Const. of 1868, art. IX, sec. 2.	Republicans (Convention)	Public schools open to all children.
N.C. Const. of 1868, art. XII, sec. 1	Republicans (Convention)	All male citizens subject to duty in state militia.
1868 N.C. Sess. Laws 35, ch. 22, §§ 7 and 17.	Republicans/William Woods Holden (Republican)	Established state militia companies segregated by race, and segregated state detailed militia.
1868–1869 N.C. Sess. Laws 185, ch. 81, § 1.	Republicans/William Woods Holden (Republican)	Directed counties in which turnpike road was located to divide labor duties on the road among those people who lived near the turnpike without discriminating based on race.
1868–1869 N.C. Sess. Laws 458, 471, ch. 184, § 50.	Republicans/William Woods Holden (Republican)	Separate schools in townships to have equal resources and teachers.
1872–73 N.C. Sess. Laws 212, ch. 134, § 1.	Conservatives/ Tod Robinson Caldwell (Republican)	Land donated for purpose of establishing a building for colored pupils in state Institution for the Deaf and Dumb and Blind.

Text	Previous Law	Subsequent Statute(s)
"The General Assembly . . . shall provide by taxation and otherwise for a general and uniform system of Public Schools, wherein tuition shall be free of charge to all the children of the State between the ages of six and twenty-one years."		
"All able bodied male citizens of the State of North Carolina between the ages of twenty one and forty years who are citizens of the United States, shall be liable to duty in the Militia . . . ."		
"The white and colored militia shall be enrolled in separate and distinct companies and shall never be compelled to serve in the same companies." (§ 7)		See also 1893 N.C. Sess. Laws 350, ch. 374, § 2 (same); 1899 N.C. Sess. Laws 543, ch. 390, § 1 (same).
* * *		
"That the white and colored members of the detailed militia shall not be compelled to serve in the same sections." (§ 17)		
"[A]llot by names . . . all such persons, liable to do labor or service on public roads . . . and no discrimination shall be made on account of race, color, or previous condition."		
"The school authorities of each and every Township shall establish a separate school or separate schools for the instruction of children and youth of each race . . . and such school or schools shall be supported, regulated and instructed in same manner and to the same extent as any other public school or schools of the same grade."		
"That a lot of land belonging to the State of North Carolina . . . is donated and appropriated to the Institution for the Deaf and Dumb and Blind for the purposes of establishing thereon buildings for the accommodation of the colored pupils of said institution."		In the next legislative session, money was appropriated for completion of "the building for the colored department." 1873-74 N.C. Sess. Laws 85, 86, ch. 59, § 2.

Law	Political Party Controling General Assembly or Convention/Governor	Purpose
1874–75 N.C. Sess. Laws 338, ch. 250, § 1.	Conservatives/ Curtis Hooks Brogden (Republican)	To (unsuccessfully) establish asylum in Wilmington for mentally ill patients of color and to remove patients of color from asylum in Raleigh; statute mandated that no other patients of color were to be admitted to Raleigh asylum.
Amendment of 1875, ch. 26, to N.C. Const. of 1868, art. IX, sec. 2.	Equal number of Republican and Conservative delegates, with three independents (Convention)	Required racially separate public schools but, in addition, at least paid lip service to idea that separate schools should be equal.
1876–77 N.C. Sess. Laws 437–38, ch. 234, §§ 1–2.	Democrats/ Zebulon Baird Vance (Democrat)	Established racially separate normal schools for the training of young men to be teachers.
1879 N.C. Sess. Laws 61, ch. 54, § 1.	Democrats/Thomas Jordan Jarvis (Democrat)	To establish a preparatory department in colored normal school.
1879 N.C. Sess. Laws 136, ch. 73, § 1.	Democrats/Thomas Jordan Jarvis (Democrat)	Colored children born before January 1, 1868, are legitimate and have right of inheritance.

Text	Previous Law	Subsequent Statute(s)
"*Provided*, That no more colored insane shall be received in the asylum in Raleigh, and that all the colored inmates now in the asylum at Raleigh, North Carolina, be removed to Wilmington...."		See 1876–77 N.C. Sess. Laws 547–48, ch. 278, § 1 (money appropriated by 1874–75 legislature had gone unused and still in treasury and so this money was to establish "an asylum for the colored insane, at some point in the state.").[2] See also 1879 N.C. Sess. Laws 331, ch. 174, § 2.
"And the children of the white race and the children of the colored race shall be taught in separate public schools; but there shall be no discrimination made in favor of, or to the prejudice of, either race."		
"[I]t shall be lawful, for the state board of education, to establish a normal school, in connection with the state university, for the purpose of teaching and training young men of the white race...." and "[I]t shall be lawful for the state board of education to establish a normal school at any place they may deem most suitable, either in connection with some one of the colored schools of high grade in the state, or otherwise, for the teaching and training young men of the colored race...."		
"[T]he provisions of an act to establish normal schools... be extended so... that a preparatory department may be established in connection with the colored normal school."		
"That the children of colored parents born at any time before the first day of January, one thousand eight hundred and sixty-eight, of persons living together as man and wife, are hereby declared legitimate children... with all the rights of heirs-at-law and next kin, with respect to the estate or estates of any such parents...."		

---

2. The correct chapter number (278) here was misprinted in the session laws volume as "CCXXLVIII."

Law	Political Party Controling General Assembly or Convention/Governor	Purpose
1879 N.C. Sess. Laws 265, 267, ch. 139, § 7.	Democrats/Thomas Jordan Jarvis (Democrat)	To outlaw racial discrimination in awarding dental licenses.
1881 N.C. Sess. Laws 290, 293, ch. 141, § 5.	Democrats/Thomas Jordan Jarvis (Democrat)	To expand normal schools so that there were four schools for each race and to appropriate $2000 each for white and colored normal schools.
1881 N.C. Sess. Laws 299, 299–300, ch. 149, § 1.	Democrats/Thomas Jordan Jarvis (Democrat)	To donate one acre to trustees of Shaw University for medical school.
1883 N.C. Sess. Laws 237, 238, ch. 156, § 3.	Democrats/Thomas Jordan Jarvis	Established separate insane asylum for colored persons.
1883 N.C. Sess. Laws 391, 392, ch. 236, § 4.	Democrats/Thomas Jordan Jarvis (Democrat)	Taxes collected in Kinston from retail liquor licenses to be divided equally between white and colored schools.
1883 N.C. Sess. Laws 587, 588, ch. 412, § 4.	Democrats/Thomas Jordan Jarvis (Democrat)	Required trustees of segregated schools in Town of Washington to be of the same race as the school(s) for which they were trustees.

Text	Previous Law	Subsequent Statute(s)
"*Provided*, that no one applying for a license to practice dentistry shall be denied such license on account of race, color or previous condition of servitude."		
"That the state board of education be directed to establish other normal schools ... and that the sum of two thousand dollars per annum is hereby appropriated for such schools for white teachers, and the sum of two thousand dollars for such schools for colored teachers ... *Provided, however*, That the number of schools shall not be less than four for each color."		
"That one square acre of ground, to be taken from the southeast corner of the lot on which the governor's mansion is now located, shall be and the same is hereby donated to the trustees of Shaw University, to be by them held in trust for the purpose of establishing a medical college for colored students."		
"'The North Carolina Insane Asylum' and 'The Western North Carolina Insane Asylum' shall be exclusively for the accommodation, maintenance, care and treatment of the white insane of the state, and 'The Eastern North Carolina Insane Asylum' shall be exclusively for the accommodation, maintenance, care and treatment of the colored insane of the state."	For prior legislative action to establish separate asylum for colored patients, see 1874-75 N.C. Sess. Laws 338, ch. 250, § 1, supra.	See 1897 N.C. Sess. Laws 702, 704, ch. 520, § 5 (department for criminal insane at state penitentiary at Raleigh to keep races "in separate apartments").
"That all money arising from retail liquor license tax collected by the commissioners of the town of Kinston" * * * "shall be equally divided between the white and colored graded schools."		For similar laws in same 1883 Session, see 1883 N.C. Sess. Laws 444, 446, ch. 282, § 10 (for township of Shoe Heel) and 1883 N.C. Sess. Laws 456, 458, ch. 292, § 10 (for Lumberton).
"*Provided always*, that all the trustees for white schools shall be white persons, and the trustees for colored schools shall be colored."		

Law	Political Party Controling General Assembly or Convention/Governor	Purpose
1883 N.C. Sess. Laws 621 (joint resolution of March 12, 1883).	Democrats/Thomas Jordan Jarvis (Democrat)	To have directors of the colored race appointed to the Boards of Trustees for both the colored insane asylum and the institute for the colored deaf.
1885 N.C. Sess. Laws 92, 93, ch. 51, §§ 2, 5.	Democrats/Alfred Moore Scales (Democrat)	Croatan Indians (today's Lumbees) to have separate schools in Robeson County.
1885 N.C. Sess. Laws 485, ch. 253, § 1.	Democrats/Alfred Moore Scales (Democrat)	Created graded schools for white and colored children in Town of Smithfield in what had been a white school district.

Text	Previous Law	Subsequent Statute(s)
"That in the appointment of directors in the colored insane asylum and the institution for the colored deaf, dumb and blind, the colored race should have some representation, and the authorities are requested to appoint some suitable and worthy representative colored men to such positions."		
"That said Indians and their descendants shall have separate schools for their children, school committees of their own race and color . . . ."		See also 1889 N.C. Sess. Laws 436, ch. 458 (separate schools for Croatan in Richmond County); 1907 N.C. Sess. Laws 737, ch. 499 (separate schools for Croatan in Cumberland County); 1911 N.C. Sess. Laws 321, ch. 263 (Public Local) (separate schools for Croatan in Sampson County) (repealed by 1913 N.C. Sess. Laws 216, ch. 100 (Public Local)); 1913 N.C. Sess. Laws 64, ch. 22 (Public Local) (separate schools for Croatan in Person County); 1917 N.C. Sess. Laws 605, 607, ch. 509, § 5 (Public Local) (two schools for Croatan in Sampson County, but "all children of the negro race to the fourth generation" excluded). But see 1889 N.C. Sess. Laws 72, ch. 60, § 1, excluding Negroes from Croatan schools.
"That all the territory embraced within the bounds of white school district number forty, in Smithfield township, Johnston county, shall be and is hereby constituted the 'Smithfield Graded School District for white and colored.'"		

Law	Political Party Controling General Assembly or Convention/Governor	Purpose
1887 N.C. Sess. Laws 699, 700–701, ch. 400, §§ 4, 10.	Democrats and Republicans split with independents holding influence/Alfred Moore Scales (Democrat)	Created a "Croatan Normal School" in Robeson County that (1) allowed trustees to appoint Croatan Indians as additional trustees and (2) was presumably a separate normal school exclusively for Croatan Indians, given that Negroes were excluded from schools for Croatan Indians under 1889 statute even though present statute did not racially restrict who could attend school.
1889 N.C. Sess. Laws 163, 167, ch. 199, § 23.	Democrats/Daniel Gould Fowle (Democrat)	Directed county boards of education to apportion one-third of school funds to help equalize lengths of school terms between white and colored schools.
1889 N.C. Sess. Laws 265, 266, ch. 254, § 5.	Democrats/Daniel Gould Fowle (Democrat)	Special tax revenues in Littleton to be divided equally between white school and colored school.
1891 N.C. Sess. Laws 233, 235, ch. 285, § 6	Democrats/Daniel Gould Fowle (Democrat)	Duty of Concord school board to apportion money in way to equalize school facilities.
1891 N.C. Sess. Laws 364, 367, ch. 337, § 13.	Democrats/Daniel Gould Fowle (Democrat)	County boards of commissioners empowered to establish and maintain homes for indigent white and colored children, even though segregated.

Text	Previous Law	Subsequent Statute(s)
"[The trustees] shall have power to select three additional trustees from the Croatan race...." * * *	1889 N.C. Sess. Laws 72, ch. 60, § 1 (excluded from Croatan schools "all children of the negro race to the fourth generation").	
"*Provided*, that no person shall be admitted into said school as a student who has not attained the age of fifteen years; and that all those who shall enjoy the privilege of said school as students shall previously obligate to teach the youth of the Croatan race for a stated period."		
"[A]t the same time the remaining one-third shall be apportioned in such manner as to equalize the average length of school terms for the two races, as far as may be practicable...."		
"That the special taxes... shall be equally divided between the schools for white and colored—one-half (1/2) to the school for the white race and one-half (1/2) to the school for the colored race."		
"That it shall be the duty of said board... [to apportion funds] between said graded schools for white and colored children, so as to equalize school facilities between the two races."		See also 1893 N.C. Sess. Laws 455, 457, ch. 301, § 10 (Private) (equalize schools in Asheboro); 1903 N.C. Sess. Laws 160, 161, ch. 95, § 7 (Private) (equalize facilities in Roxboro schools).
"*Provided*, that no white child shall be committed to any such institution established or maintained for colored children, and no colored child shall be committed to any such institution established or maintained for white children...."		

Law	Political Party Controling General Assembly or Convention/Governor	Purpose
1891 N.C. Sess. Laws 404, 405, ch. 348, § 6.	Democrats/Daniel Gould Fowle (Democrat)	Mandated that appropriation from U.S. government under second Morrill Land-Grant College statute (ch. 841, 26 Stat. 417 (1890)) would be apportioned equally based on population of white and colored in state.
1893 N.C. Sess. Laws 146, 148, ch. 189, §§ 1, 6.	Democrats/Elias Carr (Democrat, but ex-Alliance)	Established colored schools in Fayetteville where previously there had only been schools for white race; also mandated that schools for both races were to have same length of school term.
1895 N.C. Sess. Laws 185, ch. 135.	Democrats/Elias Carr (Democrat, but ex-Alliance)	Returned election of local government officials to citizens and took away General Assembly's appointment power, benefiting majority-black areas in eastern part of state.

Text	Previous Law	Subsequent Statute(s)
"[The appropriation] shall be divided into the exact ratio in this state of the white population to the colored: this provision to apply to the current and all succeeding appropriations."		This statute led, in the very same session of the General Assembly, to the establishment of two new colored schools of higher education. See 1891 N.C. Sess. Laws 213, ch. 265 (normal school at Elizabeth City) and 1891 N.C. Sess. Laws 607, ch. 549 (agricultural and mechanical college).
"[That previous statute on schools in Fayetteville] be amended by striking out the words 'for whites' whenever they occur . . . ." * * * "[T]he schools for each race herein provided for shall have the same length of school terms."	1883 N.C. Sess. Laws 252, ch. 157 (an act to incorporate public schools in Fayetteville "for whites").	See also 1895 N.C. Sess. Laws 297, 298, ch. 225, § 3 (same length of school terms in Warsaw).
"There shall be elected in each county of the state, at the general election to be held in the year one thousand eight hundred and ninety-six (1896), and every two years thereafter, by the duly qualified electors thereof, three persons to be chosen from the body of the county, who shall be styled the board of commissioners . . . ." (§ 4) (internal quotation marks omitted).	1876–77 N.C. Sess. Laws 226, 227–28, ch. 141, §§ 4–5.	See also 1895 N.C. Sess. Laws 209, ch. 157 (popular election of justices of peace).

Law	Political Party Controling General Assembly or Convention/Governor	Purpose
1895 N.C. Sess. Laws 211, ch. 159, §§ 7, 10.	Fusion/Elias Carr (Democrat, but ex-Alliance)	Liberalized election law both in terms of registration of voters (voter registration not invalidated because of failure to specify age and place of residence of elector) and with regard to election mechanics (required appointment of voting registrars and judges of election from each political party).
1895 N.C. Sess. Laws 439, 440, ch. 409, § 6.	Fusion/Elias Carr (Democrat, but ex-Alliance)	Tax dollars for segregated schools in Rutherfordton to provide both equal facilities and equal terms.
1897 N.C. Sess. Laws 381, 389, ch. 194, § 54 (Private).	Fusion/Daniel L. Russell (Republican)	Money to be apportioned to schools in Southern Pines without discrimination based on race.

Text	Previous Law	Subsequent Statute(s)
"[T]he clerks [of Superior Court] in their several counties shall appoint, upon the written recommendation or approval of the chairman of the state executive committee of each political party of the state, one citizen and qualified voter from each of said political parties of and for each election precinct . . . who shall be known, for the duties required of them under this act, as registrars of election in their respective precincts." (§ 7)	1889 N.C. Sess. Laws 289, ch. 287 (restrictive election law).	1899 N.C. Sess. Laws 658, ch. 507 (reimposed voting restrictions following 1898 Democratic victory).
* * *		
"Every registration shall specify, as near as may, the age and residence of the elector, as well as the township or county from whence he removed, in the case of a removal, since the last election, and the name by which he is commonly known; but no registration shall be invalidated because of a failure to specify the age and place of residence, etc., unless it shall appear that, upon the registrar properly questioning the elector, he declined to answer the questions pertaining to these matters." (§ 10)		
"[The school board shall use money] in such a manner as to best promote the surest interests of both races: Provided, that equal facilities with equal terms shall be given to both races."		See also 1897 N.C. Sess. Laws 573, 573–74, ch. 392, § 5 (money to be apportioned in City of High Point "so as to equalize" schools of two races); 1897 N.C. Session Laws 522, 524, ch. 343, § 10 (money to be apportioned in Town of Washington so that terms of school and school facilities are equal); 1899 N.C. Sess. Laws 225, ch. 96, § 5 (same for schools in Kinston).
"The school committee . . . shall apportion the money . . . as shall be just to the white and colored races without discrimination in favor of or to the prejudice of either race."		

Law	Political Party Controlling General Assembly or Convention/Governor	Purpose
1899 N.C. Sess. Laws 492, ch. 355, § 1.	Democrats/Daniel L. Russell (Republican)	Imposed duty on state mental hospital to treat Croatan Indians (i.e., Lumbees) who are insane, but in separate section of Raleigh hospital.
1903 N.C. Sess. Laws 188, 190–92, ch. 106, §§ 5, 7, 12 (Private).	Democrats/Charles B. Aycock (Democrat)	Greenville graded schools to maintain white and colored schools for same length, the board of trustees could appoint a committee of colored persons to advance interests of colored school, and the board of trustees empowered to admit students from outside the corporate limits of Greenville to either the white or colored school.
1907 N.C. Sess. Laws 1178, 1181, ch. 831, § 10.	Democrats/Robert B. Glenn (Democrat)	Prohibited racial discrimination in payment of benefits from Firemen's Relief Fund.
1907 N.C. Sess. Laws 1399, ch. 1004.	Democrats/Robert B. Glenn (Democrat)	Allowed Cherokee Indians who could speak and write English language to trade, contract, and barter.
1915 N.C. Sess. Laws 663, ch. 238 (Private).	Democrats/Locke Craig (Democrat)	Incorporated Wilson Tubercular Hospital for Negroes.
1919 N.C. Sess. Laws 416, ch. 211, § 1.	Democrats/Thomas Walter Bickett (Democrat)	Treatment of Cherokee Indians of Robeson County and Croatan Indians (i.e., Lumbees) at state insane hospital to be same level of care as white patients' care at same hospital.

Text	Previous Law	Subsequent Statute(s)
"[I]t shall be the duty . . . to arrange for the care and treatment of all insane and inebriate Croatan Indians at the State Hospital at Raleigh in a department separate and distict from the white insane . . . ."		1919 N.C. Sess. Laws 416, ch. 211, § 1.
"[If the Board of Trustees] deem it advisable to do so, may appoint a committee of colored persons to aid the board in looking after the interest of the colored graded school . . . ."		
* * *		
"*Provided further*, that the board of trustees shall have power to admit the children to either of the said schools who reside outside the corporate limits of said town upon such terms as they may deem fair and just."		
"Inasmuch as there are in a number of the towns and cities of this State fire companies composed exclusively of colored men, it is expressly provided that the local boards of trustees shall make no discrimination on account of color in the payment of benefits."		
"[Amended code so that existing] section shall not apply to any person of Cherokee Indian blood or any Cherokee Indian who understands the English language and who can speak and write the same intelligently."		
"It shall be the purpose of the Wilson Tubercular Hospital for Negroes to aid in the prevention and cure of tuberculosis among the negro race of North Carolina."		
"That all the insane and inebriate [Indians] . . . shall be cared for and receive same treatments as other patients in said hospital receive."		

About the Author

Richard A. Paschal is an attorney in Raleigh, North Carolina. He received his undergraduate degree from the University of North Carolina at Chapel Hill. Paschal received his J.D. from the University of Virginia School of Law, where he was Articles Editor on the *Virginia Law Review*. He earned a Ph.D. from The Johns Hopkins University, where he studied public and constitutional law in the Department of Political Science. After receiving his law degree, Paschal clerked for the Honorable James L. Dennis on the U.S. Court of Appeals for the Fifth Circuit. He has taught various courses on constitutional law and American legal history.

Index

Illustrations are indicated by italicized page numbers. Tables 1 and 2 are not included in the subject index except for case names; the page numbers of these table entries end with "t."

Abrams, Charles, 17n55
Adams, Spencer B., 98n187
African Americans
    scholarship on history of, 24–27, 43–55, 43n2
    use of term, xvii–xviii*n*7
    See also exclusion; race/racism; Reconstruction; segregation *and various institutions, public accommodations, and common carriers engaging in segregation*
Afro-Creoles as initiators of *Plessy v. Ferguson*, 32, 34
Alabama, educational system in, 130n122
Alamance County
    jury service by blacks in, 162
    Klan violence in, 65, 66, 66n42
Alexander, Michelle, xix*n*13

Alexander, Thomas B., 59n5
Amar, Vikram David, 157n239
American Baptist Publication Society, 183
American imperialism, 46n11
American Indians
    creation of Western territories for, 25
    flexible application of laws not extended to, 187n90
    jury service by, 161
    school for deaf and blind, 180, 180–181n60
    standard for determining Indian descent, 119–120n70
    use of term, xvii–xviii*n*7
    See also Croatan Indians; Native Americans
Anderson, Eric, 68n54, 73n81, 79n108, 80n110, 83–84, 164

Angelou, Maya, xviin6
apprenticeship system, 61, 61nn12–13, 114
appropriations statutes, 109, 109n18, 111n25, 169–170, 187n87
  See also specific types of institutions receiving state funding
Arkansas, educational system in, 130n122
Asheville, electric streetcar system in, 50, 50n33
asylums for the insane, 47n15, 109n18, 170–176, 187
  for blacks, 171, 174–175, 187
  care of the insane as duty of state under 1868 Constitution, 173, 173n19
  for Croatan Indians, 175–176
  desegregation (1965), 176, 176n34
  North Carolina compared to other states, 171n5
  race-neutral statutes and no need to specify races eligible for care, 171–173, 173n18
  Reconstruction period, admissions policy during, 172
  use of terminology, 170n4
Atlanta, Ga.
  fear of black supremacy in, 84, 84n118
  ordinances on racial segregation, 54, 54n54
Atlantic Coast Line Railroad, 124, 124n95
Aycock, Charles Brantley, 79n108, 81n110, 84–85, 99, 99n194, 141–142, 141n171, 141n173, 153

Ayers, Edward, 72n75, 80n110, 82, 109n18, 126n107

Baldwin, James, 193–194
Barksdale v. Commissioners of Sampson County (1885), 133–134, 133n134, 134n136, 134n139
Bassett, John Spencer, 43n2, 100, 100n198
bathrooms, racially separate for employees, 40, 116
Battle, Kemp, 162
Beale, Howard K., 45
Benson, Town of, residential segregation in, 116
black churches, establishment of, 27, 125, 125n101
Black Code (N.C.), 40n37, 60n9, 61, 117, 117n64
black officeholding, 59n4, 64, 70, 74, 74n88, 80n110, 83–84
"Black Second." See Second congressional district.
black supremacy, white fear of, 83–84, 84n118, 89–90, 193
blackface performers, xvi, xvin3
Board of Public Charities, 170
Bradley v. Milliken (1971), 22n83
Bradley v. Milliken (1973), 6n15
Brandeis, Louis, 121
Britton v. Atlanta & Charlotte Air-Line Ry. Co. (1883), 32n5, 126n104
Brogden, Curtis, 174–175
Brown, Henry Billings, 33, 33n8
Brown v. Board of Education (1954), 22, 24n90, 45, 45n10

Brown v. Board of Education
  (*Brown II*, 1955), 45
Brunson v. North Carolina (1948),
  167n289
Bryan, William Jennings, 77
Buchanan v. Warley (1917), 8n22
Buncombe County, jury service by
  blacks in, 164
Butler, Marion, 39n30, 75, 87, 153,
  155n230
Byrne, J. Peter, 17n56

Caldwell, Tod, 183
Calhoun, John C., xvii*n*5
Canby, Edward R.S., 62–63
Cardozo, Benjamin, 23
Carr, Elias, 78
Carteret County
  exclusion of blacks from jury
    service in, 164
  gerrymandering and, 68n54
Carthage, Town of, 121n79
Caswell County
  jury service by blacks in, 165,
    165n276
  Klan violence in, 65, 66
Catawba County, jury service by
  blacks in, 162
Cell, John, 49
cemeteries, segregation of, 54, 105,
  110, 114, 115, 121, 123n89, 190
Chadbourn, Town of, 115
Chamber of Commerce (Wilmington), 92
Charleston, S.C., ordinance on segregated passenger coaches and
  carriages, 49

Charlotte
  graded schools, authorization of,
    135n142
  racial ordinances, 105, 116, 118,
    118n68
Chase, Salmon P., 158, 158n244
churches, racial segregation of,
  125–126
  See also black churches
citizenship, 159n246
city ordinances
  gaps in records of, 104–105n8
  racial segregation and, 8n22, 49,
    54, 104–107
Civil Rights Act, federal (1875), 160
civil rights act (federal), 123–124
Civil Rights Cases (1883), 124n94
civil rights resolution (N.C.),
  109n18
Coates, Albert, 121–122
Cohen, Morris L., 35n20
Cohen, William, 61n14, 108n17
Colfax massacre (1873), 27
*Collie v. Commissioners of Franklin
  County* (1907), 134n136, 134n139,
  144n180
collusive lawsuit of Plessy and railroad company, 32
  See also Plessy v. Ferguson
colonization movement, 25
Colored Orphan Asylum (Oxford),
  183–184, 184n76
colored persons, use of term,
  xviii*n*7, 38n25, 106n14, 154n228
congressional elections, 68, 71, 76
Congressional Reconstruction
  (1867–77), 62–64, 117, 117n64, 173

Connor, Henry G., 38, 100, 155
Conservative Party (later Democratic Party), 59, 59n5
   gerrymandering and, 68–69
   Klan and, 65n35, 66, 67nn50–51
   in Wilmington, 68–69
Constitution of 1868
   1900 amendment, 28, 37, 37n23, 40–41, 41n38, 79n108, 115, 148–150, 153–156 (*See also* literacy test as voter eligibility requirement; poll tax)
   1915 amendment prohibiting local, private, or special acts in specified areas, 122–123
   care of the insane as duty of state, 173, 173n19
   orphanages, provision for, 182
   public schools, provision of, 63, 112, 129, 131
   ratification of, 63, 117n64, 160
   school for deaf, dumb, and blind children, provision of, 177
   silent on racial distinctions, 173
   voting extended to freedmen, 63
constitutional convention (1868), 63, 146
constitutional convention (1875), 71
consumer cooperatives, 72, 75
contract formation restrictions on blacks, 48, 61, 61n12
   See also restrictive covenants
convict labor, 4n3
Coon, Charles, 141n171, 144n180
Cooper, James Fenimore, xviin6
corporate and business interests, 75, 75n92, 78, 78n106, 80n110

corruption, 64–65, 64–65n34, 72, 145n181
Cortner, Richard, 33n9
county boards of education, 138–142, 142n172
courts
   Constitution of 1868 and, 63
   military vs. civil, 162
   separate Bibles for swearing-in black and white witnesses, 126, 126n108
   testimony by blacks, restrictions on, 48, 61, 61n12, 158, 158n243
   See also jury service
Craig, Lee A., 79n108, 88n141
Craig, Locke, 82n110, 85
Craven County
   gerrymandering and, 68n54
   school funding and segregated schools in, 132, 132n134
Crenson, Matthew, 182n66
criminal justice system
   "infamous" crime subjecting person to "infamous" punishment to remove voting rights, 4–5n6
   jails, racial segregation of, 113, 116, 190, 190n4
   juvenile detention facilities, racial segregation of, 113
   racially disparate impact of, xix–xx*n*13
   slavery as punishment for crime, 3n3
criminal statutes, 40n36, 109, 109n18
Croatan Indians
   asylum for insane for, 175–176

interracial marriage with Negro, prohibition on, 113, 114
interracial marriage with white person, prohibition on, 108, 113
segregation in state facilities, 116
separate schools for, 114, 119n70, 190
standard for determining Indian descent, 119–120n70
"crow" as term to denote African Americans, xvii, xviin6
Crow, Jeffrey J., 41n38, 78nn105-106, 79n108, 92n156, 153n221, 171n5
Cumming v. Richmond County Board of Education (1899), 34n12
Cunningham, Roger A., 15n50, 19n65
custom. *See* social and cultural norms

The Daily Record (Wilmington), 86n128, 92n155, 94–95
Daily Standard (Raleigh), 162n260
Daniels, Josephus, 37n22, 78–79, 79n108, 81n110, 84, 84n119, 88–90, 98–99, 100n198, 141n171
See also News and Observer
Darnell, State v. (1914), 106n14
de facto discrimination
definition of, 7n18, 46n13
difference from *de jure* discrimination, 47, 112
era of, 47, 54
de jure discrimination, xv–xx, 103–168
definition of, 7n18, 36, 46n13

difference from *de facto* discrimination, 47, 112
intentional state action and, 46n13
Milliken's remedy for *de jure* racial discrimination, limitations on, 7–8
in Northern cities, 48, 194
not inevitable, 24
origins in North Carolina and the South, 40, 46–47
prevalence of, 34, 37, 48, 194
prior to White Supremacy Campaigns, 40
state institutions and, 169–188
See also Jim Crow laws; jury service; law-society interaction; race-neutral laws; school funding; school segregation; voting and voter laws; White Supremacy Campaigns
definitions. *See* terminology
Democratic Party
black support for, 59, 59n6, 74
Conservative Party's name change to, 67
county boards of education dominated by, 138–139
facing two-party system in North Carolina, 71–72
Farmers' Alliance and, 72, 74–75
fusion with Populists (1898), 80–81n110, 151
loss to fusionists (1894–96), 75–78, 145
Red Shirts and, 88
splinter groups, effect of, 71

white supremacy as platform of, 72–73, 74n85, 78–79, 79n108, 80–81n110, 84, 152, 190–191
See also Conservative Party; gerrymandering; White Supremacy Campaigns
desegregation
asylums for the insane (1965), 176, 176n34
Masonic Home for Children (1995), 187
See also school desegregation
Detroit, Mich., segregation in metropolitan area of, 6–22, 193, 194
disenfranchisement, xix, xxn13, 145–157
as destruction of Republican voter base, 99n194
"infamous" punishment used to create, 4–5n6
Simmons as individual responsible for, 38–39
use of term, 120n71
See also Constitution of 1868, for 1900 amendment; de jure discrimination; jury service; voting and voter laws; White Supremacy Campaigns
Dix, Dorothea, 171
Dixon, Thomas, 26, 26n99
Dortch Act, 137, 138, 144n180, 190n8
Douglas, Robert M., 81–82n110
Du Bois, W.E. Burghardt, 45
Due Process Clause (federal), 8n22, 17n54
Dunning, William Archibald, 44n3, 57

Dunning School, 44, 44nn3–4, 57, 58n2
Duplin County
cemeteries, segregation of, 115
gerrymandering and, 68n54
school funding and segregated schools in, 140
Durden, Robert F., 92n156, 153n221
Durham
graded school law in, 136n144
school funding and segregated schools in, 138n156

economic depression (1890s), 74
Edgecombe County, gerrymandering and, 68n54
Edmonds, Helen, 73n82, 153, 154n226
education, 128–145
county boards of education, 138–142, 142n172
graded schools, introduction of, 135
legislative creation of new public school system (1868), 64
normal schools, introduction of, 135n141
North Carolina compared to other states, 130–131, 130nn122–123
public schools, provision of (Constitution of 1868), 63, 112, 129
school committees, racial composition of, 115
See also school desegregation; school funding; school segregation

INDEX | 277

elections
  1868, 63–64, 64n31
  1870, 65, 67, 67n49
  1872, 71, 72–73
  1876, 73n80
  1888, 73n81
  1894, 76, 76n97, 76n99
  1896, 76–77, 76n100, 145, 150
  1898, 78–80, 79n108, 84, 87–93, 151–152, 151–152n211
  1900, 41n38, 84, 98–99, 151–153, 156
  1904, 156
  1912, 121n76
  See also voting and voter laws
employment and labor
  involuntary servitude in Reconstruction period, 61, 61–62nn13–14
  labor unions excluding blacks, 27
  labor unions supporting Sunday closing laws, 192n14
  segregation of workers, 126, 126n107
  U.S. need for cheap black labor, 25
enticement of servant away from "master or employer" by another employer, 108, 108n17, 117n64
Episcopal Diocese of North Carolina, 125–126
Equal Protection Clause (federal), 8n23, 9n28, 31
equality. *See* inequality of African Americans; race-neutral laws; separate but equal

Escott, Paul D., 41n38, 66n39, 67nn48–49, 73n80, 75n92, 80n110
Eskridge, William N., Jr., 104n4
exclusion
  black women excluded from first-class ladies' railroad cars, 26, 32
  examples of notable laws (1868–1915), 27–28, 112–116
  labor unions excluding blacks, 27
  public accommodations applying rule of, 52, 54n53
  segregation as alternative to, 52–53, 111, 111–112n26, 127n112
  state public welfare institutions and, 169
  See also jury service; voting and voter laws

Fallon, Richard H., 107n15
Farmers' Alliance, 72, 74–75, 75n92
Farmers' Legislature (1891), 75
Fayetteville
  graded schools, authorization of, 135n142
  Republican convention (1874) held in, 124
Federal Home Loan Bank Board (FHLBB), 11n31
Federal Housing Administration (FHA), 8–15
  Underwriting Manual, 9–13, 15
Fields, Barbara J., xviiin7
Fifteenth Amendment (federal), 192
Fisher, E.C., 172
Flora Realty & Inv. Co. v. City of Ladue (1952), 16n51

Foner, Eric, 58n2, 60n10, 61n13, 66n47, 108n17, 125n101, 161
Forman, James, Jr., xxn13, 161n254
former slaves. *See* freedmen
Forsyth County, exclusion of blacks from jury service in, 167
Fourteenth Amendment (federal)
    exclusion of African Americans and, 34, 166
    ratification by North Carolina (1868), 64
    "reasonableness" judicial standard and, 192, 192n15
    refusal of Southern states to ratify, 62
    restrictive covenants in deeds in violation of, 9n28
Fowle, Daniel G., 159n246
Frampton, Thomas Ward, 157n240
Franklin, John Hope, 29n107, 43n2, 45, 128n113, 170n3
Franklin County, gerrymandering and, 69n61
fraud. *See* voting and voter laws
Free Will Baptist Children's Home, 187n89
freedmen
    Democratic Party and, 59, 59n6
    eligibility to vote, 39n30, 63, 146, 155n230, 190
    enticement statutes and, 108n17, 117n64
    Raleigh convention (1865), 60n9
Freedmen's Bureau (U.S.), 5, 52, 172, 172n13, 172n15, 178, 179n50
Freund, David M.P., 15n50, 16n52, 17n56

Friedman, Lawrence, 192n14
Furches, David M., 81–82n110
fusionists, 47n14, 75–78, 83, 142, 142n172, 145, 151

Garner, James Wilford, 44n3
Garrison, William Lloyd, xviin6
gender. *See* black women; women
General Assembly
    black members of, 64, 74, 74n87, 83, 83n114, 147
    Democratic control of, 47n14, 70–71, 93, 97, 152, 190
    Farmers' Legislature (1891), 75
    galleries, racial segregation of, 109n18
    See also elections; legislation and lawmaking; *specific political parties*
Georgia schools, 34, 130n123
gerrymandering, 68–69, 68n54, 69nn60–61, 91, 93, 190
Gilmore, Glenda, 25–26, 85n123, 86
Girsh, Appeal of (1970), 15n50
gold standard, 77
Goldsboro
    closure of schools to avoid funding both races equally, 138
    school funding and segregated schools in, 113, 135–136, 138n156
    separate asylum for insane for black patients in, 171, 175, 176n34, 187
Goodwin, Edward McKee, 180
Gordon, Daniel R., 33n9
Gordon, Robert, 193

governmental vs. nongovernmental action, use of term *de jure* to denote, xvn1, 7n18
Grand Lodge of Masons, 183, 183n69
Grant Colored Orphan Asylum (Oxford), 183
Granville County
  different Bibles required for swearing in of races, 126n108
  gerrymandering and, 69–70n61
Greene County
  gerrymandering and, 68n54
  Populist Party in, 153
Greensboro
  courthouse, segregation of, 127
  graded schools, introduction of, 135n142
  residential segregation ordinance, 106
Grissom, Eugene, 172–173
Gudger v. Penland (1891), 4n6

Haar, Charles, 17n56
Hairston, State v. (1869), 118n64
Haley, John, 99n194
Halifax County
  gerrymandering and, 68n54
  jury service by blacks in, 165, 165n276
Hall v. DeCuir (1878), 31–32n4
Hamburg (S.C.) Massacre (1876), 87n135
Hamilton, Joseph G. de Roulhac, 40n37, 44, 44nn3–4, 57, 65n36, 70n65, 80n110
Hanchett, Thomas W., 41n38

Handlin, Oscar, 36n21
Hare v. Board of Education of Gates County (1893), 119n70
Harlan, Louis, 131n125, 142n173, 143
Harriss v. Wright (1897), 92n153
Hatley, Flora J., 41n38
Hertford County, jury service by blacks in, 165, 165n276
Hillier, Amy E., 11n31
Hogan, M.K., 172n15
Holden, William W., 59–60, 63, 64, 66–67, 162n260
Holden Convention (1865–66), 117n64
Home Owners' Loan Corporation (HOLC), 10–11n31
home rule, elimination of and attempts to restore, 67n48, 70, 70n65, 91, 139, 190
hospitals, segregation of, 47n15, 116
  See also asylums for the insane
Housing and Urban Development Department, U.S., combatting segregation in Detroit suburbs, 20
housing segregation. *See* residential segregation
Howard School (Fayetteville), 111n25
Hubbard, Orville, 19

illiteracy. *See* literacy test; voting and voter laws
impeachments
  Douglas as N.C. Supreme Court justice, acquittal for, 81–82n110

Furches as N.C. Supreme Court chief justice, acquittal for, 81–82n110
Holden as governor, removed from office, 67
Indians
  use of term, xviii*n*7
  See also American Indians; Croatan Indians; Native Americans
inequality of African Americans, 193–194
  apartheid and, 25
  pre-*Plessy* treatment and, 34
  segregation as inherently unequal, 24, 112
  separate-and-unequal legislation, 34, 36
  See also separate but equal
"infamous" crime subjecting person to "infamous" punishment, 4–5n6
insane asylums. *See* asylums for the insane
Institution for the Deaf and Dumb and Blind, 53n51, 111, 176–181, 180n55, 187
  appropriation provisions, 179
  conflict between statutory and constitutional language, 177
  disparity between statutes and attending to needs of black students, 181, 187
  separate building for black students, 178–179, 179n51, 179n53
  services provided for both white and black branches, 180, 187

white deaf and dumb students' facility in Morganton, 180
integration
  to end exclusion, blacks preferring segregation over, 24n91, 52, 53, 111, 111n26
  plans for housing integration of Detroit suburbs, 20, 20n69
  possibility of, 52, 54, 124, 124–125nn95–96
  unlikelihood of, 24, 51
interracial relations
  cooperation in years after emancipation, 25
  marriage, prohibition on, 48, 108, 113, 114, 118n64, 119n70
  white fear of, 85–86, 86n128
  See also white supremacy; *various types of segregation, public accommodations, and common carriers*
intimidation
  of potential black voters, 38, 66, 67n49, 151, 153
  Red Shirts' tactics of, 87
  of Republican political candidates (1898), 92–93
  White Government Union's tactics of, 92
involuntary servitude
  distinguished from slavery, 3n3
  in Reconstruction period, 61, 61–62nn13–14

Jackson, Andrew, xvii*n*5
Jackson, Kenneth, 8, 11n31
  Crabgrass Frontier, 14

jails. *See* criminal justice system
James, David R., 121n76
Jennett, Norman, 89, 90, 90n149, 91
Jim Crow laws
   before 1890s, 117, 189
   creation of *de jure* discrimination, 23–24
   Dunning School providing foundation for, 58n2
   fluidity in race relations prior to, 45, 51–52, 54
   little interest in study of, 54n55
   not inevitable and existence of alternatives, 24, 25, 46n11
   race relations prior to, 45, 51–52
   study confined to 1865 to 1920, 28–29
   timing and origins of, xv–xx, 46–48, 47n16, 51, 54–55, 55n56
   See also de jure discrimination; race-neutral laws; White Supremacy Campaigns
"Jim Crow poet," xviin5
Johnson, Andrew, 59–60, 60n10, 117n64
Jones County, gerrymandering and, 68n54
Joyner, James Y., 143
"Jump Jim Crow" (song), xv–xvii, xvinn2–3
"jump Jim Crow" as expression, xviii–xix
jury service, 157–167
   Chase's order for integrated juries, 158
   Civil Rights Act (1875) and, 160
   as essential democratic institution, 157
   exclusion of blacks from, 34, 34n14, 157, 162–167, 191
   "infamous" punishment used to remove person's right to serve, 4–5n6
   integrated juries, 51, 51n39, 158, 159n246, 161–166
   newspapers reporting on black jurors as unusual occurrence, 166–167, 167n288
   qualifications in law, 160, 160n252
   race-neutral statutes on, 157–158, 160, 164, 193
   Sickles' order (General Orders No. 32) for jury lists to include all poll tax payors, 158–159, 159n246
   white attitudes toward blacks on juries, 162–163
Justesen, Benjamin R., 83n114

Keyes v. School District No. 1, Denver, Colorado (1973), xvn1, 7n18, 46n13
King, William Eskridge, 138n157, 139n163
Kinston, Town of, funding of schools by race, 136, 138n156
Kirk, George, 66
Kirk-Holden War, 67
Kirkbride, T.S., 176
Kitchin, Claude, 79n108
Kitchin, William Walton, 122
Klarman, Michael J., 33n11, 164n273

Kousser, Morgan, 71, 76n99, 140, 141n171, 142, 144n180, 145, 149, 151, 151–152n211, 153, 155
Krehbiel, Keith, 104n3
Ku Klux Klan
    amnesty and pardon for crimes committed by, 67n51
    Dixon and, 26, 26n99
    formation and politics of, 65nn35–36
    rebirth in 1920s, 29, 29n107
    Red Shirts compared to, 87
    violence in Piedmont region by, 65–67

labor. *See* employment and labor
Lane v. Stanley (1871), 132, 132–133n134, 134
Lassiter v. Northampton County Bd. of Elections (1959), 37n24
law-society interaction
    facial vs. as-applied challenges to law, 107n15
    gap between law's text and its operation, 28–29, 36–37, 104, 167–168, 169, 187, 190–191
    implementation of law as way to assess true impact of law, 5–6, 23, 27, 40, 192–193
    jury service and, 163, 167
    public welfare institutions and, 176, 181, 187–188
    residential segregation resulting from, 6–22, 193
    in response to White Supremacy Campaigns (1898–1900), 28, 128, 168, 190–191
    schools and, 144, 167
    voting and, 145–146, 151, 156–157, 167–168
    See also social and cultural norms
Lefler, Hugh Talmage, 64n34, 67n49
legislation and lawmaking
    categorization of statutes, 35–36, 111–112, 122
    as distillation of society's values, 36, 103–104
    facial vs. as-applied challenges to law, 107n15
    importance of law in assessing racist attitudes, 27, 36, 40, 128, 192–193
    no great wave of new laws following 1900, 37, 40–41, 101, 118–119, 191
    private, local, or special acts, 35, 121–123, 122n80
    race-conscious statutes, 27–28, 107–112
    See also de jure discrimination; race-neutral laws
Leloudis, James, 59n6, 139, 143
Lenoir County, gerrymandering and, 68n54
Leuchtenburg, William E., 29n107
Levi, Edward H., 169
Liberal Anti-Prohibitionist Party, 71n72
Link, William A., 72n79
Lionshead Lake, Inc. v. Township of Wayne (1952), 16n51
literacy test as voter eligibility requirement, 28, 28n105, 37–39, 37n23, 38n26, 39n30, 41, 97, 115,

118, 120, 141n171, 146, 151–156, 167, 191, 193
Litwack, Leon F., xviiin7, xix, 48, 49, 111–112
local officials
   appointment of, 70, 74, 91, 139, 190
   blacks as, 59n4, 64, 70, 74, 74n88, 80n110, 83–84
   See also home rule
localized approach to legislation. *See* legislation and lawmaking
Logan, Frenise A., 40n37, 59n4, 59n6, 136n143, 140, 147n190
Louisiana
   black voter levels in, 156
   governor's power to appoint local officials in, 70n63
   passenger railroad segregation in, 31, 31nn3–4
Louisville, New Orleans and Texas Ry. Co. v. Mississippi (1890), 31n4
Lumbee Tribe. *See* Croatan Indians

Manly, Alexander, 86n128, 92n155, 94–95, 96n181
Manuel, State v. (1838), 159n246
Margo, Robert A., 143
marriage, interracial. *See* interracial relations
Martin County, jury service by blacks in, 159n246, 161
Masonic Home for Children, 187
Massachusetts
   interracial juries in, 158n242
   interracial marriage, prohibition on, 48

railroad cars, racial segregation abandoned in, 49n24
McCulloch, Margaret Callender, 171n7
McKinley, William, 77
Melton, John R., 95
Memorial Industrial School (Winston-Salem), 183n71
mentally ill, institutions for. *See* asylums for the insane
Merton, Robert, 39
migration of African Americans from North Carolina, 28
militia, segregation of, 113, 115
Milliken v. Bradley (1974), 6–7, 7n18, 21, 22n83
Milliken v. Bradley (1977), xvn1, 7n18, 46n13
Mississippi
   black voter levels in, 156
   literacy requirement for voting in, 120
Moore v. City of East Cleveland (1977), 17n54
Mooresville residential segregation ordinance, 105–106
Morehead, John Motley, 176
Morgan, J.P., 78
Morganton, Town of
   asylum for the insane in, 174–175, 175n29
   cemeteries, segregation of, 110, 114, 121, 190
   white deaf and dumb students' facility in, 180
Morrison, Cameron, 88
mortgages and mortgage insurance, 8–14, 17, 21, 23

Murray, Pauli, 35, 35n19
Myrdal, Gunnar, 10n31, 43

Nash, Steven E., 69n61
Native Americans
　use of term, xviii*n*7
　See also American Indians;
　　Croatan Indians
Negroes
　standard for determining Negro
　　descent, 119–120n70
　use of term, xviii*n*7, 38n26
New Bern/NewBerne, funding of
　schools by race, 136
New Hanover County
　1900 constitutional amendment,
　　vote on, 153
　gerrymandering and, 68–69,
　　69n60, 190
　jury service by blacks in, 165,
　　165n276
　juvenile detention facility in,
　　113
　orphanage for colored children
　　in, 115
　Republican candidates in (1898),
　　92
New Negro movement, 26–27
New Orleans
　fear of black supremacy in, 84
　ordinances on racial segrega-
　　tion, 49
New State Ice Co. v. Liebmann
　(1932), 121n78
Newbold, N.C., 130
Newby, Paul Martin, 3n3, 123n88
News and Observer (Raleigh),
　79n108, 81–82n110, 86n128,
88–90, 88n142, 89–91, 96, 98–99,
　139
Newsom, State v. (1844), 159n246
Newsome, Albert Ray, 64n34, 67n49
newspapers
　reporting on black jurors as un-
　　usual occurrence, 166–167
　reporting on deviations from
　　racial segregation, 124–125,
　　124–125nn95–96, 125nn99–100
　in White Supremacy Campaigns,
　　79n108, 81–82n110, 88–90,
　　89–91, 98–99
　See also specific newspapers by
　　name
Noble, M.C.S., 136n143
nonwhites, use of term, 20–21,
　20nn71–72
Norris v. Alabama (1935), 166
North Carolina Advisory Commit-
　tee to the U.S. Commission on
　Civil Rights, 167
North Carolina Baptist State Con-
　vention, 126
North Carolina Constitution. *See*
　Constitution of 1868
North Carolina courts. *See* courts
North Carolina General Assembly.
　See General Assembly
North Carolina session laws. *See*
　legislation and lawmaking
Northampton County, gerryman-
　dering and, 68n54

officeholding
　blacks in local positions, 59n4,
　　64, 70, 74, 74n88, 80n110,
　　83–84

end of home rule, 67n48, 70, 70n65, 91, 139, 190
"infamous" punishment used to remove person's right to hold office, 4–5n6
O'Hara, James, 124, 180
Olsen, Otto H., 65n35, 67n50
Olson, Kent C., 35n20
Onslow County, gerrymandering and, 68n54
Orange County, Klan violence in, 66
orphanages, 181–188
    Colored Orphan Asylum of North Carolina, 183–184, 183nn70–71, 184n76
    constitutional duty to provide for, 182
    Free Will Baptist Children's Home, 187n89
    New Hanover County "home" for orphaned colored children, 115
    no state orphanage publicly established, 53n49, 182
    Oxford Orphan Asylum (for white children), 183, 183nn68–69
    Oxford Orphanage, 187, 187nn88–89
    private orphanages, state subsidies to, 109n18, 182–188, 184n76, 184n84, 187n89
    racially separate institutions, 182–183
    social purpose of, 182n66
    state-created inequality through funding, 186–188

Orr, Oliver H., Jr., 81n110
Orth, John V., 3n3, 64n32, 123n88
Outlaw, Wyatt, 65–66, 65n38, 66n46
Oxford, orphanages in, 182–184, 183nn68–71
Oxford Orphanage, 187, 187nn88–89

Padover v. Township of Farmington (1965), 19n65
Palmer, W.J., 178
Parents Involved in Community Schools v. Seattle School District No. 1 (2007), xvn1, 7n18, 46n13
Park View Heights Corp. v. City of Black Jack (1972), 15n50
parks, segregation of, 116
Pembroke Indian School, 180, 181n60
Pender County
    Democratic strategy in, 68–69
    gerrymandering and, 190n5
Pennsylvania voting laws, 48
Perman, Michael, 155
Person County, funding of schools by race, 138, 138n156
Piedmont counties, 58, 65, 65n35, 66–67, 66n39, 78
Plessy, Homer, 32, 32n7
Plessy v. Ferguson (1896), 31–34, 31n1, 33nn8–9, 40, 192, 192n15
political system of North Carolina, 58–82, 145–146
    See also elections; White Supremacy Campaigns; *specific political parties*
Polk, Leonidas LaFayette, 72, 75

poll tax, 37, 37n23, 41, 115, 118, 120, 131–132, 134n139, 154, 155, 159

Populist Party, 46n11, 75–78, 78n105, 80–81n110, 81, 145, 152–153

See also fusionists

Pound, Roscoe, 29, 192–193

Prather, H. Leon, Sr., 87n130, 88n140, 91n152, 91n157, 135n140, 140n169

"prejudiced nondiscriminator," use of term, 39

Presidential Reconstruction (1865–67), 60–62

President's Committee on Civil Rights, 187n87

Pritchard, Jeter, 77, 87, 155

Pritchett, Jonathan B., 144n180

property ownership
  blacks less likely than whites to own real property, 149
  freehold qualification of land ownership, 159, 160
  in Oregon, 48
  by race in Upper South (1870), 136n145
  See also restrictive covenants

public accommodations
  racial customs prior to 1890, 52, 123–127, 123n90, 124–125nn95–96, 126n104, 127n112
  See also specific types

public welfare institutions, 111–112, 169–188
  asylums for the insane, 170–176, 187
  North Carolina compared to other states, 170, 171n5
  racially separate institutions, 171, 175, 176n34, 178–179, 179n51, 179n53, 182–183, 187–188
  schools for the deaf, dumb, and blind, 176–181, 187
  See also orphanages

Puitt v. Commissioners of Gaston County (1886), 113n37, 137–138, 217t

punishment
  imprisonment and ability of person to vote, hold office, or serve on jury, 4n6
  "infamous" crime subjecting person to "infamous" punishment, 4–5n6
  slavery as punishment for crime, 3n3
  whipping as punishment to disqualify voting rights, 4–5, 4n5

Rabinowitz, Howard, 24n91, 52–54, 52–53n46, 111, 127n112, 173–174n21

race-neutral laws
  asylums for the insane and, 171–173, 173n18
  institutions for the blind and, 177
  jury service and, 157–158, 160, 164, 193
  literacy requirement for voting, 28, 193
  non-explicit language allowing for discretionary application, 5, 108, 108n17, 193
  research methodology and, 110
  school funding and, 28, 63, 193

weaponization against African
    Americans, 193
  zoning ordinances, 17
race/racism
  change of white attitudes due
    to White Supremacy Cam-
    paigns unleashing racial
    animus, 100–101, 100n198
  concept of, xviii*n*7
  definition of "race" in statutes
    on descent, 119–120n70
  examples of notable laws
    (1868–1915), 27–28, 112–
    116
  hidden racism in American
    history, 192
  "Jim Crow" used to signify any
    law or governmental action
    of, xix
  Populists and, 77
  post–World War I racial con-
    flicts, 29n107
  property value and, 9
  restrictive covenants prohibiting
    property sales, 8, 8n23, 9,
    9n28
  as smokescreen issue for class
    and economic interests,
    80n110
  state institutions and, 169–188
  superiority of white race, belief
    in, 79–80, 99n193
  as topic of historical scholarship,
    23–24, 43–45
  Woodward's thesis on, 45–48
  See also de jure discrimination;
    jury service; residential seg-
    regation; school segregation;
    voting and voter laws; white
    supremacy; White Supremacy
    Campaigns
race riots (1919), 28, 29n107
racial districting. *See* gerrymandering
racial homogeneity in housing,
  9–10, 12, 14, 20
  See also residential segregation
racial steering by real estate agents,
  27
racially disparate impact of American criminal justice system,
  xix–xx*n*13
railroads
  Afro-Creoles colluding in *Plessy*
    lawsuit with, 32
  black servants allowed in white
    passenger cars, 189
  contact between races traveling
    on, 88n143
  Farmers' Alliance to counter
    interests of, 72
  Jim Crow and, xvii, 24, 24n89,
    48, 48n24, 127n109
  Louisiana laws on racial segrega-
    tion of, 31, 31nn3–4
  regulatory commission, failure
    to establish, 72
  segregation of, 26, 32, 114, 115,
    118, 126, 126n104, 152, 189
  state-owned railroad leased to
    Southern Railway Company,
    78, 78n106
  Tennessee laws on racial segre-
    gation of, 25n91
  women, separate cars for, 26, 32,
    32n6

Raleigh
    asylum for the insane in, 171–173, 172n11, 172n15
    cemeteries, segregation of, 54, 105
    Institution for the Blind in, 180
    Institution for the Deaf and Dumb and Blind in, 176–177, 179
    racial segregation in, 52, 53n46
    school funding and discretion to apportion money to maintain schools for both races, 114, 140, 140n166
    State Library, segregation of, 115, 118, 128
    train station, segregation of, 127
rape of white women. See white woman
readmission of North Carolina into the Union, 64
reapportionment. See gerrymandering
reasonableness standard, 34, 192
Reconstruction, 26n99, 33n8, 57–101
    American public's knowledge of, 57
    asylums for the insane, admission policies during, 171, 172
    Congressional Reconstruction (1867–77), 62–64, 117, 117n64, 173
    freedmen not capable of participating in government, 57–58
    histories of, 44, 44nn3–4
    in North Carolina, 57–101
    Presidential Reconstruction (1865–67), 60–62
    race relations during, 52n43, 161
    in South Carolina, 51
    white memory of, used to manipulate voting, 73–74, 73nn82–83, 75
Red Shirts, 87–88, 87n132, 87n135, 87n137, 99
"Red Summer" (1919), 29n107
Redding, Kent, 121n76
Redemption and Redeemers, 46n11, 47, 47nn14–15, 67, 71, 72–73, 73–74n84, 91n152
    See also white supremacy
redlining, 11n31
Reich, David, xviiin7
Republican Party
    freedmen belonging to, 59
    fusion with Populists, 75–78, 78n105, 145
    in local offices, 64
    in Piedmont region, 67
    rebirth as "Lily-white" party (1902), 99n194
    in Reconstruction period, 44, 51
    refusal to support Negro office-seekers, 59n4
    segregation policies of, 52
    strength in North Carolina, 58, 62, 63, 145
    tensions within (1896), 77n104
    Unionist whites belonging to, 62
    in Wilmington, 68–69, 91–92
    withdrawal from 1898 election in Wilmington, 92–93
research methodology, 107–112

categorization of types of statutes, 35–36, 111–112, 122
criticism and shortcomings of earlier scholarship, 24–25, 34–35, 45–55, 118, 121n76, 164–167, 170, 187–188
cutoff date of 1920, choice of, 28–29
examples of notable laws (from Table 1) establishing racial exclusion and discrimination, 27–28, 112–116
statutes advancing interests of African Americans and Native Americans (Table 2), 27–28, 53n51, 107–112, 247–267
statutes discriminating on basis of race (Table 1), 107–112, 195–245
systematic approach to state laws and their implementation, 35–36, 54–55, 161, 192–194

residential segregation
of Detroit, 6–22, 193, 194
fair housing, FHA policies as detrimental to, 9, 9n28
Federal Housing Administration (FHA) role in, 8–15
negative effects of, 52
North Carolina city ordinances on, 104–107, 106n14
ordinances, 8n22
racial homogeneity, 9–10, 12, 14, 20
racial steering by real estate agents, 27
single-family houses vs. multifamily apartments, 13–17, 14n46, 15n50
towns mandating, 116
urban annexation and, 52–53n46

restrictive covenants prohibiting property sales to African Americans, 8, 8n23, 9, 9n28
Revised Code, legal status of, 177n41
Reynolds, Charles A., 127n110
Reynolds, William Bradford, 33n9
Rice, Thomas Dartmouth ("Daddy"), xv–xvi, xvi*nn*2–3
Richmond, Va.
fear of black supremacy in, 84
ordinance on segregated passenger coaches and carriages, 49
Riggsbee v. Town of Durham (1886), 113n37, 217t
road crews, segregation of, 116
Robeson County, segregation of Croatan Indians in, 116, 119n70, 176
Roche, John P., 33n10
Romney, George, 20, 20n69
Rothstein, Richard: *The Color of Law*, 7–8
Royal Oak Chamber of Commerce (Oakland County, Michigan), 19–20
Russell, Daniel, 77n104, 78n105, 81n110, 87–88, 92–93, 93n161, 145
Rutherford County, Klan violence in, 66
Ryan, James E., 21n82

Salisbury, school funding by race in, 113
saloons, segregation in, 105, 105n12
Savannah, Ga., ordinance on segregated passenger coaches and carriages, 49
Schoenbrod, David S., 16n51
school desegregation, 6–8
  See also Brown v. Board of Education
school for deaf, dumb, and blind, 176–181
  See also Institution for the Deaf and Dumb and Blind
school funding, 131–142, 190–191
  capitation tax limits in state constitution, 131, 131n129, 133n134, 134n139
  fusionists' approach to (1894), 77
  impoverishment of black schools, 129–130, 134–136, 139, 139n163, 141–142, 141n171, 144n180, 190–191
  post-1900, 140–145, 191
  pre-1900, 77, 77n102, 114, 145
  race-neutral statutes allowing discretionary application, 28, 63, 193
  responsibility to keep schools open, 132–133n134, 134nn136–137
  school taxes from each race to be allocated to school for that same race, 113, 129–130, 135–138, 190, 190n8
  unlikelihood of Negro challenge to discriminatory funding system, 144
school segregation, 128–145
  1869 law requiring separate schools for each race, 112, 113
  1875 constitutional amendment requiring separate schools for each race, 129
  1903 law prohibiting child "with negro blood" from attending school for white race, 119, 119–120n70
  black support for, 51, 52
  Croatan Indians, separate schools for, 114, 119n70, 190
  discriminatory effect of, 112, 142
  housing segregation as way to accomplish, 21–22
  laws mandating, xvn1, 46n13, 113–114, 116, 190
  long-term effects on black economic status, 191
  See also Brown v. Board of Education; school funding
Schweninger, Loren, 136n145
Scotland County
  1900 constitutional amendment, vote on, 153–154
  jury service by blacks in, 165, 165n276
Second congressional district, 68, 68n54, 83, 190n5
Secret Nine (Wilmington 1898), 94n169

segregation
    as alternative to exclusion, 52–53,
        111, 111–112n26, 127n112
    black support for, 24n91, 52–53
    as inherently unequal, 24, 112
    "Jim Crow" used to signify, xvii,
        xix
    mental health field viewing as
        necessary, 176
    ordinances on, 49
    prevalence of, 41n38, 54
    Republican policies during
        Reconstruction and, 52
    response to *Brown* decision,
        45n10
    as rule after Redemption, 47n15
    as urban phenomenon, 48
    See also public welfare institu-
        tions; research methodology;
        residential segregation; school
        segregation; separate but
        equal; *specific types of common
        carriers and public accommo-
        dations*
separate but equal
    benefits of, to blacks, 53,
        111–112n26
    common law of carriers and, 32
    Constitution of 1868 on public
        schools, 138n155
    harm done by, 28, 53, 112, 192
    Louisiana law mandating racial
        segregation of passenger rail-
        road cars, 31, 31n3
    North Carolina laws separating
        black from white facilities,
        41n38

    origins of doctrine, 33–34
    See also public welfare institu-
        tions; school funding; school
        segregation
Shelley v. Kraemer (1948), 8n23,
    9n28
Shepsle, Kenneth A., 103n2
Shipp v. M'Craw (1819), 211t
Sickles, Daniel E., 62–63, 158
silver standard (free silver), 77,
    79n108, 81n110
Simmons, Furnifold, 38–39, 39n30,
    73, 78, 79n108, 80–81n110, 85n123,
    97–98, 154–155
Skinner v. White (1836), 4n6
slavery
    churchgoing with owners,
        125n101
    criminal offense to teach slave to
        read or write, 128–129, 129n115,
        177, 177n38
    as punishment for crime, 3n3
    See also involuntary servitude
social and cultural norms
    application of law in response to,
        39, 41, 103, 112, 168, 191
    avoidance of economic and
        social situations likely to cause
        confrontation, 51
    color line in minds of individu-
        als of each race, 25n92
    contact points between races,
        27n101, 48, 49, 83, 88n143
    education of blacks, negatives
        associated with, 129–130
    folkways enforcing racial atti-
        tudes, 27, 49, 54, 125

Jim Crow laws and, 25–27, 51
public accommodations,
    customs regarding race prior
    to 1890, 52, 123–127, 123n90,
    124–125nn95–96, 126n104,
    127n112
segregation prior to Jim Crow
    laws, 47n16, 127n112
subordination of blacks by,
    xix, 27, 27n101, 51, 51n38, 156,
    189–190
white attitudes, 26, 28, 40, 58,
    100–101, 156, 190
    See also law-society interaction;
    white supremacy; White
    Supremacy Campaigns *for
    application of laws following
    1898 and 1900 elections*
Social Darwinism, 79
South Carolina
    antidiscrimination law, black
        subordination despite of, 51,
        51n38
    educational system in,
        130nn122–123
    as segregated state at end of
        Reconstruction, 51
Southern cities, size in 1890s,
    50n32
Spaulding, Kenneth B., 187n89
Spencer, Herbert, 79
Sprunt, James, 92–93
State v. ___. *See name of opposing
    party*
state archives, segregation of,
    128n113

State ex rel. See name of relator
State Colored Normal School (now
    Fayetteville State University),
    111n25
state debt after Civil War, 64, 64n32,
    117n64
State Library. *See* Raleigh
statutory terminology, use of,
    xviiin7
    See also terminology
steamboats
    black servants allowed in white
        passenger sections, 189
    Louisiana passenger laws and,
        32n4
    newspapers reporting deviations
        from racial segregation on,
        124
    segregation of, 48, 115, 118, 152,
        189
Stephens, John W., 65
Stephenson, Gilbert Thomas,
    164–165
Stevens, Thaddeus, 5
Strauder v. West Virginia (1880),
    5n9, 34n14
streetcars
    contact between races traveling
        on, 88n143
    racial segregation mandated for,
        40, 48, 116, 118, 128
suburbs
    white exodus to, 12
    zoning restrictions, 15–20
suffrage. *See* voting and voter laws
Sugrue, Thomas, 10n31, 12n37, 20

Sunday closing (blue) laws, 192n14
Sweetwater Sabre Club, 87n135

Talmadge, Herman, 45n10
taxation
    for interest payments on state debt, 64
    jury service requiring individual to have paid taxes, 158–160, 160n252
    uniformity required in, 137
    See also poll tax; school funding
Tennessee, passenger railroad segregation in, 25n91
terminology, xv–xx, 7n18
    African Americans, xvii–xviiin7
    American Indians, xvii–xviiin7
    asylums for the insane, 170n4
    colored persons, xviiin7, 38n25, 106n14, 154n228
    "crow" used to denote African Americans, xvii, xviin6
    de facto discrimination, 7n18, 46n13
    de jure discrimination, 7n18, 36, 46n13
    disenfranchisement, 120n71
    Indians, xviiin7
    "Jim Crow," xv–xx
    Negroes, xviiin7, 38n26
    nonwhites, 20–21, 20nn71–72
    "prejudiced nondiscriminator," 39
    "race" in statutes on descent, 119–120n70

    "scalawags" and "carpetbaggers," 62n19
    in U.S. Census, xviiin7, 38nn25–26, 154nn228–229
Thuesen, Sarah Caroline, 41n38
Thirteenth Amendment (federal), 3, 3n3, 4n5
Tillman, Ben, 85–86, 86n128, 87, 87n132, 87n135, 92n155, 94
Tise, Larry E., 171n5
toilet facilities, segregation of, 40, 116
Trelease, Allen W., 73n83, 76n99
trial participation by blacks. See courts
"tyranny of intractable facts," 36

Umfleet, LeRae Sikes, 94n169, 95n175
Underwood, State v. (1869), 199t
Union League, 65n35, 65n38
United States Commission on Civil Rights, 11
University of Virginia lectures by Woodward, 45
urban areas
    in 1890s, 50, 50n32
    racial discrimination in, 48–49, 52–53n46
    See also city ordinances
U.S. Army, 52
U.S. Census
    illiteracy rates of voting-age colored males, 38, 154
    terminology, xviiin7, 38nn25–26, 154nn228–229

U.S. Commission on Civil Rights,
North Carolina Advisory
Committee, 167
U.S. Supreme Court
on *de jure* segregation, xv*n*1,
46n13
ignoring law and governmental
action's effect on housing and
schooling, 22, 22n83
invalidation of federal civil
rights law (1883), 124

vagrancy laws, 61, 61n12, 61–62n14,
108n17
Van Bokkelen, State ex rel. v. Canaday (1875), 209t
Vance, Zebulon, 69n61, 72–73
Vance County
creation and name of, 69n61
jury service by blacks in, 166
veto points, 103–104
Village of Euclid v. Ambler Realty Co. (1926), 15n50
Virginia
black voter levels in, 156
educational system in, 130n123
literacy requirement for voting
in, 120–121
Virginia v. Rives (1880), 34n14
voting and voter laws, xx*n*13,
145–157
ballots and ballot box
procedures, 97, 98n184,
150–152, 151nn209–210
black voting levels, 145–149,
153–156, 155n230

change from 1877 to 1889
election procedure, 148–150,
150nn206–208
change of election date for state
offices, 97–98
constitutional amendment on
voting requirements (1900),
148–150, 153–156
Democrat-controlled General
Assembly (1899) changing
election laws, 152
exclusion of blacks from, 34, 37,
38, 70n61, 98–99, 148–157, 191
federal Reconstruction Act
(1867), 146
fraud, 64–65n34, 145, 145n181,
151, 153–154, 157
freedmen's voting rights, 39n30,
63, 146, 155n230, 190
fusionists' approach to (1894)
and increase in black voters,
77, 97, 150
gerrymandering of district
lines, 68–69, 68n54, 69nn60–
61, 91, 93, 190
illiteracy and, 37–38, 98n184, 115,
120, 146, 151, 154
"infamous" punishment used to
remove person's voting rights,
4–5n6
North Carolina compared to
other Southern states, 156
in Pennsylvania, 48
poll tax requirements, 37, 37n23,
41, 115, 118, 120, 131–132,
134n139, 154, 155, 159

Populist Party's assistance to black voters (1900), 152–153
race-neutral statutes on, 28, 193
reregistration of all voters (1900), 115, 152–153
right to vote distinguished from citizenship, 159n246
Simmons Election Law, 97–98
voting registrars, appointment and power of, 97, 150–152, 150n206, 155–156
See also elections; intimidation; literacy test as voter eligibility requirement

Waddell, Alfred Moore, 93, 94n167, 95–96
Wade, Richard C., 48–49
Wake Baptist Association, 183
Wake County, segregated road crews in, 116
Wallenstein, Peter, 3n3, 119n70
Warren County
　black population of, 163n263
　gerrymandering and, 68n54, 69–70n61
　jury service by blacks in, 163, 165–166, 165n276
Washington, Town of
　racial distribution of school committee in, 115
　school trustees to be same race as school for which they serve as trustee, 114

Watson, Richard L., 76n99, 79n108, 98n186
Wayne County
　black population of, 68n56
　gerrymandering and, 68n54
Weldon dining room at railroad stop, black and white customers seated together, 124, 124–125nn95–96
Welke, Barbara Y., 32n6
Whigs, 59n5
whipping
　Ku Klux Klan's use of, 66
　as legal punishment to disqualify voting rights, 4–5, 4n5
　Red Shirts' use of, 87
White, Garland H., 59n6
White, George, 99
White, Richard, 58
White, Theophilus, 81–82n110
White v. Ayer (1900), 81n110
White v. Hill (1899), 81n110
"White Declaration of Independence," 94–95, 94n169
White Government Unions, 87, 92
white supremacy
　1900 constitutional amendment, role of. *See* Constitution of 1868, *for 1900 amendment*
　Conservative Party as Redeemers, 67, 67n48
　Democrats as party of, 72–73, 74n85, 78–79, 79n108, 80–81n110, 84, 152, 190–191
　fusion of Democrats and Populists around, 80–81n110

as political strategy to combat rise of Populist Party, 46n11, 78–82

reliance on distortion and falsehoods, 26, 26n99, 193

in response to fear of black supremacy, 28, 83–84, 84n118, 89–90, 193

Wilmington coup and violence (1898) and, 94–97

Wilmington in 1898 election and, 91–93

White Supremacy Campaigns (1898 & 1900)

1888 campaign presaging, 73n81

adoption of 1900 constitutional amendment and, 41n38

Daniels's role in, 78–79, 79n108, 81n110, 84, 84n119, 88–90, 98–99

Democrats' strategy to win elections, 78–82, 84–101

difference between 1898 and 1900 campaign, 98

motivations of, 80–81n110

no great wave of new laws following, 37, 40–41, 101, 118–119, 128, 145

racial animus and *de jure* discrimination in response to, 28, 37, 39–41, 100–101, 107, 128, 168, 190–191

Simmons's role in, 78, 79n108

white women, protection of, 61, 61n12, 85–86, 85n123

Wiecek, William, 103

Williams, Norman, Jr., 17n55

Williams, Rachel Marie-Crane, 90n149

Williamson, Joel, 25n92, 41n38, 50–51

Wilmington

1898 coup and violence, 94–97, 96n181

1898 election, 91–93, 91n152, 92n155

black population, 91, 96–97n181

gerrymandering to weaken Republican stronghold in, 68–69, 69n60

integrated juries in, 162

newspaper reporting on deviations from racial segregation in public setting, 125, 125nn99–100

proposed colored insane asylum in, 174n21, 174n28

Wilmington Journal, 162–163

Wilmington Messenger's response to Manly's editorial, 86n128

Wilmington Race Riot Commission, 94n169, 95n175

Wilson, Town of, funding of schools by race, 136

Wilson County

black population of, 68n56

gerrymandering and, 68n54

Winston (later Winston-Salem)

cemeteries, segregation of, 121n79

electric streetcar system in, 50, 50n33

Memorial Industrial School, 183n71

residential segregation ordinance, 106, 106n14
saloons, segregation of, 105, 105n12
trolley parks, segregation of, 127, 127n110
witnesses in court. *See* courts
women
- black women and segregation policies, 25–26, 32
- first-class ladies' railroad cars, 26, 32, 32n6
- ineligible to vote, 59n4
- white women, protection of, 61, 61n12, 85–86, 85n123

Woods, Louis Lee, II, 10n31
Woodward, C. Vann, 23–25, 45–55
- *Origins of the New South*, 59n5, 62n19, 73n84, 74n88
- *The Strange Career of Jim Crow*, xix, xx*n*13, 23–24, 34–35, 34n15, 45–52, 45n6, 50n31, 54, 117–118, 128, 162, 170, 187–188
- *Thinking Back: The Perils of Writing History*, 44n3

Worth, Jonathan, 60, 61–62, 63, 158–159, 159n246
Wright, Silas, 92, 94

zoning restrictions, 15–20, 23
- family defined for purposes of, 16–17, 16n53, 18
- large-lot zoning, 16nn51–52, 19
- Michigan Supreme Court on, 19n65
- multifamily buildings, 15n50, 17–18
- segregation accomplished through, 17n56, 193

Zucchino, David, 41n38, 95n175